MOON

H A

PHILADELPHIA

KARRIE GAVIN

Contents

Maps

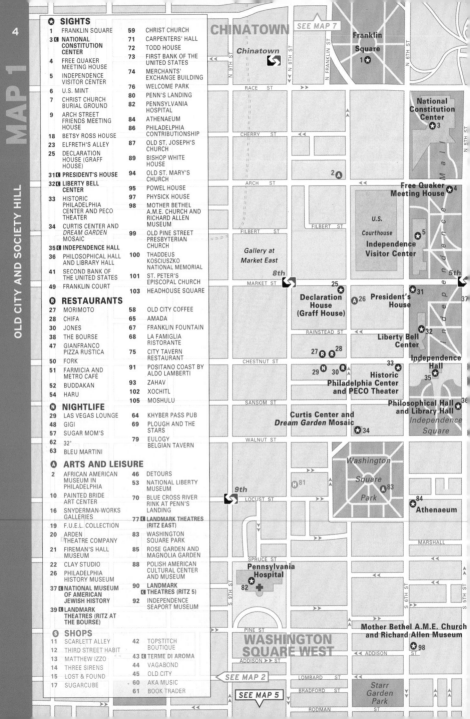

✪ SIGHTS

1 FRANKLIN SQUARE
3 NATIONAL CONSTITUTION CENTER
4 FREE QUAKER MEETING HOUSE
5 INDEPENDENCE VISITOR CENTER
6 U.S. MINT
7 CHRIST CHURCH BURIAL GROUND
9 ARCH STREET FRIENDS MEETING HOUSE
18 BETSY ROSS HOUSE
23 ELFRETH'S ALLEY
25 DECLARATION HOUSE (GRAFF HOUSE)
31 PRESIDENT'S HOUSE
32 LIBERTY BELL CENTER
33 HISTORIC PHILADELPHIA CENTER AND PECO THEATER
34 CURTIS CENTER AND *DREAM GARDEN* MOSAIC
35 INDEPENDENCE HALL
36 PHILOSOPHICAL HALL AND LIBRARY HALL
41 SECOND BANK OF THE UNITED STATES
49 FRANKLIN COURT
59 CHRIST CHURCH
71 CARPENTERS' HALL
72 TODD HOUSE
73 FIRST BANK OF THE UNITED STATES
74 MERCHANTS' EXCHANGE BUILDING
76 WELCOME PARK
80 PENN'S LANDING
82 PENNSYLVANIA HOSPITAL
84 ATHENAEUM
86 PHILADELPHIA CONTRIBUTIONSHIP
87 OLD ST. JOSEPH'S CHURCH
89 BISHOP WHITE HOUSE
94 OLD ST. MARY'S CHURCH
95 POWEL HOUSE
97 PHYSICK HOUSE
98 MOTHER BETHEL A.M.E. CHURCH AND RICHARD ALLEN MUSEUM
99 OLD PINE STREET PRESBYTERIAN CHURCH
100 THADDEUS KOSCIUSZKO NATIONAL MEMORIAL
101 ST. PETER'S EPISCOPAL CHURCH
103 HEADHOUSE SQUARE

ⓡ RESTAURANTS

27 MORIMOTO
28 CHIFA
30 JONES
38 THE BOURSE
47 GIANFRANCO PIZZA RUSTICA
50 FORK
52 BUDDAKAN
54 HARU
58 OLD CITY COFFEE
65 AMADA
67 FRANKLIN FOUNTAIN
68 LA FAMIGLIA RISTORANTE
75 CITY TAVERN RESTAURANT
91 POSITANO COAST BY ALDO LAMBERTI
93 ZAHAV
102 XOCHITL
105 MOSHULU

ⓝ NIGHTLIFE

29 LAS VEGAS LOUNGE
48 GIGI
57 SUGAR MOM'S
62 32°
63 BLEU MARTINI
64 KHYBER PASS PUB
69 PLOUGH AND THE STARS
79 EULOGY BELGIAN TAVERN

ⓐ ARTS AND LEISURE

2 AFRICAN AMERICAN MUSEUM IN PHILADELPHIA
10 PAINTED BRIDE ART CENTER
16 SNYDERMAN-WORKS GALLERIES
19 F.U.E.L. COLLECTION
20 ARDEN THEATRE COMPANY
21 FIREMAN'S HALL MUSEUM
22 CLAY STUDIO
26 PHILADELPHIA HISTORY MUSEUM
37 NATIONAL MUSEUM OF AMERICAN JEWISH HISTORY
39 LANDMARK THEATRES (RITZ AT THE BOURSE)
46 DETOURS
53 NATIONAL LIBERTY MUSEUM
70 BLUE CROSS RIVER RINK AT PENN'S LANDING
77 LANDMARK THEATRES (RITZ EAST)
83 WASHINGTON SQUARE PARK
85 ROSE GARDEN AND MAGNOLIA GARDEN
88 POLISH AMERICAN CULTURAL CENTER AND MUSEUM
90 LANDMARK THEATRES (RITZ 5)
92 INDEPENDENCE SEAPORT MUSEUM

ⓢ SHOPS

11 SCARLETT ALLEY
12 THIRD STREET HABIT
13 MATTHEW IZZO
14 THREE SIRENS
15 LOST & FOUND
17 SUGARCUBE
42 TOPSTITCH BOUTIQUE
43 TERME DI AROMA
44 VAGABOND
45 OLD CITY
60 AKA MUSIC
61 BOOK TRADER

CHINATOWN

SEE MAP 7

Chinatown

Franklin Square

National Constitution Center 3

Free Quaker Meeting House 4

Independence Visitor Center 5

U.S. Courthouse

RACE ST
CHERRY ST
ARCH ST
FILBERT ST
MARKET ST
RAINSTEAD ST
CHESTNUT ST
SANSOM ST
WALNUT ST
LOCUST ST
SPRUCE ST
PINE ST
ADDISON ST
LOMBARD ST
BRADFORD ST
RODMAN ST

Gallery at Market East

8th

Declaration House (Graff House) 25

President's House 31

Liberty Bell Center 32

Historic Philadelphia Center and PECO Theater 33

Independence Hall 35

Philosophical Hall and Library Hall 36

Independence Square

Curtis Center and *Dream Garden* Mosaic 34

Washington Square Park

Athenaeum 84

MARSHALL

9th

Pennsylvania Hospital 82

WASHINGTON SQUARE WEST

SEE MAP 2

SEE MAP 5

Mother Bethel A.M.E. Church and Richard Allen Museum 98

Starr Garden Park

NEW ST

SEE MAP 7

Pier 12 N

BENJAMIN FRANKLIN BRIDGE

FLORIST ST

676 30

RACE ST

Pier 11 N

11 S

COLUMBUS BLVD

24

12
13
QUARRY

21

U.S. Mint
6

14
16
15
17
CHERRY ST

22
23
Elfreth's Alley

N BREAD ST

N 2ND ST

N FRONT ST

Betsy Ross House
18   19

Arch Street Friends Meeting House

ARCH ST

OLD CITY

20

7
Christ Church Burial Ground

9

42

CUTHBERT ST

FILBERT ST

Christ Church

43
44 57
58 59

3RD ST

AMERICAN ST

COMMERCE ST

45

46
47
48

CHURCH ST

60
61

66

2nd

67

70

MARKET ST

2nd ST

S STRAWBERRY ST

LETITIA

S FRONT ST

95

LUDLOW ST

49
50
Franklin Court
51

62

68

38 The Bourse

R

RANSTEAD ST

39

52 53
54 55
56

63

64

69

BANK ST

65

Penn's Landing

40

CHESTNUT ST

79
78

80

41
econd Bank of the United States

Carpenters Hall

73
71

U.S. Customs House

IONIC ST

77

PENN'S LANDING

First Bank of the United States
75

Todd House
72

89 74

Merchants' Exchange Building

Welcome Park

76

Independence Seaport Museum

92

Old St. Joseph's ose Church
87
88

Bishop White House
90   91

WALNUT ST

THOMAS ST

Delaware River

86

Philadelphia Contributionship
85

ST JAMES PL

93

SOCIETY HILL

DOCK ST

International Sculpture Garden

Boat Basin

Mary's Magnolia Gardens

Powel House
94   95

Old St. Mary's Church

LOCUST ST

38TH PARALLEL PL

City Park

SPRUCE ST

96

CYPRESS ST

Physick House
97

DELANCEY ST

Thaddeus Kosciuszko National Memorial
100

PINE ST

99
ld Pine Street Presbyterian Church

101
St. Peter's Episcopal Church

102

STAMPER ST

Headhouse

Moshulu
105

GASKILL ST

SOUTH STREET

Square
103

104

SEE MAP 5

Pier 22 S

CHRISTOPHER COLUMBUS BLVD

95

0   100 yds
0   100 m

DISTANCE ACROSS MAP
Approximate: 1.3 mi or 2 km

© AVALON TRAVEL

HOTELS

8   HOLIDAY INN HISTORIC DISTRICT
24   COMFORT INN DOWNTOWN-HISTORIC AREA
40   OMNI HOTEL AT INDEPENDENCE PARK
55   BEST WESTERN INDEPENDENCE PARK HOTEL
56   APPLE HOSTELS OF PHILADELPHIA

66   PENN'S VIEW HOTEL
78   THOMAS BOND HOUSE BED AND BREAKFAST
81   MORRIS HOUSE HOTEL
96   APPEL'S SOCIETY HILL BED & BREAKFAST
104 MADAME SAITO BED & BREAKFAST

Chinatown

Franklin Square

National Constitution Center

U.S. Mint

SEE MAP 1

RACE ST

CHERRY ST

FILBERT ST

U.S. Courthouse

Independence Visitor Center

Gallery at Market East

8th

MARKET ST

5th

Liberty Bell

Independence Hall

Independence Square

JEWELER'S ROW

Independence Square

Washington Square

9th

MARSHALL CT

Pennsylvania Hospital

PINE ST

ADDISON ST

Starr Garden Park

BRADFORD ST

RODMAN ST

GASKILL ST

SEE MAP 5

SEE MAP 1

SOUTH STREET

SIGHTS

3 ARCH STREET UNITED METHODIST CHURCH
4 MASONIC TEMPLE
7 READING TERMINAL MARKET
13 CHINATOWN FRIENDSHIP GATE
17 CITY HALL
22 ST. STEPHEN'S EPISCOPAL CHURCH
46 LIBRARY COMPANY OF PHILADELPHIA

RESTAURANTS

8 VIETNAM
12 SINGAPORE KOSHER VEGETARIAN RESTAURANT
14 SZECHUAN TASTY HOUSE
15 RAY'S CAFÉ AND TEA HOUSE
30 LOLITA
33 BARBUZZO
35 CAPOGIRO
36 1225 RAW SUSHI AND SAKE LOUNGE
37 SAMPAN
40 XIX
56 GARCES TRADING COMPANY
59 VALANNI
61 MERCATO
69 MS. TOOTSIE'S RBL

NIGHTLIFE

9 YAKITORI BOY
10 TROCADERO THEATRE
38 VINTAGE
39 FERGIE'S
43 WOODY'S
44 SISTERS
47 Q LOUNGE
49 UNCLES
51 VOYEUR
53 THE BIKE STOP
60 TAVERN ON CAMAC
64 DIRTY FRANK'S

ARTS AND LEISURE

1 PENNSYLVANIA ACADEMY OF THE FINE ARTS
5 FABRIC WORKSHOP AND MUSEUM
11 SPACE 1026
23 LUCKY STRIKE LANES
45 ACADEMY OF MUSIC
52 12TH STREET GYM
55 FORREST THEATRE
57 WALNUT STREET THEATRE
58 WILMA THEATER
63 KIMMEL CENTER
68 PHILADELPHIA THEATRE COMPANY AND SUZANNE ROBERTS THEATRE

SHOPS

6 AIA BOOKSTORE AND DESIGN CENTER
16 GALLERY AT MARKET EAST
19 MACY'S
21 SOUND OF MARKET STREET (JAZSOUND)
24 WEST ELM
25 I. GOLDBERG
26 MITCHELL & NESS
27 GROCERY
28 OPEN HOUSE
29 SCARLET FIORELLA
31 DUROSS & LANGEL
32 VERDE
34 ROBIN'S BOOKSTORE
41 NAKED CHOCOLATE CAFÉ
42 MIDTOWN VILLAGE
54 TEN THOUSAND VILLAGES
65 GIOVANNI'S ROOM
67 HELLO WORLD

HOTELS

2 LE MÉRIDIEN
18 THE RITZ-CARLTON OF PHILADELPHIA
20 LOEWS HOTEL
48 THE INDEPENDENT HOTEL
50 UNCLE'S UPSTAIRS INN
62 ALEXANDER INN
66 CLINTON STREET BED & BREAKFAST

0 100 yds
0 100 m
DISTANCE ACROSS MAP
Approximate: 4.2 mi or 6.9 km

30th

Schuylkill River

MARKET ST

LUDLOW ST

LUDLOW ST

RANSTEAD ST

CHESTNUT ST

SANSOM ST

MORAVIAN ST

WALNUT ST

SEE MAP 6

UNIVERSITY CITY

LOCUST ST

RITTENHOUSE SQUARE

SPRUCE ST

FITLER SQUARE

CYPRESS ST

DELANCEY ST

DELANCEY ST

PANAMA ST

Fitler Square

PINE ST

LOMBARD ST

NAUDAIN ST

SOUTH ST

KATER ST

BAINBRIDGE ST

GRAYS FERRY

PEMBERTON ST

FITZWATER ST

CLYMER ST

CATHARINE ST

WEBSTER ST

KAUFFMAN ST

CHRISTIAN ST

◆ SIGHTS
1 COMCAST CENTER

◆ RESTAURANTS
4	MAMA'S VEGETARIAN	51	LE BEC-FIN
6	FUJI MOUNTAIN	59	TEQUILAS RESTAURANT
8	VIC SUSHI BAR	60	MONK'S CAFÉ
9	TINTO	63	SEAFOOD UNLIMITED
15	LA COLOMBE	64	AUDREY CLAIRE
21	DI BRUNO BROS.	65	METROPOLITAN BAKERY
25	TONY JR.'S	67	MERITAGE RESTAURANT AND WINE BAR
28	LEBUS		
32	OYSTER HOUSE	69	PUMPKIN RESTAURANT
34	SHANK'S ORIGINAL UPTOWN	71	JAMAICAN JERK HUT
		73	ANTS PANTS
37	ROUGE	75	BETTY'S SPEAKEASY
45	THE BLACK SHEEP		

◆ NIGHTLIFE
5	FIRST UNITARIAN CHURCH	52	GOOD DOG
		61	MCGLINCHEY'S
10	VILLAGE WHISKEY	68	PUB AND KITCHEN
12	THE BARDS	70	BOB & BARBARA'S
22	FRANKLIN MORTGAGE & INVESTMENT CO.	72	GRACE TAVERN
		74	TEN STONE
26	TRIA	76	RESURRECTION ALE HOUSE
33	NODDING HEAD BREWERY		
		77	SIDECAR BAR & GRILLE
38	WALNUT ROOM		

◆ ARTS AND LEISURE
2	SCHUYLKILL RIVER TRAIL	55	RITTENHOUSE SQUARE
		56	CURTIS INSTITUTE OF MUSIC
3	MUTTER MUSEUM		
11	ADRIENNE THEATRE	62	RITTENHOUSE FITNESS CLUB
46	DHYANA YOGA		

◆ SHOPS
7	BALANCE HEALTH CENTER	35	ANTHROPOLOGIE
		36	KIEHL'S
13	BODY KLINIC	39	KNIT WIT
14	BORN YESTERDAY	40	BLUEMERCURY APOTHECARY AND SPA
16	TOPPERS SPA AND SALON		
17	BOYD'S	41	CHILDREN'S BOUTIQUE
18	BUFFALO EXCHANGE	42	HEAD START SHOES
20	THE SHOPS AT LIBERTY PLACE	44	URBAN OUTFITTERS
		47	APPLE STORE
23	PREMIUM STEAP	48	JOAN SHEPP
24	BENJAMIN LOVELL SHOES	49	RITTENHOUSE ROW
		50	UBIQ
29	JOSEPH FOX BOOKSHOP	53	THE SHOPS AT THE BELLEVUE
30	PETULIA'S FOLLY		
31	PLAGE TAHITI	58	RESCUE RITTENHOUSE SPA

◆ HOTELS
19	WESTIN	57	RITTENHOUSE 1715
27	HOTEL PALOMAR	66	LA RESERVE CENTER CITY BED AND BREAKFAST
43	THE LATHAM		
54	RITTENHOUSE HOTEL		

© AVALON TRAVEL

3 Philadelphia Zoo

4 Lemon Hill Mansion

5 Boathouse Row

A 6

Fairmount Water Works Interpretive Center

7

8

9

Philadelphia Museum of Art

SEDGLEY DR

LEMON HILL DR

KELLY

ZOOLOGICAL ST

RIVER

676

WALLACE ST

HAVERFORD AVE

SPRING GARDEN ST

HAMILTON ST

BARING ST

POWELTON AVE

POWELTON VILLAGE

RACE ST

WARREN ST

LANCASTER AVE

SEE MAP 6

34th

LUDLOW

UNIVERSITY CITY   SEE MAP 3

MARKET

30th

30th Street Station

AQUARIUM DR

PARRISH ST

PENNSYLVANIA AVE

ASPEN ST

MANTUA AVE

WEST

ART

DR

N 34TH ST

N 31ST ST

N 32ND ST

N 33RD ST

N 36TH ST

N 37TH ST

N 38TH ST

© AVALON TRAVEL

○ SIGHTS

3	◉ PHILADELPHIA ZOO	10	EAKINS OVAL
4	LEMON HILL MANSION	13	◉ EASTERN STATE PENITENTIARY
5	BOATHOUSE ROW	23	FREE LIBRARY OF PHILADELPHIA
7	FAIRMOUNT WATER WORKS INTERPRETIVE CENTER	27	CATHEDRAL BASILICA OF SAINTS PETER AND PAUL
9	◉ PHILADELPHIA MUSEUM OF ART		

○ RESTAURANTS

8	◉ WATER WORKS RESTAURANT	16	MUGSHOTS COFFEEHOUSE & CAFÉ
11	◉ BRIDGID'S	21	DARLING'S CAFÉ
12	LONDON GRILL	25	FOUNTAIN AT THE FOUR SEASONS
15	JACK'S FIREHOUSE		

○ NIGHTLIFE

| 1 | NORTH STAR BAR |

○ ARTS AND LEISURE

2	WAKE UP YOGA	18	FAIRMOUNT BICYCLES
6	LLOYD HALL BIKE SHACK	20	RODIN MUSEUM
14	TERROR BEHIND THE WALLS AT EASTERN STATE PENITENTIARY	22	◉ FRANKLIN INSTITUTE
		24	ACADEMY OF NATURAL SCIENCES

○ SHOPS

| 17 | ALI'S WAGON |

○ HOTELS

| 19 | BEST WESTERN CENTER CITY | 26 | FOUR SEASONS |
| | | 28 | WINDSOR SUITES |

N 1

A 2

POPLAR ST

N TANEY ST

N 22ND ST

N 21ST ST

PARRISH ST

N 20TH ST

RIDGE AVE

PERKIOMEN

BROWN ST

N 25TH ST

ASPEN ST

FAIRMOUNT

RINGGOLD ST

CORINTHIAN AVE

N 19TH ST

WYLIE ST

FRANCIS ST

MEREDITH ST **R** 11

N 25TH ST

12 R

FAIRMOUNT

13 14
A
Eastern State
Penitentiary

17 **G A** 18 AVE

NORTH ST

R 15 **R** 16

WALLACE ST

N 24TH ST

N 23RD ST

MOUNT VERNON ST

SPRING GARDEN

GREEN ST

WILCOX ST

N 22ND ST

BRANDYWINE ST

Eakins Oval
10

PENNSYLVANIA AVE

SPRING GARDEN ST

SEE MAP 7

H 19

N 21ST ST

HAMILTON ST

N 20TH ST

N 19TH ST

N 18TH ST

N 17TH ST

BENJAMIN

PARK TOWNE PL

BENJAMIN

A 20

FRANKLIN

PENNSYLVANIA AVE

FRANKLINTOWN

FRANKLIN

CALLOWHILL ST

FRANKLIN TOWN BLVD

PKWY

WOOD ST

PKWY

Schuylkill River

23
A
Free Library
of Philadelphia

76

WINTER ST

VINE ST

SPRING ST

R 21

22
A

Logan
Square

VINE ST

676

RACE ST

N 23RD ST

N 22ND ST

27
A
Cathedral Basilica of
Saints Peter and Paul

CHERRY ST

24 A

25 R 26

BENJAMIN FRANKLIN PKWY

MUSEUM
DISTRICT

ARCH ST

H 28

JOHN F KENNEDY BLVD

SEE MAP 2

0   200 yds

0   200 m

DISTANCE ACROSS MAP
Approximate: 1.7 mi or 2.7 km

Lombard-South

SEE MAP 2

RODMAN ST

SEE MAP 1

Philadelphia's
Magic Gardens ✦ 1

SOUTH ST

KATER ST

2 Ⓢ

3 Ⓡ

BAINBRIDGE ST

SEE MAP 3

FITZWATER ST

Ⓡ
21

Ⓡ 22

23 Ⓗ

25 Ⓡ

CATHARINE ST

28 Ⓐ
CATHARINE ST

CHRISTIAN ST

Ⓡ 24

29 Ⓡ

HAWTHORNE

Ⓡ 26

Ⓡ 27
MONTROSE ST

HALL ST

CARPENTER ST

KIMBALL ST

KIMBALL ST

WASHINGTON AVE

LEAGUE ST

33 Ⓡ

Ⓡ 34

611

ELLSWORTH ST

Ellsworth-Federal

Ⓝ
35

ANNIN ST

WHARTON

ANNIN ST

FEDERAL ST

36 Ⓡ E. PASSYUNK AVE

WHARTON ST

Passyunk
Square

SEARS ST

SEARS ST

EARP ST

Ⓢ
37

REED ST

0   100 yds
0   100 m

DISTANCE ACROSS MAP
Approximate: 1.7 mi or 2.7 km

WILDER ST

DICKINSON ST

Ⓝ 38

GREENICH ST

© AVALON TRAVEL

To Ⓡ 39 Marra's
Pizza

CROSS ST

TASKER ST

GASKILL ST

SOUTH STREET

Headhouse Square

MONROE ST

FABRIC ROW

FITZWATER ST

QUEEN ST

ITALIAN MARKET

CHRISTIAN ST

CARPENTER ST

Gloria Dei (Old Swedes' Episcopal Church)

WASHINGTON AVE

Jefferson Square Park

MANTON ST

TITAN ST

SEARS ST

REED ST

WILDER ST

GREENWICH ST

CROSS ST

PENNSPORT

S 6TH ST | S 5TH ST | S 4TH ST | S 3RD ST | S 2ND ST | S FRONT ST | WATER ST | COLUMBUS BLVD | CHRISTOPHER ST

☼ SIGHTS
1 PHILADELPHIA'S MAGIC GARDENS

℞ RESTAURANTS
3 CHAPTERHOUSE CAFÉ
6 BEAU MONDE
13 MARRAKESH RESTAURANT
14 JIM'S STEAKS
18 FAMOUS 4TH ST. DELICATESSEN
19 DMITRI'S
21 HAWTHORNES CAFÉ
22 SAM'S MORNING GLORY DINER

Ⓝ NIGHTLIFE
7 L'ETAGE
9 TATTOOED MOM
15 FILLMORE AT THE TLA

Ⓐ ARTS AND LEISURE
28 FLEISHER ART MEMORIAL
31 MUMMERS MUSEUM

Ⓢ SHOPS
2 VIA BICYCLE
4 SOUTH STREET
5 ANASTACIA'S ANTIQUES
8 GARLAND OF LETTERS
10 REPO RECORDS

Ⓗ HOTELS
23 BELLA VISTA BED & BREAKFAST

20 GLORIA DEI (OLD SWEDES' EPISCOPAL CHURCH)
24 ISGRO PATICCERIA
25 RALPH'S
26 Ⓒ SABRINA'S CAFÉ
27 ANTHONY'S ITALIAN COFFEE HOUSE
29 JOHN'S WATER ICE
33 NAM PHUONG
34 PLAZA GARIBALDI
36 PAT'S KING OF STEAKS
39 MARRA'S PIZZA

16 FLUID
30 ROYAL TAVERN
35 DEVIL'S DEN
38 PUB ON PASSYUNK EAST

32 UNITED ARTISTS RIVERVIEW STADIUM 17

11 Ⓒ PHILADELPHIA RECORD EXCHANGE
12 PHILADELPHIA AIDS THRIFT
17 BRICKBAT BOOKS
37 EAST PASSYUNK AVENUE

◎ SIGHTS

3	30TH STREET STATION	23	WOODLANDS CEMETERY AND MANSION
19	UNIVERSITY OF PENNSYLVANIA		

◎ RESTAURANTS

2	JG DOMESTIC	21	MARIGOLD KITCHEN
4	DISTRITO	22	GREEN LINE CAFE
10	LA TERRASSE	26	DAHLAK
11	WHITE DOG CAFÉ	27	VIENTIANE CAFÉ

◎ NIGHTLIFE

5	CAVANAUGH'S	14	WORLD CAFÉ LIVE
12	NEW DECK TAVERN	15	ROTUNDA

◎ ARTS AND LEISURE

6	INTERNATIONAL HOUSE	17	STRIKES BOWLING LOUNGE
9	INSTITUTE OF CONTEMPORARY ART	18	NEIGHBORHOOD BIKE WORKS
13	UNIVERSITY OF PENNSYLVANIA ARENA	20	UNIVERSITY MUSEUM OF ARCHAEOLOGY AND ANTHROPOLOGY
16	RAVE MOTION PICTURES UNIVERSITY CITY 6	24	CLARK PARK

◎ HOTELS

1	CORNERSTONE BED & BREAKFAST	8	THE HILTON INN AT PENN
7	INTERNATIONAL HOUSE	25	GABLES

Lee Park

FAIRMOUNT AVE

WALLACE

MOUNT VERNON ST

HARVERFORD ST

BRANDYWINE ST

BARING ST

POWELTON AVE

FILBERT ST

46th

40th

MARKET ST

LUDLOW ST

CHESTNUT ST

SANSOM ST

WALNUT ST

LOCUST ST

LOCUST WALK

SPRUCE ST

WEST PHILADELPHIA

PINE ST

OSAGE ST

LARCHWOOD AVE

BALTIMORE AVE

40th

HAZEL AVE

CEDAR AVE

BALTIMORE AVE

Clark Park

Woodlands Cemetery and Mansion
23

0   200 yds

0   200 m

DISTANCE ACROSS MAP
Approximate: 2.3 mi or 3.7 km

© AVALON TRAVEL

SEE MAP 4

Fairmount

Park

76

676

76

MANTUA

WALLACE ST

MOUNT VERNON ST

SPRING GARDEN ST

HAMILTON ST

BARING ST

PEARL ST

POWELTON AVE

1 H

LANCASTER AVE

WARREN ST

RACE ST

CHERRY ST

ARCH ST

2 R

ARCH ST

A

30th Street
Station

3

Amtrak
Station

KENNEDY BLVD

3

UNIVERSITY
CITY

34th

MARKET ST

JOHN

30th

MARKET ST

3

3

33rd

Drexel
University

LUDLOW ST

6 A H 7

9 A

36th

CHESTER ST

Main
Post
Office

8 H

10   R   R   N
11   12

14 N

WALNUT ST

19 ✦ University of
Pennsylvania

13 A

LOCUST ST

37th

SPRUCE ST

RITTENHOUSE

SPRUCE ST

A 20

PINE ST

River

LOMBARD ST

Philadelphia
Civic Center

SOUTH ST

SEE MAP 3

Schuylkill

SCHUYLKILL EXPRESSWAY

SCHUYLKILL AVE

CHRISTIAN ST

76

CARPENTER ST

GRAYS

SOUTHWEST
CENTER CITY

WASHINGTON AVE

W MASTER ST

611

W THOMPSON ST

A 1
A 2

Girard

OLD
KENSINGTON

W MASTER ST

W THOMPSON ST

Girard Medical Center

W GIRARD AVE

W GIRARD AVE

4
National Shrine
of St. John Neumann

3

W HARPER AVE

POPLAR ST

MYRTLE ST

PARISH ST

SPRING
GARDEN

OGDEN ST

Fairmount

BROWN

FAIRMOUNT

NORTHERN
LIBERTIES

SEE MAP 4

NORTH ST

WALLACE ST

POPLAR

MOUNT   VERNON   ST

WALLACE ST

LUDLOW

19
Rodeph Shalom
Synagogue

GREEN   ST

BRANDYWINE   ST

Edgar Allan Poe
National Historic Site
18

17 N

Spring
Garden

SPRING GARDEN ST

BUTTONWOOD ST

HAMILTON   ST

20

NOBLE   ST

21 N

22

611

WILLOW ST

CARLTON

CALLOWHILL ST

A 23

WOOD

676 30

VINE   ST

Franklin
Square

Race-Vine

CHINATOWN

SPRING   ST

Chinatown

SEE MAP 2

RACE

© AVALON TRAVEL

FISHTOWN

Girard

Penn
Treaty
Park

GEORGE ST

WILEY ST

LAUREL ST

POPLAR ST

I-95

GREEN ST

Spring
Garden

Piers 37 N to 57 N

Delaware River

Pier 35 1/2 N

Pier 12N

Pier 11N

BENJAMIN FRANKLIN
BRIDGE

676 30

95

SEE MAP 1

DISTANCE ACROSS MAP
Approximate: 1.7 mi or 2.8 km

0	200 yds
0	200 m

☼ SIGHTS
4   NATIONAL SHRINE OF ST.
    JOHN NEUMANN
18 EDGAR ALLEN POE
    NATIONAL HISTORIC SITE

19 RODEPH SHALOM
    SYNAGOGUE

Ⓡ RESTAURANTS
3 ◖ TIFFIN
8   BAR FERDINAND

11 STANDARD TAP
12 HONEY'S SIT 'N EAT
13 NORTH THIRD

Ⓝ NIGHTLIFE
5   KUNG FU NECKTIE
6 ◖ JOHNNY BRENDA'S
9   THE BARBARY
14 700 CLUB

17 ◖ SILK CITY
20 STARLIGHT BALLROOM
21 SHAMPOO
22 ELECTRIC FACTORY

Ⓐ ARTS AND LEISURE
1   NEW FREEDOM THEATRE
2   THE LEGENDARY BLUE
    HORIZON

10 ◖ NORTH BOWL
23 VOX POPULI AND KHMER
    GALLERY

Ⓢ SHOPS
7 ◖ THE PIAZZA AT SCHMIDTS
15 ART STAR
16 ◖ R.E. LOAD BAGGAGE, INC.

RESTAURANTS
2 MCNALLY'S TAVERN
3 OSAKA JAPANESE RESTAURANT

ARTS AND LEISURE
1 MORRIS ARBORETUM
7 WISSAHICKON PARK
8 WISSAHICKON ICE SKATING RINK

SHOPS
4 HIDEAWAY MUSIC
5 CHESTNUT HILL

HOTELS
6 CHESTNUT HILL HOTEL

© AVALON TRAVEL

RESTAURANTS
2 JAKE'S AND COOPER'S WINE BAR
5 THE COUCH TOMATO CAFÉ
6 BAYOU BAR & GRILL
8 MANAYUNK BREWERY AND RESTAURANT

ARTS AND LEISURE
7 HUMAN ZOOM

SHOPS
1 MAIN STREET MUSIC
3 SALON L'ETOILE & SPA
4 MANAYUNK

© AVALON TRAVEL

DISTANCE ACROSS MAP
Approximate: 1.2 mi or 1.9 km

| 0 | 300 yds |
| 0 | 300 m |

✪ SIGHTS
- 2 LAUREL HILL CEMETERY
- 3 STRAWBERRY MANSION
- 4 WOODFORD MANSION
- 5 LAUREL HILL MANSION
- 7 MOUNT PLEASANT
- 10 BELMONT MANSION
- 15 SMITH CIVIL WAR MEMORIAL
- 16 CEDAR GROVE
- 17 SWEETBRIAR

ⒶARTS AND LEISURE
- 6 FAIRMOUNT PARK
- 8 SMITH: THE KIDS' PLAY PLACE IN THE PARK
- 9 SEDGELEY WOODS DISC GOLF COURSE
- 11 PHILADELPHIA HORTICULTURE CENTER
- 12 SHOFUSO JAPANESE HOUSE AND GARDENS
- 13 MANN CENTER FOR THE PERFORMING ARTS
- 14 ◖ PLEASE TOUCH MUSEUM

ⒽHOTELS
- 1 ◖ CHAMOUNIX MANSION

© AVALON TRAVEL

PENNSYLVANIA

276

73

23   476
Plymouth
Meeting

Chestnut
Hill

309

Beth Sholom
Synagogue

Conshohocken

GERMANTOWN AVE

Elkins
3

611

MONTGOMERY CO
PHILADELPHIA CO

76

4
R
Fairmount

Germantown

Manayunk

Wissahickon Valley

23

Park

To Villanova

5
R

Schuylkill River

1

Bryn Mawr

West
Manayunk

76

HENRY AVE

PHILADELPHIA

Narberth

LEHIGH   AVE

7   A

30

CITY LINE AVE

Fairmount

Havertown

DARBY RD

1

LANCASTER AVE

Park

GIRARD   AVE

3

476

Upper
Darby

9   N

CHESTNUT ST

WALNUT ST

676   30

BENJAMIN
FRANKLIN
BRIDGE

13

Springfield

BALTIMORE PIKE

Drexel Hill

Darby

12   A

LINDBERGH BLVD

S BROAD AVE

611

Battleship
New Jersey

95

13   R

SASSYPUNK AVE

S 26TH AVE

76

ESSINGTON AVE

14
A

WALT
WHITMAN
BRIDGE

13

Glenoden

BARTRAM AVE

PENROSE   AVE

16   A
A

15
A   17

Franklin
Delano
Roosevelt
Park

Delaware

To
Delaware

95

To   A 18 Union
and PPL Park

Philadelphia
International
Airport

135

Abington

Huntington
Valley

Bensalem
Ⓐ 1

232

Bristol

132

63

1

Ⓢ 2

95

Cheltenham

73

13

Willingboro

To Burlington

232

Delran

13 1

6 Ⓐ

130

TACONY-
PALMYRA
BRIDGE

Cinnaminson

95

Palmyra

BETS ROSS
BRIDGE

73

8 Ⓡ

90

Pennsauken

NEW JERSEY

dventure
quarium

Camden

130

76

676

168

30

295

◆ SIGHTS

| 3 | BETH SHOLOM SYNAGOGUE | 11 | BATTLESHIP *NEW JERSEY* |
| 10 | ADVENTURE AQUARIUM | | |

Ⓡ RESTAURANTS

| 4 | VALLEY GREEN INN | 8 Ⓒ | TACCONELLI'S PIZZERIA |
| 5 | CHUBBY'S STEAKS | 13 | JOHN'S ROAST PORK |

Ⓝ NIGHTLIFE

| 9 | TOWER THEATER | | |

Ⓐ ARTS AND LEISURE

1	PARX RACING	16	76ERS
6	PENNYPACK PARK	16	FLYERS
7	BARNES FOUNDATION	16	SOUL
12	BARTRAM'S GARDEN	16	WELLS FARGO CENTER
14	AMERICAN SWEDISH HISTORY MUSEUM	16	WINGS
15	PHILLIES	17	EAGLES
		18	UNION

Ⓢ SHOPS

| 2 | FRANKLIN MILLS OUTLET MALL | | |

DISTANCE ACROSS MAP
Approximate: 23.6 mi or 38 km

0   2 mi

0   2 km

SEPTA Regional Rail & Rail Transit

MAP 10
TRANSPORTATION MAP

23

One Day - Unlimited Travel
Independence Pass

www.septa.org/pass

LEGEND

- ○ **Market-Frankford Line**
- ○ **Broad Street Line & Broad-Ridge Spur**
- ○ **Norristown High Speed Line**
  between 69th Street and Norristown
- ○ **Trolley Lines** (Routes 10, 11, 13, 15, 34, 36, 101 and 102)
- ● **Regional Rail Lines**
  (end shows route destination)
- ○ **PATCO Line**
  train to New Jersey (not a SEPTA service)
- ⊃ **Free Interchange**
  (no transfer needed between transit services)
- ● **Pedestrian Connection**
  (additional fare needed for connecting service)
- & **Wheelchair accessible station**

INFORMATION

Customer Service:	**215-580-7800**
TDD/TTY:	**215-580-7853**
Website:	**www.septa.org**

Current as of June 2011

Discover Philadelphia

Home to more than 1.5 million people, Philadelphia is the sixth largest city in the country, yet it has been described as "the biggest small town in America." Perhaps that is because it's a city of close-knit neighborhoods, where everyone seems to know everyone and many families have been rooted for generations. But whatever the cause, the result is a bustling city that offers every cultural amenity while somehow remaining cozy, friendly, and more accessible than most major metropolises.

Philadelphia is considered the birthplace of the nation, and its most famous historical landmarks are located in Independence National Historical Park, "the nation's most historic square mile." In addition to Independence Hall, the Liberty Bell, and a multitude of other attractions, the area comes complete with horse-drawn carriages and tour guides dressed in colonial garb. As you're exploring the streets (some paved and some still cobblestone), history is always present. While Philadelphia has a modern, world-class downtown, the shiny new skyscrapers, restaurants, theaters, shops, and hotels still mingle with the well-preserved homes and churches of our founding fathers.

You've probably come to Philadelphia to see the Bell, eat the world-famous cheesesteaks, and run up the Art Museum steps à la Rocky Balboa, and by all means, do all of that while you're here. But be sure to also take time to experience the activities that locals enjoy on a daily basis. Relax in Rittenhouse Square. Grab lunch in Reading Terminal Market. See a play on the Avenue of the Arts. Shop at the Italian Market. Take a hike in Wissahickon Park. And visit the colorful neighborhoods beyond Center City to find family-run greasy spoons where you'll be called "Hon," charming neighborhood BYOBs, and dive bars where Quizzo and karaoke rival the 76ers, Eagles, Phillies, and Flyers as serious competitive sports.

Philadelphia has gotten a lot of recent press about becoming America's "next great city." And while locals are the first to admit (okay, brag) that the city has seen a myriad of welcome improvements in the past few decades, the qualities at the very essence of the city's charm — its rich history and diverse neighborhoods filled with passionate, colorful characters — have been long established. As any proud local will tell you — and we are all proud — Philly has *always* been a great city; it just keeps getting better all the time.

We couldn't be happier that millions of visitors are flocking to see for themselves what we've known all along, but let's be clear: Philadelphia will never become "the next" New York, Boston, or San Francisco. There is no other city in the world quite like Philly — and that's just the way we like it.

Planning Your Trip

▶ WHERE TO GO

Old City

Most first-time visits to Philadelphia begin in Old City. Home to Independence National Historical Park, "the nation's most historic square mile," this is where you'll find Independence Hall, the Liberty Bell, the National Constitution Center, and many other historic attractions. Old City also has a wealth of dining, shopping, hotels, and nightlife.

Society Hill

A tranquil neighbor to Old City, Society Hill boasts many of the finest and oldest homes and cathedrals in the city. Bordered by leafy Washington Square Park to the west and the Penn's Landing waterfront strip to the east, it is a lovely place to soak up American history.

Center City East

Broad Street, known as Avenue of the Arts in the blocks south of City Hall that are home

Independence Hall

to the city's biggest theater and opera houses, divides the downtown business district into East and West. Center City East is home to Reading Terminal Market, Chinatown,

Chinatown Friendship Gate

Rittenhouse Square

Midtown Village, Antique Row and Washington Square West, which is the center of local gay culture.

Center City West

The skyscrapers, hotels, restaurants, bars, and shops are the biggest and generally the most upscale on the west side of Broad Street in Center City West. The action centers around tree-lined Rittenhouse Square and the chic Rittenhouse Row shopping district, also home to many restaurants, hotels, and bars.

Museum District

Lined with flowers, sculptures, and flags from around the world, the Benjamin Franklin Parkway is the broad, diagonal street connecting City Hall with the Philadelphia Museum of Art. Home to the Franklin Institute, Rodin Museum, Academy of Natural Sciences, and the newly relocated Barnes Foundation, the Museum District is considered the cultural center of the city. Just north in the Fairmount neighborhood is the spooky Eastern State Penitentiary.

South Philadelphia

South Street, known for its eclectic mix of tattoo parlors, independent record stores, dive bars, and upscale restaurants, forms the northern border of South Philly. The Italian Market embodies the area's diverse mix of Italian and Asian influences. Farther south, East Passyunk Avenue has hip new restaurants and chic boutiques alongside centuries-old family-run pizza joints and tchotchke shops.

University City

The University of Pennsylvania and Drexel University are just blocks apart in University City, the section of West Philly nearest to Center City. While the area is dominated by student life, there are also museums, restaurants, shopping, and bed-and-breakfasts for all ages to enjoy.

Northern Liberties

For many years considered the up-and-coming neighborhood, No-Libs has officially come up. Chic boutiques and the Edgar Allen Poe House draw a sprinkling of visitors by day, but the area—with its excellent restaurants and nightlife—truly comes alive at night.

Fairmount Park

The largest urban park system in the nation boasts miles of hiking, biking, and jogging trails. The Schuylkill River Bike Path is a paved loop that spreads out on both sides of the river. In addition to endless recreational opportunities, the park is home to historic sights, gardens, and the Philadelphia Zoo.

Chestnut Hill and Manayunk

A short drive from Center City along I-76 or Kelly Drive, Manayunk and Chestnut Hill are well worth the trip. Main Street is Manayunk's trendy strip of boutiques, bars, and restaurants, and Germantown Avenue is Chestnut Hill's upper-crust shopping district. While you're in the northwest part of the city, take a hike in peaceful Wissahickon Park and visit the historic homes in nearby Germantown.

the Channel 6 Zooballoon at the Philadelphia Zoo

▶ WHEN TO GO

To enjoy the mildest weather and avoid the largest crowds, visit in spring or fall. To be assured that all attractions are open, visit May–October, as a small selection of tourist sites are only open seasonally. If you don't mind longer lines for popular attractions and hotel rates that rise along with the temperature, the city comes alive in summer with festivals, fireworks, and parades—especially during the week of Independence Day. And if you don't mind bundling up, winter offers the lowest hotel rates, fewest crowds, and, if you're lucky, perhaps a beautiful snowfall.

a city street in fall

Laurel Hill Cemetery in winter

spring at the Horticulture Center

Explore Philadelphia

▶ THE THREE-DAY BEST OF PHILADELPHIA

It would take at least a week to experience all the major sights and neighborhoods in Philadelphia, but you can experience many of the highlights in just three days. Stay in or near Center City, where it's easy to get anywhere in the city on foot, by bike, on public transportation, or by the seasonal hop-on hop-off tour buses that stop at major attractions around the city.

You can easily spend an entire afternoon or even a day at the biggest and best sights, including the National Constitution Center, Franklin Institute, and especially the Philadelphia Museum of Art, so you'll have to keep moving if you want to hit multiple sights in a short time. While this itinerary covers primarily sights and dining, you'll be in many areas that happen to be shopping havens, so feel free to skip some of the sights and hit the stores instead.

Day 1

▶ Any first-time visit to Philadelphia should begin in Old City, where Philly's most famous historic sights are conveniently located within a few square blocks dubbed Independence National Historical Park.

▶ Have breakfast at Metro Café and then head to the Independence Visitor Center. Here, you'll find information and maps, watch a short historical film, sign up for tours, buy tickets for tour buses, and most important, reserve your free timed ticket for Independence Hall.

▶ Spend the rest of the morning at the National Constitution Center or take a Mural Tour in an open-air trolley.

▶ Eat lunch at The Bourse food court, then spend the afternoon visiting the Liberty Bell and Independence Hall. If time allows, stop at nearby Franklin Court or the Betsy Ross House.

▶ Old City is filled with restaurants and nightlife, so you have plenty to choose from. Try Amada for exquisite tapas, Zahav for modern Middle Eastern cuisine, or continue to immerse yourself in history with dinner at historic City Tavern Restaurant.

▶ Finish the night with the Lights of Liberty nighttime walking tour, or if you're ready to return to the present, go bar hopping at the trendy Old City clubs.

The *Common Threads* mural by Meg Saligman, located at Broad and Spring Garden Streets, is one of the highlights of the open-air trolley Mural Tour.

CHEESESTEAKS AND BEYOND

With many of its top restaurants receiving national acclaim, Philly has become a real foodie town. But when you're in need of a quick bite, it's hard to beat the longtime culinary classics that are as iconic to Philly as the Liberty Bell. Be sure to try all of the following at least once while you're here.

CHEESESTEAKS

You're never far from a great cheesesteak in Philly, and it's true that they are simply not as good anywhere else. They're served in every neighborhood, at diners and in bars, out of food trucks and storefront windows, and in restaurants serving upscale twists on the classic. **Pat's King of Steaks** (1237 E. Passyunk Ave.) and **Geno's Steaks** (1219 S. 9th St.), the famous dueling spots in South Philly, are worth a visit for the cultural experience, but **Jim's Steaks** (400 South St.), another regular stop for visiting celebs, serves superior steaks in my opinion. Others to try are **Tony Jr.'s** (118 S. 18th St.), **Shank's Original Uptown** (120 S. 15th St.), **John's Roast Pork** (14 E. Snyder Ave.), and **Chubby's Steaks** (5826 Henry Ave.). And remember, you're in Philly, so it's just a cheesesteak, not a "Philly cheesesteak."

HOAGIES

Most locals would argue that hoagies, loosely translated as Philly's version of the "hero" or "sub," are in a league of their own in the sandwich family. Exactly why hoagies are better than other sandwiches is debatable, but the bread certainly plays a large part. Many use Amoroso's rolls (a Philly institution since 1904) or their own gourmet bread, but never airy, tasteless rolls. A few spots to try are: **Sarcone's** (734 S. 9th St.), **Shank's** (120 S. 15th St.) and **Koch's Deli** (4309 Locust St.).

SOFT PRETZELS

With a history dating to early German settlers to the area, the soft pretzel remains a strong local tradition. Indulge in a perfectly browned, chewy soft pretzel, topped with rock salt and smothered with yellow mustard. It should be chewy – not hard or soggy – and is always best fresh out of the oven. Try **Center City Pretzel Co.** (816 Washington Ave.) or the **Philly Pretzel Factory** (1532 Sansom St.), a mostly local chain with multiple locations.

WATER ICE

Pronounced locally as "wooder ice," water ice is an essential part of summer in the city. Vastly superior to the supermarket variety of Italian ice or snow cones (syrup drizzled over ice), a proper water ice has a perfectly smooth, creamy consistency – often blended with real bits of fruit. Try **John's Water Ice** (701 Christian St.) or **Rita's** (239 South St.), a Philly-born chain that's spreading real water ice throughout the country. Most places are open from late spring through early fall, which is fine, because no one wants to anything with the word "ice" in it in winter.

Just order a cheesesteak "whiz wit" for the classic with Cheez Whiz and fried onions.

Day 2

▶ Spend the day in the Museum District. Walk along the picturesque Benjamin Franklin Parkway and take your pick from the many museums while stopping for photo-ops along the way.

▶ Don't miss the world-class Philadelphia Museum of Art, and before you run up those famous steps, snap some pictures with the Rocky statue.

▶ Visit the small but lovely Rodin Museum, or if you prefer science to art, go to the Franklin Institute or the Academy of Natural Sciences instead.

▶ Have lunch at Darling's Café or the classy Four Seasons hotel, and then stroll behind the Art Museum to see Fairmount Water Works Interpretive Center and Boathouse Row.

▶ If time allows, walk a few blocks north to the Eastern State Penitentiary and have dinner at London Grill or one of the other restaurants and bars on Fairmount Avenue.

Day 3

▶ Begin your day with breakfast at Reading Terminal Market. Stop to explore City Hall, and on weekdays take a tour or ride the elevator to the base of the William Penn statue for a spectacular view of the city.

▶ Next, tour the Masonic Temple across the street or the nearby Pennsylvania Academy of the Fine Arts.

▶ Grab lunch at one of the many area food trucks or at Di Bruno Bros. market and take it to Rittenhouse Square for a picnic. Spend the afternoon strolling and

TOP 10 FOR KIDS

- Join in a real archaeological dig at the **Academy of Natural Sciences** (page 142).

- Take the RiverLink ferry across the Delaware to the **Adventure Aquarium** in Camden, New Jersey (page 76).

- Tour the **Betsy Ross House,** with an audio tour and scavenger hunt designed just for kids (page 47).

- See historic Philadelphia in a whole new light on the **Lights of Liberty** 3-D nighttime walking tour (page 50).

- Walk through the giant human heart model and visit the IMAX theater at the **Franklin Institute** science museum (page 142).

- Ride the carousel and play mini-golf at the historic-themed course in **Franklin Square** (page 49).

- Take part in interactive exhibits at the **National Constitution Center** (page 43).

- Visit the hands-on petting zoo and Treehouse and ride in the Zooballoon at the **Philadelphia Zoo** (page 66).

- Discover one of the world's best interactive kids' museums, the **Please Touch Museum** (page 143).

- Play in Fairmount Park's sprawling indoor and outdoor **Smith: The Kids' Play Place in the Park** (page 156).

mom and baby giraffes at the Philadelphia Zoo

shopping on Rittenhouse Row, or visit the nearby Mutter Museum.

▶ In the evening, catch a show at any of the lovely theaters on the Avenue of the Arts. Have at dinner at one of the many great restaurants in Rittenhouse or head to Chinatown. Or—if you somehow haven't yet, have a cheesesteak already! Tony Jr.'s is a Rittenhouse area favorite, or venture into South Philly for a one-of-a-kind experience at Pat's King of Steaks.

FUN AND FREE: PHILLY ON A BUDGET

You don't have to be rich to have fun in Philly. All of the following sights and activities are free – yes, you heard right, free.

SIGHTS

With the exception of the National Constitution Center, all of the sights operated by **Independence National Historical Park** are free, including the **Liberty Bell Center, Independence Hall, Franklin Court, Carpenters' Hall, Bishop White House, the U.S. Mint,** and the **Edgar Allen Poe House.** The **Independence Visitor Center** also has a free mini-museum and film to help visitors get acquainted with the area. Most of the historic cathedrals and places of worship throughout the city are open to the public free of charge, including **Arch Street Friends Meeting House, Old Pine Street Presbyterian,** and **Mother Bethel A.M.E.**

On the Avenue of the Arts, free themed tours are offered of the **Kimmel Center** and the **Academy of Music,** two of the city's most beautiful theaters, and the Kimmel Center offers free performances.

MUSEUMS

Pay whatever you wish (zero is a number too) at the **Philadelphia Museum of Art,** including the **Perelman Building,** on the first Sunday of each month, and at the **Independence Seaport Museum** every Sunday 10 A.M.-noon. The **University Museum of Archaeology and Anthropology** is free during the last hour of each day, and the **Fairmount Waterworks Interpretive Center** and the **Institute of Contemporary Art** are always free. At the **Rodin Museum,** a $5 donation is suggested but not required.

GALLERIES

Most of the city's art galleries are free, including the **Morris Gallery** and ground floor of the Pennsylvania Academy of the Fine Arts, which presents rotating exhibitions of regional artists. The best time to visit the smaller galleries, mostly located in Old City and Northern Liberties, is on the **First Friday** of the month, when they are open to the public, many with the added lure of snacks and wine, which are also free.

the Rodin Museum

SIGHTS

Millions of visitors from the United States and abroad come each year to soak in the rich history of our nation's birthplace—and for good reason. A 2009 *Travel + Leisure* survey ranked Philadelphia third among U.S. cities for its wealth of historical sights and monuments. Our nation was formed largely out of events that took place on local ground, including Revolutionary War battles and the drafting of the Declaration of Independence and Constitution, and a wealth of monuments and museums keep that history alive.

The largest concentration of sights can be found in Independence National Historical Park, rightfully dubbed "America's most historic square mile." Many of the city's most famous attractions—including the Liberty Bell and Independence Hall—are conveniently located within this compact and attractive area, where tour guides in colonial garb and horse-drawn carriages make it easy to imagine the Philadelphia of our founding fathers. Even the least patriotic among us find it hard not to feel a surge of national pride after spending time in this part of town.

The past decade has brought still more life to Independence Park, with the addition of the interactive multimedia National Constitution Center; the Liberty Bell Center, a mini-museum to house the Liberty Bell; and a major renovation of Franklin Square. The President's House monument and the National Museum of American Jewish History both opened in 2010, bringing even more diverse stories of early Philadelphia and U.S. history than ever before. The Historic Philadelphia Center

© KARRIE GAVIN

HIGHLIGHTS

LOOK FOR TO FIND RECOMMENDED SIGHTS.

🌙 **Most Momentous Building:** Both the Declaration of Independence and the Constitution were debated and drafted in **Independence Hall,** and our nation was born (page 38).

🌙 **Most Iconic Philadelphia Landmark:** The Liberty Bell is practically synonymous with the City of Brotherly Love. At the **Liberty Bell Center,** you'll learn about its history and the many freedom movements that claim the bell as their symbol (page 42).

🌙 **Most Modern Old City Attraction:** Offering a refreshing and fascinating contrast to the many historic buildings, the world-class **National Constitution Center** delights with its high-tech interactive exhibits highlighting the history and meaning of the U.S. Constitution (page 43).

🌙 **Most Complicated Site:** Many of the same men who fought so hard for our nation's independence on the premise that "all men are created equal" owned their own slaves. The **President's House** aims to explore this paradox on the ground where the nation's first White House once stood (page 45).

🌙 **Most Beautiful Office Building:** Philadelphia's **City Hall** is the largest municipal building in the nation and arguably the most breathtaking. This impressive work of architecture is crowned by a 37-foot-tall figure of William Penn – the largest statue atop any building in the world (page 56).

🌙 **Most Secretive Sight:** A tour of the **Masonic Temple** reveals a lot about the magnificent building and a little about the oldest, most mysterious fraternal order in the world – the masons. The building is considered one of the three most impressive Masonic temples in the world (page 58).

🌙 **Most Historic Market:** Where else but the **Reading Terminal Market** can you eat delicious international fare and shop for unique goods in a former railroad station more than 100 years old? Go hungry: The smells are simply irresistible (page 59).

🌙 **Spookiest Sight:** The **Eastern State Penitentiary** mixes past and present with artist installations placed throughout the grounds in addition to all those creepy ghosts you'll encounter on a tour (page 62).

🌙 **Best Art Museum – Inside and Out:** Before entering the world-renowned **Philadelphia Museum of Art,** be sure to take in the stunning Greek Revival building – and stand at the top of the "Rocky steps" to survey the city (page 64).

🌙 **Best Place to See Animals and Get High:** The **Philadelphia Zoo** is the nation's oldest zoo, but it is regularly updated with all-new, cutting-edge attractions, including the Zooballoon, a hot-air balloon that rises high above the city offering breathtaking views of the skyline, Schuylkill River, and Fairmount Park (page 66).

© CHRISTOPHER WOODS

lion at the Philadelphia Zoo

reopened its technologically advanced Lights of Liberty walking tour and added Liberty 360, a 3-D panoramic film—two attractions that bring the past up to date with the present with groundbreaking technology.

While Old City is the nexus of action for tourists, you're never far from history anywhere in Philadelphia, with markers of the city's long life apparent from South Philadelphia to Germantown. As you explore, look for the National Historic Landmark symbols on homes, churches, cemeteries, hotels, and even some of the buildings that now house modern shops and restaurants.

In addition to the 300-plus-year-old sites, you will see 19th-century architectural gems like City Hall and the Grand Masonic Temple sharing the skyline with ultramodern skyscrapers like the Cira Center and the Comcast Center. Extending out from Center City, the Benjamin Franklin Parkway, often called the Museum or Cultural District, is a sight in its own right. Inspired by Paris's Champs-Élysées, it connects City Hall with the world-renowned Philadelphia Museum of Art, which expanded in 2007 with the addition of the Perelman Building across the street. On or near the Parkway, you can also visit the Franklin Institute, the Academy of Natural Sciences, and the Rodin Museum, which will soon be joined by the world-renowned Barnes Collection, slated to relocate from just outside the city to its new home by 2012.

Fairmount Park extends on both sides of the Schuylkill River and into the northwest section of the city, and in addition to its vast recreational opportunities, it is home to the Philadelphia Zoo, historic homes, gardens, and sculptures. Still more historic homes—including stops on the Underground Railroad and sites of Revolutionary battles—are open for tours in Germantown. Meanwhile, local institutions like Reading Terminal Market have remained popular for more than a century, helping connect Philadelphia's history with the present. In a place that has done an extraordinary job of preserving its past while keeping up with the times, there is no shortage of interesting sights to see.

Old City · Map 1

INDEPENDENCE NATIONAL HISTORICAL PARK

Operated by National Park Services (215/965-2305, www.nps.gov/inde), Independence National Historical Park includes many of the most important sights in the heart of Old City, including the Liberty Bell and Independence Hall. Because this is a government organization dedicated to preserving American history, all of the sites with the exception of the National Constitution Center, are free. Major sites are open 9 A.M.–5 P.M. daily, some with extended hours in summertime, while hours of more minor sites change seasonally and some close completely in winter. A free automated cell phone tour (267/519-4295) operates around the clock. Explore the sites in any order you like and look for numbered signs posted on buildings. When prompted, punch in the number of the site to hear more stories and information about the site for no more than the cost of minutes on your phone.

Start your day at **Independence Visitor Center** (215/537-7676, www.independence visitorcenter.com) to find information, sign up for tours, and pick up the free timed-entrance tickets required for Independence Hall March–December. Come early in summertime as it's first-come, first-served, and tickets are often gone for the day by lunchtime. Beyond the national park, there are many additional attractions in the surrounding blocks of Old City and Society Hill. The area is easily explored on foot, but if you prefer, take the **PHLASH** (800/537-7676, www.phillyphlash.com, $2 per trip, $5 per day, $10 all-day family pass for five people). The big purple trolley offers continuous service May–October 10 A.M.–6 P.M. with

Independence Visitor Center

27 stops at major attractions within the park and throughout the city.

BISHOP WHITE HOUSE

309 Walnut St., 215/965-2305, www.nps.gov/inde
HOURS: Tour only, call ahead
COST: Free; tickets required, available at Independence Visitor Center

Reverend William White (1748–1836) was the first Episcopal bishop of Pennsylvania and founder of the American Episcopal Church. For nearly 50 years he lived in this home conveniently located between the two churches where he served as rector—Christ Church and St. Peter's Church. Many prominent 18th-century figures, among them George Washington and Benjamin Franklin, visited him here. Restored to its 1787 appearance, the elegant Federal-style mansion offers a glimpse into the life of an upper-class 18th-century Philadelphia family. It contains White's library, personal items, and an early version of a flush toilet, or privy—one of the very first in a Philadelphia home. Tours are limited to 10 people at a time on a first-come, first-served basis in combination with a tour of the Todd House.

CARPENTERS' HALL

320 Chestnut St., 215/925-0167, www.carpentershall.org
HOURS: Mar.-Dec. Tues.-Sun. 10 A.M.-4 P.M., Jan.-Feb. Wed.-Sun. 10 A.M.-4 P.M.
COST: Free

Before the meeting of the Second Continental Congress at Independence Hall, the First Continental Congress met in 1774 at Carpenters' Hall. George Washington, John Adams, Samuel Adams, and Patrick Henry were among the group, which included delegates from 12 colonies who met to discuss their discontent with their ruler, King George. They were particularly disgruntled about the "taxation without representation" imposed on the colonies. The meeting resulted in one of the earliest formal acts of rebellion against British rule—a trade embargo—and was the precursor to the Second Continental Congress, which met two years later and declared war. The Georgian-style building was designed by Robert Smith and built in 1770 to serve as headquarters for the Carpenters' Company of Philadelphia. Founded in 1724, the Carpenters' Company exists today as the nation's oldest trade guild. Over its long history, it has also been home to Franklin's Library Company, the American Philosophical Society, the First and Second Banks of the United States, and a hospital for American forces during the Revolutionary War. Inside, you'll find a scale model of the building, the original Windsor chairs used by members of the Continental Congress, and a banner carried during the 1788 parade celebrating the ratification of the Constitution.

A modest brick building next to Carpenters' Hall introduces visitors to one of the most significant developments of the colonial era: the beginning of the U.S. military. The **New Hall Military Museum** includes exhibits on the Army, Navy, and Marine Corps, past and present. Educational seminars are given during the summer. The building is a reconstruction of the original built by the Carpenters' Company in 1791, which housed the office of the first Secretary of War, Henry Knox.

CITYPASS OR PHILADELPHIA PASS

Purchasing a **CityPass** (888/330-5008, www.citypass.com/philadelphia) is a convenient and economical option if you're planning to visit most or all of the attractions that are included. It buys you one day of hop-on, hop-off service on the Philadelphia Trolley Works and Big Bus Company, which connects all of the other attractions, and admission to the Franklin Institute, Adventure Aquarium, and the Philadelphia Zoo, as well as your choice of admission to either the Academy of Natural Sciences or the National Constitution Center and your choice of the Please Touch Museum or Eastern State Penitentiary. Good for a total of six attractions and valid for nine days, the passes are available at the Independence Visitor Center, online, or at any of the participating attractions. At a cost of $59 for adults and $39 for kids 2-12, visiting three of the six attractions makes the pass worthwhile, and visiting all six will save almost half off full admission prices.

Another option is the **Philadelphia Pass** (888/567-7277, www.philadelphiapass.com), which includes admission to more than 40 popular attractions, including all of those offered with the CityPass, as well as discounts at other sights, tours, shops, and restaurants. This may be a better choice if you're short on time and planning a quick whirlwind tour, but you'll have to move quickly since it is only valid for one, two, three, or five consecutive days. Prices range $49-115 for adults and $39-95 for kids 2-12 depending on how many days you purchase. The more days, the more you can save, with the five-day pass getting you access to most of the city's sights for just $23 per day. Purchase online in advance and the pass can be sent to you or you can print out an email confirmation and pick it up at Independence Visitor Center. An extra perk of either of these passes is skipping the lines at most attractions.

Keep in mind that these passes are economical when you're planning to pay for admission to several of the sites included, but if it is just an easy means of transportation you're looking for, the **PHLASH** buses (800/537-7676, www.phillyphlash.com, $2 per trip or $5 per day, all-day family pass $10) are a convenient option. Offering continuous service May-October every 12 minutes 10 A.M.-6 P.M., the big purple buses cover a lot of ground, stopping at 27 attractions across the city.

DECLARATION HOUSE (GRAFF HOUSE)
701 Market St., 215/965-2305, www.nps.gov/inde
HOURS: Daily 9 A.M.-noon, with extended summer hours
COST: Free

When bricklayer Jacob Graff Jr. decided to rent out rooms in the modest home he built for himself in 1775, he never could have anticipated what would happen under his roof. Thomas Jefferson—a Virginia delegate to the Continental Congress and future president of the United States—was his boarder, and it was in these rooms that he drafted the Declaration of Independence. A small exhibit on the 1st floor contains rough drafts of the seminal document and a small theater for viewing the short film *The Extraordinary Creation*. The film reveals important details—like the fact that Jefferson's original version called for the abolition of slavery, but it was eliminated because the committee, including Benjamin Franklin and John Adams, didn't feel people were ready for the change. Upstairs, you can see Jefferson's bedroom and parlor, which include reproduction furnishings of his desk and swivel chair.

FRANKLIN COURT
314-322 Market St., 215/965-2305, www.nps.gov/inde
HOURS: Hours vary by building and season, most exhibits open daily 9 A.M.-5 P.M. in summer
COST: Free

Philadelphia's favorite son—a printer, diplomat, inventor, publisher, author, statesman, and postmaster—founded the Library Company, Pennsylvania Hospital, Philosophical Society, the University of Pennsylvania, and much, much more, so it's fitting that an entire court occupying a large portion of a city block is dedicated to him. This is where Ben Franklin's home stood for the final five years of his life after he returned from nearly 20 years of working as a commissary in France and England. On the spot, a "ghost structure" made of steel designed by world-famous architect Robert Venturi for the bicentennial outlines the area. Remains of the original foundation, underground kitchen, and privy pit (toilet) can be seen through viewing pits in the ground, and flagstones around the house have been carved with bits of correspondence between Ben and his wife, Deborah, mostly discussing renovations to their home while he was away.

At the opposite end of the court, a row of homes built by Franklin in the late 1780s has been transformed into the **Franklin Court Museum Shop** and the **B. Free Franklin Post Office and Museum.** Note that the post office is the only one in the country that does not display an American flag—the flag had not yet been created at the time it was founded. The court also contains an archaeological display called "Fragments of Franklin Court" and a **Printing Office and Bindery.** The **Underground Museum** showcases interactive exhibits and a 22-minute film entitled *The Real Ben Franklin.* A phone bank plays audio testimonies about Franklin based on the words of other famous people in history. As you will learn at the site, like most major public figures Franklin was highly praised and highly criticized. But there is no doubt he left quite a mark on Philadelphia, and the world.

FREE QUAKER MEETING HOUSE
500 Arch St., 215/965-2305, www.nps.gov/inde
HOURS: Wed.-Sun. 11 A.M.-4 P.M.
COST: Free

The Revolutionary War raised a major dilemma for many Quakers—whether to uphold their religious values or fight those darn Brits. Since one of the most important tenets of the religion is pacifism, those who decided to join the fight for independence were often excommunicated from their meeting houses, so in 1783, those ousted for their political beliefs founded one of their own. The simple brick Georgian structure designed by Samuel Wetherill had 200-plus members at one time, including Betsy Ross and Constitution-signer Thomas Mifflin, who became known as the "fighting Quakers." After the war, most returned to their former meeting houses, and by 1834 services were no longer held here. It has since been a school, an apprentice library, a plumbing warehouse, and headquarters for the Junior League of Philadelphia. Take a peek at the two original benches and original window and the five-pointed-star tissue pattern that Betsy Ross is believed to have used to make the first American flag. Descendants of the original group still hold annual meetings here.

◖ INDEPENDENCE HALL
Chestnut St. btwn. 5th and 6th Sts., 877/444-6777, www.nps.gov/inde
HOURS: Daily 9 A.M.-5 P.M.; tours start every 15-30 minutes, last tour at 4:30 P.M.
COST: Free, timed-ticket required Mar.-Dec.; reserve at Independence Visitor Center the day of visit (tickets go fast in summer so come early) or in advance online or by phone ($1.50 charge)

Independence Hall is the centerpiece of Independence National Historical Park. Just in case you slept through grade-school history classes, this is where the Declaration of Independence and the Constitution were debated, drafted, and signed, and where the United States' independence from England became official. The principles that our nation was founded on were formed inside these walls.

Originally called the State House, the classic Georgian structure was designed by Andrew Hamilton and Edmund Wooley and built 1732–1756. Of the many restorations it has undergone, the most notable were those by Greek Revival architect John Havilland in 1830 and by the National Park Service in 1950; the latter greatly restored the building to its late 18th-century appearance. The furniture is largely reproduction pieces, since most of the original

© KARRIE GAVIN

The Declaration of Independence and the U.S. Constitution were drafted inside Independence Hall, formerly the State House.

furniture was burnt during the winter of 1777–1778 when Philadelphia was briefly occupied by the British Army. Independence Hall was the meeting place for the Second Continental Congress 1775–1783, except during that brief British occupation. The most important decisions were made in the 1st-floor **Assembly Room,** home to George Washington's famous "Rising Sun" chair. This is where he was appointed commander in chief of the Continental Army (1775), the Declaration of Independence was adopted (July 4, 1776), the design of the American flag was agreed upon (1777), the Articles of Confederation were adopted (1781), and the U.S. Constitution was drafted (1787). Original copies of the Articles of Confederation, Declaration of Independence, and the Constitution are on display in the **Great Essentials Exhibit** in the West Wing. You can also see the Syng silver inkstand that the founding fathers dipped their ink into to sign the Declaration of Independence and the Constitution.

Independence Hall is actually the center of a trio of matching Georgian buildings that housed the three branches of early government, and it makes sense to visit all of them together. On the corner of Chestnut and 5th Streets sits **Old City Hall.** Built in 1790 by master carpenter David Evans, it was home to the United States Supreme Court 1791–1800. Once the capital moved to D.C., this building became Philadelphia's City Hall until 1870.

On the corner of Chestnut and 6th Streets is **Congress Hall,** where the two branches of Congress met (1790–1800). The House of Representatives was on the 1st floor and the Senate on the 2nd floor. Built in 1787, Congress Hall was the site of the presidential inaugurations of George Washington (second term) and John Adams. It is also where the Bill of Rights was ratified. On the 2nd floor, there are many symbolic designs, including a 19th-century fresco of an eagle holding an olive branch signifying peace and a plaster medallion on the ceiling with an oval sunburst with 13 stars to honor the 13 original states. The carpet features 13 state shields and cornucopias

SIGHTSEEING TOURS

Taking a guided tour can be a fun and educational way to start your visit to Philadelphia. Options range from your basic history tour to a bar crawl led by guides in colonial garb. Old City is usually best explored on foot, with lots of sights within close proximity of one another, but to cover farther-reaching areas of the city – or when hot summer temperatures make it unpleasant to do much walking at all – there are also bike, bus, trolley, carriage, boat, and even kayak tours to choose from.

ON FOOT

Guided 75-minute **Constitutional Walking Tours** (215/525-1776, www.theconstitutional.com, Apr.-Nov., $17.50 pp, children 3-12 $12.50, $55 family of four) start at Independence Visitor Center (6th and Market Sts.) and cover about 20 sites, including the Betsy Ross House, Christ Church, and the National Constitution Center. For $15, download the tour to your MP3 and go at your own pace. Note that price of the tour does not include admission tickets.

On a 90-minute **Candlelight Ghost Tour** (215/413-1997, www.ghosttour.com/Philadelphia.html, Apr.-Oct. daily 7:30 P.M., additional times in summer, Nov.-Mar. days and times vary, $17 adult, $8 children 4-12) of Independence Park and Society Hill, you'll hear tales of ghosts believed to roam "America's most historic and most haunted city," with stops including Independence Hall and St. Peter's Cemetery. The same company offers a Haunted Trolley Tour, also 90 minutes, which covers more ground with less time at each site ($30 adult, $20 children 4-12). Walking tours depart from Signers Garden (5th and Chestnut Sts.), and trolley tours depart from outside the Bourse (11 S. 5th St.). Purchase tickets at the Independence Visitor Center, Omni Hotel Gift Shop (415 Chestnut St.), or online.

A variety of unique tours depart from **Historic Philadelphia Center** (Chestnut and 6th Sts., 215/629-4026, www.onceuponanation.org, Apr.-Oct., times vary). Costumed actors debate over war with England on a walk to Independence Hall on the **Turmoil and Treason Tour** ($20 adults, $18 senior/student/military, $15 children 12 and under). The **Colonial Kids Quest** ($17, children 2 and under free) lets kids play detective and look for a missing copy of the Declaration of Independence, while on the **Tipplers Tour** ($34 adult, $30 senior/military/student), adults enjoy a drink at four different bars while learning about the role of the local watering holes in colonial Philadelphia. The **Independence After Hours Tour** ($75 adult, $50 children 12 and under, $70 senior/military/student) includes a three-course dinner at City Tavern with Revolutionary-era reenactments between courses, followed by a walk to Independence Hall where you'll "sneak" inside to watch the founding fathers debate the Declaration of Independence. In addition, the **Lights of Liberty** underwent a $10 million makeover with a new and improved tour debuting in 2011 that tells the story of the American Revolution through an audio track, giant laser-light images, and groundbreaking 3-D technology.

For a free tour of Independence Park, **Twilight Tours** (early July–Labor Day, daily 6 P.M., free) are offered by **Friends of Independence National Historical Park** (143 S. 3rd St., 215/861-4971, www.friendsofindependence.org). The volunteer-led walking tours meet at Signers Garden (5th and Chestnut St.) and last about an hour.

Philadelphia Society for the Preservation of Landmarks tours (1616 Walnut St., 215/546-1146, www.preservationalliance.com, prices and tours vary) are a hit with those interested in an in-depth tour focusing on architecture and history featuring off-the-beaten places that most visitors and many locals never see.

ON WHEELS

Philadelphia Trolley Works and 76 Carriage Company (215/389-8687, www.phillytour.com) operates narrated tours on open-air Victorian trolleys, double-decker London-style buses (**Big Bus Company**), and horse-drawn carriages (**76 Carriage Company**). Bus and trolley tours depart from the Independence

© ANDREW KAZMIERSKI/123RF.COM

a horse-drawn carriage

Visitor Center (5th and Market Sts.) and allow you to hop off at any of 21 stops around the city, including Independence National Historical Park, Chinatown, City Hall, Eastern State Penitentiary, Philadelphia Museum of Art, Philadelphia Zoo, Franklin Institute, and Penn's Landing. An all-day pass costs $27 (adult), $25 (seniors), or $10 (children 4-12), and a two-day pass is $43, $40, or $18 respectively. Carriage rides through Old City and Society Hill depart from 5th and Chestnut Streets and cost $30-80 for four people, depending on the length of tour, and an additional $10 for each additional rider. Avoid taking a carriage ride on the hottest summer days – the horse will be even hotter than you are. Check the website for the full variety of specialty tours offered by this company.

Tours on Segways (those two-wheeled, self-balancing electric scooters) are offered by two local companies. **I-Glide Tours** (215/735-1700, www.iglidetours.com, $49 evening, $69 daytime) offers 2.5-hour guided tours through the Art Museum District that depart from Eakins Oval. **Detours** (22 N. 3rd St., 267/324-5408, http://detourstouring.com, 1.5-3 hours, $55-75 pp) offers Segway tours (along with bicycle and running tours) that depart from Old City with the choice of two routes, one to the Art Museum District and the other within Old City and Independence Park.

ON WATER

Schuylkill Banks River Tours (River at Walnut St., 888/748-7445, www.schuylkillbanks. org) offers three seasonal boat tours: a general river tour; a trip to Bartram's Garden with time to explore; and a jazz cruise. Kayak tours led by a certified instructor depart from the same spot.

There are several ways to tour the Delaware River, including the **Riverboat Queen Fleet** (200 N. Columbus Blvd., Penn's Landing, 215/923-2628, www.riverboatqueenfleet.com, summer only), which offers the **New River Loop,** a replica of a paddlewheel boat offering trips starting at $15 per person with options to add on food and drinks. Pedal boats are also available for private rental.

Not exactly a tour, but more of a party on water, the **Spirit of Philadelphia** (Pier 3, Columbus Blvd., Penn's Landing, 866/455-3866, www.spiritofphiladelphia.com, prices vary) is a large ship spread out over two floors offering lunch, dinner, late-night cruises, and special theater and holiday cruises along the Delaware River. The staff entertains with Philadelphia facts and dance routines before the dance floor opens to everyone. A similar setup with food, music, dance, and a variety of sightseeing and meal cruises, the **Philadelphia Belle** (Pier 3, Penn's Landing, 888/868-7764, http://philadelphiabelle.com/index.html) is a beautiful grand riverboat that debuted in 2010.

wishing for abundance in the new land, and is a reproduction of the original made in the 1790s by William Sprague, who was founder of the first woven carpet mill in Philadelphia, credited with bringing the carpet industry to the United States.

INDEPENDENCE VISITOR CENTER

6th and Market Sts., 800/537-7676,
www.independencevisitorcenter.com
HOURS: Opens daily at 8:30 A.M., closes at 7 P.M.
Memorial Day–Labor Day, 5 P.M. in winter, and 6 P.M.
during remainder of year
COST: Free

Just across the street from the Liberty Bell and steps from Independence Hall and the Constitution Center, the visitor center should be the first stop on any visit to historic Philadelphia. You can pick up maps, sign up for tours, check out the latest schedule of events, and ask the helpful park rangers questions. Visit the free mini-museum and watch the short film *Independence* for an introduction to the history of the area. Automated kiosks provide loads of information and allow you to book tickets to

area attractions, not just within the historic area but across the Philadelphia region. The center has a gift shop, café, and wireless Internet, and is also where you go to reserve your free timed tickets to Independence Hall and to sign up for tours of the Todd and Bishop White Houses.

◖ LIBERTY BELL CENTER

501 Market St., 215/965-2305, www.nps.gov/inde
HOURS: Mon.-Fri. 9 A.M.-5 P.M.
COST: Free

You have to see the Liberty Bell if you're visiting Philadelphia; it's just one of those things. Just don't set your hopes too high—it is just a bell after all—and not a very well-made one at that. But the real attraction here is not the 2,080-pound piece of metal; it is what it has come to symbolize for people. The iconic symbol of United States' independence and the birth of democracy, the bell has also been adopted as a symbol for other groups' fights for freedom, including freedom from slavery and the women's rights movement. In fact, the abolitionists were the ones who began calling it the "Liberty Bell."

The iconic symbol of liberty is one of Philadelphia's most popular attractions.

There is some debate over the details of the bell's history, but it goes something like this: Originally built for the tower of the State House (now Independence Hall), it was cast in London and arrived in Philadelphia in 1752. It was built to commemorate the 50-year anniversary of William Penn's Charter of Privileges, a document that had established unprecedented freedoms to the people of Pennsylvania and whose principles form a basis for some of the content of the National Constitution that would follow.

As for the cracks, the first occurred during its first ring in a test run. It was recast two years later by two local guys, John Stow and John Pass, who took the opportunity to carve their own names into it, which can be seen today. The bell purportedly was rung for several important events, including the first public reading of the Declaration of Independence in 1776. No one is sure when it rang for the last time, but some claim it was for George Washington's birthday in 1846, at which point the cracks were so bad that the bell was rendered useless.

Housed in Independence Hall for more than 200 years, it was moved to Liberty Bell Pavilion in 1976 for the bicentennial. In 2003 it was moved again to its current home in the Liberty Bell Center, a modern glass-enclosed mini-museum and multimedia gallery containing documents, images, and a short History Channel film exploring facts and myths surrounding the bell, available in nine languages. The bell's strategic position offers an uninterrupted view of Independence Hall, making it one of the most photographed spots in the city. On the bell, Pennsylvania is spelled "Pensylvania," which was one of several acceptable spellings at the time. It is engraved with the message "Proclaim Liberty throughout all the Land unto all the Inhabitants thereof."

MERCHANTS' EXCHANGE BUILDING

143 S. 3rd St., 215/965-2305, www.nps.gov/inde
HOURS: Mon.-Fri. 8 A.M.-4:30 P.M.
COST: Free

This magnificent Greek Revival building designed by William Strickland (also responsible for the Second Bank of the United States and the steeple atop Independence Hall) was essentially the first stock exchange building in the country. Merchants came here to barter or sell their wares—previously done on the streets and in coffee shops and taverns. Now headquarters for the National Park Service, it holds a small exhibition inside on the building's history. Built 1832–1834, the tower is based on the Choragic Monument of Lysicrates in Athens. At the dedication speech in 1832, solicitor John Kane aptly predicted: "The building which we have founded shall stand among the relics of antiquities, another memorial to posterity of the skill of its architect—and proof of the liberal spirit, and cultivated taste, which, in our days, distinguish the mercantile community."

◖ NATIONAL CONSTITUTION CENTER

525 Arch St., 215/409-6600,
www.constitutioncenter.org
HOURS: Mon.-Fri. 9:30 A.M.-5 P.M., Sat. 9:30 A.M.-6 P.M., Sun. noon-5 P.M.
COST: $12 adult, $11 senior, $8 child, free children 4 and under and active military

The only national museum entirely dedicated to telling the story of the U.S. Constitution, this modern structure sits just across from Independence Hall where the seminal document was drafted. The museum opened July 4, 2003, and immediately became one of the area's most popular attractions, bringing in more than a million visitors a year. Inscribed on the outside of the two-story building are the first three words of the Constitution, "We the People."

A visit begins with *Freedom Rising,* a live-actor show complete with film, music, and lights that runs twice an hour. The Hollywood-style show, complete with dramatic voiceovers and inspirational music, is actually quite entertaining and educational. The 360-degree theater is surrounded by a circular exhibit space, where you can learn anything you ever wanted to know about the Constitution; the events, people, and ideas that led to its creation; and the ideals from it that remain central to the function of government today.

© CHRISTOPHER WOODS

the National Constitution Center at night

You will see photographs, artifacts, and an original copy of the Constitution, and can participate in interactive and multimedia exhibits that kids and adults will both enjoy. Try on judicial robes; take a photograph of yourself projected onto a screen so it looks like you're taking the oath of office; and vote for your favorite president. In Signers' Hall, choose for yourself whether to sign or dissent to the Constitution and snap pictures with life-size bronze figures of the founding fathers.

PHILOSOPHICAL HALL AND LIBRARY HALL

105 S. 5th St., 215/440-3400, www.amphilsoc.org
HOURS: Philosophical Hall: call for hours;
Library Hall Mon.-Fri. 9 A.M.-4:45 P.M.
COST: Free

Property of the American Philosophical Society, Philosophical Hall is the only privately owned building on Independence Square. Founded in 1743 by Benjamin Franklin to "promote useful knowledge," it is the oldest learned society in the country. The word "philosophy" once had a much broader context, and the society was intended to encourage thinking about all sorts of topics, including science, nature, machinery, industry, and government. Its esteemed list of past and present members includes Benjamin Franklin, Charles Darwin, Madame Curie, Albert Einstein, Toni Morrison, Nelson Mandela, more than a dozen U.S. presidents, and 200 Nobel Prize winners. The Federal-style building was constructed 1786–1789 by Samuel Vaughan and remodeled in 1949 by Sydney Martin. It houses one of the nation's first museums, founded in 1784 by Charles Wilson Peale—artist, naturalist, and Philosophical Society member—and features rotating exhibits exploring art, science, and early U.S. history, including scientific specimens and instruments, patent models, portraits, maps, rare books, and millions of manuscripts.

Just across the street, Library Hall houses many of the society's most important collections, including original journals of Lewis and Clark, a copy of the Declaration of

Independence in Jefferson's handwriting, and first editions of Sir Isaac Newton's *Principia* and Charles Darwin's *On the Origin of Species*. The building is a reproduction of the original Library Hall, built in 1790 by architect William Thornton and original home to the Library Company of Philadelphia. As the first public library in the country, founded by Benjamin Franklin, it served as Library of Congress when Philadelphia was the capital. While only researchers who contact the library in advance have access to the materials, there are rotating exhibits in the entrance hall that are open to the public when the library is open.

PRESIDENT'S HOUSE

6th and Market Sts., 215/965-2305, www.nps.gov/inde
HOURS: 24 hours, open-air site
COST: Free

"The President's House; Freedom and Slavery in the Making of a New Nation" is the newest addition to Independence Park. It opened in late 2010 just next to the Liberty Bell. An oversight committee took great care in planning and debating the details of the site with the dual and often conflicting goals of honoring the earliest executive branch of government while evoking critical thought about the complex paradoxes that existed around the practice of slavery in our nation's early history. Many of our founding fathers, the same men who fought for American independence and democracy based on the premise that "all men are created equal," owned slaves, and this site that stands on the ground inhabited by the nation's first White House sets out to explore this contradiction.

While it's extremely modest by modern standards, George Washington once called the three-story brick mansion owned by financier Robert Morris that occupied this spot "the best single house in the city." During the first 10 years of our nation, before the capital relocated to Washington, D.C., George Washington (1790–1797) and John Adams (1797–1800) lived and worked here. Future presidents Thomas Jefferson, James Madison, James Monroe, and John Quincy Adams

were among other famous dignitaries who spent time here. Adams did not have slaves, but George and Martha Washington had at least nine, including a cook and Martha's personal servant. While many slave owners in the northern states chose to emancipate their slaves much earlier as the consciousness around the immorality of the practice shifted in the years leading to the Civil War, George Washington did not free his slaves until after his death, as stipulated in his will.

Archaeologists have discovered over 10,000 artifacts to help recreate the history and layout of the house, including the location of the slave quarters. At the open-air site, visitors will see structural fragments of the home, learn about events through illustrated glass panels, timelines, and video reenactments, and can visit an area for silent reflection. One of the display panels reads: "It is difficult to understand how men who spoke so passionately of liberty and freedom were unable to see the contradiction, the injustice, the immorality of their actions. We cannot ignore the past; we can only honor the memory and lives of those who endured bondage in a land where freedom rings for some, not all."

SECOND BANK OF THE UNITED STATES

420 Chestnut St., 215/965-2305, www.nps.gov/inde
HOURS: Wed.-Sun. 11 A.M.-4 P.M.
COST: $2

Designed by William Strickland and built 1819–1824, this is considered one of the finest examples of Greek Revival architecture in the United States. Modeled on the Parthenon, the building served as a model for countless other U.S. financial institutions. The bank was chartered in 1816 during a time of massive currency fluctuations to provide credit for government and businesses—think of the Fed today. In 1832, President Andrew Jackson vetoed a bill to recharter the bank because he feared it was creating an unconstitutional monopoly. While it has greatly evolved over the years, the banking system of today operates under many of the same structures and ideas.

Today, the building is owned by the

© JULIANE JACOBS/123RF.COM

The Second Bank of the United States was modeled on the Greek Parthenon.

National Park Service and houses the portrait gallery "People of Independence." The 185 paintings of colonial and federal leaders, scientists, explorers, and officers include George Washington, Alexander Hamilton, Thomas Mifflin, Thomas Jefferson, Robert Morris, and the Marquis de Lafayette. Charles Wilson Peale (1741–1827), the most famous portraitist of the 18th century, painted 85 of them. If you've ever wondered what the founding fathers looked like, this is a good place to find out.

THADDEUS KOSCIUSZKO NATIONAL MEMORIAL

301 Pine St., 215/597-7130, www.nps.gov/thko

HOURS: Wed.-Sun. noon-4 P.M.

COST: Free

Thomas Jefferson called Polish-born Thaddeus Kosciuszko "as pure a son of liberty as I have ever known." A former Polish count, Kosciuszko developed innovative military engineering that contributed to several important victories in Revolutionary War battles. After the war, he returned to Poland, but came back several years later to collect his military payment and consult with Dr. Benjamin Rush about injuries he suffered while unsuccessfully defending his homeland against czarist Russia. During his stay he was treated as a hero and visited by local leaders, including Vice President Jefferson.

The small Georgian-style boarding home where he stayed, built 1775–1776 by Joseph Few, has been converted into a memorial and museum maintained by Independence National Historical Park. The 1st floor displays his military innovations, the 2nd floor his bedroom. In addition to entertaining the leaders of the day, he is rumored to have entertained many a young lady here as well. A short video reveals additional details about his life.

TODD HOUSE

4th and Walnut Sts., 215/965-2305, www.nps.gov/inde

HOURS: Tour only, call ahead

COST: Free; tickets available at Independence Visitor Center (corner of 6th and Market Sts.), first-come, first-served, combined with tour of the Bishop White House

From 1791 to 1793, future first lady Dolley Payne lived in this Georgian home with her husband, lawyer John Todd. Todd died during the 1793 yellow fever epidemic, leaving young Dolley to care for their son. She quickly attracted the attentions of many men, including a lawyer from Virginia, James Madison. They were married; he became president of the United States and she became one of the favorite first ladies in history. The parlor of the house is believed to be where Madison—17 years her senior—first wooed young Dolley. On the tour you can see a reproduction of John Todd's law office and leather fire buckets hanging from the ceiling. The home exemplifies a middle-class American home in the late 18th century.

MORE OLD CITY SIGHTS
ARCH STREET
FRIENDS MEETING HOUSE

320 Arch St., 215/627-2667, www.archstreetfriends.org
HOURS: Mon.-Sat. 10 A.M.-4 P.M., worship meetings
Wed. 7 P.M. and Sun. 10:30 A.M.
COST: $2 donation suggested

The oldest and largest Quaker meeting house in the world fittingly occupies a piece of land donated by Quaker founder William Penn. In 1793, Penn donated the site to the Religious Society of Friends to be used as a Quaker burial ground with a large wall surrounding it to keep cats and dogs out of the graves. Constructed in 1804 by architect Owen Biddle, the building sits at a slight elevation to accommodate the layers of graves underneath. The modest, symmetrical brick structure reflects the early Quaker values of simplicity.

There are three distinct sections inside. The East Wing is the most interesting to visitors, with dioramas depicting the major events in the life of William Penn as well as the "Drinker Dollhouse," a reproduction of the 18th-century home of a Philadelphia Quaker, Elizabeth Drinker. The West Wing was used for women-only meetings, some of which were attended by famous abolitionist Lucretia Mott. Today, men and women attend worship together in the Center section. Worship meetings are open to the public and last 45–60 minutes.

BETSY ROSS HOUSE

239 Arch St., 215/686-1252, www.betsyrosshouse.org
HOURS: Apr.-Sept. daily 10 A.M.-5 P.M.,
Oct.-Mar. Tues.-Sun. 10 A.M.-5 P.M.
COST: $4 adult, $3 child (12 and under), student, or senior; $6 audio tour includes admission

Did she or didn't she? The debate over whether or not Betsy Ross actually sewed the first American flag rages on, but the fact that she led a fascinating life is indisputable. Married and widowed three times, Betsy was shunned because her first husband was not a Quaker. She was eventually welcomed back into the Society of Friends when she married her third husband—a Quaker—John Claypoole.

Built in 1740, her "bandbox"-style home had one room on each floor and a winding staircase from the basement to the top. Betsy made a living as an upholsterer while she lived here 1773–1785, but she wasn't the only one; a variety of shopkeepers and artisans lived and worked in the home over its long history, including a shoemaker, an apothecary, and a cigar-maker. Period furniture, including some of Betsy's belongings, can be seen in the seven tiny rooms connected by narrow hallways and low doorways. A 25-minute audio tour provides a history of the house and Betsy's life, with an alternative audio tour complete with a scavenger hunt available for kids.

CHRIST CHURCH

20 N. American St., 215/922-1695,
www.christchurchphila.org
HOURS: Mon.-Sat. 9 A.M.-5 P.M., Sun. 1-5 P.M.,
closed Mon. and Tues. in Jan. and Feb.
COST: Free, suggested donation $3 adult, $2 student

In its heyday, Christ Church counted many of Philadelphia's elite among its members—including 15 of the signers of the Declaration of Independence. Basically, everyone who was anyone came here to pray. The first parish of the Anglican Church in Pennsylvania and the birthplace of the American Episcopal Church, it is referred to as "The Nation's Church."

At its founding in 1695, the modest brick-and-wood structure resembled the typical Quaker meeting houses that dominated early

Philadelphia. That is a far cry from what you'll see today—one of the finest and most elaborate examples of colonial Georgian architecture in the world. Rebuilt 1727–1744, the church was designed by Dr. John Kearsley and modeled on the work of famed British architect Christopher Wren. The tower was added in 1754 with funds raised from a lottery organized by Benjamin Franklin, making the church the tallest structure in the colonies for 75 years to follow.

Inside, you'll see William Penn's baptismal font (donated in 1697 by All Hallows Church in London), a chandelier installed in 1740, and a pulpit built by Thomas Folwell in 1769. William White, church rector for 57 years, first bishop of Pennsylvania, and chaplain of the Continental Congress, is also buried here. When the parish grew too large, St. Peter's Church was established as an offshoot for Society Hill members. The church remains active to this day, and 20-minute guided tours are offered when service is not in session.

CHRIST CHURCH BURIAL GROUND

Arch St. btwn. 4th and 5th Sts., 215/922-1695,
www.christchurchphila.org
HOURS: Mar.-Nov. Mon.-Sat. 10 A.M.-4 P.M.,
Sun. noon-4 P.M., Dec. Sun.-Fri. noon-4 P.M., Sat.
10 A.M.-4 P.M., weather permitting; closed Jan. and Feb.
COST: $2 adult, $1 student, $10 for groups up to 25

In 1790, Ben Franklin's funeral was attended by more than 20,000 people. Here he rests, alongside his wife and young son and more than 5,000 other early Philadelphians. In 1719, the overcrowded grounds of Christ Church a few blocks away could no longer fit more bodies, so this plot was purchased on the "outskirts of town" to accommodate its members. The site was closed to the public for 25 years, but it reopened in 2003 after an intensive renovation. More than 1,400 markers remain, many so old and worn down that the names are no longer visible. During a tour you'll learn about the prominent figures and ordinary folks who were buried here. While 80 percent of the burials took place before 1840, the most recent was in 1994. Legend has it that it's good luck to throw a penny on Ben's grave.

CURTIS CENTER AND DREAM GARDEN MOSAIC

601-45 Walnut St., 215/238-6450
HOURS: Mon.-Fri. 8 A.M.-6 P.M., Sat. 10 A.M.-1 P.M.
COST: Free

The building was commissioned by Curtis Publishing, one of the largest and most influential publishers of the early 20th century. Curtis was responsible for the still-popular *Ladies Home Journal*, founded in 1883, and the *Saturday Evening Post*, founded in 1728 but purchased by Curtis in 1897. Curtis Publishing operated out of this building, built in the 1890s, for many years. It's an office building today, and the only reason to visit is for a glimpse of the *Dream Garden* mosaic just inside the 6th Street entrance. Tiffany Studios and artist Maxfield Parrish combined artistic visions to brighten the Curtis Center lobby with the dazzling *Dream Garden* mosaic. The 15-by-49-foot intricately designed mosaic combines light, glass, and color in a mesmerizing landscape. Louis Comfort Tiffany was hired to work with Philadelphian Parrish to execute a design based on Parrish's painting *The Dream Garden*. The mosaic was completed in 1916 and has been on display ever since—despite casino-owner Steve Wynn's attempt to take it to Vegas. Wynn purchased the masterpiece in 1988, but public outcry inspired Pew Charitable Trust to pay $3.5 million to keep it in place.

ELFRETH'S ALLEY

Btwn. Front and N. 2nd Sts. and Quarry and Arch Sts.,
museum and shop in Houses 124 and 126,
215/574-0560, www.elfrethsalley.org
HOURS: Museum: Mar.-Oct. Mon.-Sat. 10 A.M.-5 P.M.,
Sun. noon-5 P.M., Nov.-Feb. Thurs.-Sat. 10 A.M.-5 P.M.,
Sun. noon-5 P.M.
COST: Guided tours $5 adult, $2 child (6-12), $12 family,
offered on the hour and half hour; self-guided tour $3
adult, $1 child 6-12

Clichéd but true, walking through this narrow cobblestone street is like stepping back in time. Occupied since 1702, Elfreth's Alley is the oldest continuously occupied residential street in the United States. Federal and

© JULIA GAVIN

Elfreth's Alley

Georgian homes—complete with horse posts and shoe scrapes—have been immaculately preserved, and the entire street is on the Philadelphia Register of Historic Properties. Small by today's standards, one of the homes is said to have housed up to 27 people from eight different families at one time. There's very little car traffic, and no modern appliances are visible in the windows looking out on the narrow alley, making the bustle of today's Old City feel far away.

The street was named after blacksmith Jeremiah Elfreth, who lived here and was responsible for building many of the homes. In 1755, he built the home that stands today as a museum and the only home regularly open to the public. The others are private homes. Many residents open their doors during two annual fundraisers for preservation programs. **Fete Day** is a celebration with music, parade, and historical reenactments usually held on the first or second Saturday in June, and **Deck the Alley** is a holiday event held in early December.

FIRST BANK OF THE UNITED STATES
116 S. 3rd. St.

Although it's closed to the public, the architecture of the oldest national bank in the country is worth a peek as you stroll through Old City. Designed by Samuel Blodgett and James Windrim in the Classical Revival style influenced by the ancient Greeks, the building was constructed 1795–1797. An eagle, the relatively new national symbol at the time, sits atop the portico. The bank as an institution began in 1791 during Alexander Hamilton's term as treasury secretary. It was part of an attempt to deal with the massive debt the government accrued during the Revolutionary War and to create standard currency for all of the states. George Washington signed the first bank charter, drafted by Congress in 1791, and the bank opened in Carpenters' Hall until it moved here in 1795. The bank charter lasted 30 years but was abandoned by Congress in 1811. The building was restored for the bicentennial in 1976.

FRANKLIN SQUARE
6th and Race Sts., 215/629-4026,
www.onceuponanation.org
HOURS: Playgrounds open daily 6 A.M.–9 P.M., extended until 10 P.M. in summer; other attractions vary with season
COST: Park free; carousel $3 adult, $2 child, free 2 and under; mini-golf $8 adult, $6 child (3-12)

Franklin Square was a desolate, neglected piece of prime real estate in the heart of Old City for many years. But in 2006, a $6 million renovation project transformed it into a lovely landscaped park with kid-friendly attractions, including an 18-hole mini-golf course, two playgrounds, and an old-fashioned carousel. Four brick paths lead to an original restored 1838 marble fountain in the center. SquareBurger, a Stephen Starr–owned snack bar, offers burgers, fries, and frozen treats. One of the five squares of green space William Penn planned for Philadelphia, Franklin Square was originally named Northeast Square; it was renamed in honor of Benjamin Franklin in 1825.

HISTORIC PHILADELPHIA CENTER AND PECO THEATER

6th and Chestnut Sts., 215/629-4026,
http://historicphiladelphia.org
HOURS: Daily 9 A.M.-7 P.M., until 9 P.M. in late spring
and summer

Just across the street from Independence Hall
and the Liberty Bell is the headquarters of
Historic Philadelphia, Inc., a nonprofit dedicated to making the visitor experience more
fun, interesting, and interactive. Offering information, a souvenir shop, and tickets for tours,
the organization is responsible for the Betsy
Ross House, Franklin Square, and the story-
telling benches staffed with guides in colonial
costumes stationed throughout Independence
Park. Their interesting tours include the new
and improved **Lights of Liberty** tour, a nighttime walking tour that uses 3-D technology to
tell the story of American independence. In addition, while you're there, don't miss the latest
addition, **Liberty 360** ($7 adult, $6 student
senior, military, child 12 and under), which debuted in 2010. The 15-minute film is shown

every 20 minutes in the PECO theater, taking
viewers on a journey through Revolutionary
history led by Ben Franklin in a groundbreaking 3-D, 360-degree panoramic theater.

PENN'S LANDING

Visitors center: 301 S. Columbus Blvd. near Spruce St.,
215/928-8801, www.pennslandingcorp.com

Penn always dreamed of building an attractive waterfront area lined with trees, but it
didn't actually happen until about 300 years
after he first landed here. The area was vacant
and dilapidated until the late 1960s, when
the city and developers saw its potential and
began to build. Penn's Landing is now home
to recreational parks, an ice-skating rink, several historic attractions, modern dining and
entertainment options, and expensive condominiums. It includes roughly 10 blocks along
the Delaware River from Vine Street to South
Street, and several footbridges connect it to
Old City and Society Hill over I-95.

From Penn's Landing, check out the
Benjamin Franklin Bridge, the largest

Penn's Landing is bustling during summer.

suspension bridge in the world at the time it was completed in 1926. Designed by Paul Philippe Cret, who also designed the Benjamin Franklin Parkway, it was built to connect Center City with Camden, New Jersey. A lighting system added for the bicentennial celebration makes the view especially beautiful at night.

The **Great Plaza** at Chestnut Street is home to a tiered amphitheater that hosts numerous festivals, including a New Orleans–inspired festival on Memorial Day and a weekend-long blues festival in July. In summertime, concerts and events are often held here, including the fireworks display for the Sunoco Welcome America Independence Day celebration. Inscribed stones in the ground highlight Philadelphia as a "City of Firsts." A few blocks south, check out the **International Sculpture Garden,** an open-air art installation that aims to honor the impact of other cultures on the American experience. The diverse collection includes two pre-Columbian spheres (300–1525), the largest Nandi sculpture (c. 1500) ever to leave India, and two Korean Chosen Dynasty memorial figures, among others.

U.S. MINT
151 N. Independence Mall East (enter on 5th and Arch Sts.), 215/408-0110, www.usmint.gov
HOURS: Mon.-Fri. 9 A.M.-4:30 P.M., closed on federal holidays
COST: Free; government-issued ID required
From half-eagles of yore to George Washingtons of today, there isn't a penny, shilling, or bird

you can't find in the U.S. Mint. Behind the concrete columns, enormous printing and coin presses make every variety of coin and bill in U.S. currency. Elite craftsmen etch microscopic details into each mold and print, and money is processed, printed, and shipped five days a week. In less than 24 hours the mint will have made one million dollars, so they can easily afford the free admission for guests. The U.S. Mint is more than a workshop; it showcases the history of our nation's currency-making process. On display are the presses and tools that crafted the first gold eagle coins (each coin was nearly handmade), as well as information on the development of the National Treasury and early mint facilities. This facility opened in 1969 as Philadelphia's fourth mint.

WELCOME PARK
2nd St. and Sansom Alley
In 1982 the Friends of Independence National Historical Park created Welcome Park in honor of the 300th anniversary of William Penn's founding of Pennsylvania. Named after his ship, *The Welcome,* the open-air monument was built on the spot where his home stood 1699–1701. A dollhouse-sized replica of the home, the Slate Roof House, is part of the display. Penn's original plan for Philadelphia is etched in marble on the ground, and a miniature version of the statue of Penn above City Hall occupies the center. Along two walls, a timeline of his life and of early Philadelphia history is displayed.

Society Hill

Map 1

ATHENAEUM
219 S. 6th St., 215/925-2688, www.philaathenaeum.org
HOURS: Mon.-Fri. 9 A.M.-5 P.M., first Sat. of month 10 A.M.-2 P.M.
COST: Free; valid photo ID required
The Athenaeum is a must-see for architecture and design enthusiasts, or anyone looking for a glimpse into the finest in 19th-century living. Established as a research library in 1814, its

first member was renowned architect William Strickland in 1820. Strickland's 1839 proposal for a building to house the library on Washington Square was the first drawing acquired by the Athenaeum. It now contains more than a million books, architectural drawings, photographs, and manuscripts representing the work of more than 1,000 American architects, and is considered the premier landmark devoted to American architecture 1800–1945. The 1st-floor gallery is open to the public with rotating exhibits, but you'll need to make an appointment in advance to tour other areas. Designed by architect John Notman in 1845, the building is one of Philadelphia's first brownstones. The relatively simple exterior belies the ornate reading rooms and 24-foot ceilings inside.

HEADHOUSE SQUARE
2nd St. btwn. Pine and Lombard Sts.

One of the nation's earliest social scenes, Headhouse Square has brought the Society Hill community together since the 18th century. Most of the founders lived within walking distance of this colonial square, and since 1745, traders, artisans, and craftspeople have sold and traded goods here on weekends. "The Shambles," a covered brick courtyard stretching along 2nd Street between Pine and Lombard Streets, was built in 1803 for the community's "market master," the bazaar's official goods inspector. Now home to stylish restaurants, cafés, bars, and shops, the area maintains much of the energy it must have had 250 years ago. The

market tradition continues today as locals and tourists stroll the charming cobblestone street during seasonal craft shows, art exhibitions, and a great farmers market, which is usually held on Sundays May–Dec. 10 A.M.–2 P.M.

MOTHER BETHEL A.M.E. CHURCH AND RICHARD ALLEN MUSEUM
419 S. 6th St., 215/925-0616, www.motherbethel.org
HOURS: Museum Tues.-Sat. 10 A.M.-3 P.M., and after Sun. service noon-1 P.M.; call ahead to request tour
COST: Free

Former slave and preacher Reverend Richard Allen was forced to sit in the balcony of the mixed-race church he attended, St. George's Methodist. So in 1797, along with Absalom Jones and others, he founded Mother Bethel A.M.E., a place where African Americans could worship without restrictions. Mother Bethel, the first African Methodist church in America, occupies the oldest piece of land continuously owned by African Americans in the country. The original building built on this piece of land was a modest converted blacksmith shop, but the current building—the church's fourth

The Mother Bethel A.M.E. Church occupies the oldest piece of land in the nation continuously owned by African Americans.

incarnation, built in the 1890s—is a stunning example of 19th-century Romanesque Revival architecture. Light streams through the expansive stained-glass windows and creates a warm glow on the elaborate woodwork.

The church basement contains the Richard Allen Museum, home to Allen's tomb, along with a small but fascinating collection of exhibits highlighting the history of the church and African American history. Allen, born in 1760, was a slave in the Germantown section of Philadelphia who bought his own freedom in 1782 and became a prominent politician and abolitionist activist. His church became an important station on the Underground Railroad and was used as a school where slaves were taught to read. It also played a significant role in the birth of the first black periodical and insurance company, and Frederick Douglass and Sojourner Truth were among the many famous leaders who spoke here. The museum's artifacts include the original pulpit constructed by Allen, his Bible, ballot boxes used to elect church officers, and a wooden pew from the original blacksmith's shop.

OLD PINE STREET
PRESBYTERIAN CHURCH

412 Pine St., 215/925-8051, www.oldpine.org
HOURS: Mon.-Sat. 10 A.M.-5 P.M.; call ahead
COST: Free

Old Pine, as its commonly called, was once known as the "Church of the Patriots" because so many of its parishioners, including John Adams, were strong supporters of the Revolution. It was the third Presbyterian church in Philadelphia, but is the oldest one still standing today. Established in 1768, the pale-yellow church stands on its original foundation and has its original brick walls, but was expanded twice during the 19th century. The church was almost destroyed after the British occupied it and used it as a hospital during the Revolutionary War, burning many of the pews for warmth during the cold winter. The shaded graveyard holds more than 3,000 early Philadelphians, including at least 50 Revolutionary War soldiers, making it a

site that inspires many ghost stories. No formal tours are offered, but Old Pine welcomes visitors to come in and look around.

OLD ST. JOSEPH'S CHURCH

321 Willings Alley, off 4th St. btwn. Walnut and Locust Sts., 215/923-1733, www.oldstjoseph.org
HOURS: Daily 11 A.M.-4 P.M. when no service; call ahead
COST: Free

This tiny chapel served as the city's first Catholic parish in 1733 for just 11 Philadelphia families. Despite the general unpopularity of Catholics in Philadelphia at the time, William Penn's 1701 Charter of Privileges called for religious tolerance and granted land to as few as 10 people wishing to start a religious congregation. This church became the only place under British rule where Catholic mass was legal. Ben Franklin advised church leaders to install an iron gate, which turned out to be a good call, considering Quakers once had to prevent a Protestant mob from interrupting services here. The church was, however, damaged during anti-Catholic riots in the 1830s. The current building is the third on this site, dating from 1839, and the parish remains active but visitors are free to explore when no mass is in service. Notice the stained-glass windows above the altar, glass mosaics on the north and south walls, and the ceiling painting, *The Exaltation of Saint Joseph into Heaven,* by Italian artist Philippo Paggini, whose work also appears in the Capitol in Washington, D.C.

OLD ST. MARY'S CHURCH

252 S. 4th St., 215/923-7930
HOURS: Mon.-Sat. 9 A.M.-4:30 P.M. when no service; call ahead
COST: Free

While Old St. Joseph's was the first, Old St. Mary's was the second Catholic parish in Philadelphia. The two churches were run as one unit until 1830. Built in 1763 by master carpenter Charles Johnson, the church was enlarged in 1810 and has seen several renovations since. Notice the marble pieta crafted by French sculptor Boucher, the crucifix carved by William Rush, and two stories of stained-glass windows. The church contains a 1791 baptismal font, brass chandeliers from Independence Hall, and Bishop Conwell's chair.

The cemetery has been in use since 1759, when graves were transported here from crowded Old St. Joseph's and Washington Square. It is higher than street level because a top layer of graves was added after the 1793 yellow fever epidemic required much more space for bodies. Notable people buried here include Commodore John Barry (known as father to the U.S. Navy), General Moylan (aid to George Washington), Thomas Fitzsimmons (a member of the Continental Congress who helped draft the Constitution), and Michael Bouvier, great-great-grandfather of Jacqueline Kennedy Onassis. Church is open to visitors when there is no service.

PENNSYLVANIA HOSPITAL

800 Spruce St., 215/829-3370,
www.uphs.upenn.edu/paharc
HOURS: Mon.-Fri. 9 A.M.-4 P.M.
COST: Free, $4 suggested donation for tours

Although Benjamin Franklin was best known as an inventor and scientist, he also dabbled in medicine. Realizing the importance of a medical care facility, he consulted esteemed doctor Thomas Bond, and together they founded the nation's first hospital in 1751. The hospital sparked a boom of medical advancements and made Philadelphia the hub of medicine and surgery in the western hemisphere.

Now part of the University of Pennsylvania health-care system, the hospital remains an integral center of medical research and teaching and one of the city's best hospitals in many fields. Since it is a functioning hospital, only a few areas are open to the public. Guided tours can be scheduled by appointment Thursday and Friday at 10 A.M. and 1 P.M., or a brochure that details the hospital's history can be purchased in the gift shop for a self-tour (each for a suggested donation of $4). On a tour, you'll see Benjamin West's epic painting *Christ Healing the Sick in the Temple* and the oldest existing surgical amphitheater in the United States—constructed on the top floor in 1804 to take advantage of natural light.

PHILADELPHIA CONTRIBUTIONSHIP

212 S. 4th St., 215/627-1752, www.contributionship.com
HOURS: Mon.-Fri. 9 A.M.-4 P.M.
COST: Free

In 1736, Ben Franklin founded Philadelphia's first fire brigade, the Union Fire Company, and in 1752, he helped establish the first property insurance company in the country. The Philadelphia Contributionship for the Insurance of Houses from Loss by Fire laid the groundwork for modern insurance companies. Fire and fireproofing buildings were longtime interests of Ben Franklin, who once told a friend that in case of fire: "You may be forced to leap out of windows and hazard your neck to avoid being overroasted." John Stow, who recast the Liberty Bell after it cracked, was responsible for casting the Contributionship's official symbol, the hand-in-hand fire mark, which can be seen on buildings around town.

Constructed in 1836, the building remains the headquarters of the Contributionship, still an active insurance company. It also contains a small ground-floor museum open to the public. Among the memorabilia are fire marks, firefighters' hats, miniature engines, lanterns, and a silver "speaking trumpet" used to convey orders at fire sites. You'll learn interesting tidbits about the history of firefighting—like how rival fire companies fought one another at the scenes of fires because whoever put out the fire received payment; some members went on to form the city's most violent gangs. The museum maintains home surveys for many old Philadelphia residences, including those of Ben Franklin and John Penn (William Penn's son). The elegant 2nd-floor rooms are open by appointment only.

PHYSICK HOUSE

321 S. 4th St., 215/925-7866, www.philalandmarks.org
HOURS: Thurs.-Sat. noon-4 P.M., Sun. 1-4 P.M., tours on the hour, last tour 3 P.M.
COST: $5 adult, $4 student and senior, $3 pp for group of 10 or more, $12 family, free under 6

Named after the "father of American surgery," Dr. Philip Syng Physick, the four-story Federal-style home was built in 1768 by wine importer

Henry Hill and served as the home and office of Dr. Physick 1815–1837. Here, he designed numerous revolutionary operative instruments, invented the stomach pump, pioneered the use of autopsy for research, and advanced cataract surgery. He also offered medical advice to presidents and created America's first carbonated beverage. He even began an anti-smoking campaign way before its time.

The home was rehabilitated by the Annenberg family during the late 1960s and has been largely restored to its original character. French and colonial art and Neoclassical furniture decorate the 1st floor, while the 2nd floor is entirely dedicated to Physick's work, showcasing his surgical inventions. The home contains one of the largest gardens in 19th-century Philadelphia.

POWEL HOUSE

244 S. 3rd St., 215/627-0364, www.philalandmarks.org
HOURS: Thurs.-Sat. noon-4 P.M., Sun. 1-4 P.M., tours on the hour, last one at 3 P.M.
COST: $5 adult, $4 student and senior, $3 pp for group of 10 or more, $12 families, free child 6 and under

Built in 1765, this stately Georgian mansion was home to Samuel and Elizabeth Powel, a prominent 18th-century couple, and is the finest surviving example of an upper-class colonial townhouse. Samuel Powel was a third-generation Philadelphian who spent years traveling in Europe like many wealthy young men of his time. He married Elizabeth Willing upon his return and became mayor of Philadelphia during the Revolution. The Powels were friendly with all the VIPs of the period, including Benjamin Franklin, John Adams, the Marquis de Lafayette, and George and Martha Washington, and political discussions and grand parties often took place here. Martha and George Washington even celebrated a wedding anniversary here, and a thank-you note written by George himself after a lovely night is on display in the home.

The British briefly took over the home during their occupation of Philadelphia during the war, and kindly allowed the Powels to stay in their own servants' quarters. By the early 20th century, the home was in terrible disrepair and was almost converted into a parking lot. Frances Wister, founder of the Philadelphia Society for the Preservation of Landmarks, raised money to buy it in 1931, and over the next decade restored it to its early appearance. Among the trademarks of upper-class colonial America seen here are a decorative arts collection (including a china set given as a gift by Martha Washington), portraits of the Powels, and a formal walled garden.

ST. PETER'S EPISCOPAL CHURCH

313 Pine St., 215/925-5968, www.stpetersphila.org
HOURS: Tues.-Sat. 9 A.M.-noon
COST: Free

Designed by Scottish-born architect Robert Smith, this Georgian-style building opened in 1761 as an alternative to the overcrowded Christ Church, a far walk in the mud on rainy days for some members. It was run jointly with Christ Church until 1832. In stark contrast with the Quaker ideals that shun hierarchy in the nearby Friends' meeting houses, the church pews here were available for purchase, so the richest members literally bought the best seats in the house. The towering spire designed by William Strickland in 1842 was built to house a gift of eight bells given to the church by the Whitechapel Foundry in London, where the Liberty Bell was made. Among the famous members buried in the church graveyard are portraitist Charles Wilson Peale; chiefs of the seven Iroquois tribes who died during the smallpox epidemic in 1793; James Polk's vice president, George Mifflin Dallas; Benjamin Chew, owner of Cliveden, the site of the 1777 Battle of Germantown; and Nicholas Biddle, president of the Second Bank of the United States. No guided tours are offered, but you can call 215/554-6161 from your cell phone for an audio tour or download it to your MP3 player from the website in advance. Feel free to knock if the door is locked.

Center City East Map 2

ARCH STREET UNITED METHODIST CHURCH

55 N. Broad St., 215/568-6250,
www.archstreetumc.org

HOURS: Tours Wed. 10 A.M.-1 P.M.

COST: Free

North of the Masonic Temple and City Hall on Broad Street stands another architectural gem, the Arch Street United Methodist Church. The Gothic Revival structure has a white-marble exterior and impressive stained-glass windows, and it houses a multi-stop Stanbridge organ made in 1870. The church was founded in 1862 and built on a former coal yard 1864–1870. The active congregation hosts many community and social events, including regular workshops about Native American heritage. View it from the outside any time, but for a tour of the inside, you'll have to go on Wednesday morning.

CHINATOWN FRIENDSHIP GATE

10th and Arch Sts.

There's no question you're in Chinatown when you see the colorful Friendship Gate, which forms an arch 40 feet above 10th Street near Arch Street with the words "Philadelphia Chinatown" appearing in Chinese characters. A collaboration between leading architect Sabrina Soong, other Chinese engineers and artisans and members of the local community, it was built in 1984. In celebrating the traditional Qing Dynasty style, this grand gateway to Chinatown was partially constructed with tiles from Philadelphia's sister city, Tianjin. It was the first gate constructed by Chinese artisans outside of China.

◖ CITY HALL

Broad and Market Sts., 215/686-2840,
www.philadelphiacityhall.org

HOURS: Tower tours Mon.-Fri. 9:30 A.M.-4:15 P.M.; building tour including tower Mon.-Fri. at 12:30 P.M.

COST: Building tour $10 adult, $8 seniors and children 3-18; tower tour only $5 adult, $4 children 3-18, $3 seniors

City Hall stands proudly on the site of the

Philadelphia City Hall

© RITU JETHANI/123RF.COM

original Center Square, named as one of the five original squares William Penn planned for the city in 1682. The city was originally concentrated in Old City along the Delaware River, where its earliest residents settled, so it made sense that local government offices were located nearby in Independence Hall, originally called the State House. But Penn predicted that the city would eventually expand westward towards the Schuylkill River, and he envisioned this space at its geometric center as the perfect locale for city government. Even though Penn left the city for good in 1701, his well-laid plan came to fruition two centuries later, when construction of current City Hall was completed for city offices in 1901.

Renowned architects John McArthur Jr. and Thomas U. Walter designed the masterpiece that stands today—one of the world's finest examples of French Second Empire architecture. Construction began in 1871 and took 30 years and at least 1,000 people to complete. The design was influenced by the Palais des Tuileries and the New Louvre in Paris, evidenced in the turreted courtyard stair towers, slate mansard roof with dormer windows, and the paired columns that create the cozy illusion that the building is just three stories high instead of eight. A solid-granite ground floor is 22 feet thick in some areas—strong enough to support the brick structure faced with marble. The 548-foot center tower stands as the tallest masonry structure in the world supported without a steel frame.

Famed sculptor Alexander Milne Calder designed the more than 250 sculptures on the building's exterior. The symbolically rich sculptures include representations of seasons, continents, allegorical figures, and of course the crown jewel—the 37-foot-tall, 27-ton **William Penn statue** at the top. There was for many years an unofficial but long-respected agreement that no building would be built

SCULPTURE AND SYMBOLISM NEAR CITY HALL

More than 250 sculptures designed by Alexander Milne Calder adorn the magnificent City Hall. While you're in the area, be sure to check out some of the other unique nearby sculptures.

CLOTHESPIN

Across 15th Street on the west side of City Hall stands Claes Oldenburg's 45-foot steel *Clothespin*. Sleek and modern, it offers a stark contrast to City Hall's ornate design. Oldenburg has compared his clothespin to Constantin Brancusi's *The Kiss*, and many agree that the shape is reminiscent of lovers holding one another. The *Clothespin* has also been viewed as a symbol of holding, or clipping, the old with the new in Philadelphia.

LOVE

At the intersection of 15th Street and John F. Kennedy Boulevard is John F. Kennedy Plaza, known to locals as Love Park because of the sculpture by Robert Indiana that stands proudly at its center. It is said that the crooked "O" in the bright-red letters that spell "love" is there to remind us that nothing – including love – is perfect. Positioned at an angle so the Benjamin Franklin Parkway spreads out behind it with the Art Museum in the distance, the sculpture was installed for the city's bicentennial in 1976 and quickly became an iconic image of the City of Brotherly Love.

GOVERNMENT OF THE PEOPLE

Just north of City Hall across John F. Kennedy Boulevard, you can't miss Jacques Lipchitz's

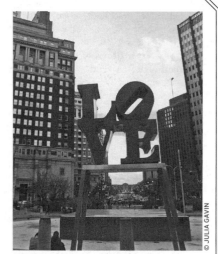

© JULIA GAVIN

LOVE sculpture by Robert Indiana

large *Government of the People,* one of several art installations in the plaza of the Municipal Services Building. The abstract bronze sculpture of hands and limbs gripping each other was built in the 1970s during the era of the polarizing mayor Frank Rizzo. Nearby stands a large replica of Rizzo himself, who fittingly has his back to Lipchitz's statue. He purportedly cut off city funding for the statue that he hated and was quoted as saying, "It looks like some plasterer dropped a load of plaster." Ah, the history of Philadelphia municipal politics.

taller than Penn's head, but the city's growth eventually demanded that it grow up (both literally and figuratively). In 1987, Liberty One was built, the first of a series of skyscrapers that now tower high above Billy Penn.

While City Hall looks small in today's skyline, it remains one of the most impressive and unique buildings in all of Philadelphia and perhaps the world. It is also the largest municipal building in the country, covering more than 14.5 acres of space on its eight floors. Just as Independence Hall once housed the three branches of national government when Philadelphia was the nation's capital in the early 19th century, City Hall today houses segments of all three branches of city government. It is the home base of the mayor, city council, and civil trial courtrooms.

While the vast majority of the 700 rooms are standard offices, several of the spaces are truly spectacular. City Council Chambers, the Mayor's Reception Room, Conversation Hall, the Caucus Room, and the Supreme Court Room are lavish, impressive meeting rooms. Security measures require that you visit the building as part of a tour, which is offered on weekdays at 12:30 P.M. It covers all the impressive rooms of the building that are not in use at the time of the tour, including the tower. The full tour takes about 90 minutes, but a tower tour alone, offered throughout the day, lasts about 15 minutes. A small elevator (capacity of only four; claustrophobics beware) takes visitors to an observation deck at the base of the Penn statue for a panoramic view of the city. The view from the top makes the site's prime location at the very center of Penn's original Philadelphia apparent. Tours depart from room 121 of the East Portal. Summer months can be busy, so plan to stop early in the morning to reserve a tour spot for later in the day.

LIBRARY COMPANY OF PHILADELPHIA
1314 Locust St., 215/546-3181, www.librarycompany.org
HOURS: Mon.-Fri. 9 A.M.-4:45 P.M., print room by appt. only
COST: Free

The country's very first lending library was founded by Benjamin Franklin in 1731, when he was only 25 years old. In its original Old City location, which is today called Library Hall, it served as the Library of Congress during the time that Philadelphia was the nation's capital. The only intact colonial-era library and the oldest circulating library in the nation, it was the largest library in the nation until 1850. In its current location on Locust Street, it remains an excellent resource on 17th- to 19th-century American society and culture with more than half a million rare books, graphics, manuscripts, and an array of artwork, prints, and photographs of early Philadelphia. While you'll need an appointment to get into the print room, there are free revolving exhibits that draw from the collections and are open to the public.

◖ MASONIC TEMPLE
1 N. Broad St., 215/988-1917, www.pagrandlodge.org
HOURS: Tours Tues.-Fri. 10 A.M., 11 A.M., 1 P.M., 2 P.M., and 3 P.M., Sat. 10 A.M. and 11 A.M., tours not available at times due to special events; call ahead
COST: Library and museum only $3; tour including library and museum $8 adult, $6 student, $5 child and senior, $20 family, free for active Pennsylvania masons, military, and children under 5

Philadelphia's Masonic Temple is a magnificent work of art and architecture both inside and out, which is no surprise considering it was built for and by the world's top masons. While masons of today represent practically every profession, the earliest members were highly skilled stoneworkers. The Grand Lodge of England (GLE) was founded in 1717 and spread to the U.S. colonies by the 1730s, making Freemasonry the oldest continuous fraternal organization in the world.

The building, designed by James Windrim, was completed in 1873, and the interior was decorated under the supervision of artist George Herzog over a 20-year period. The library and museum contain artifacts from the early masons, including George Washington's Masonic apron, and while this part can be visited alone, you would be missing out on the best part without a guided tour of the entire

© RITU JETHANI/123RF.COM

Philadelphia's ornate Masonic Temple

building. Paintings of former Masonic Grand Masters, including Ben Franklin and George Washington, line the grand staircase and hallways, and hand-painted wooden sculptures by William Rush, the "father of American sculpture," are on display. Seven spectacular meeting rooms stand as a tribute to the seven "ideal" forms of architecture. Oriental Hall replicates parts of the Alhambra; Gothic Hall is a tribute to the European Knights Templar made famous in Dan Brown's *The Da Vinci Code*; and Egyptian Hall is adorned with hieroglyphics so accurate that archaeology students from the University of Pennsylvania visit to study them. Other styles include Renaissance, Ionic, Corinthian, and Norman, and on a tour, you'll find each room more fascinating and breathtaking than the one before. There is one minor, intentional mistake in the design of each room, to acknowledge that only God is perfect and all human work is flawed.

The masons are shrouded in mystery. While the knowledgeable and friendly tour guides are willing to share information about many aspects of their history, don't bother asking them to reveal all their secrets, or to explain why women are still not admitted—believe me, I tried.

◖ READING TERMINAL MARKET

12th and Arch Sts., 215/922-2317, www.readingterminalmarket.org
HOURS: Mon.-Sat. 8 A.M.-6 P.M., Sun. 9 A.M.-5 P.M.

Picture the Reading Terminal Market more than a century ago amid a mass of trains bringing goods and people in and out of the city, and you'll see how far it has come in its long history. Today, it is flanked on one side by the Gallery, a massive urban mall, and on the other by the state-of-the-art Convention Center. It has survived the Great Depression, World War II, and the decline of the railroads, and it is as much a marvel today as it was at the turn of the 20th century.

Reading Terminal opened its doors in 1892 in response to a backlash against outdoor markets, which were beginning to be viewed as a health hazard. The new market was laid out in a tidy grid system similar to the streets of downtown Philadelphia. Twelve aisles and four larger avenues were aligned in the spacious cavern beneath the elevated train shed of the Reading Railroad. Proximity to the railroad made it the perfect place for shipping and receiving goods and provided easy access for Pennsylvania Dutch merchants to sell their wares.

In the 1970s, the Reading Railroad filed for bankruptcy and attempted to dismantle the market to make it easier to sell the terminal. Fortunately, they changed their minds and began efforts to revitalize it in the 1980s. What remains is one of Philadelphia's most proud and well-utilized sites. Now, the railroad runs underneath the market instead of above it, and Amish merchants still have a significant presence, bringing some of the best baked goods, meat, and produce. They have been joined by vendors selling everything from cheesesteaks to Vietnamese cuisine to fresh-baked cookies, making it an excellent place to stop for lunch. It's also one of the best spots in Philadelphia to buy affordable and delicious produce, meats, seafood, and a dizzying array of prepared foods.

Philadelphia chefs from many local restaurants visit the market early each morning to pick up the freshest ingredients to serve. Non-food goods are also available, including jewelry, books, artisan candles, gourmet cookware, and crafts from around the globe.

ST. STEPHEN'S EPISCOPAL CHURCH

19 S. 10th St., 215/922-3807, www.ststephensphl.org
HOURS: By appt.
COST: Free

This is the only church designed by William Strickland, Philadelphia's leading colonial architect, that remains standing in Philadelphia today. Completed in 1823, it was modeled after St. Stephen's Church in Vienna and enlarged in 1878 by architect Frank Furness, who was responsible for the ornate stencils on the walls. The church's design marked the end of the Neoclassical style and was one of the earliest examples of what became known as Gothic Revival architecture. The site also happens to be where Benjamin Franklin flew the first kite.

Center City West   Map 3

COMCAST CENTER

17th and JFK Blvd., 215/496-1810,
www.themarketatcomcastcenter.com
HOURS: Market and shops Mon.-Fri. 8 A.M.-7 P.M., Sat. 8 A.M.-5 P.M.
COST: Free

Designed by Robert A. M. Stern Architects, Pennsylvania's tallest building opened in 2007 at 975 feet and 58 stories tall. With its sustainable design based on LEED principles, it is one of the tallest green office buildings in the United States. It was built as headquarters to the largest U.S. cable company, Comcast, but it is more than just an office building.

Stop inside the lobby to see **The Comcast Experience,** an LED wall measuring 83.3 feet wide and 25.4 feet high that broadcasts a variety of images throughout the day—from historic sites to nature footage to a holiday show that runs every 15 minutes between Thanksgiving and the New Year. Witness "Humanity in Motion," an art installation of life-sized figures that appear to be striding along girders high above the lobby. The building includes a half-acre landscaped public park, a grand new entrance to Philadelphia's Suburban Station, and a few high-end shops and a food court.

Museum District

Map 4

SIGHTS

BOATHOUSE ROW

Kelly Dr. along the Schuylkill River behind the Art Museum, www.boathouserow.org

The converted historic homes that serve as clubhouses to some of Philadelphia's rowing clubs also provide one of the city's most famous sights—Boathouse Row. The homes are old, and some are very interesting architecturally, but the sight is especially pretty, and most famous, for the way it looks at night from I-76 when the lights outlining the homes reflect onto the Schuylkill River. Designed in 1979 by architectural lighting designer Raymond Grenald, the lights helped revitalize Boathouse Row and brought them renewed status as a city attraction. The busiest stretch of the Schuylkill River Trail runs along Boathouse Row and is always crowded with walkers, runners, bikers, and others out to enjoy the scenery when the weather is pleasant.

CATHEDRAL BASILICA OF SAINTS PETER AND PAUL

18th and Benjamin Franklin Pkwy., 215/561-1313, www.sspeterpaulcathedral.catholicweb.com

HOURS: Mon.-Fri. 7 A.M.-5 P.M., Sat. 9:30 A.M.-6:30 P.M., Sun. 7 A.M.-6:30 P.M., guided tour after Sun. 11 A.M. mass and by appt.

COST: Free

The Cathedral Basilica of Saints Peter and Paul is Philadelphia's largest brownstone and its most architecturally impressive Italian Renaissance structure. Home to the Archdiocese of Philadelphia, it was built 1846–1864 and modeled after the Lombard Church of St. Charles (San Carla al Corso) in Rome. Four massive Corinthian columns, a vaulted copper dome, and eight side chapels are just the beginning of the church's grandeur. Constantino Brumidi, also credited with painting the dome of the Capitol in Washington, led the design team.

© KARRIE GAVIN

Boathouse Row

The ornate cathedral accommodates 2,000 people. The Crypt of the Bishops in the lower level holds the bodies of six Philadelphia bishops and archbishops.

EAKINS OVAL

Benjamin Franklin Pkwy. in front of the
Philadelphia Museum of Art

The large oval with a monument across the street from the Art Museum was named for Thomas Eakins (1844–1916), the famous Philadelphia realist painter best known for *The Gross Clinic* and *The Agnew Clinic*. It was dedicated in 1897 at the Green Street entrance to Fairmount Park and moved to this spot in 1928 when construction on the parkway was completed. The centerpiece is **Washington Monument,** designed by German sculptor Rudolf Siemering in 1897. The bronze and granite replica of George Washington in uniform on a horse sits high atop a granite pedestal looking towards City Hall, and his face was made from an impression taken during his life. Surrounding him, four pairs of Native American figures and animals each guard a pool of water representing the four great waterways of America—the Mississippi, the Potomac, the Delaware, and the Hudson. The 13 steps that lead to the pedestal represent the original 13 states, and each side represents aspects of the American journey—victory in the war, warning against the dangers of slavery, westward movement, and the march of the army. Sit on this symbolic statue with the Art Museum in one direction and the parkway and City Hall in the other for a great photo op.

◀ EASTERN STATE PENITENTIARY

N. 22nd St. and Fairmount Ave., 215/236-3300,
www.easternstate.org

HOURS: Apr.-Nov. daily 10 A.M.-5 P.M., last entry 4 P.M.,
June-Aug. daily 10 A.M.-8 P.M., last entry 7 P.M.

COST: $12 adult, $10 senior, $8 students and children
7-12, not recommended for children under 7

A walk through Eastern State Penitentiary offers a glimpse into a world rarely seen by ordinary citizens. This eye-opening site forces visitors to imagine the lives of those behind bars and to consider the controversial history

a shadowy hallway in Eastern State Penitentiary

© KARRIE GAVIN

and ideals of the past and present criminal justice system.

When it opened in 1829, the penitentiary's novel design and philosophy were considered radical experiments. Benjamin Franklin and Benjamin Rush were among the members of the first prison reform group in history—the Philadelphia Society for Alleviating the Miseries of Public Prisons—who supported the prison. Famed architect John Havilland won the design competition to build the prison, and one of his competitors, William Strickland, oversaw construction. The castle-like structure occupies 11 acres in what was then considered the outskirts of town, and today is the Fairmount neighborhood. It was the most expensive structure ever built in the country at the time.

An alternative to the overcrowded prisons of the time, the Quaker-inspired goal of Eastern State was to reform criminals through strict isolation. It was founded on the belief that when left to their own devices without the influence of the outside world, prisoners would become "penitent," or remorseful. Prisoners ate, worked, and lived in their cells, with an hour each day in a small private outdoor courtyard. When it was necessary to move through public spaces, hoods were placed over prisoners' heads so they couldn't see one another. The concept and the architecture became a model for prisons worldwide, and approximately 300 prisons on four continents were modeled on the innovative floor plan in which a central guard post is flanked with multiple sections extending from the center.

While the intentions of the founders were presumably good, the failings of the isolation system quickly became clear and the prison faced accusations of inhumane treatment of prisoners. The first investigation into the possibility of questionable practices took place in 1832; in 1842 Charles Dickens visited and said: "The system is rigid, strict, and hopeless solitary confinement, and I believe it, in its effects, to be cruel and wrong." It wasn't until 1913 that the confinement system was abandoned.

In 1970, the prison closed, and there was talk of tearing it down and using the space for commercial property. Fortunately, a task force set out to preserve what is now considered a National Historic Landmark. In 1994, Eastern State opened for daily tours. Visitors are required to sign a waiver stating that they are aware of the poor condition of the building before entering, but areas deemed unsafe are closed to the public.

Different tours take place throughout the day in which guides tell stories of prisoners, escapes, and more, but the well-made self-guided audio tour, "Voices of Eastern State," is a great option. Actor Steve Buscemi's voice, along with those of real prisoners and guards that served here, will guide you to more than 20 fascinating sites throughout the prison that reveal its rich history. Among the famous prisoners who did time here was Al Capone, who was apparently given royal treatment during his eight-month stay. A peek into his restored cell reveals a cushy apartment with antiques, rugs, oil paintings, and the sounds of a waltz that he frequently played on his radio.

If you happen to be in town and have a high tolerance for fear, the already-spooky site is transformed into the annual **Terror Behind the Walls,** a haunted house, every night in October.

FAIRMOUNT WATER WORKS INTERPRETIVE CENTER
640 Waterworks Dr., 215/685-0723, www.fairmountwaterworks.org
HOURS: Tues.-Sat. 10 A.M.-5 P.M., Sun. 1-5 P.M.
COST: Free

Stroll above the scenic Fairmount Dam just behind the Art Museum and learn about Philadelphia's 200-year relationship with the Schuylkill River. You will be in good company; out-of-town admirers have included Mark Twain and Charles Dickens, who praised the site for its technical ingenuity and natural and architectural beauty. The nation's first municipal water-delivery system, now a National Historic Landmark, was completed in 1822. Using steam engines and later waterwheels, it pumped water uphill from the Schuylkill River into a reservoir where the Art Museum now stands. The kid-friendly exhibits in the interpretive center explain the importance of waterways to urban centers and illustrate the storied history of this once cutting-edge facility. The site is also home to the upscale, appropriately named Water Works Restaurant.

FREE LIBRARY OF PHILADELPHIA
1901 Vine St., 215/686-5322, www.library.phila.gov
HOURS: Mon.-Thurs. 9 A.M.-9 P.M., Fri. 9 A.M.-6 P.M., Sat. 9 A.M.-5 P.M., Sun. 1-5 P.M., tour rare books collection Mon.-Fri. 11 A.M. or by appt.

The central branch of the Free Library of Philadelphia, just off the Benjamin Franklin Parkway, opened in 1927 and contains more than seven million items and special collections. While parts of it are in need of repair or updating, many signs of the Beaux Arts building's original grandeur can still be seen in the lobby and many of the reading rooms. Twenty different signs posted throughout the building describe each space and its history.

During an hour-long tour of the Rare Books Collection on the 3rd floor, you'll see a cuneiform from 2800 B.C.; *Book of the Dead* scrolls; Charles Dickens's mummified pet raven, Grip, believed to have inspired Edgar Allen Poe's famous poem *The Raven*; and original manuscripts and first editions of both Dickens and

Poe. The collection also contains the **William McIntyre Elkins Library,** which was transported from the collector's home in Briar Hill just outside Philadelphia and recreated panel by panel. It contains an extensive Dickens collection and Dickens's own desk and lamp.

The library regularly hosts free films, lectures, and children's programs, and rotating exhibits in the 1st-floor Fleisher Gallery. A roof deck affords a great view of the city, but is only open for special events—or if you can sweet-talk a staff member into taking you up for a peek. Stop at the H.O.M.E Page Café in the East Wing for lunch, coffee, snacks, and wireless Internet service. A massive renovation and restoration project is in the works to add a modern, state-of-the-art addition to the library, connected by bridges to the original building.

LEMON HILL MANSION

Sedgeley and Lemon Hill Drives, 215/232-4337, www.lemonhill.org
HOURS: Apr.-mid-Dec. Wed.-Sun. 10 A.M.-4 P.M., Jan.-Mar. by appt.
COST: $5 adult, $3 student and senior

Lemon Hill was built in 1800 by wealthy merchant Henry Pratt on land formerly owned by Declaration of Independence signatory Robert Morris. Of particular architectural note are the curved doors, windows, and fireplaces in the two oval rooms that look out over the lush gardens. The property was the first purchased by the city for the creation of its Fairmount Park system, and holds a special place in local, mercantile, and horticultural histories. Check it out high on the hill across the street from the Schuylkill River Path near Boathouse Row—recognizable by its lemon-colored paint.

◖ PHILADELPHIA MUSEUM OF ART

26th St. and Benjamin Franklin Pkwy., 215/763-8100, www.philamuseum.org
HOURS: Tues.-Sun. 10 A.M.-5 P.M., Fri. open until 8:45 P.M.
COST: $16 adult, $14 senior, $12 student and child (13-18), free 12 and under, pay what you wish first Sun. of month, additional fee for special exhibits

Whether you've come to see the world-renowned art collection, take photographs outside at one of the most picturesque spots in the city, or to run up the steps in the footsteps of Philly's Rocky Balboa (hopefully you'll do all of the above), just be sure to come. Easily Philadelphia's most impressive museum and

© KARRIE GAVIN

The Philadelphia Museum of Art is a sight to see both inside and out.

ROCKY'S HOME

Ben Franklin is certainly Philadelphia's most famous historical son, but almost equally revered is the city's most famous fictional son, Rocky Balboa. More than just a character in a movie, Rocky has come to represent Philly's scrappy, fighting, underdog spirit. In the classic 1976 movie, Rocky, played by Sylvester

© KARRIE GAVIN

Rocky statue, by sculptor A. Thomas Schomberg, at the base of the Art Museum steps

Stallone, is shown training (often as the sun comes up with inspirational music playing) in and around many Philadelphia landmarks, from the Italian Market to the steps of the Philadelphia Museum of Art.

In 1982, a bronze 8-foot, 6-inch, 1,500-pound statue of Rocky was constructed, and much debate ensued over where his replica belongs. For many years, it was at the top of the Art Museum steps, fists raised above his head in the classic pose from the movie, but some people deemed it uncouth to have him so prominently displayed in front of a world-class museum of art. *Rocky* was eventually relegated to a spot outside of the Spectrum sports arena in South Philadelphia, which some considered more fitting since he is an athlete (albeit a fictional one). But that was still not quite right and many visitors who went looking for him at the Art Museum, which many termed the "Rocky Steps," were not happy to find him missing from his post.

A compromise was reached in 2006 and *Rocky* was returned to the Art Museum, but rather than standing prominently at the top of the steps, he now stands on a more modest street-level pedestal next to the East Entrance. It seems that Rocky has finally found a permanent home.

Feel free to run up the steps for a classic photo op. And don't be embarrassed – even locals have done it at least once in their lives. Just don't make the mistake that some visitors do and forget to actually go into the museum. While *Rocky* deserves a few snaps of the camera, the museum beyond the steps is the real draw.

the third-largest museum of art in the United States, the Philadelphia Museum of Art is a sight to behold inside and out. Rising high at the end of the Benjamin Franklin Parkway and serving as the gateway to Fairmount Park, it is known to locals simply as "the Art Museum."

Founded during the nation's first centennial in 1876, originally as a museum of decorative arts housed in Fairmount Park's Memorial Hall, it relocated to its current location in 1928. Its chief designer, Julian Abele, was the first African American graduate of the University of Pennsylvania's architecture school. Inspired by temples he saw while traveling in Greece, he designed the museum to look like three linked Greek temples. Made of Minnesota dolomite, the massive Greek Revival building is adorned with rich color in the detailed friezes.

Be sure to walk around outside and take in all the elaborate details, and don't miss the intricate brightly painted sculptures along the top. If you're looking for the 8-foot, 6-inch, 1,500-pound statue of Rocky, it is located on a street-level pedestal next to the East Entrance steps.

Inside, take in what you can of the more than 200 galleries showcasing more than 225,000 works of art. Don't miss some of the 80-plus carefully decorated period rooms, which will transport you through time and all over the world. The museum hosts some of the most famous traveling exhibits in the art world, often serving as one of, if not the only, U.S. stop, so be sure to check the website to find out what is there. Every Friday evening, you can come for **Art After 5** (5–8:45 P.M.) for live music (usually international or jazz), food, and wine in the Great Stair Hall, as well as access to select galleries, all for the price of admission.

Now there is still more to see just across the street with the 2007 addition of the **Ruth and Raymond G. Perelman Building** (Fairmount and Pennsylvania Aves., included in price of ticket to Main Building; for Perelman alone $8 adult, $7 senior, $6 student and child 13–18, pay what you wish first Sun. of month). The preserved art deco building is the first major expansion in 80 years. Modern gallery spaces, state-of-the-art visitor amenities, study centers, and educational resources are just some of the features offered in the impressive new space, which can be reached on foot or by free shuttle from the Main Building every 15 minutes Tuesday–Sunday 10 A.M.–5 P.M.

◖ PHILADELPHIA ZOO

3400 W. Girard Ave., 215/243-1100,
www.philadelphiazoo.org
HOURS: Mar.-Oct. daily 9:30 A.M.-5 P.M.,
Nov.-Feb. daily 9:30 A.M.-4 P.M.
COST: $18 adult, $15 child 2-11 in season, $14 for all
Nov.-Feb.

Founded in 1874, the oldest zoo in the country has only recently joined the ranks of the very best in the country. In the past decade, each

cheetahs at the Philadelphia Zoo

year has brought new and increasingly exotic animals along with updated exhibits and attractions. The latest and greatest is the **Channel 6 Zooballoon** (Apr.–Oct. weather permitting, $15 pp, $50 family of four), which takes visitors on an exhilarating 15-minute trip 400 feet above the ground for a 360-degree view of the city. In addition to being a fun ride, the balloon is a historical tribute to the first North American passenger balloon flight, taken by Philadelphia pilot Jean-Pierre Blanchard in 1785; President George Washington was among the onlookers.

The zoo occupies 42 acres in West Fairmount Park, complete with winding landscaped paths and historic architecture, including the country home of William Penn's grandson. The botanical collections include more than 500 plant species, and animal sculptures include Heinz Warneke's giant *Cow Elephant and Calf* and Henry Mitchell's popular *Impala Fountain and Hippo Mother and Baby.* The long history of the zoo includes the first orangutan and chimp births in a U.S. zoo (1928), the world's first children's zoo (1957), and the first U.S. exhibit of white lions (1993).

You could easily spend a day watching the carnivores feed in Carnivore Kingdom, walking among flying birds in the Jungle Bird Walk, and hanging out with the primates in the interactive PECO Primate Center. Kids love to feed and ride the animals in the Children's Zoo, play in the giant Treehouse, and ride the Amazon Rainforest Carousel on the ground and the Express Train up in the air. Guided tours on a wide range of topics ($5) are available.

South Philadelphia   Map 5

GLORIA DEI
(OLD SWEDES' EPISCOPAL CHURCH)
Columbus Blvd. and Christian St., 215/389-1513,
www.old-swedes.org
HOURS: Jun.-Aug. daily, Sept.-May Tues.-Sun.
9 A.M.-4 P.M.; call ahead
COST: Free

Swedes settled along the banks of the Schuylkill and Delaware Rivers as early as 1638, long before William Penn arrived. The earliest church still standing in Pennsylvania was built for a group of early settlers 1698–1700. Check out the massive Swedish-style marble baptismal font, which was crafted in Philadelphia and added to the church in 1731. Miniature wooden replicas of ships that carried Swedish settlers here in the early 17th century hang from the ceilings. The church is home to a one-room museum operated by Independence National Historical Park that displays a historical map and other artifacts from the church's early days. Sea captains and Revolutionary War soldiers are among those buried in the cemetery. The church is used regularly for worship and other community activities, but the doors are open to the public.

PHILADELPHIA'S MAGIC GARDENS
1020 South St., 215/733-0390,
www.philadelphiasmagicgardens.org
HOURS: Apr.-Oct. Sun.-Thurs. 11 A.M.-6 P.M.,
Fri.-Sat. 11 A.M.-8 P.M., Nov.-Mar. closes an hour
earlier Sun.-Thurs.
COST: Self-guided tour $5 adult, $2 child, guided site tour $8 adult, $5 child, guided walking tour $10 adult, child $6

In the 1960s, a group of young artists moved into a run-down section of South Street and helped transform the neighborhood into something beautiful. At the forefront were Isaiah Zagar and his wife, Julia, who returned from the Peace Corps in 1969 and opened the Eyes Gallery at 4th and South Streets to sell the textiles, woodcarvings, and ceramics they collected in South America. They decorated their store with anything and everything they found in the neighborhood, especially the many pieces they discovered in an abandoned glass warehouse. Isaiah began creating mosaics with a variety of materials—glass being his material of choice—and hasn't stopped since.

Zagar's trademark mosaics can be seen all over the city on homes, businesses, and in murals, but the pinnacle is his beautiful, trippy home and studio—the Magic Gardens. Every square inch has been covered with colorful tiles, bottles, mirrors, and other everyday materials to create an abstract collage. Take a self-guided or guided tour of the Magic Gardens and grab a brochure that lists the addresses of more than 60 nearby murals of Zagar's unmistakable public artworks, which you can explore on your own any time of the year. On weekends April–October, you can also take an hour-long guided walking tour of the gardens and nearby murals.

University City   Map 6

30TH STREET STATION

2955 Market St., 215/386-6426, www.amtrak.com

HOURS: 24 hours

Locals probably forget to stop and appreciate the beauty of Philadelphia's 30th Street Station while they run for their trains, but it happens to be one of America's finest transportation hubs and one of the few remaining grand railroad stations in the country. The Pennsylvania Railroad needed a location between New York and Washington on what is now known as the Northeast Corridor, and Philadelphia was the obvious choice. Serving as a stop on the regional rail line within the city and suburbs, and as the main hub into and out of the city by rail, 30th Street has all the modern necessities—eateries, bookstore, and gift shops—along with magnificent architecture.

The Neoclassical structure was built 1929–1934 by Graham, Anderson, Probst & White and is now listed on the National Register of Historic Places. The 90-foot-high ceilings create an old-school sophistication, making it easy to imagine an early-20th-century bustle not all that different from today. Inside, there is a sculpture by Walker Hancock created in 1950 to honor Pennsylvania Railroad employees killed during World War II; it includes archangel Michael lifting the body of a soldier from the flames of war.

The station has had its share of movie fame; featured in the 1983 film *Trading Places* and M. Night Shyamalan's *Unbreakable* (2000), its most famous screen moment is from the classic scene in *Witness* (1985), in which a young Amish boy traveling through Philadelphia with his mom witnesses a murder in the bathroom of the station. Fortunately, it was just a movie and the station is generally a safe place.

UNIVERSITY OF PENNSYLVANIA

Btwn. 34th and 38th Sts. and Walnut and Spruce Sts., 215/898-5000, www.upenn.edu

A member of the Ivy League, the University of Pennsylvania, more commonly known as "Penn," is the oldest and most esteemed of Philadelphia's universities. With Ben Franklin among its founders, it was the first official university in the country when it opened in 1740. Franklin helped design an educational program that included practical applications in commerce and public service along with classics and theology, laying the groundwork for the multidisciplinary and liberal arts curriculums practiced at many modern universities today (blame Ben for all those annoying general-ed requirements). The campus moved to its current site in West Philly in the 1870s after more than a century in Center City. Accessible to Center City by several bridges that can be crossed by car, on bike, or on foot, the neighborhood is called University City for Penn (and nearby Drexel University).

The centerpiece of campus is **Locust Walk,** an idyllic ivy-covered walkway spanning several blocks through the heart of campus, lined with trees and stately architecture. If school is in session, you're likely to see students there promoting fraternity parties, clubs, and events, and no matter when you come, you'll see several monuments to Ben Franklin along the way, including the bronze sculpture on a bench near 36th and Walnut Streets (a popular photo op), and a large statue on a pedestal near 34th and Walnut Streets.

Across from that statue, you'll see a sculpture of a large broken button, courtesy of Claes Oldenberg, also responsible for the *Clothespin* sculpture near City Hall. Just beyond the button is the **Van Pelt Library,** an excellent place to study, read, use free Internet, or to visit the rare books room on the 6th floor. The library is open to the public with a photo ID. There are many notable buildings worth exploring on campus, including the rotating exhibit in the Arthur Ross Gallery in the stunning **Fisher Fine Arts Library** (just across College Green from the Van Pelt Library). And all true sports fans will want to see the historic basketball arena, the **Palestra** (220 S. 32nd St.).

WOODLANDS CEMETERY AND MANSION
4000 Woodland Ave., 215/386-2181,
www.woodlandsphila.org
HOURS: Cemetery open daily, mansion hours vary;
call ahead
COST: Free

A National Historic Landmark, Woodlands consists of 300 hundred sprawling acres of land along the west bank of the Schuylkill River, home to a cemetery, gardens, and a Neoclassical mansion. Famous Philadelphia lawyer Andrew Hamilton purchased the land in 1735, and the mansion was built in 1787 by his grandson William. The 16-room manor was one of

CITY OF MURALS

Philadelphia boasts more than 3,000 murals – more than any other city in the entire world. The colorful, larger-than-life artworks brighten schools, community centers, businesses, and homes from Center City and the Avenue of the Arts to outlying neighborhoods that most tourists and even some residents rarely see. Especially in parts of the city where urban blight is at its worst, the murals bring beauty and a sense of community pride to neighborhoods that need it most, and the Mural Tours provide visitors with an interesting and safe way to explore these areas.

The **Mural Arts Program** traces its roots to the mid-1980s, when the city was plastered with graffiti. Muralist and community activist Jane Golden was hired to redirect the energies of graffitists into mural painting. She still runs the program, which has not only alleviated much of the graffiti problem but also empowered young artists and contributed to neighborhood revitalization in many parts of the city. Professional artists are hired to work closely with residents to create murals that tell the stories of the spaces they inhabit.

While the magnificent works of art speak for themselves, a guided tour is the best way to experience them. The Mural Arts Program (877/887-8225, www.muralarts.org) offers **trolley tours** ($25 pp, seniors $23, children 12 and under $15) of various sections of the city on Saturdays and Sundays April–November and Wednesdays May–November. They begin at 10 A.M. and last 90 minutes to two hours. The **Mural Mile Walk** ($17 pp), offered May–October daily at 11:30 A.M., covers 2.5 miles and 17 murals in Center City. If the guided tour is sold out, you can rent an MP3 player and headphones for a **self-guided version** ($10). Trolley and

PHOTO BY JACK RAMSDALE FOR MURAL ARTS PROGRAM
© CITY OF PHILADELPHIA MURAL ARTS PROGRAM

Jackie Robinson, by David McShane, is located at 2804 North Broad Street.

walking tours depart from the Independence Visitor Center at 6th and Market Streets, rain or shine. Reservations are strongly recommended. **Bike tours** ($17 pp) are offered on occasion. One new, unique tour option is known as **Love Letter** ($17 pp) and features 50 rooftop murals in West Philly. Participants take in the artworks from SEPTA's elevated train and several platforms. The tour departs from the Love Park Welcome Center at 1600 JFK Boulevard at 10 A.M. Saturday year-round.

Be sure to check the website for a full schedule of tours and special events, as the Mural Arts Program is always expanding to offer more murals and more ways to experience them.

Philadelphia's finest estates for many years. An active botanist, Andrew's gardens and greenhouses contained more than 10,000 different plant species, including several grown from seeds harvested during Lewis and Clark's expeditions. His was considered the largest collection of plants on the continent at the time.

After William's death in 1813, much of the property was sold, and in 1840, Woodlands Cemetery Company purchased the remaining grounds. Woodlands, along with Laurel Hill Cemetery, served as an innovative improvement to the overcrowded city-church cemeteries that dominated early Philadelphia. Both cemeteries were unique in their elaborate landscaping and architecture and in their isolated locations.

Today, winding brick paths from the original landscape are lined with headstones of many notable Philadelphians that were buried here, including Thomas Eakins, Rembrandt Peale, the Drexel and Biddle families, surgical pioneer Dr. Samuel Gross, and railroad magnates Asa Whitney and John Edgar Thompson.

If you visit when the office is open, grab a map showing where the famous people are buried. You can also tour the mansion, which is undergoing a much-needed renovation but serves as an impressive example of Neoclassical architecture.

Northern Liberties   Map 7

EDGAR ALLEN POE
NATIONAL HISTORIC SITE
532 N. 7th St., 215/597-8780, www.nps.gov/edal
HOURS: Wed.-Sun. 9 A.M.-5 P.M.
COST: Free

One of America's most famous and unique writers, Edgar Allen Poe (1809–1849), lived in this three-story brick home with his wife, Virginia, and his mother-in-law, Maria Clemm. He was a Philadelphia resident for only a year before moving to New York City in 1843, but this was one of the most productive years in his writing life. It was here that he wrote *The Black Cat,* which describes a basement very similar to the one in the home, as well as three of his most acclaimed masterpieces: *The Tell-Tale Heart, The Fall of the House of Usher,* and *The Gold Bug.* This is the only one of the three homes Poe lived in throughout his life that stands today. Visitors can tour the rooms, cellar, and exhibits and watch a short film about Poe, his family, and contemporaries. The site is operated by Independence National Historical Park.

NATIONAL SHRINE OF
ST. JOHN NEUMANN
St. Peter's Catholic Church, 1019 N. 5th St.,
215/627-3080, www.stjohnneumann.org

HOURS: By appt.
COST: Free

Catholics come from far and wide to pray to the shrine of St. John Neumann (1811–1860). Born in Bohemia, Neumann became an American Catholic Church bishop in Philadelphia in 1852. His credits, according to some, include founding the Catholic school system and a religious order for women. The beloved bishop died at the age of 48 and was enshrined in a crypt in the basement of Saint Peter's Church, as he had requested. Devoted followers have come to pray to him ever since, and many believe their prayers were answered. Word spread of the believed "miracles" and the saint's popularity soared. In 1977, he was canonized and declared "America's first saint" by Pope Paul VI. People continue to come from all over the world to pray to him. Scenes from his life are depicted on stained-glass windows next to the glass case that holds his preserved body. The church is an active parish and not a big tourist stop, so if you're fascinated by the shrine or you believe in miracles, call first to see if it is okay to come for a visit.

RODEPH SHALOM SYNAGOGUE
615 N. Broad St., 215/627-6747,
www.rodephshalom.org

HOURS: Call ahead
COST: Free

The oldest Ashkenazic congregation in the western hemisphere, founded in 1795, has had several homes over its long history. The current synagogue, located just north of Center City and built in 1927, is a striking example of Moorish architecture. A large dome, starburst skylights, stained-glass windows, an ark supported on marble columns, and bronze-and-enamel doors are just a few of the highlights. The Broad Street Foyer houses the Leon J. and Julia S. Obermayer Collection of Jewish ritual art, containing more than 500 ceremonial objects dating to the 1700s. Call in advance to schedule a tour at this active congregation.

Fairmount Park   Map 8

LAUREL HILL CEMETERY
3822 Ridge Ave., 215/228-8200,
www.thelaurelhillcemetery.org
HOURS: Mon.-Fri. 8 A.M.-4:30 P.M.,
Sat.-Sun. 9:30 A.M.-4:30 P.M., closed major holidays
COST: Free admission, $5 self-guided tour and map,
$15-20 for most guided tours

If wandering around a cemetery isn't your idea of a good time, then clearly you've never visited Laurel Hill. The centuries-old architecture and beautiful view of the Schuylkill River from the raised, sprawling grounds make it a worthwhile stop. On a tour of the ancient mausoleums and gravestones, you'll learn about the fascinating lives—and deaths—of many of Philadelphia's earliest and most notable residents, including almost 40 Civil War–era generals, six *Titanic* survivors, and members of the prominent Rittenhouse, Elkins, Widener, and Strawbridge families. Self-guided tours are always available, and special themed tours are offered several times a month.

Until the 1830s, city cemeteries were as crowded and unsanitary as the streets they butted up against. Bodies filled small churchyards in packed residential and commercial areas, and when space ran out, additional layers of graves were often added on top of the existing graves. A picturesque, rural burial ground was a revolutionary idea at the time. Laurel Hill was intended to be a dignified resting place for the departed as well as a country retreat for the living. Today, it attracts joggers and horticulturalists as much as architecture and history buffs. Its vast archives of contracts, maps, photographs, and documents are a resource for historians, genealogists, and scholars.

SMITH CIVIL WAR MEMORIAL
N. Concourse Dr., W. Fairmount Park

Framing the street on the way to Memorial Hall (home of the Please Touch Museum) from Center City stands the large bronze Smith Civil War Memorial. Erected 1897–1912 with funds provided by its wealthy namesake, Richard Smith, it includes a bronze statue of Smith himself, along with accomplished war heroes Generals Hancock and McClellan, and others. The memorial is made up of two separate towers on each side of the street, and the base of each tower is a curved wall with a built-in bench. They're known as the whispering benches; if you sit at one end and whisper, someone at the other end can hear you.

HISTORIC HOMES OF FAIRMOUNT PARK

In the 18th and early 19th centuries, many wealthy Philadelphians built retreat homes along the elevated, picturesque banks of the Schuylkill River in Fairmount Park. They offered a quick escape from the ills of urban life, including summer heat and epidemics like typhoid and yellow fever. A number of these historic houses have been preserved and are open to the public. The homes offer a glimpse into the lives of early Philadelphians, while showcasing early architectural styles and period furnishings. Cedar Grove, Sweetbriar, and Belmont are on the west side of the river, while

HISTORIC GERMANTOWN

Home to stops on the Underground Railroad, Philadelphia's only Revolutionary War battle, and the country's first paper mill, Germantown is rich with history. Founded by German settlers in 1881, today it is an urban neighborhood in the northwest section of the city that is well worth the 15-minute drive from Center City for history lovers. While you're in the neighborhood, stop for a hike in the Wissahickon or have lunch in nearby Mt. Airy, Chestnut Hill, or Manayunk.

The Germantown Historical Society (5501 Germantown Ave., 215/844-1683, www.germantownhistory.org, Tues. 9 A.M.-1 P.M., Thurs. 1-5 P.M., and by appt., $3 adult, $2 senior and student, free under 10) has an extensive collection of artifacts and a small museum open to the public. It is headquarters for **Historic Germantown** (www.freedomsbackyard.com), a partnership of 14 local attractions, including all of those highlighted here. A passport for admission to all 14 ($15 pp, $25 family) can be purchased in person or online.

Upper Germantown

Historic RittenhouseTown (206 Lincoln Dr., 215/438-5711, www.rittenhousetown.org, most weekends in summer noon-4 P.M., $5 adult, $3 senior/child) pays homage to the area's earliest settlers — the German immigrants drawn to Pennsylvania for religious freedom. William Rittenhouse (originally Wilhelm Rittenhausen), leader and minister of a small Mennonite community, built North America's first paper mill in this wooded enclave on the edge of Wissahickon Creek in 1690. He developed a self-sufficient industrial village containing more than 40 buildings, including homesteads, workers' cottages, a church, a school, and a firehouse. Seven buildings remain and are open for tours.

During the Revolutionary War, the Battle of Germantown took place on the grounds of **Cliveden** (6401 Germantown Ave., 215/848-1777, www.cliveden.org, Apr.-Dec. Thurs.-Sun. noon-4 P.M., and by appt., $10 adult, $8 student). The stately Georgian home was built 1764-1767 for Benjamin Chew, who was banished during the war due to his British ties. Lucky for him, he was absent during the

bloody battle of October 1777. British troops on their way to Philadelphia broke into Cliveden for protection while American troops fired muskets and cannons from across the street at **Upsala**, another historic home.

The **Johnson House** (6306 Germantown Ave., 215/438-1768, www.johnsonhouse.org, Thurs.-Fri. 10 A.M.-4 P.M., Sat. 1-4 P.M., and by appt., $8 adult, $6 senior, $4 student), built 1765-1768, was home to three generations of Quaker abolitionists and became an important station on the Underground Railroad in the 1850s.

Wyck (6026 Germantown Ave., 215/848-1690, www.wyck.org, Apr.-mid-Dec. grounds: Mon.-Sat. 10 A.M.-4 P.M.; mansion: Tues., Thurs., and Sat. 1-4 P.M., $5 adult, $4 senior, free during farmers market Jun.-Nov. Fri. 1-4 P.M.) was used by British troops as a field hospital during the Battle of Germantown, but its real interest lies in the nine generations of a Quaker family that lived there, seen through 100,000-plus artifacts accumulated over 300 years. Mansion tours are offered Tuesday, Thursday, Friday (self-guided only), and Saturday 1-4 P.M.

Just off of Germantown Avenue, the **Ebenezer Maxwell Mansion** (200 W. Tulpehocken St., 215/438-1861, www.ebenezermaxwellmansion.org, Thurs.-Sat. noon-4 P.M., last tour 3:15 P.M., $6), built in 1859, is a classic example of the lavish Victorian architecture popular in the area in the mid-19th century and contains a small exhibit space.

Lower Germantown

The **Deshler-Morris House** (5442 Germantown Ave., 215/597-4159, www.nps.gov/demo, Apr.-Dec. Wed.-Sun. noon-4 P.M. and by appt., free), also called the "Germantown White House," was home to George Washington on two occasions; in 1793 when he came to escape the yellow fever epidemic and again for vacation the following summer. Ironically, his enemy, British general Howe, also stayed here after winning the Battle of Germantown.

With a name straight out of a Harry Potter book, **Grumblethorpe** (5267 Germantown Ave., 215/843-4820, www.philalandmarks.org, call ahead, $4 student/senior, $12 family, free

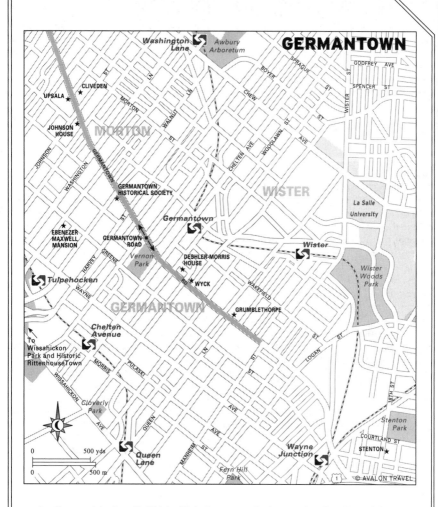

under 6) was originally called "John Wister's Big House" because it had multiple stories. Built in 1744 for wine importer John Wister, it's a classic example of 18th-century Pennsylvania German architecture. General James Agnew stayed here after being wounded in the Battle of Germantown; he died in the front parlor and his blood stains remain on the floor.

Stenton (4601 N. 18th St., 215/329-7312, www.stenton.org, Apr.-Dec. Tues.-Sat. 1-4 P.M. and by appt., $5 adult, $4 student/senior, free under 6) is one of the best-preserved Georgian mansions in Philadelphia. Built in 1730 for James Logan, secretary to William Penn, the mansion, grounds, and barn are open for tours. The barn contains an exhibit of agricultural tools dating from the 18th and early 19th centuries.

the rest are on the east side. The houses are operated by various civic organizations and have various hours and admission costs. To see a particular house, contact that house directly, or for information about seasonal guided trolley tours of multiple homes in summer and during the winter holiday, call **Fairmount Park Council for Historic Sites** (215/879-1280, www.fairmountparkhistoricsites.org).

BELMONT MANSION

2000 Belmont Mansion Dr., 215/878-8844,
www.belmontmansion.org
HOURS: Tues.-Sun. 11 A.M.-5 P.M.,
in winter weekends noon-5 P.M.
COST: $7 adult, $5 student, senior, and child,
free under 6

Built in the late 18th century, Belmont Mansion is one of the finest examples of Palladian architecture in the United States standing today. The land was purchased in 1742 by William Peters, a English lawyer and land agent for William Penn's family. He designed the mansion and formal gardens, and later passed it on to his son, Richard. In the turbulent times of the Revolution, Richard served as Secretary of the Board of War for the Revolutionary Army and Pennsylvania Delegate to Congress under the Articles of Confederation. George Washington, John Adams, Thomas Jefferson, and James Madison all stayed here at various times. After the Revolution, Richard became Speaker of the Pennsylvania Assembly, Pennsylvania State Senator, Judge of the United States District Court, and an environmental scientist and prominent abolitionist. In 2007, after a long restoration project, the American Women's Heritage Society opened the house as an interpretive and educational center and **Underground Railroad Museum.** On a tour, you'll learn about the role of the home and its owners and slaves in history and in the abolitionist movement.

CEDAR GROVE

1 Cedar Grove Dr., 215/763-8100,
www.philamuseum.org/parkhouses
HOURS: Tues.-Sun. 10 A.M.-5 P.M.
COST: $5 adult, $3 senior, $2 child 6-12

In 1746, wealthy widow Elizabeth Coates Paschall acquired land in the Frankford section of the city, where she built a large house for herself and her three children. Over subsequent generations, Cedar Grove grew with multiple additions and renovations, most notably when Elizabeth's granddaughter Sarah and her husband, Isaac Wistar Morris, doubled its size around 1800. They added a formal parlor, new kitchen, and a 3rd floor. The house was in Frankford until the 1920s, when it was moved brick by brick to Fairmount Park. Today, tourists and history buffs can stroll through the mansion and take in the fine mix of Federal, Baroque, and Rococo architectural styles, including notable features like the large kitchen with original utensils and a two-sided wall of closets on the 2nd floor.

LAUREL HILL MANSION

7201 N. Randolph Dr., 215/235-1776,
www.fairmountpark.org/LaurelHill.asp
HOURS: July-mid-Dec. Wed.-Sun. 10 A.M.-4 P.M.,
Apr.-June Sat.-Sun. 10 A.M.-4 P.M.
COST: $5 adult, $3 senior, $2 child (6-12)

Laurel Hill Mansion was built by Rebecca Rawle around 1767, after she lost her first husband. During the Revolutionary War the house was seized from her and her second husband, Philadelphia mayor Samuel Shoemaker, because they were considered British sympathizers. It was later returned to the family and occupied by Rebecca's son William Rawle, who became a noted lawyer and founded the Philadelphia Bar Association. The elegant Georgian structure was augmented with wings on the southern and northern sides. Its position on a bluff overlooking the Schuylkill River makes it particularly notable.

MOUNT PLEASANT

3800 Mount Pleasant Dr., 215/763-8100,
www.philamuseum.org/parkhouses
HOURS: Tues.-Sun. 10 A.M.-5 P.M.
COST: $5 adult, $3 senior, $2 child 6-12

Before John Adams became president, he declared Mount Pleasant to be "the most elegant seat in Pennsylvania," validating its owners' high ambitions. Built 1762–1765 by Scottish ship captain John Macphearson and his wife, Margaret, the house was intended to make a grand statement with its exquisite architecture high above the Schuylkill River. Architect Thomas Neville, a protégé of Independence Hall architect Edmund Woolley, designed his own interesting Scottish interpretation of the Georgian style. Among many noteworthy owners were national traitor Benedict Arnold and Jonathan Williams, a great-nephew of Benjamin Franklin and first superintendent of West Point. It is currently unfurnished, so visitors have to imagine what it would look like with all the finest furnishings.

STRAWBERRY MANSION

2450 Strawberry Mansion Bridge Dr., 215/228-8364, www.historicstrawberrymansion.org

HOURS: July-mid-Dec. Wed.-Fri. 10 A.M.-4 P.M.

COST: $5 adult, $3 senior, $2 child 6-12

Although Strawberry Mansion shares a name with a nearby section of the city that has been long distressed by poverty and crime, the largest of Fairmount Park's historic houses knew nothing of urban decay in its heyday in a then-rural setting. Dating to around 1790, it was built for renowned lawyer Judge William Lewis, now best remembered for drafting the United States' first law abolishing slavery. Lewis built the middle section of the house, and the Greek Revival–styled wings were added by the next owner, Judge Joseph Hemphill. With two floors of furniture and decorative arts from the Federal, Regency, and Empire styles, the home offers a glimpse into another time. The name Strawberry Mansion comes from Mrs. Grimes, a resident who sold strawberries and cream from the house in the mid-19th century.

SWEETBRIAR

1 Sweetbriar Dr., 215/222-1333, www.sweetbriarmansion.org

HOURS: July-mid-Dec. Wed.-Sun. 10 A.M.-4 P.M.

COST: $3

Boston-born merchant Samuel Breck built his country estate overlooking the Schuylkill in 1797 to escape the yellow fever ravaging Philadelphia. He chose the Neoclassical style, rather than the then-dominant Georgian, and installed an entryway colonnade, large Italianate windows, and a stairway with a balcony. Breck hosted fabulous salons and dinners here, and entertained many friends, including luminaries like Marquis de Lafayette. He kept thorough diaries detailing the life of Philadelphia in the post-Revolutionary period. Though Sweetbriar, along with other "country estates," was built in part for its owners to escape the epidemics sweeping the city proper, Breck's own daughter died of typhus, and the brokenhearted parents closed the house and sold it 10 years later. Today, the house holds arts and crafts, a significant library, and architectural and artistic details like the elegant Etruscan room.

WOODFORD MANSION

33rd and Dauphin Sts., 215/229-6115, www.woodfordmansion.org

HOURS: Tues.-Sun. 10 A.M.-4 P.M.

COST: $5 adult, $3 senior, $2 child 6-12

Woodford is a classic example of early Georgian architecture built for Philadelphia's elite class. William Coleman, a local merchant and friend of Benjamin Franklin, bought this tract of land and built his home here 1756–1758. David Franks purchased the home in 1771 and added the second story and back wing, but only lived there until 1778, when he was sent to England and the house was confiscated because he was a British sympathizer. It was later acquired by Isaac Wharton, whose mother, Rebecca Rawle, built nearby Laurel Hill Mansion. The home stayed in that family until it was acquired by the city in 1868. Inside, you will see a large collection of 18th- and early 19th-century English, Continental, and American decorative arts.

Greater Philadelphia Map 9

ELKINS PARK

BETH SHOLOM SYNAGOGUE

8231 Old York Rd., Elkins Park, 215/887-1342,
www.bethsholomcongregation.org

HOURS: Call ahead

COST: Free

While Jewish synagogues in the Philly region are plentiful, especially in the nearby northern suburbs, only one of them was designed by legendary architect Frank Lloyd Wright. Beth Sholom Synagogue, meaning "House of Peace" in Hebrew, was built to house the congregation when it moved from North Philadelphia to Elkins Park in the 1950s. It is the only synagogue Wright ever designed, and it was the last project he completed before his death. The design is heavy with sacred imagery. A large glass pyramid calls to mind both a mountain and a tent, which Wright referred to as a "luminous Mount Sinai." The congregation is of the Conservative doctrine, with a membership of about 1,000 families. As it's an active congregation, be sure to call ahead if you wish to go inside.

CAMDEN RIVERFRONT

In summertime, the best and fastest way to cross the Delaware River to reach Camden, New Jersey, is on the **RiverLink Ferry** (215/925-5465, www.riverlinkferry.com), which runs daily Memorial Day–Labor Day and on weekends for the rest of the months of May and September. It can also be reached via a short drive cross the Ben Franklin Bridge or the **high-speed train** line to New Jersey (PATCO, 215/922-4600, www.ridepatco.org).

ADVENTURE AQUARIUM

1 Riverside Dr., Camden, NJ, 856/365-3300,
www.adventureaquarium.com

HOURS: Daily 9:30 A.M.-5 P.M.

COST: $21.95 adult, $17.95 child (2-12), free under 2, $5 extra for 4-D theater show

During its first 10 years, the New Jersey State Aquarium at Camden played perpetual second fiddle to larger aquariums in Baltimore and

Washington, D.C., but after a full renovation and expansion, it reopened in 2005 as the new and much-improved Adventure Aquarium. Anchoring the steadily developing Camden waterfront, the aquarium holds over 8,000 animals in a variety of aqueous and semi-aqueous habitats. Besides the countless varieties of fish, it is also home to seals, penguins, and polar bears. Exhibits include the humongous Ocean Realm featuring native Atlantic fish, the Amazon-themed Irazu River Falls, the Touch-a-Shark interactive tank, the West African River Experience with huge Nile hippos and exotic river fish, and much more. Adventure Aquarium also features a 150-seat "4-D" theater showing nature documentaries and commercial-run movies in addition to kid-friendly interactive shows ($5 additional theater admission).

BATTLESHIP *NEW JERSEY*

62 Battleship Pl., Camden, NJ, 866/877-6262,
www.battleshipnewjersey.org

HOURS: May-Labor Day daily 9:30 A.M.-5 P.M.,
Sept.-Dec. daily 9:30 A.M.-3 P.M., Feb.-Mar. Sat.-Sun.
9:30 A.M.-3 P.M., Apr. daily 9:30 A.M.-3 P.M., closed Jan.

COST: $18.50 adult, $14 senior, veteran, and child 6-11,
free child under 6 and military

Considered "America's most decorated battleship," the *New Jersey* earned 19 battle and campaign stars for outstanding service throughout World War II, the Korean War, Vietnam, and the Gulf War. Built in the Philadelphia Naval Yard and launched on December 7, 1942, today it is docked in Camden and open to the public for tours, events, and even overnight visits. At 887 feet and 45,000 tons, the longest battleship ever built is the length of nearly three football fields and more than 11 stories high. On a tour, you'll see exhibits detailing the ship's history, while you explore. Climb up ladders and into the 16-inch gun turret and watch the 4-D flight simulator, "Seahawk," recreate a World War II–era dogfight over Iwo Jima. For a surcharge, you can take the expanded Firepower Tour, which highlights the ship's weapon systems.

RESTAURANTS

Beginning with the "Restaurant Renaissance" of the 1990s and continuing ever since, the Philly food scene has evolved into one of the best in the country, attracting increasing numbers of foodies to sample the diverse cuisine. Centuries-old mom-and-pop eateries share the streets with stylish bistros and fine-dining restaurants courtesy of world-renowned chefs and restaurateurs, including Iron Chef Jose Garces, who has opened seven restaurants in Philly just since 2005.

Philly has one of the best BYOB scenes in the country, due to strict limits on local liquor licenses, which is great for us because it means a generally inexpensive way to dine out and save money on jacked up drink prices. Gastropubs, bars that serve high-quality cuisine—forget the old standard fare from the deep fryer—also make an excellent option for dining in a lively, causal setting. In fact, the dining scene is generally laid-back and casual, with a few exceptions at the very high or trendy end, mostly around Rittenhouse Square and Old City. For the most part, anything goes as far as dress, including jeans and sneakers.

And while it goes without saying that the Philadelphia food scene today extends far beyond cheesesteaks, unless you're a strict vegetarian there is no excuse for not sampling at least one of the greasy delights; they're just not the same anywhere else. Philly's other long-standing culinary trademarks include hoagies (subs in other parts of the country), soft pretzels, and water ice, all of which can be found just about anywhere. No visit to Philadelphia is complete without a stop at two other historic

HIGHLIGHTS

LOOK FOR ◖ TO FIND RECOMMENDED RESTAURANTS.

◖ **Best BYOB: Mercato** never disappoints, with its savory Old World Italian dishes and mouthwatering desserts. Plus you get to bring your own bottle and save your money for all that delicious food you'll want to try (page 87).

◖ **Best Special Occasion Restaurant:** Take the elevator up to **XIX**, or Nineteen, named for its location on the 19th floor of the Park Hyatt at the Bellevue. You'll be treated to panoramic views of the city along with unique, perfectly prepared cuisine in one of the city's most elegant settings (page 89).

◖ **Best Coffee:** For true strong-coffee lovers, **La Colombe** is the spot. This is the coffee served by many of the city's other great coffee shops, so why not go straight to the source (page 91)?

◖ **Best Neighborhood Restaurant:** The Fairmount neighborhood has a sprinkling of great restaurants and bars, and **Bridgid's** is a shining star among them, with a stellar beer selection and a small but high-quality lunch and dinner menu. The prices and friendly atmosphere are top-notch (page 97).

◖ **Most Romantic Waterfront Dining:** The elegant **Water Works Restaurant,** attached to the Water Works National Historic Landmark, overlooks the Schuylkill River just behind the Art Museum; snag a window seat for views of Boathouse Row (pages 99).

◖ **Best Brunch: Sabrina's Café** offers heaping portions of delicious omelettes and stuffed French toast to eager locals. Be prepared to wait for a table on weekends — but it's worth it (page 99).

◖ **Most Socially Conscious Restaurant:** A University City mainstay, **White Dog Café** is a place where you can feel good about what you're eating and who you're supporting. The focus is on locally sourced ingredients and progressive business practices; the result is ultrafresh, delicious food (page 108).

◖ **Best Delivery:** While most places only deliver within a short range of their shop, **Tiffin** offers service to all of Center City and well beyond. It also happens to serve the best affordable Indian food in town (page 109).

◖ **Best Old World Pizzeria:** For an authentic Philly experience and the city's best pizza, you'll have to get off the beaten path. The family-owned **Tacconelli's Pizzeria,** in its fifth generation in the Port Richmond neighborhood, still serves up the best thin-crust pizza around (page 113).

© JULIA GAVIN

La Colombe serves some of the best coffee in Philly.

PRICE KEY

$ Entrées less than $10
$$ Entrées $10-20
$$$ Entrées more than $20

landmarks, Reading Terminal Market and the Italian Market, for a vast variety of affordable ethnic cuisine and a totally unique atmosphere.

The number of healthy options has also increased, with many restaurants focusing on fresh, locally grown ingredients in keeping with the national trend in this direction. Considering the many nearby farms in Pennsylvania and New Jersey, this isn't hard to do. A great number of farmers markets are available across the city, especially in the warmer months, many from our Amish neighbors who come into the city to sell their goods. In 2010, the local Tourism Board launched an excellent website, Philly Homegrown (http://food.visitphilly.com), to encourage people to support the local food movement and help them find local farmers markets and other food purveyors.

Beyond the select sampling of restaurants, coffee shops, and markets I've included to help get you started, there are approximately 4,000 others for you to discover on your own. In addition, the food trucks on many corners of Center City and University City should not be overlooked, as many of them offer amazingly tasty fare for unbeatable prices; just join the longest lines and you can't go wrong. Now go out and eat.

Old City   Map 1

For as many historic sites as there are in Old City, there are at least as many restaurants. With stylish bistros, fine dining, gastropubs, pizza joints, and practically every ethnic specialty, there is something for every taste and budget. Options line Market and Chestnut Streets between Front and 5th Streets, as well as the nearby side streets.

ASIAN
BUDDAKAN $$$

325 Chestnut St., 215/574-9440, www.buddakan.com
HOURS: Mon.-Thurs. 11:30 A.M.-2:30 P.M. and 5-11 P.M.,
Fri. 11:30 A.M.-2:30 P.M. and 5 P.M.-midnight,
Sat. 5 P.M.-midnight, Sun. 4-10 P.M.

Perhaps the most famous member of Stephen Starr's renowned restaurant empire, Buddakan has a modern Asian-themed atmosphere complete with a massive statue of Buddha. The over-the-top, if borderline cheesy, decor contributes to an unforgettable experience in the low-lit dining room. The large menu features fusion dishes like wasabi-crusted filet mignon, raw tuna on flatbread, and whole sizzling fish with sweet black-bean sauce. There is certainly more authentic Asian cuisine in the city, but Buddakan offers a fun night-on-the-town atmosphere, delicious but pricey drinks, and undeniably tasty, creative dishes.

HARU $$$

241-243 Chestnut St., 215/861-8990,
www.harusushi.com
HOURS: Mon.-Wed. 11:30 A.M.-3 P.M. and 5-10 P.M.,
Thurs. 11:30 A.M.-3 P.M. and 5-11 P.M., Fri. 11:30 A.M.-3 P.M.
and 5 P.M.-1 A.M., Sat. noon-1 A.M., Sun. noon-10 P.M.

This elite sushi chain has seven New York locations, one in Boston, and the other here in Philadelphia. Housed on a busy Old City corner in a former bank, the Philly outpost is a grand bilevel space with soaring ceilings, massive arched windows, and comfortable, squishy booths that look deceivingly like bamboo. In addition to the dramatic main area, there is additional seating near the sushi bar and a 2nd-floor bar area. From traditional miso to lobster miso soup, and from classic, fresh sashimi to modern, inventive rolls and hot fusion entrées, the menu is diverse and delicious. A full drink menu includes a variety of sake cocktails.

MORIMOTO $$$

723 Chestnut St., 215/413-9070,
www.morimotorestaurant.com

HOURS: Mon.-Wed. 11:30 A.M.-2 P.M. and 5-10 P.M., Thurs. 11:30 A.M.-2 P.M. and 5-11 P.M., Fri. 11:30 A.M.-2 P.M. and 5 P.M.-midnight, Sat. 5 P.M.-midnight, Sun. 4-10 P.M.

Though the Iron Chef himself now spends most of his time in the New York location, his original eponymous restaurant, also a Stephen Starr spectacle, is still a jewel. The space will wow you before you even sit down, with its ultramodern dining room dimly lit with alternating multicolor lights and a cutting-edge design with lots of curved edges. It only gets better from there, with amazing sushi, sashimi, seafood, steak, salads, and several eat-till-you-die *omakase* (chef's tasting) options. Though your wallet will suffer for it, Morimoto is a must for any real restaurant lover—it's an experience.

CAFÉS
OLD CITY COFFEE $

221 Church St., 215/629-9292, www.oldcitycoffee.com

HOURS: Mon.-Fri. 6:30 A.M.-7 P.M., Sat. 7 A.M.-7 P.M., Sun. 7 A.M.-6 P.M.

Since 1984, this popular Old City coffeehouse has been roasting and brewing what many locals consider the city's best java. Sit inside the warm and cozy shop or snag a seat outside for great people-watching. A small but tasty selection of bagels, scones, muffins, and cookies is served along with a few breakfast and lunch options such as salads, soups, and breakfast sandwiches. Free wireless Internet is available, so get comfortable and stay awhile. Old City Coffee also has a booth in Reading Terminal Market, offering take-away and very limited seating.

COLONIAL AMERICAN
CITY TAVERN RESTAURANT $$$

138 S. 2nd St., 215/413-1443, www.citytavern.com

HOURS: Mon.-Thurs. 11:30 A.M.-9 P.M., Fri.-Sun. 11:30 A.M.-10 P.M.

The previous regulars at this historic tavern and restaurant include some guys you may have heard of, including George Washington, Benjamin Franklin, John Adams, and Thomas Jefferson. The original tavern, completed in 1773, was much the same as the current restored replica completed in 1976. In its early incarnation, the tavern was more than just a bar and eatery as we know it today. Without modern office buildings, this was where people met to discuss important business. The colonial-garbed waiters and period furnishings are true to the era, as is the menu inspired by foods popular in colonial times. Chef Staib turns out West Indies Pepper Pot Soup, Martha Washington Style Colonial Turkey Pot Pie, Braised Rabbit, and Pan-Seared Brook Trout. A place like this is in real danger of being kitschy, but with the food and atmosphere as good as they are, no one seems to mind. Don't miss the sweet-potato-and-pecan biscuits, supposedly a favorite of Thomas Jefferson.

FOOD COURT
THE BOURSE $

111 S. Independence Mall East (5th St. btwn. Market and Chestnut Sts.), 215/625-0300, www.bourse-pa.com

HOURS: Year-round Mon.-Sat. 10 A.M.-6 P.M., Mar.-Nov. additional hours Sun. 11 A.M.-5 P.M.

If you're looking for a quick bite in the middle of sightseeing or need to feed a big, choosy family, the Bourse is a cheap, convenient option. Just across the street from the Liberty Bell, Independence Hall, and the Constitution Center, you'll find a mall-like food court offering the standards: fast food, pizza, cheesesteaks, Chinese food, and a candy shop. Several touristy knickknack and memento shops can also be found inside the grand old building. Built in 1895, the Bourse (meaning "place of exchange" in Middle French) was the brainchild of George E. Bartol. During a visit to Hamburg, he decided that Philadelphia needed a *bourse* of its own. It once housed Philadelphia's stock, grain, and maritime exchanges and was renovated into its current form in the 1980s.

food court and shops at the Bourse in Old City

ITALIAN
GIANFRANCO PIZZA RUSTICA $

6 N. 3rd St., 215/592-0048, www.gianfrancopa.com
HOURS: Mon.-Thurs. 10 A.M.-10 P.M., Fri. 10 A.M.-11 P.M., Sat. 10 A.M.-10 P.M., Sun. 1-9 P.M.

Serving up the best pizza in Old City, this is a great place to grab a quick slice in the middle of sightseeing or bar-hopping. The thin crust, fresh tomato sauce, and a vast variety of standard and interesting toppings (including pesto, artichokes, broccoli rabe, and prosciutto) keep customers coming back. Calzones, stromboli, and sandwiches round out the tasty offerings. You may have to wait a bit for your order at lunch time on weekdays, but it's well worth it. Two additional outposts can be found in Center City East (248 S. 11th St., 215/923-9134) and in South Philly (2124 S. Broad St., 215/551-2300).

LA FAMIGLIA RISTORANTE $$$

8 S. Front St., 215/922-2803, www.lafamiglia.com
HOURS: Mon. 5:30-9:30 P.M., Tues.-Thurs. noon-2:30 P.M. and 5:30-9:30 P.M., Fri. noon-2:30 P.M. and 5:30-10 P.M., Sat. 5:30-10 P.M.

Luxurious and elegant, La Famiglia pampers guests with old-school Italian charm, classic decor, and tuxedoed waitstaff. The Sena family serves an authentic taste of traditional Naples, with perfectly prepared antipasti, pasta, seafood, veal, and steak dishes. Choose a glass or bottle of wine from the expansive cellar dating from the 1940s. Save room to sample the dessert cart, or enjoy a cheese course, sorbet, ice cream, or traditional biscotti. Considering the steep price, this is a place best reserved for special occasions, but this Italian indulgence makes for an unforgettable evening.

POSITANO COAST BY ALDO LAMBERTI $$

212 Walnut St., 215/238-0499, www.positanocoast.net
HOURS: Mon.-Thurs. 11:30 A.M.-10:30 P.M., Fri. 11:30 A.M.-11 P.M., Sat. noon-11 P.M., Sun. 12:30-10:30 P.M.

Near the center of Old City's club scene, Positano Coast by Aldo Lamberti offers a refined take on contemporary southern Italian cuisine, with dishes including grilled lamb, pan-seared skate, eggplant Napoleon, and spicy crab cakes. Choose between large plates and small plates for sharing. An ample outdoor covered seating area on the 2nd floor allows patrons to feel the breeze and observe the passersby, or snag one of the comfy couches or a table in the back lounge. Extensive selections of fine wines and organic cocktails are available, and Positano Coast also offers diners a BYOB option on Sunday and Monday. Happy hour Monday–Friday 5–7 P.M. includes $3 glasses of wine, along with food and cocktail specials.

LATIN-ASIAN
CHIFA $$$

707 Chestnut St., 215/925-5555, www.chifarestaurant.com
HOURS: Mon.-Thurs. 11:30 A.M.-2:30 P.M. and 5-10 P.M., Fri.-Sat. 11:30 A.M.-2:30 P.M. and 5-11 P.M., Sun. 5-10 P.M.

Another Jose Garces hit, Chifa offers

RESTAURANTS

RESTAURANTS

© GARCES RESTAURANT GROUP

The booths at Chifa make a cozy place to enjoy the delicious Peruvian-Cantonese fare.

Peruvian-Cantonese tapas in a stylish setting. With a bar and small tables in the front and cozy booths in the back, the atmosphere is lively and modern. Stop in for a few tapas and creative cocktails, like the spicy margarita with a chile garnish or the traditional pisco sour, a Peruvian alcohol with fresh lime juice. Better yet, come in for a full dinner. Either way, don't miss the delectable *bao* buns, with pork belly, duck, or tofu, the *pulpo* (octopus), or the multiple ceviches. Choose a few hot items and a few cold ones for balance, and if you really want to maximize the experience, order the tasting menu for the table for $45, $55, or $65, and drown in the waves of creative and delicious flavor combinations.

MIDDLE EASTERN
ZAHAV $$$
237 St. James Pl., 215/625-8800,
www.zahavrestaurant.com
HOURS: Sun.-Thurs. 5-10 P.M., Fri.-Sat. 5-11 P.M.
Meaning "gold" in Hebrew, Zahav opened in 2008 to rave reviews. Among its many

accolades, it was named one of the country's best new restaurants by *Esquire* in 2008, the city's best restaurant in 2009 by *Philadelphia* magazine, and the chef received multiple James Beard award nominations, including Best Chef Mid-Atlantic in 2010. It's tucked away on an Old City side street in a beautiful space with ultra-high ceilings and ultra-low lighting. Israeli-born chef Solomonov offers a modern take on his authentic native cuisine. Start with the amazing hummus and house-baked *laffa*, and the *salatim*, a daily selection of eight small salads. Next, choose several small plates and skewers or go for the ultimate tasting experience—*mesibah* (meaning "party time"). You'll be treated to an array of the restaurant's best small plates along with the signature dish, a mouthwatering whole-roasted lamb shoulder—yum.

NEW AMERICAN
FARMICIA AND METRO CAFÉ $$
15 S. 3rd St., 215/627-6274,

www.farmiciarestaurant.com
HOURS: Farmicia: Tues.-Thurs. 11:30 A.M.-3 P.M. and
5:30-10 P.M., Fri. 11:30 A.M.-3 P.M. and 5:30-11 P.M.,
Sat. 8:30 A.M.-3 P.M. and 5:30-11 P.M.,
Sun. 8:30 A.M.-3 P.M. and 5-9 P.M.; Metro Café:
Tues.-Fri. 11:30 A.M.-4 P.M., Sat.-Sun. 8:30 A.M.-4 P.M.

Farmicia and Metro Café, an expanded version of Metropolitan Bakery that also offers breakfast and lunch, operate out of the same great Old City space. It's one of the least typical "Old City" spots in Old City; the simple, fresh flavors of the food and drinks and the friendly, casual atmosphere are a refreshing change from the sometimes over-prepared, trendy offerings at some nearby establishments. Between the café and restaurant, you can get snacks, breakfast, coffee, lunch, brunch, dinner, or a bar menu practically any time of day. The focus of the food is organic, locally grown, and artisan ingredients, and of course, using only the best breads from Metropolitan. Best of all, at no additional charge, you can BYOB any time. An excellent happy hour is offered at the bar Tuesday–Friday 5–7 P.M., with reduced-price food and drinks.

FORK 💲💲💲

306 Market St., 215/625-9425,
www.forkrestaurant.com
HOURS: Mon.-Thurs. 11:30 A.M.-10:30 P.M.,
Fri. 11:30 A.M.-11:30 P.M., Sat. 5-11:30 P.M., Sun. 11 A.M.-3 P.M.
and 5-10:30 P.M.

Hip, sophisticated bistros come and go like the breeze in trendy Old City, but Fork has remained a hit for more than a decade. High ceilings, velvet curtains, wrought-iron chandeliers and pendant lighting create an elegant yet cozy atmosphere. Owner Ellen Yin and Chef Terence Feury offer a seasonal menu that changes daily and focuses on locally sourced ingredients. Don't miss the extensive and generous fruit-and-cheese platter or the strong specialty cocktails. You can watch the action in the open kitchen or really be part of it by coming to the bistro dinner at 7:30 P.M. on Wednesday nights—it's an excellent way to experience the best Fork has to offer at a lower price, with two

starters, an entrée, dessert, and wine served at a large communal table for $40. And be sure to check out **Fork, Etc.** (308 Market St., 215/625-9425) around the corner for gourmet take-out lunch and snacks.

JONES 💲💲

700 Chestnut St., 215/223-5663,
www.jones-restaurant.com
HOURS: Mon.-Thurs. 11:30 A.M.-midnight,
Fri. 11:30 A.M.-1 A.M., Sat. 10 A.M.-3 P.M. and 5 P.M.-1 A.M.,
Sun. 10 A.M.-3 P.M. and 4-11 P.M.

With its Brady Bunch–inspired decor, Jones is the homiest outpost in local restaurateur Stephen Starr's vast and trendy gastronomic empire. Shag carpeting and stone fireplaces set the tone, but while the interior takes its cues from '70s suburbia, the reasonably priced comfort food includes some decidedly contemporary twists. Alongside mashed potatoes, meatloaf, and fried chicken and waffles, you can find pistachio-crusted tilapia and seared tuna tacos. There's also a good selection of tasty if overpriced drinks, including the Happy, the Chai Teani, and the Morning Glory.

SNACKS AND SWEETS
FRANKLIN FOUNTAIN 💲

116 Market St., 215/627-1899, www.franklinfountain.com
HOURS: Daily 11 A.M.-midnight

The perfect addition to historic Old City, Franklin Fountain has the feel of an authentic old-school ice cream and soda shop, even though it's only been around for a few years. Sit at the marble countertop and enjoy a banana split or sundae made with creamy homemade ice cream. Or try a classic egg cream, made with milk, flavored syrup, and club soda. Servers dressed in traditional soda-jerk gear and the building's early details, including tin walls and ceiling and a mosaic tile floor, help set the mood. If you haven't satisfied your sweet tooth with the ice cream, candy, or homemade fudge, stop into **Shane Candies** (110 Market St., 215/922-1048) a few doors down; the oldest candy shop in Philadelphia has been owned and operated by the same family for nearly 100 years.

© GARCES RESTAURANT GROUP

Have tapas at the bar or at a table at Amada in Old City.

SPANISH

AMADA $$$

217-219 Chestnut St., 215/625-2450,
www.amadarestaurant.com

HOURS: Mon.-Thurs. 11:30 A.M.-2:30 P.M. and 5-10 P.M.,
Fri.-Sat. 11:30 A.M.-2:30 P.M. and 5 P.M.-midnight,
Sun. 4-10 P.M.

Upon opening in 2005, Amada quickly became one of the hottest restaurants in the city, which is saying a lot. The vibe is always stylish, fun, and energetic, but even more so on Wednesday and Friday with live flamenco dancers. But the main reason it's so hard to get a table here at times is the food—delectable, authentic Spanish tapas created by internationally acclaimed chef Jose Garces, who has since become arguably Philly's hottest chef. Watch through the open kitchen as chefs prepare cured meats, artisan cheeses, and traditional and creative inventions in beautiful preparations. Whether you want savory, salty, or sweet, the robust flavors on the menu are sure to please. A full bar offers an extensive wine list, as well as red and white sangria, the perfect accompaniment to any dish.

Society Hill   Map 1

Society Hill is primarily residential except for the areas that border Old City, Washington Square, and South Street. Headhouse Square, encompassing several blocks of 2nd Street just north of South Street, is packed with bars and restaurants, and Penn's Landing, the waterfront strip along the Delaware, has a few worthwhile offerings just a short walk across a footbridge from Society Hill.

MEXICAN

XOCHITL $$$

408 S. 2nd St., 215/238-7280, www.xochitlphilly.com

HOURS: Sun.-Wed. 5 P.M.-midnight,
Thurs.-Sat. 5 P.M.-1 A.M.

This Headhouse Square restaurant (pronounced SO-cheet) offers upscale, creative twists on authentic Mexican cuisine in a cozy setting. Start with the delicious guacamole made tableside or fresh ceviche. An extensive tequila list can be served by the shot or flight or made into a variety of margaritas or specialty drinks. Save room for dessert; the apple cider *churros* are just divine. The tequila bar downstairs is a good alternative for tequila lovers who would rather drink and hear a DJ spin than eat a full dinner. Go for happy hour for great drink specials at the upstairs bar daily 5–7 P.M. or in the lounge Thursday, Friday, and Saturday 10 P.M.–midnight.

NEW AMERICAN
MOSHULU $$$

401 S. Columbus Blvd., 215/923-2500, www.moshulu.com

HOURS: Mon.-Fri. 11:30 A.M.-3 P.M. and 5:30-10 P.M., Sat. 11:30 A.M.-2:30 P.M. and 5-10:30 P.M., Sun. 10:30 A.M.-2:30 P.M. and 5-9 P.M.

Dining on a docked ship offers the romantic experience of being surrounded by water without the seasickness that comes with a typical dinner cruise. Built in 1904, the *Moshulu* had been used for shipping goods; it served as a warehouse on water; and it was confiscated twice during wars over the course of its long life. But interesting as its history is, the real reason to come is for quality food in the heart of Penn's Landing. What could have easily become a cheesy tourist trap is instead an elegant restaurant offering classics like filet mignon, crab cakes, and salmon in updated, tasteful variations. On Sunday, an upscale buffet brunch is offered for $35 per person, and while prices are a bit steep, the experience is memorable. To experience the boat for less money, visit the Bongo Bar on the upper deck for drinks and a lower-priced, tasty bar menu. It sometimes features live music.

Center City East   Map 2

This expansive area is packed with restaurants, with the majority concentrated in Chinatown, Washington Square West, and along the Avenue of the Arts. In addition to Chinese restaurants, Chinatown has Cambodian, Vietnamese, Burmese, and other offerings. Washington Square West, also known as the Gayborhood, offers plenty of restaurants, BYOBs, and bars serving great food, especially along Pine Street, Spruce Street, and 13th Street south of Market. Avenue of the Arts offers mostly large, upscale, and often overpriced chains catering to the thick wallets of the theater crowd.

ASIAN
SAMPAN $$$

124 S. 13th St., 215/732-3501, http://sampanphilly.com

HOURS: Mon.-Thurs. 11:30 A.M.-4 P.M. and 5-11 P.M., Fri. 11:30 A.M.-4 P.M. and 5 P.M.-midnight, Sat. 5 P.M.-midnight, Sun. 5-10 P.M.

Renowned chef Michael Schulson served as chef at many other acclaimed restaurants and opened the stunningly successful Izakaya in Atlantic City before returning to Philly (which he calls home) to open Sampan in the heart of Midtown Village in 2009. The upscale modern Asian menu specializes in "Asian street flavors." The menu changes seasonally, but you may find tasty small plates like crab wonton tacos or beef or lobster carpaccio, along with entrées like miso glazed salmon and Korean fried chicken. Lunch is also popular with *bahn mi,* the Vietnamese-style hoagie, a favorite. An outdoor "graffiti bar," with walls covered in graffiti by local artists, is a great place to kick back and have a drink while waiting for your table.

SINGAPORE KOSHER VEGETARIAN RESTAURANT $

1006 Race St., 215/922-3288

HOURS: Sun.-Thurs. 11:30 A.M.-10 P.M., Fri.-Sat. 11:30 A.M.-11 P.M.

Singapore Chinese Vegetarian offers a delicious range of vegetarian options. Besides

RESTAURANTS

BRING YOUR OWN BOTTLE

While it's easy to spend a few hundred bucks on dinner for two at Philadelphia's top restaurants, it's just as easy to keep it under $50 by bringing your own bottle to one of the city's many BYOBs, which often rival and at times surpass their liquor-serving counterparts in quality of cuisine. While locals have long complained about Pennsylvania's strict liquor licensing laws and high taxes on liquor sales, the fringe benefits are out of this world. The law makes it difficult and expensive for a new business to serve liquor, with a set number of liquor licenses available that must be bought from another business that is going out of business. As a result, Philly has arguably the largest and best BYOB scene in the entire country, with something for every taste and budget. With so many BYOBs, restaurants have to maintain very high food standards to compete. Most BYOBs, or BYOs, maintain a casual, comfortable neighborhood vibe, even though many are centrally located in the major neighborhoods, and very few of them have "corkage fees," an annoying charge of around $5 for opening your wine. This charge is more likely at a place that has a bar of its own but also allows the BYO option, and the fee should always be clearly noted on the menu.

There are BYOBs in every Philly neighborhood, and a few not to miss include **Mercato, Audrey Claire, Pumpkin Restaurant,** and **Dmitri's** (South Philly location). Some restaurants, like **Farmicia,** offer a full bar but also let you bring your own bottle if you prefer. While wine is the drink of choice for most BYOB-ers, there are also spots where other drinks are commonly brought to the table. It is common to bring beer to casual spots like **Jamaican Jerk Hut, Tacconelli's Pizzeria,** and **Plaza Garibaldi** or to bring the booze of your choice to Mexican **Lolita** or Indian **Bindi** (105 S. 13th St., 215/922-6061, Sun., Tues.-Thurs. 5-10 P.M, Fri.-Sat. 5-11 P.M., $10-20), which you can add to the restaurant's homemade mixers.

Purchasing alcohol in Pennsylvania is not always simple. There are beer distributors and state-run Wine & Spirits shops, but beer cannot be sold at the same store as wine and booze. Hours are limited, with most of the spirits shops closing between 7 and 9 P.M. Very few beer or wine stores are open on Sunday, so plan ahead. Many bars sell six-packs to go, but you can expect to pay higher premiums for the convenience. Visit www.pawineandspirits.com for the state store locations, or ask a local to point you in the right direction.

And be sure to check out the latest addition to the BYOB scene in Philly in the form of **Garces Trading Company.** A novel concept and the only one of its kind in the city, the restaurant has a wine boutique attached to the restaurant, offering an excellent selection minus the steep restaurant markups, so you have the best of both worlds. You can BYO without having to plan in advance. Just grab a bottle and take it to your table, where your waiter will open it for you; you pay about the same as you would at any wine store.

standards like steamed or sautéed vegetables with rice, Singapore makes some of the most delicious soy/wheat/gluten/seitan fake meats you'll ever have the pleasure to taste. Mock beef and chicken in every flavor permutation populate the menu.

SZECHUAN TASTY HOUSE §

902 Arch St., 215/925-2839

HOURS: Tues.-Sun. 11 A.M.-midnight

Feelin' hot, hot, hot? Szechuan Tasty House has some of the most flavorful, spicy food in Chinatown. Tell your server if you want more or less spice; they sometimes discourage their American guests from the super-spicy because they don't believe you can take it, so be clear about what you want. Most dishes are not just hot, but also wonderfully flavored. Don't miss the dumplings in hot-pepper oil as an appetizer and the three-pepper chicken or classic Szechuan beef as entrées. A variety of noodle dishes and vegetarian dishes, including well-prepared tofu, are also excellent choices.

1225 RAW SUSHI AND
SAKE LOUNGE ⊖⊕⊕

1225 Sansom St., 215/238-1903, www.rawlounge.net
HOURS: Mon.-Wed. 11:30 A.M.-2:30 P.M. and 5-9:45 P.M.,
Thurs. 11:30 A.M.-2:30 P.M. and 5-10:45 P.M.,
Fri. 11:30 A.M.-2:30 P.M. and 5-11:30 P.M., Sat. noon-3 P.M.
and 5-11:30 P.M., Sun. noon-3 P.M. and 5-9:45 P.M.

The sleek, modern lounge-like decor comes complete with red walls, a bamboo ceiling, and high-backed booths, with a welcoming outdoor courtyard with additional seating. Creative salads, meat dishes, and cooked plates do not disappoint, but the highlight of the menu is definitely the sushi. The chef turns out generous and beautiful portions of fresh sashimi, maki, and nigiri in inventive combinations. The full bar serves beer, wine, and specialty drinks, many made with sake from the extensive selection. Try a flight of four different types of sake ($18 standard/ $31 premium).

VIETNAM ⊖⊕

221 N. 11th St., 215/592-1163, www.eatatvietnam.com
HOURS: Sun.-Thurs. 11 A.M.-9:30 P.M.,
Fri.-Sat. 11 A.M.-10:30 P.M.

One of the city's most popular Vietnamese restaurants occupies a warm, inviting space in the heart of Chinatown. It's hard to go wrong with anything on the reasonably priced menu. Crispy spring rolls and tender summer rolls are top-notch, as is the grilled barbecue platter that lets you sample a range of appetizers. For entrées, catfish cooked in a clay pot and a variety of vermicelli and *pho* dishes do not disappoint. You may have to wait for a table on weekends, but order a strong specialty drink from the full bar to pass the time. Vietnam's main competitor is **Vietnam Palace** (222 N. 11th St., 215/592-9596), just across the street. It's also a local favorite, and each has staunch supporters, so try both if you have time. And if you happen to be in University City when your Vietnamese food craving hits, you can now try **Vietnam Café** (816 S. 47th St., 215/729-0260), a stylish bar and restaurant by the owners of Vietnam Restaurant that became an instant success upon its opening in 2009.

CAFÉS
RAY'S CAFÉ AND TEA HOUSE ⊕

141 N. 9th St., 215/922-5122, www.rayscafe.com
HOURS: Mon.-Tues. 8:30 A.M.-8 P.M.,
Wed. 8:30 A.M.-6 P.M., Thurs. 8:30 A.M.-8 P.M.,
Fri. 8:30 A.M.-9 P.M., Sat. 11:30 A.M.-9 P.M.

Ray's serves the best, and most expensive, coffee in Chinatown, along with a wide selection of teas, bubble teas, and a small Thai food menu. Coffee is made to order from exotic ground beans using the siphon method and brewed with spring water. Some brews are rather pricey, but true coffee connoisseurs will find it worth it. Coffee and tea drinks are all served in an elegant display with a fruit tart or homemade cookie.

EUROPEAN BISTRO
GARCES TRADING COMPANY ⊖⊕⊕

1111 Locust St., 215/574-1088,
www.garcestradingcompany.com
HOURS: Daily 8 A.M.-10 P.M.

Jose Garces outdoes himself with his gourmet market and upscale café with an attached wine store—the only restaurant of its kind in the entire city. The restaurant functions as a BYOB, but you can choose from a great selection of beer or wine on the premises and pay retail price rather than marked-up restaurant prices. The delicious menu features artisanal cheese and charcuterie from France, Spain, Italy, and the United States, as well as antipasti, deep-dish pizzas, pastas, and grilled entrées. Try the tasting menu for a little bit of some of the best items on the menu. In addition to lunch and dinner, brunch (weekends 11 A.M.–3 P.M.) is a popular way to experience this excellent European-style bistro.

ITALIAN
⊆ MERCATO ⊖⊕⊕

1216 Spruce St., 215/985-2962, www.mercatobyob.com
HOURS: Mon.-Thurs. 5-10:30 P.M., Fri.-Sat. 5-11 P.M.,
Sun. 5-10 P.M.

This tiny cash-only BYOB is always noisy and crowded—due to close tables, an open kitchen, and its immense popularity. Start with a plate of bread and artisan cheese paired with an olive oil tasting. Then choose from an array of pasta, fish, and meat dishes that combine

RESTAURANTS

Old World Italian slow-cooking with totally unique, updated flavors and preparations. While you can't go wrong with anything on the menu, favorites include the whole grilled artichoke appetizer and the pan-seared diver scallops over wild mushroom and pea risotto. A bittersweet molten chocolate lava cake and a mascarpone cheesecake are just two of the excellent desserts. Reservations are not taken, so you'll often have to wait for a table—especially on weekends—but it's well worth it.

MEDITERRANEAN
BARBUZZO $$$

110 S. 13th St., 215/546-9300, www.barbuzzo.com
HOURS: Mon.-Fri. noon-3 P.M. and 5 P.M.-midnight, Sat.-Sun. 5 P.M.-midnight

Marcie Turney and Valerie Safran—the restaurateurs responsible for Lolita (Mexican) and Bindi (Indian), also on 13th Street—have done it again, perhaps better than ever before. Barbuzzo opened in 2010 to instant acclaim and was even called the best restaurant in Philly by several local critics. The cozy farmhouse motif with weathered wood walls and an open kitchen is instantly inviting. Tables are narrow and set close together but the din is loud enough—even on a Monday night—to converse without the people at the next table hearing every word. The small plates are meant to be shared, which is good, because you'll want to taste every single savory dish that arrives at the table, from the well-balanced meat, cheese, and vegetable boards to creative pizzas and perfectly prepared pasta, fish, and meat dishes. Save room for the *budino* (pudding)—named Dessert of the Year by local food blog Foobooz in 2010; the pot of creamy, salty, crunchy deliciousness is a taste you'll remember long after the meal is over. From 10:30 P.M. to midnight Sunday–Thursday, you'll find reduced prices on drinks and rotating menu items.

VALANNI $$

1229 Spruce St., 215/790-9494, www.valanni.com
HOURS: Mon.-Sat. 5 P.M.-1 A.M., Sun. 11 A.M.-3 P.M. and 5 P.M.-1 A.M.

With one wall of exposed brick, dim pendant

Barbuzzo is a stylish Mediterranean restaurant and bar in Midtown Village.

© JASON VARNEY

lighting, and plenty of candlelight, the mood is romantic yet fun at this stylish Mediterranean-Latin restaurant and bar. The bar is often filled with regulars who come for the strong, delicious specialty cocktails. Small plates, which can be eaten as appetizers or alone as a tapas-style meal, include lobster-and-crab macaroni and cheese, spicy pulled chicken empanadas, and grilled beef kabobs, and large plates include several varieties of paella. Desserts are enormous and delicious, especially the deep-fried oreo beignets and the caramelized rum bananas. Happy hour, Monday–Friday 5–7 P.M., offers half-priced tapas and $5 drinks.

MEXICAN
LOLITA $$

106 S. 13th St., 215/546-7100, www.lolitabyob.com
HOURS: Sun.-Tues. 5-10 P.M., Wed.-Thurs. 5-10:30 P.M., Fri.-Sat. 5-11 P.M.

Exposed brick walls, a bright open kitchen, and just-right lighting set the mood in this popular BYOB owned by Valerie Safran and chef Marcie Turney. High-quality ingredients and savory flavors make the contemporary Mexican dishes—like grilled spice-rubbed pork chop or shiitake and lancaster jack cheese enchiladas—stand out. The *fundido con queso y chorizo*—homemade tortillas served with a generous portion of melted Oaxaca and Chihuahua cheeses, roasted poblano, smoked brandied chorizo, and Mexican oregano for dipping—is a delicious but filling appetizer meant to be shared. Bring your own wine, or even better, bring your own tequila to mix with Lolita's homemade fresh margarita mix in combinations of flavors including orange, watermelon, basil, and mint.

NEW AMERICAN
⬛ XIX $$$

Broad and Walnut Sts. (19th fl. in the Park Hyatt Philadelphia at the Bellevue), 215/790-1919, www.hyatt.com/gallery/nineteen
HOURS: Daily 6:30 A.M.-11 P.M., afternoon tea 2-4 P.M.

The 19th floor of the Park Hyatt at the Bellevue is dripping with elegance befitting a restaurant occupying one of the city's finest and oldest hotels. Perfect for a celebration or romantic dinner, XIX (pronounced "nineteen") offers outstanding modern American cuisine, and the knowledgeable sommelier makes excellent pairing recommendations from the extensive wine list. Innovative chef Marc Plessis takes full advantage of seasonal and local ingredients, and his creative flavor combinations always seem to hit the mark. A raw bar occupies the center of the main dining room under the high domed ceiling. But the most alluring aspect of the room is the spectacular view of the city through the expansive windows. If you don't have a few hundred dollars to drop on dinner for two, you can still enjoy the elegant atmosphere with breakfast, lunch, or brunch or a visit to the bar, which offers an ample, delicious menu at much lower prices. A classic afternoon tea is served by reservation only.

SNACKS AND SWEETS
CAPOGIRO $

119 S. 13th St., 215/351-0900, www.capogirogelato.com
HOURS: Mon.-Thurs. 7:30 A.M.-10 P.M., Fri. 7:30 A.M.-midnight, Sat. 9 A.M.-midnight, Sun. 10 A.M.-10 P.M.

Capogiro Gelato Artisans provides customers with deliciously dense, creamy, traditional Italian ice creams in countless fruity and savory flavors that change with the seasons. In additional to traditional flavors like hazelnut and strawberry, there are innovative offerings like rosemary/honey/goat's milk and mascarpone fig. Not your grandmother's ice cream cone, a very small cup will cost you around $5, but it is worth every cent. Ideal for a sweet ending to a date or a break in the middle of a day of shopping, Capogiro has three additional locations for your pleasure (Center City West: 117 S. 20th St., 215/636-9250; University City Philly: 3925 Walnut St., 215/222-0252; and South Philly: 1625 E. Passyunk Ave., 215/462-3790).

SOUL FOOD
MS. TOOTSIE'S RBL $$
1312 South St., 215/731-9045, www.kevenparker.net
HOURS: Mon.-Thurs. 5 P.M.-midnight, Fri.-Sat.
noon-2 A.M., Sun. noon-midnight

Philadelphia is definitely an eating town, but it's not generally known for its soul food; Keven Parker wants to change that. Ms. Tootsie's RBL (for Restaurant Bar Lounge) combines a stylish, upscale lounge setting with a full bar complete with bottle service, along with comforting, affordable soul food like southern fried chicken, smothered pork chops, and fried catfish. Sides like candied yams, collard greens, and mouth-watering macaroni and cheese all hit the spot, and while it won't be easy, save room for the sweet potato cheesecake for dessert if you can. Take-out is also available.

Center City West   Map 3

This part of town is chock-full of good restaurants. In addition to the city's most elegant eating establishments, you will find trendy bistros, casual coffee shops to grab a tasty lunch, and plenty of bars serving food. Walnut Street and the surrounding side streets are lined with restaurants between Broad and 18th Streets, including several directly on Rittenhouse Square, with some of the best on 20th Street just off the square.

ASIAN
FUJI MOUNTAIN $$$
2030 Chestnut St., 215/751-0939, www.fujimt.com
HOURS: Mon.-Fri. 11:30 A.M.-1:45 P.M. and daily
5 P.M.-1:30 A.M.

This sushi bar and restaurant is one more attraction signaling the rebirth of this section of Chestnut Street west of Broad, which used to shut down once the happy hour crowds left for the day. Besides serving up some of the city's best sushi and sashimi, the four-floor restaurant boasts a karaoke room available for private rental for up to 30 people, where you can belt out the best Japanese and American pop favorites while enjoying a full bar and food menu. Other rooms in the complex offer traditional Japanese dining, with delicious entrées, appetizers, bottle service, and cocktails. Fuji Mountain takes online orders and delivers to nearby addresses.

VIC SUSHI BAR $$
2035 Sansom St., 215/564-4339, www.vic-sushi.com
HOURS: Mon.-Thurs. 11:30 A.M.-9:30 P.M., Fri.
11:30 A.M.-10 P.M., Sat. 2:30-10 P.M.

With Vic, Philadelphians no longer have to spend all their money at Morimoto or cross the bridge into New Jersey to enjoy excellent sushi at an even more excellent price. The friendly staff welcomes you to sit at one of the six bar seats, and BYOB if you like, but with delivery and take-out options, it doesn't matter that the seats are often filled. Don't miss the sashimi appetizer, with two perfect pieces each of everyone's favorites—yellowtail, tuna, and salmon—for $8.95. Continue with the unbeatable deal of three basic eight-piece rolls of your choice for $10.95 (yes, that's all three rolls for a total of $10.95). Or have fun with creative specialty rolls (like the Lover Roll—spicy tuna, avocado, and cucumber roll topped with salmon, eel, and avocado), which are unique, delicious, and filling and range in price $9–14.

CAFÉS
ANTS PANTS $
2212 South St., 215/875-8002, www.antspantscafe.com
HOURS: Mon.-Fri. 7 A.M.-4 P.M., Sat.-Sun. 8 A.M.-3 P.M.

As the website of this seemingly oddly named café explains, "ants' pants" is an Australian colloquial term meaning "the best" or "height of fashion." Well, if I were Australian I would say that the coffee, food, and atmosphere at this small local haunt are "the ants' pants." They serve breakfast, lunch, and brunch, and while snagging a seat on the weekend is often challenging, at most other times, this is a place

FOOD TRUCK FARE

Those small, sparkling-metal mini-kitchens-on-wheels throughout the city often serve surprisingly good food at prices that cannot be beat. Frequented by everyone from students to the white-collar elite, food trucks can be found in the downtown business district and near the universities. With seasoned professionals and impossibly hot grills, food trucks churn out meals in a jiffy, so even the longest lines usually move fast. Choose from bagels, egg-and-cheese sandwiches, cheesesteaks, and hoagies to practically every ethnic food under the sun – even sushi. Aside from the standard greasy fare, there are healthy options at some trucks, from affordable fresh fruit to the **Magic Carpet,** a University City favorite with two locations (34th and Walnut Sts. and 36th and Spruce Sts.) that serves up delicious vegetarian and vegan cuisine. A good rule of thumb when choosing a food truck is to join the longest lines; they not only serve the best-tasting fare, but you can rest assured that the hygiene levels are satisfactory if locals keep coming back.

where you can sit for hours over your coffee, book, or laptop (free wireless Internet is provided). Don't miss the crème brûlée–battered French toast, the salmon BLAT (smoked salmon, bacon, lettuce, and tomato), or the delicious spinach salads. When the weather is nice, sit outside in the small back patio area.

BETTY'S SPEAKEASY ❸

2241 Grays Ferry Ave., 215/735-9060,
www.bettysfudge.com

HOURS: Tues.-Sat. 9 A.M.-7 P.M.

A self-proclaimed "local, organic, fair-trade speakeasy," the small café is best known for its homemade fudge and award-winning cupcakes (Best of Philly 2009) that come in a variety of unique flavors. The fudge sauce, made with local butter, honey, and goat's milk, comes in flavors like Lavender Mint and the Peanut Butterer; try it in the shop mixed into chocolate

milk or an espresso drink or buy a jar to eat at home or give as a gift. A small menu of salads, soups, sandwiches, and a cheese plate is also available and tasty, but be sure to save room for dessert. The friendly staff is happy to tell you which local, organic ingredients are used in each treat. This is a neighborhood gem you can feel good about supporting, although your waistline may pay for it after a few visits. (Trust me; I speak from experience.)

◀ LA COLOMBE ❸

130 S. 19th St., 215/563-0860, www.lacolombe.com

HOURS: Mon.-Fri. 7 A.M.-7 P.M., Sat.-Sun. 8 A.M.-7 P.M.

The most popular Center City coffee shop caters to one type only—coffee lovers. Just off Rittenhouse Square, it's filled with the Rittenhouse elite, hipsters, bohemians, and regulars—some that look like they might be just out of bed. Basically, everyone comes to La Colombe. One of the few coffee shops where the coffee is so good that they don't need to offer wireless Internet or a large food menu to keep customers happy, La Colombe keeps it simple with strong freshly roasted gourmet coffee and espresso drinks and just a tiny case of croissants and scones at the counter. A medium-sized roaster that provides coffee to many of the city's other coffee shops and some grocery stores, La Colombe proves that not everyone is looking for Starbucks.

CARIBBEAN
JAMAICAN JERK HUT ❸❸

1436 South St., 215/545-8644, jamaicanjerkhutinc.com

HOURS: Mon.-Thurs. 11 A.M.-10 P.M.,
Fri.-Sat. 11 A.M.-11 P.M., Sun. 5-10 P.M.

When the weather is nice, continue past the somewhat cramped interior to the choice seating area—the large backyard patio filled with tables for dining alfresco. You might wait awhile for your food, but if you've got sunshine or a pleasant breezy night, good friends, and a few Red Stripes to pass the time at this unique BYOB, time will fly. Flaky patties stuffed with beef, chicken, or vegetables are a great starter, and the menu features something for meat lovers and vegetarians alike. Spice-sensitive diners should avoid the jerked dishes—they pack a punch. Curried dishes, while still flavorful, are more manageable, and all the homemade juices are worth sampling. While the place is a bit run-down and the outdoor space is surrounded by a chain fence and the sides of houses, the place has got character—so much in fact that this is where the wedding was held in the last scene of *In Her Shoes.* Remember that movie, girls?

CHEESESTEAKS AND SANDWICHES

SHANK'S ORIGINAL UPTOWN ❸

120 S. 15th St., 215/629-1093, www.shanksoriginal.com
HOURS: Mon.-Sat. 10 A.M.-6:30 P.M.

Shank's and Evelyn's was a tiny storefront breakfast and lunch joint near the Italian Market since 1962. Well, ever since the classic South Philly spot moved to the heart of Center City in 2009, the secret is out. Signature menu items include cheesesteaks (considered the best in Philly by many) and chicken cutlet or pork sandwiches with a variety of toppings (try Italiano style with broccoli rabe and sharp provolone). Serving some of the best breakfast sandwiches in town, it also makes a great morning stop. **Shank's Original Pier 40** (901 S. Columbus Blvd., 215/218-4000, daily 7:30 A.M.–midnight) offers almost the same menu at its waterfront location.

TONY JR.'S ❸

118 S. 18th St., 215/568-4630, www.tonyjrsphilly.com
HOURS: Mon.-Fri. 8 A.M.-9 P.M., Sat. 9 A.M.-9 P.M., Sun. 11 A.M.-7 P.M.

You no longer have to go to deep South Philly to get a perfect cheesesteak. This centrally located sandwich shop offers classic cheesesteaks along with dressed-up varieties with additions like broccoli rabe or roasted peppers. In addition to cheesesteaks, the roasted pork, sausage and pepper, breakfast, and veggie sandwiches are also popular.

FRENCH

LE BEC-FIN ❸❸❸

1523 Walnut St., 215/567-1000, www.lebecfin.com
HOURS: Tues.-Sat. 11:30 A.M.-2 P.M. and 5:30-10 P.M.

If you're wealthy or working with a liberal business expense account, a trip to Philadelphia isn't complete without a stop at the city's ultimate fine-dining restaurant. Since opening in the 1970s, George Perrier's famous French restaurant has pretty consistently received the highest honors in the hospitality industry. In a historic building in the heart of Rittenhouse Row, Le Bec-Fin exudes elegance and sophistication, from its high ceilings flanked with grand chandeliers to the attentive tuxedo-clad servers. The classic French cuisine is fresh, elegant, and perfectly prepared, and usually served as part of a multi-course tasting menu that includes all-you-can-eat dessert and cheese carts that will make your eyes (and the button of your pants) pop. The restaurant has had ups and downs in its 40-plus years. Long considered the best overall restaurant in the city and one of the nation's best French restaurants, it has struggled in recent years as tastes have veered away from the formal, fine-dining style. The restaurant was close to closing in 2010, but an outcry of public support led Perrier to recommit to staying open. While the essence of his fine French food and atmosphere hasn't changed, he is working to keep up with the times with measures that include downgrading the jacket-and-tie dress code to business casual and offering special discounted menus to draw more guests. Hopefully, it works, as it would be a shame to see this longtime Philly staple close. Alas, if you're not a trust-fund baby or a CEO, consider stopping for the somewhat less prohibitive lunch menu or visiting **Le Bar Lyonnais** for happy hour (Tues.–Sat. 5–7 P.M.); located on the lower floor, the bar and lounge offers tasty drinks and a small food menu prepared in the same kitchen as its wealthy upstairs neighbor.

IRISH

THE BLACK SHEEP ❸

247 S. 17th St., 215/545-9473,
www.theblacksheeppub.com
HOURS: Daily 11:30 A.M.-2 A.M.

A block from always-jumping Rittenhouse Square, The Black Sheep is a multidimensional Irish pub. It has three levels where you can drink, watch a game, play darts, or sample traditional Irish dishes like shepherd's pie, Guinness stew, and bangers and mash. Sunday brunch offers staples like traditional Irish breakfast and eggs Benedict, but the menu is not strictly limited to traditional Irish fare, with fish tacos and grilled filet mignon sliders also pleasing options. Wednesday nights feature Quizzo, a group trivia game that goes well with a perfect pint of Guinness.

MARKET

DI BRUNO BROS. $

1730 Chestnut St., 215/665-9220, www.dibruno.com

HOURS: Mon.-Fri. 9 A.M.-9 P.M., Sat. 9 A.M.-7 P.M., Sun. 9 A.M.-6 P.M.

Philadelphia's answer to Dean & Deluca began as a small family-run cheese shop in the Italian Market in 1939. The original shop (930 S. 9th St., 888/322-4337) still exists in the heart of the market and offers a modest sampling of the massive array of cheeses, stuffed olives, flavored oils, spreads, charcuterie, produce, and prepared foods offered in this two-floor mega-store on Chestnut Street that opened in 2004 to immediate success. While the Italian Market location cannot be beat for character, the Chestnut Street store sells everything the original store offers along with a separate fish and meat market, a coffee, baked goods, and gelato bar, and an upstairs café with full salad bar, deli, cooked entrées, and sushi bar. Whether you're looking for a quick bite, a fully prepared meal to eat in Rittenhouse Square, all the ingredients you need to throw a big party, or a perfect gift basket for your food-loving friend, Di Bruno Bros. has it all. It's a bit pricey, but both stores are stocked with enough free samples of breads, oils, and cheeses that you may find you're no longer hungry for lunch by the time you make it to the cash register.

MEDITERRANEAN

AUDREY CLAIRE $$

276 S. 20th St., 215/731-1222, www.audreyclaire.com

HOURS: Sun.-Thurs. 5-10 P.M., Fri.-Sat. 5-10:30 P.M.

Audrey Claire was at the forefront of Philadelphia's popular BYOB onslaught when she opened her eponymous cash-only restaurant in 1996. She continues to pack guests into the small but airy corner location near Rittenhouse Square, with guests vying for outside tables when the weather is nice. The seasonal menu is divided into small and large plates, and each section offers standouts. You may find seared brussels sprouts unlike anything your mother tried to feed you, or a pear-and-gorgonzola flatbread blending sweet and tart flavors to perfection. Among the large dishes, grilled rack of lamb and a hearty pork chop are both stellar, and the nightly specials often utilize the season's freshest ingredients. **Twenty Manning Grill** (261 S. 20th St., 215/731-0900), also owned by Audrey, is just a block north across 20th Street. A stylish bistro, also with an open, airy feel, Twenty Manning has a full bar and modern dishes heavy on seafood, including a small raw bar.

MEXICAN

TEQUILAS RESTAURANT $$$

1602 Locust St., 215/546-0181, www.tequilasphilly.com

HOURS: Mon.-Thurs. 11:30 A.M.-2 P.M. and 5-10 P.M., Fri. 11:30 A.M.-2 P.M. and 5-11 P.M., Sat. 5-11 P.M., Sun. 5-10 P.M.

Upscale authentic Mexican cuisine is served in an eclectic yet elegant setting in a converted old brownstone. High ceilings and dim lighting welcome you into the grand, mirrored bar area offering more than 100 different tequilas. Partitioned into three separate additional dining areas, the large restaurant maintains a cozy feel. But the reason locals and visitors keep coming back is the food. Choose from excellent meat and seafood entrées, and do not miss the fresh, limey ceviche or the divine guacamole to start. Order sangria and margaritas by the glass, pitcher, or carafe. Oh, and be sure to mention it if it happens to be your birthday: The staff will sing to you in Spanish and bring out a free shot of tasty, sweet tequila mixed with cinnamon and other tasty, secret ingredients. With perhaps the longest happy hour in the city, Tequilas offers half-priced drinks and discounted appetizers Monday–Friday 2–6:30 P.M.

RESTAURANTS

NEW AMERICAN
MERITAGE RESTAURANT AND WINE BAR 💲💲💲

500 S. 20th St., 215/985-1922,
www.meritagephiladelphia.com
HOURS: Tues.-Thurs. 5-10 P.M., Fri.-Sat. 5-11 P.M.

Meritage, along with Pub and Kitchen across this street, has brought life to this once-quiet corner not far from Rittenhouse Square. The menu has something for everyone, with contemporary American dishes that change seasonally and are heavily influenced by French and Asian styles. Choose from snacks, small plates, and large plates, all excellent for sharing. The small bar area is often packed and noisy, especially on weekends, but the dining room in the back has a quieter, more romantic, atmosphere. Dine alfresco when the weather is nice, surrounded by white lights when the sun goes down. Meritage's extensive wine list has received accolades from both *Wine Spectator* and *Wine Enthusiast,* so come in for a few glasses and snacks or for a full meal.

MONK'S CAFÉ 💲💲

264 S. 16th St., 215/545-7005, www.monkscafe.com
HOURS: Daily 11:30 A.M.-2 A.M., food served until 1 A.M.

You'll often have to wait while crammed into the front entrance like sardines at this extremely popular spot, but it's worth it. If you're lucky, you'll nab a bar seat and drink from the extensive Belgian beer collection until your table is ready (or eat at the bar). Avoid weekends, or go at an off time unless you can stand crowds and the smells of delicious food wafting past your empty stomach for up to an hour. Don't miss the famous farm-raised mussels available in a variety of delicious sauces made with different kinds of beer, garlic, and other exciting ingredients; they are served with the also-famous *pommes frites* with bourbon mayonnaise dipping sauce, but it's hard to go wrong with anything on the reasonably priced menu. The salads, burgers with a variety of toppings, and sandwiches are as delicious as the entrées.

PUMPKIN RESTAURANT 💲💲💲

1713 South St., 215/545-4448,
http://pumpkinphilly.com
HOURS: Tues.-Thurs. 6 P.M.-midnight,
Fri.-Sun. 5:30 P.M.-midnight

A favorite in Philadelphia's vibrant BYOB scene, Pumpkin's orange-accented storefront exterior and small—some might say cramped—interior do not do justice to the work of its kitchen. The relatively small menu (usually about five appetizers, five entrées, and several sides) features seasonal, mostly local ingredients that change every single day. You can check the website to find out what is being offered on any given day, and you will always find a mix of perfectly prepared, creative meat and seafood dishes, with scallops making frequent appearances. The husband-and-wife owners (he is the chef, she runs the front of the house) accept cash only, and reservations are highly recommended. If you don?t have time to fit in a dinner at Pumpkin Restaurant, you can still buy fresh, local and delicious produce, baked goods, dairy, meat, and prepared foods, or sit down for coffee, breakfast (served all day), lunch, or a casual dinner at **Pumpkin Market and Café** (1610 South St., 215/545-3924, Tues.-Fri. 7 A.M.-8 P.M., Sat.-Sun. 9 A.M.-8 P.M.).

ROUGE 💲💲💲

205 S. 18th St., 215/732-6622, www.rouge98.com
HOURS: Mon.-Fri. 11:30 A.M.-2 A.M.,
Sat.-Sun. 10 A.M.-2 A.M.

One of the few establishments occupying the prime location directly on Rittenhouse Square, Rouge is always packed. Snagging a table from happy hour onwards can be difficult, especially on weekends. Enjoy a drink at the elegant bar while you wait for a table, or go for lunch when prices are lower and it's not usually quite as busy. The scene is dominated by beautiful, wealthy yuppies letting their highlighted hair down after work, but the view of the square from the bar—or better yet, a sidewalk table—is excellent, and may just make you forget about the steep prices (try $16 for a hamburger and at least $12 for a martini). You'll pay the premium for the location, but the American cuisine with a French flair is quite good, and far superior to its nearby neighbors. The generous tuna tartare appetizer is reason enough to stop in.

SEAFOOD

OYSTER HOUSE 💲💲💲

1516 Sansom St., 215/567-7683,
www.oysterhousephilly.com

HOURS: Mon.-Sat. 11:30 A.M.-11 P.M.

The Mink family has been serving fresh oysters in Philadelphia since 1947. Sam Mink sold oysters out of a South Philly spot called Kelly's, and his son David opened the Sansom Street Oyster House in 1976. The restaurant was sold in 2000, but it came back to the Mink family in 2009 when David's son Sam bought it back in 2009 and opened it as Oyster House. Today's Oyster House offers fresh, traditional comfort seafood with modern embellishments along with a clean, bright, modern look. David brings his own vision and youth to the spot while still maintaining the focus on high quality seafood passed down through his family. An extensive raw bar is offered alongside old-school staples like snapper turtle soup and a lobster roll. The restaurant draws a big "Oyster Hour" crowd for $1 oysters of the day, $3 draft beers, and $3 oyster shooters Monday–Friday 5–7 P.M. and Saturday 9–11 P.M.

SEAFOOD UNLIMITED 💲💲

270 S. 20th St., 215/732-3663,
www.seafoodunlimited.com

HOURS: Mon.-Tues. 5-9:30 P.M.,
Wed.-Thurs. 11:30 A.M.-2:30 P.M. and 5-9:30 P.M.,
Fri.-Sat. 11:30 A.M.-2:30 P.M. and 5-10:30 P.M.,
Sun. 5-9 P.M.

This casual, friendly Rittenhouse Square seafood restaurant serves perfectly fresh fish with a menu that changes daily. Each dish is done just right, and with prices that are relatively low—especially for this area—it is a long-time local favorite. The New England and Manhattan clam chowders are excellent; fresh oysters on the half shell never disappoint; and the steamed lobster stuffed with crab imperial is a classic. But the best way to go is to check out the fish case up front and see for yourself what looks best on any given day. Then choose to have it grilled, fried, pan-seared, or broiled with herb butter. You will not be disappointed. An excellent happy hour is offered every day from 5 P.M. to close with $5 cocktails and wines, $3 Yuengling lager drafts, and $4 small plates, including steamed mussels, buffalo shrimp, and oysters on the half shell for $1.25.

SNACKS, SWEETS, AND BREAD

LEBUS 💲

135 S. 18th St., 215/569-8299, www.lebusbakery.com

HOURS: Mon.-Fri. 7 A.M.-7 P.M., Sat. 8 A.M.-6 P.M.,
Sun. 9 A.M.-5:30 P.M.

A classic grassroots independent-business success story, LeBus started serving food to University of Pennsylvania students out of a school bus more than 25 years ago. Today, in addition to several retail locations, it supplies wholesome artisan breads to more than 500 clients, including the Four Seasons and Saladworks. Using ancient European recipes and natural ingredients, LeBus breads are known for their full flavors, from the signature French baguette and raisin walnut bread to croissants, muffins, and bagels. The Rittenhouse store is a popular morning stop for coffee, baked goods, and sweet treats and for lunch for its homemade soups, quiches, and sandwiches. Be warned: Snagging croissants or bagels after noon can be difficult. Take out only, no inside seating. If you're in Manayunk, stop at **Winnie's LeBus** (4266 Main St., 215/487-2663, www .lebusmanayunk.com) for breakfast, lunch, dinner, or weekend brunch and you'll be treated to LeBus breads served in or with many of the dishes.

METROPOLITAN BAKERY 💲

262 S. 19th St., 215/545-6655,
www.metropolitanbakery.com

HOURS: Mon.-Fri. 7:30 A.M.-7 P.M., Sat.-Sun. 8 A.M.-6 P.M.

With five locations throughout the city, you're never far from the delicious breads, bagels, pastries, and coffee of Metropolitan Bakery. More than 30 varieties of bread are sold at the shops and also served and sold at many other local restaurants and markets. Well known for their signature French berry rolls, homemade granola, and croissants, Metropolitan offers an array of single rolls as well as whole loaves along with other gourmet treats like olive oils, coffees, teas, jams, cheeses, and spreads. Each shop is a little different, but all offer amazing gourmet treats. Additional locations: Home Page Café in the Free Library of Philadelphia (1901 Vine St., Mon.–Sat. 8 A.M.–5 P.M., Sun. 1–5 P.M.), University City (4013 Walnut St., Mon.–Fri. 7:30 A.M.–7 P.M., Sat.–Sun. 8 A.M.–7 P.M.), Reading Terminal Market (12th and Arch Sts., Mon.–Sat. 8 A.M.–6 P.M., Sun. 9 A.M.–5 P.M.), and Chestnut Hill (8607 Germantown Ave., 215/753-9001, Mon.–Fri. 7:30 A.M.–7 P.M., Sat. 8 A.M.–6 P.M., Sun. 8 A.M.–5 P.M.).

TAPAS
TINTO ❸❸❸
114 S. 20th St., 215/665-9150, www.tintorestaurant.com
HOURS: Sun. 10:30 A.M.-2:30 P.M. and 5-10 P.M., Mon.-Thurs. 5-10 P.M., Fri.-Sat. 5 P.M.-midnight

Spanish for red wine, Tinto—Philadelphia's hottest restaurant and wine bar—lives up to its name. More than 100 varieties of Spanish and French wines fill the handcrafted wooden grids that completely surround the intimate space. Reminiscent of an elegant yet rustic wine cellar, the dining area is complete with high tasting tables and a 22-foot bar covered in black-and-white Spanish tiles. The second venture after Amada of acclaimed chef/owner Jose Garces, the inventive Basque menu featuring *pinxtos* (the Basque equivalent of tapas), charcuterie, cheeses, *mariscos* (shellfish), brochettes, and *bocadillos* (sandwiches) remains one of the most popular restaurants in the city.

VEGETARIAN
MAMA'S VEGETARIAN ❸
18 S. 20th St., 215/751-0477, www.mamasvegetarian.com
HOURS: Sun. noon-7 P.M., Mon.-Thurs. 11 A.M.-9 P.M., Fri. 11 A.M.-3 P.M., closed on Jewish holidays

If you find yourself in need of a quick bite in Center City, you could do a lot worse than Mama's, whether you're a vegetarian or not. This no-frills kosher eatery stars hefty portions of falafel on freshly baked pita. The sandwich is filling; the platter, which comes with hummus and vegetables, is almost enough for two. The menu is limited, but standouts include the eggplant and the crisp french fries. The small, packed eatery is not the best place to linger, especially during the lunch rush, but it is a cheap, tasty place to refuel.

Museum District   Map 4

Museum hopping makes you hungry. While most of the museums have at least a café, and the Art Museum has several decent dining options, there are many more options nearby, lining Fairmount Avenue and the surrounding streets.

CAFÉS
DARLING'S CAFÉ ❸
2100 Spring St., 215/496-9611, www.darlingscheesecake.com
HOURS: Mon.-Fri. 7 A.M.-3 P.M., Sat.-Sun. 8 A.M.-5 P.M.

Darling's proudly claims to be purveyors of the "Original Philly Cheesecake"—yes, you heard right, cheesecake, not cheesesteak. I didn't know before trying it that there was such a thing, but apparently it's lighter in color and creamier in texture than the New York variety, and regardless, it's delicious. There is a selection of other delicious desserts as well, all of which you can order by the slice or a whole pie in advance. Try the award-winning Bananas Foster cheesecake, the Forbidden Fruit, or the Peanut Butter Silk. You're not going to be able to come in without trying the desserts, but the café also serves good breakfast and lunch fare, including soup, salad, and hot and cold sandwiches along with a full coffee bar. There is also wireless Internet available.

© KARRIE GAVIN

Mugshots is a great lunch or coffee stop after a visit to Eastern State Penitentiary.

MUGSHOTS COFFEEHOUSE & CAFÉ $

2100 Fairmount Ave., 267/514-7145,
www.mugshotscoffeehouse.com

HOURS: Mon.-Fri. 6:30 A.M.-10 P.M., Sat.
7:30 A.M.-10 P.M., Sun. 7:30 A.M.-8 P.M.

The original Mugshots is a classic neighborhood coffeehouse that happens to sit just across the street from the Eastern State Penitentiary, making it a convenient stop for visitors to this major historic site. Stop in for coffee, lunch, or a snack from the tasty menu of salads, sandwiches, wraps, and baked goods. Take a break to read, study, chat, or go online (there is free wireless Internet as well as one computer available to the public with a 15-minute suggested time limit). In addition, the environmentally and socially conscious business serves only fair-trade, organic coffees, supports local farms, and recycles absolutely everything. There are two additional locations, one just off Main Street in Manayunk (110 Cotton St., 215/482-3964, Mon.–Thurs. 6:30 A.M.–8 P.M., Fri. 6:30 A.M.–6 P.M., Sat.–Sun. 8 A.M.–6 P.M.) and the newest in Brewerytown (2831 Girard Ave., 215/717-3327, Mon.–Fri. 7 A.M.–8 P.M., Sat.–Sun. 8 A.M.–6 P.M.).

NEW AMERICAN
BRIDGID'S $$

726 N. 24th St., 215/232-3232, www.bridgids.com

HOURS: Mon. 4:30-11 P.M., Tues.-Fri. 11:30 A.M.-3 P.M. and 4:30-11 P.M., Sat. 4:30-11 P.M., Sun. 11 A.M.-2 P.M. and 4-9 P.M.

This neighborhood restaurant and bar has all the right ingredients: affordable, delicious food, an impressive beer list, and a cozy, friendly atmosphere complete with fireplace. It's no wonder it's such a popular local favorite. The first but not the last Philadelphia establishment to specialize in Belgian beers, Bridgid's offers an excellent selection of brews from around the world. The menu changes daily, but you can expect to find fresh salmon or tuna, prepared a little differently each day, along with cozy comfort food like honey-fried chicken and filet roquefort. Stop in for delicious salad, soups, and sandwiches for lunch, or for a unique and delicious Sunday brunch menu.

FOUNTAIN AT THE FOUR SEASONS $$$

18th St. and the Benjamin Franklin Pkwy.,
215/963-1500,
www.fourseasons.com/philadelphia/dining
HOURS: Mon. 6:30-11 A.M. and 11:30 A.M.-2:30 P.M.,
Tues.-Fri. 6:30-11 A.M., 11:30 A.M.-2:30 P.M., and
5:45-10 P.M., Sat. 7-11 A.M., 11:30 A.M.-2:30 P.M., and
5:45-10 P.M., Sun. 7 A.M.-noon and 5:45-10 P.M.

For anyone who is independently wealthy or celebrating a rare and very special occasion, indulge in this idyllic dining experience if you have a fat wallet. Continuously ranked among the nation's best restaurants, the Fountain's kitchen creates perfect, inventive American dishes with a French influence while the staff provides impeccable service, giving each guest the royal treatment. A jacket and tie should be worn for dinner, and smart casual dress is suggested for breakfast, brunch, and lunch in this elegant establishment. The Swann Café and the Swann Lounge, also both in the Four Seasons, offer slightly more relaxed but still elegant dining and drinking options, including a Sunday brunch buffet served in the lounge. It is exquisite, as it had better be for a whopping $68 per person.

JACK'S FIREHOUSE $$

2130 Fairmount Ave., 215/232-9000,
www.jacksfirehouse.com
HOURS: Mon.-Fri. 11:30 A.M.-4 P.M. and 5-10:30 P.M.,
Sat. 11 A.M.-3 P.M. and 5-10:30 P.M., Sun. 11 A.M.-3 P.M. and
4-9 P.M.; bar menu Mon.-Sat. 3-10:30 P.M., Sun. 3-9 P.M.

Occupying a 19th-century firehouse that still features the original mahogany interior and brass fire pole, Jack's Firehouse is a unique dining experience in Philadelphia, inside and out. The spacious outdoor dining area offers views of historic Eastern State Penitentiary across the street. Renowned chef Jack McDavid offers generous portions of American food with a southern flair using local, farm-fresh ingredients. North Carolina–style crab cakes, Cajun grilled shrimp, and the ever popular ribs are highlights. Or try the Chef's Special, a hearty four-course meal for $40 per person. Lunch and weekend brunch menus are big hits with locals as well as with visitors to the Eastern State Penitentiary.

LONDON GRILL $$

2301 Fairmount Ave., 215/978-4545,
www.londongrill.com
HOURS: Mon. 4 P.M.-2 A.M., Tues.-Fri. 11:30 A.M.-2 A.M.,
Sat. 11 A.M.-2 A.M., Sun. 11 A.M.-2 A.M.

Since 1991, London Grill has been a Fairmount staple. One of the first of an onslaught of bars and restaurants on this stretch of Fairmount Avenue, it remains one of the best. The restaurant has evolved since its early days, with Asian, Latin American, and Mediterranean twists on the modern American menu. There are several different cozy dining areas to choose from; the back dining room, surrounded by glass and resembling a greenhouse, is my favorite for a quiet meal, and the sidewalk tables are popular when the weather is nice. The restaurant is open for dinner daily, lunch Tuesday–Friday, and brunch on weekends. The bar/café area offers a lively atmosphere, sometimes with live music; a solid beer list; and an all-day menu until 11 P.M. on weeknights and 1 A.M. on weekends. Don't miss happy hour with $3 drinks 5–7 P.M. and $3 small plates 4–7 P.M. on weekdays.

London Grill serves food and drinks near the Museum District.

◖ WATER WORKS RESTAURANT ❸❸❸

640 Water Works Dr. (at Kelly Dr.), 215/236-9000,
www.thewaterworksrestaurant.com

HOURS: Tues.-Thurs. 11:30 A.M.-2:30 P.M. and 5-10 P.M.,
Fri. 11:30 A.M.-2:30 P.M. and 5-11 P.M., Sat. 11 A.M.-2 P.M. and
5-11 P.M., Sun. 11 A.M.-2:30 P.M. and 5-9 P.M.

After major renovations of the architecturally
magnificent building, Water Works Restaurant
opened in 2006 to much acclaim. Part of the
Fairmount Water Works National Historic
Landmark complex that once supplied water to
the entire city, the restaurant occupies a lovely
spot steps from the Philadelphia Museum of Art
and Boathouse Row on the edge of the Schuylkill
River. The restaurant serves delicious New
American cuisine with Mediterranean influences,
and several different seating areas offer different
vibes: There's a dramatic, main dining room; a
romantic glassed-in porch offering views of the
river; and a stylish bar area. When the weather
is nice, you can dine alfresco on the river. The
prices are steep for dinner, but brunch offers another way to experience the unique atmosphere
without completely breaking your budget.

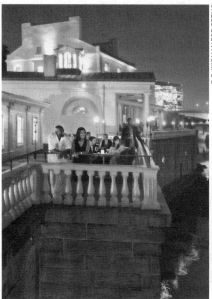

© G. WIDMAN FOR GPTMC

RESTAURANTS

**Water Works Restaurant offers fine dining
on a historic site.**

South Philadelphia

Map 5

South Philly is many locals' favorite place to eat.
There is an abundance of traditional and contemporary Italian restaurants in and around the
Italian Market on 9th Street, with a concentration of affordable Asian and Mexican eateries
on nearby Washington Avenue. South Street
and East Passyunk Avenue are also chock-full
of restaurants, gastropubs, and BYOBs. South
Philly is also, of course, home to an abundance
of cheesesteak joints, including the dueling Pat's
and Geno's on opposing corners at 9th Street
and Passyunk Avenue.

BRUNCH
◖ SABRINA'S CAFÉ ❸

910 Christian St., 215/574-1599, www.sabrinascafe.com

HOURS: Tues.-Sat. 8 A.M.-10 P.M.,
Sun.-Mon. 8 A.M.-4 P.M.

Oh, Sabrina's… Just the thought of your

delicious food and ridiculously oversized portions is enough to lift many a hungover local
from bed to come and wait an hour or more to
be seated for brunch. Considered by many to
be the best brunch spot in Philadelphia (with
Honey's Sit 'n Eat a close competitor), Sabrina's
offers every configuration of standard breakfast
fare, as well as proprietary specialties like its famous challah French toast stuffed with cream
cheese and bananas and covered with vanilla
bean maple syrup—yum. Best known for its exquisite all-day brunch menu, lunch and dinner
at Sabrina's are also quite good, with a nice variety of soups, sandwiches, wraps, and entrées.
The cozy eatery stretches by twists and turns
across several former row houses and offers outdoor seating that's great for people-watching
on nice days. It has been such a success that
in 2007, the owners opened **Sabrina's Café**

and Spencer's Too (215/574-1599) at 18th and Callowhill in the Fairmount neighborhood, which offers many of the same delicious menu items along with a few different options.

SAM'S MORNING GLORY DINER $
10th and Fitzwater Sts., 215/413-3999,
www.themorningglorydiner.com
HOURS: Mon.-Fri. 7 A.M.-4 P.M., Sat.-Sun. 8 A.M.-3 P.M.
There is something indescribably cozy about drinking coffee from a metal mug, camping style. The home-cooked meals have a flair that makes them more upscale than your average greasy-spoon diner, but still a little grittier than nearby Sabrina's, around the corner. Brunch is the house specialty here, and it's made with plenty of fresh, local ingredients. Check your diet at the door and sink your teeth into the gigantic breakfast burrito, one of several frittatas, or the pecan waffle with whipped peach butter. The wait for weekend brunch can be brutal, so go early and wait with everyone else, or better yet, go on a weekday. Oh, and the only other negative is the homemade ketchup; it simply does not compare to good old Heinz in my opinion.

CAFÉS

ANTHONY'S ITALIAN COFFEE HOUSE $
903 S. 9th St., 800/833-5030,
www.italiancoffeehouse.com
HOURS: Mon.-Thurs. 7:30 A.M.-6 P.M.,
Fri.-Sat. 7:30 A.M.-10 P.M., Sun. 7:30 A.M.-5 P.M.
Enjoy a perfectly brewed espresso, cappuccino, or regular cup of joe in an authentic old-school Italian Market coffeehouse. Dark-wood paneling and pictures of the Italian Market's early days set the mood, while delicious panini, cannoli, cookies, and perfect coffee are the real draw. If you need more to satisfy your sweet tooth, visit **Anthony's Chocolate House** (915 South St.) a few doors down for a wide array of delicious homemade chocolates and sweets.

CHAPTERHOUSE CAFÉ $
620 S. 9th St., 215/238-2626,
www.myspace.com/chapterhouse
HOURS: Daily 7 A.M.-10 P.M.
One of the city's best coffee shops, Chapterhouse

Café is barely a block from the bustling concrete jungle of South Street, but it might as well be on a different planet. The minimalist white walls, dark-wood floors, and spare but comfortable black-and-silver seats are brightened by rotating installations of paintings and mobiles by local artists hanging on the walls. You're likely to see multiple people with square-framed glasses sipping lattes and being creative, or at least looking like they are. Besides great coffee, you'll find cocoa, Italian sodas, teas, and a small selection of sandwiches. And though you'll have to show up early before they run out of bagels, there's always a good selection of pastries and muffins available.

HAWTHORNES CAFÉ $$
738 S. 11th St., 215/627-3012, http://hawthornecafe.com
HOURS: Tues.-Sat. 9 A.M.-11 P.M., Sun. 9 A.M.-6 P.M.
Foodies and beer lovers alike will find a little slice of heaven at this self-proclaimed "beer boutique and gourmet eatery," which opened in 2009 on a quiet corner near South Street. Owners Chris and Heather Hawthorne converted an empty warehouse space into a cozy little café complete with hardwood floors, fireplace, and cute personal touches. A unique concept in Philadelphia, it functions as both a six-pack shop and a restaurant. In addition to a small selection of draft beers, you can choose from the expansive beer refrigerator stocked with over 1,000 domestic and exotic brews. Grab some to go or pick one out to drink there over breakfast, lunch, brunch, or dinner. Brunch on weekends is extremely popular, but there is not a bad time to visit. The tasty modern American menu changes seasonally, with a focus on fresh, local ingredients, and the prices are very reasonable for the high-quality cuisine.

CHEESESTEAKS AND SANDWICHES

FAMOUS 4TH ST. DELICATESSEN $
700 S. 4th St., 215/922-3274,
www.famous4thstreetdelicatessen.com
HOURS: Daily 8 A.M.-9 P.M.
Simple, bright, and cheery, this corner

sandwich shop may not look like much, but it has a long list of notable clientele. City politicians, prominent business folk, and regular old people have found their way to this classic Jewish deli since it opened in 1923. Owned by the same family for more than 80 years, it changed hands in 2005, but the food is still top-notch. Sandwiches are stacked high and while the prices are a little steep for corned beef or pastrami on rye (over $10), they're large enough to split and still have leftovers. A newer Center City location offers the same

CHEESESTEAKS 101

As much as I'd love to give you a definitive answer to the question of where to get the best cheesesteak in Philly, there just isn't one. The argument will never be settled because it's truly a matter of personal preference. Some like the rolls toasted and crispy, while others prefer them soft and chewy. Some like it dripping with grease, while others complain that too much grease makes the roll soggy. Some like the meat diced as thinly as possible, while others prefer slightly larger slices or even small chunks. Some love fake, yellow Cheez Whiz, but most opt for American or provolone cheese. Regardless, the one indisputable fact is that cheesesteaks are just not the same anywhere else. The closest I've come to a perfect cheesesteak outside of Philly is at the New Jersey shore, and not surprisingly, it turned out the chef hailed from Philly. While it's a fact that locals eat cheesesteaks regularly, we try to keep our consumption in check. Let's be honest; they're not exactly health food.

WHAT MAKES A
GREAT CHEESESTEAK

All good cheesesteaks start with a roll that is chewy – not airy or tough – and many of the best spots in town use Amoroso's brand, a local company that's been around since 1904. The meat should generously fill the roll – leaving an inch of meatless roll is a definite no-no. Fried onions and either hot or sweet peppers are common additions, but beyond that, you're getting into fancy-schmancy territory. Some like to add pizza sauce, making it a pizza steak, or tomato, lettuce, onion, and mayo, making it a cheesesteak hoagie. Others opt for the only slightly healthier chicken cheesesteak, in which chicken is substituted for the beef. (It's technically a misnomer to call it a chicken cheesesteak since there is no steak involved,

but cheesechicken just doesn't have the same ring to it.) While each of these varieties is delicious in its own right, cheesesteak virgins are advised to keep it simple and stick with the classic beef cheesesteak (with fried onions and hot or sweet peppers if you like) and American cheese.

HOW TO ORDER

While not everyone is hard-core about ordering correctly, in South Philly or anywhere there is a long line, it's best to know what you're doing. First, don't *ever* order a "Philly cheesesteak" – you're in Philly, so that part goes without saying. The basic rule of thumb is to minimize the words you need to convey what you want, so don't bother saying the word "cheesesteak" if that is the main thing the establishment serves. Cheesesteak is implied, so you can just give the specs: "Whiz wit," means Cheez Whiz with fried onions, and "prov without" means – yes, you guessed it – provolone cheese without fried onions. These rules are most strictly observed at Pat's and Geno's, the famous dueling spots that share the intersection of 9th Street and Passyunk Avenue in South Philly. Of the two, I prefer Pat's to the neon-bedazzled Geno's, in part because the meat at Pat's is chopped more finely and in part because of the questionable sign at Geno's that reads "This is America, when ordering please speak English." While there are certainly better cheesesteaks out there, this corner offers a worthwhile cultural experience. Perhaps best of all, it is the only place where you can find cheesesteaks (and cheese fries if you really want to go all out) 24 hours a day. While you wait in line, be sure to check out the autographed photos of celebs on the walls of both – everyone from Justin Timberlake to Oprah has been here.

great sandwiches (38. S. 19th St., 215/568-3271, Mon.–Fri. 11 A.M.–9 P.M., Sat.–Sun. 11 A.M.–9 P.M.) and makes a great place to pick up lunch for a picnic in Rittenhouse Square.

JIM'S STEAKS $

400 South St., 215/928-1911, www.jimssteaks.com
HOURS: Mon.-Thurs. 10 A.M.-1 A.M., Fri.-Sat. 10 A.M.-3 A.M., Sun. 10 A.M.-10 P.M.

Although there are three additional outposts in Northeast Philadelphia, Springfield, and West Philadelphia (the original, 431 N. 62nd St., 215/747-6617), it's the South Street location that is famous. With a line that wraps around the corner on weekend nights, Jim's Steaks is a Philadelphia landmark that is rarely left out of any "great cheesesteak" debate. Signed photographs of famous people who have dined here line the walls on two floors. The menu offers more options than famous competitors Pat's and Geno's a few blocks to the south, with more fixin's, along with hoagies, soups, Italian sausage, and vegetarian steaks, but the classic cheesesteak with fried onions and Cheez Whiz is hard to beat. Bright fluorescent lights can be tough on the eyes during late-night visits, but if you're passing by after a night out on the town, you will find it hard to resist the smell wafting out onto the street.

PAT'S KING OF STEAKS $

1237 E. Passyunk Ave., 215/468-1546, www.patskingofsteaks.com
HOURS: 24 hours

Pat's occupies the most famous cheesesteak corner in Philly, and hence the world, along with its rival **Geno's Steaks** (1219 S. 9th St., 215/389-4166, www.genosteaks.com, also 24 hours) across the street. As the story goes, in 1930, Pat Olivieri owned a South Philly hot-dog stand. One day he wanted something different for lunch and put chopped meat in a bun instead of a dog, and the cheesesteak was born, or so it goes. While the cheesesteaks on this corner are not necessarily the best in Philly, they are pretty darn good and there is always a crowd. Everyone has their fave

between the two; I prefer Pat's as much for the simple old-school decor (compared with the neon headache that is Geno's, especially after a few beers) as for the slightly superior sandwiches. Whichever you choose, visiting this corner is a worthwhile cultural experience for all newcomers to Philly.

FRENCH
BEAU MONDE $

624 S. 6th St., 215/592-0656, www.creperie-beaumonde.com
HOURS: Tues.-Fri. noon-11 P.M., Sat. 10 A.M.-11 P.M., Sun. 10 A.M.-10 P.M.

At this French crêperie, the elegant interior—with its foil prints and bright windows—perfectly complements its delicious food. Though the menu does include other items (including a cheese plate and chicken satay), it is primarily a place to enjoy perfect, thin crepes in a variety of sweet and savory combinations. Fillings include cheeses, flavored butter, chicken, nutella, grilled vegetables, and fruits, and any combination your heart desires can be yours, for dinner, lunch, brunch, or just dessert. And, to top it all off, if you have to wait for a table, you can have a drink upstairs at L'Etage, a kickin' little bar and lounge.

ITALIAN
RALPH'S $$

760 S. 9th St., 215/627-6011, www.ralphsrestaurant.com
HOURS: Sun.-Thurs. 11:45 A.M.-9:45 P.M., Fri.-Sat. 11:45 A.M.-10:45 P.M.

Ralph's opened in 1900, laying its claim as the oldest family-owned Italian restaurant in the United States. While the food might no longer be the very best Southern Italian fare in the city, it is still reliably good, hearty, and authentic. Best of all, this traditional two-floor eatery has unbeatable, old-school ambience. It will transport you to a Mafioso-inspired time, which, minus the killing and espionage, makes for a fun, classy atmosphere and offers a glimpse into a piece of local history. Your first bite of the stellar eggplant parm or spaghetti and meatballs makes the debate over whether you're eating sauce or gravy immediately irrelevant; it's delicious either way. And don't forget to order mussels in garlicky red sauce and sop it up with bread. The service can be patchy and credit cards are not accepted, so bring your easy-going attitude and some cash and you're in for a good night.

MEXICAN
PLAZA GARIBALDI ❸

935 Washington Ave., 215/922-2370
HOURS: 11 A.M.–11 P.M.

Some of the best laid-back, authentic Mexican in the city can be found on Washington Avenue. With its colorful, cozy decor, the

ITALIAN MARKET

One of the oldest and largest outdoor markets in the United States dates back more than a century. An influx of Italian immigrants arrived in Philadelphia in the early 20th century, and the market developed to cater to the new community. It has been bustling ever since, and many of the vendors and shops have remained the same. A living, breathing historic site, the market offers a glimpse into a time before supermarkets, when eating was a community effort. It spans about nine blocks, with the bulk of the action centering on 9th Street between Christian Street and Washington Avenue. The numerous stalls and shops include fish, meat, and cheese shops, cafés, and a few selling books or household goods. Though parts of it are dilapidated and the street is often in dire need of a good scrub, it holds all the delicacies of Italy: paper-thin slices of prosciutto, juicy

mounds of mozzarella, succulent olives, and some of the freshest bread, pasta, and produce in Philadelphia.

Locals, tourists, and gourmands alike can explore and discover the myriad goodies and shops in the Italian Market while soaking in the unique atmosphere. Notice the giant mural of Frank Rizzo, the controversial, polarizing 1970s Philadelphia mayor whose likeness occupies a full wall at 9th and Montrose Streets, and recall Rocky Balboa's famous jog down the street. If you visit in winter, you may even see old men warming their hands over giant barrels of fire. The area continues to attract immigrants of many origins, and a significant number of Vietnamese, Korean, Chinese, and Mexican business owners have set up shop alongside the Italian shops – enriching the culinary and cultural experience for everyone.

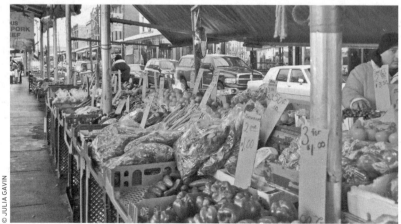

© JULIA GAVIN

Shop for meat, cheese, produce, and more at the historic Italian Market.

atmosphere is nice enough to bring your own bottle and dine in, but with burritos at around $6 and only a few entrées topping $10, it is also cheap enough to order pick-up or delivery on an ordinary weeknight. Try the moist, slightly sweet chicken mole burrito or the enchiladas suizas swimming in a tart, creamy green sauce. The nachos are a meal in and of themselves, covered with meat galore. For a quicker, order-at-the-counter authentic burrito experience, also with a few tables for a quick sit-down bite, try the fluorescent-lit **Taqueria Veracruzana** (908 Washington Ave.) across the street.

MOROCCAN

MARRAKESH RESTAURANT $$$

517 S. Leithgow St., 215/925-5929,
www.marrakesheastcoast.com
HOURS: Sun.-Thurs. 5:30-11 P.M.,
Fri.-Sat. 5:30 P.M.-midnight

Tucked away in a small alley just off South Street, accessible by a nearly unmarked door that you may have to knock on to enter, Marrakesh is a hidden gem for those who can actually find it. Belly dancers make their way through the dimly lit mazelike interior. Comfortable seating strewn with cushions makes for a cozy, romantic atmosphere. Waiters in traditional Moroccan garb serve a lovely, lengthy seven-course meal (around $30 per person) that you eat with your hands. Go hungry, allow at least two hours, and pace yourself. Each course is delicious, from the stuffed phyllo pastry to the moist chicken to the tender lamb, to the baklava and mint tea at the end. Drown in the waves of delicious food, but don't try to finish everything or you'll never make it to the seventh course. You can BYOB or order from the small wine list.

PIZZA

MARRA'S PIZZA $

1734 E. Passyunk Ave., 215/463-9249,
www.marrasone.com
HOURS: Tues.-Sat. 11:30 A.M.-11:30 P.M., Sun. 2-10 P.M.

On the recently hip stretch of Passyunk Avenue that now is home to many new, often upscale, trendy restaurants, Marra's is a taste of the old South Philly neighborhood. Generations of the Marra family have run the joint since the 1920s and built the brick oven with bricks from Mt. Vesuvius. Join the ranks of locals, visitors, and even celebs—including Frank Sinatra and John Travolta—who have come to sit in red-vinyl booths to eat huge portions of homemade pasta, mussels, calamari, and antipasti. While the hearty Italian dishes are very good, the best reason to come is for the delicious thin-crust pizza.

SEAFOOD

DMITRI'S $$

795 S. 3rd St., 215/625-0556,
www.dmitrisrestaurant.com
HOURS: Mon.-Thurs. 5:30-10 P.M., Fri.-Sat. 5:30-11 P.M., Sun. 5-10 P.M.

It's not easy to get a table at this tiny, cash-only BYOB that doesn't accept reservations, but it's well worth the wait. Be sure to come at least an hour before you're hungry, and don't even bother trying on weekends during prime dinner hours. Once seated, you will be treated to an affordable menu of fresh, grilled Mediterranean-inspired seafood like shrimp, scallops, bluefish, and octopus. Most dishes are sautéed and marinated with fresh, simple flavors like olive oil, garlic, lemon, and red-wine vinegar. Don't miss the perfect hummus and baba ghanoush served with grilled pita wedges or the avocado citrus salad for starters. There are two additional locations with almost identical menus if not quite as much character as the original. The Center City West location (2227 Pine St., 215/985-3680, Mon.–Thurs. 5:30–10 P.M., Fri.–Sat. 5:30–11 P.M., Sun. 5–10 P.M.) doesn't take reservations but the wait isn't nearly as long. It also has outside seating, a full bar, and accepts credit cards. The newest location in Northern Liberties (944 N. 2nd St., 215/592-4550, Tues.–Thurs. 5:30–10 P.M., Fri.–Sat. 5:30–11 P.M., Sun. 5–10 P.M.) is a BYOB that *does* accept reservations and credit cards. Got all that?

SNACKS AND SWEETS
ISGRO PATICCERIA $

1009 Christian St., 215/923-3092,
www.isgropastries.com
HOURS: Mon.-Thurs. 8:30 A.M.-6 P.M.,
Fri.-Sat. 8:30 A.M.-8 P.M., Sun. 8:30 A.M.-4 P.M.

Opened in 1904 by Mario Isgro, who studied culinary arts in Vienna and Messina before coming to Philadelphia, this popular old-school South Philly bakery has been owned and operated by members of the same family for over a century. Recipes for the award-winning cannolis (my personal fave), cookies, and cakes have been passed down through generations and have garnered a loyal following in generations of Philadelphians. Sweet aromas fill the street outside the row-house storefront, and inside, traditional Italian ricotta *baba au rhum, fogliatella,* jelly-filled croissants, hazelnut genoise, and chocolate cake with layers of ganache and raspberry jam fill the glass cases. Be warned; the line often wraps well around the block during the holidays.

JOHN'S WATER ICE $

701 Christian St., 215/925-6955,
www.johnswaterice.com
HOURS: Open in summertime, hours vary

Who needs a tiny $5 cup of Capogiro gelato when you can have a John's water ice for $1.50? Well, both are wonderful, but just make sure you get to John's at least once if you're in Philly in summertime. On a hot day or night, there is nothing better than a cool, light water ice, and there is no place better to get one than John's. The corner storefront serves perfectly smooth water ice with no ice chunks and just the right amount of sweetness. There are only four regular flavors—cherry, lemon, chocolate, and pineapple—and sometimes a few special flavors on weekends. Vanilla, chocolate, or butter pecan ice cream can be mixed with any water ice flavor for a gelati, which is also delicious, but if you're a water-ice virgin, stick with the basics.

VIETNAMESE
NAM PHUONG $

1110-1120 Washington Ave., 215/468-0410,
www.namphuongphilly.com
HOURS: Daily 10 A.M.-10 P.M.

A great location for hungry groups on a budget, Nam Phuong is renowned for its extensive menu, heaping portions, and economical prices. The fact that the food is actually stellar is an additional bonus. With over 200 dishes to choose from, it's easy for a diner to become a little overwhelmed. Fortunately, the attentive waitstaff will guide you in the right direction. *Pho* (soup) and *bun* (a rice-noodle dish offered with a variety of meats) are common crowd favorites, and the papaya salad and summer rolls with a thick, perfect peanut sauce are not to be missed.

University City

Map 6

People rarely venture across the bridge to U City just for dinner even though it's just a hop away; there is something about the area being separated from Center City by a body of water that creates a mental block. But when they do, they wonder why they don't do it more often. With so many affordable restaurants serving a variety of ethnic cuisine, it is well worth "the trip." There are great options on Sansom Street off 34th just off Penn's campus, on the Baltimore Avenue corridor, and in the area around 40th and Walnut Streets.

ASIAN
VIENTIANE CAFÉ $

4728 Baltimore Ave., 215/726-1095
HOURS: Mon.-Sat. 11 A.M.-3 P.M. and 5-10 P.M.

This tiny West Philly eatery serves excellent Laotian, Vietnamese, and Thai dishes, at equally excellent prices. With most entrées under $10, it is a favorite for both students and neighbors, and makes a great date spot for Penn students on a budget. Plus, it's a BYOB, making it even more affordable. Meat-lovers and vegetarians will find

RESTAURANTS

plenty of choices on the menu, from perfect pad Thai, soups, satay, spring rolls, and well-spiced curry dishes.

CAFÉS
GREEN LINE CAFE $

4239 Baltimore Ave., 215/222-3431,
www.greenlinecafe.com

HOURS: Mon.-Sat. 7 A.M.-11 P.M., Sun. 8 A.M.-8 P.M.

Named for the #34 trolley that runs by outside on Baltimore Avenue, this comfortable coffee shop is a gathering place for the University City community. It serves Penn and Drexel students, professors, families, punk anarchists, kids, and just about everyone else in the neighborhood. Standard coffee shop pastries and lunch fare are offered, and the café hosts a variety of events and artist exhibits. The concept proved so successful that other locations opened: **Green Line on Locust** (4426 Locust St., 215/222-0799, Mon.-Sat. 7 A.M.-10 P.M., Sun. 8 A.M.-8 P.M.) and **Green Line-Powelton Village** (3649 Lancaster Ave., 215/382-2143, Mon.-Fri. 7 A.M.-5 P.M., Sat.-Sun. 8 A.M.-3 P.M.).

Green Line Cafe is a favorite U. City hangout.

ETHIOPIAN
DAHLAK $

4708 Baltimore Ave, 215/726-6464,
www.dahlakrestaurant.com

HOURS: Daily 4 P.M.-2:30 A.M.

Dahlak is a local gem a bit beyond the environs of the universities offering delicious and authentic Ethiopian/Eritrean fare, which there isn't a lot of in Philly. For those who don't know, East African food usually comes in the form of flavorful stews, eaten by hand with moist, spongy *injera* bread rather than utensils. Dahlak offers a good selection of meat and meat-free dishes, which can be anywhere from mild to pretty darn hot, so be clear on the level of spice you want. The kitchen closes at 10 P.M., but the bar, which is popular with students and local hipsters, serves appetizers all night. Another location in Germantown (5547 Germantown Ave., 215/849-0788, noon-4 P.M. and 5-10 P.M.) is also quite good if you're in the neighborhood.

FRENCH
MARIGOLD KITCHEN $$$

501 S. 45th St., 215/222-3699,
www.marigoldkitchenbyob.com

HOURS: Wed.-Thurs. 5:30-9:30 P.M., Fri.-Sat. 5:30-10:30 P.M., Sun. 10:30 A.M.-2:30 P.M. and 5:30-9:30 P.M.

The oldest continually operating BYOB in the city (which says a lot in a city as old as Philadelphia), Marigold Kitchen is a local favorite. The tiny kitchen of the converted University City row home sits on a tree-lined residential street. While the style of cuisine has seen many incarnations and been under many different chefs throughout the restaurant's long history, the cozy atmosphere remains a constant. The menu changes almost daily with only the freshest ingredients used in the inventive French cuisine. Sunday brunch is not to be missed.

MEDITERRANEAN
LA TERRASSE $$$

3432 Sansom St., 215/386-5000,
www.laterrasserestaurant.com

HOURS: Mon.-Sat. 11:30 A.M.-2 A.M.

Nestled on a narrow side street near the heart

of Penn's bustling campus, La Terrasse offers an alternative to the post-adolescent energy of the college scene that dominates many nearby bars and restaurants. Instead, it caters more to the faculty, staff, grad students, and locals, with a mature selection of wine and food. It opened in 1966 and began as a French bistro, one of the first in the city, but its menu has evolved and diversified into what they now call Mediterranean. Popular for lunch, post-work drinks, and dinner, the menu includes offerings like littleneck clams, apple-and-brie salad, homemade gnocchi, and chicken marsala. The lunch menu features well-constructed sandwiches with a variety of tasty spreads and ingredients. Enjoy one on the terrace when the weather is nice.

MEXICAN
DISTRITO ❸❸❸

3945 Chestnut St., 215/222-1657

HOURS: Sun. 11 A.M.-2:30 P.M. and 5-10 P.M., Mon.-Thurs. 11:30 A.M.-2:30 P.M. and 5-10 P.M., Fri. 11:30 A.M.-2:30 P.M. and 5-11 P.M., Sat. 11 A.M.-2:30 P.M. and 5-11 P.M., bar menu Sun.-Thurs. 2:30-10 P.M.

Iron Chef Jose Garces's establishment is a perfect fit for the university-dominated community. The two-story restaurant exudes a fun, high-energy vibe with fluorescent green and pink décor complete with a bustling open kitchen and a variety of seating, from traditional tables to cozy circular booths to a car revamped as a booth. It's kitschy but fun for a night out on the town; Distrito's modern Mexican tapas are really tasty. Distrito continues Garces's trademark tapas style, so order lots of small plates and share. Two tasting menus offer a chance to sample smaller portions of many dishes. Don't miss the fresh ceviches, tuna tostada, or the *huaraches los hongos*. Expensive but tasty margaritas and the spicy, strong, and delicious Hemingway cocktail, each around $10, are highlights of the creative cocktail menu.

NEW AMERICAN
JG DOMESTIC ❸❸❸

2929 Arch St., 215/222-2363, www.jgdomestic.com

HOURS: Mon.-Fri. 11:30 A.M.-3 P.M. and 5-10 P.M., Sat. 5-10 P.M.

In a bright open setting on the ground floor of the Cira Center, just across the bridge from

© DAVID JOSEPH

Distrito serves modern Mexican fare in a fun University City setting.

RESTAURANTS

PHILLY'S IRON CHEF

The Philly restaurant scene has been blessed with quite a few nationally renowned chefs over the years, but perhaps none are more impressive than our very own Jose Garces. Born to Ecuadorian parents and raised in Chicago, Chef Garces began his culinary training in his grandmother's kitchen and has come a long way since then. In 2009, Garces was named "Best Chef Mid-Atlantic" by the James Beard Foundation and (drumroll, please) he went on to defeat Bobby Flay in the final round and win Food Network's "The Next Iron Chef" competition – all by his mid-30s. Lucky for us, seven of his eight restaurant ventures are located right here in Philly.

Garces's first venture, **Amada,** an enormously successful Andalusian tapas bar and restaurant in Old City, opened in 2005. Much to everyone's delight, by 2010, he had opened six more restaurants, each with its own unique style and cuisine, all bringing a burst of life to the local dining scene. In Center City West, **Tinto,** a wine bar and restaurant inspired by the Basque region of Spain and France, sits just next door to **Village Whiskey,** a bar serving over 80 whiskies, upscale bar snacks, and arguably the best burgers in the city. For modern Mexican at its best, Garces offers **Distrito** in University City, and for innovative and delicious Latin-Asian tapas, don't miss **Chifa** in Center City East. **JG Domestic,** on the ground floor of the Cira Center just across the bridge in University City, offers the best food and spirits from local (get it, domestic?) growers.

It's easy to run up a high tab at any of these spots with the excellent beer, wine, and cocktail selections offered, so if you'd rather spend money on food and save a bit in the booze department, visit **Garces Trading Company** in Center City East. A gourmet market and café featuring artisanal cheese, charcuterie, and deep-dish pizza, to name a few highlights, it also offers an attached market with a wine store inside – the only restaurant of its kind in the entire city. Just grab a bottle and enjoy it with your meal.

Center City in University City, JG Domestic proves that American food can be just as flavorful and creative as any food. Iron Chef Jose Garces has another success just across the street from 30th Street Station, by serving the very best food and spirits from domestic purveyors. The delicious menu changes daily and includes snacks, small and large plates, and a cheese cart. Even the drinks are American-made beer, wine, and spirits. An array of plants and wood set the tone, adding to the feel that you're eating only the freshest food available, close to the source.

◖ WHITE DOG CAFÉ $$$

3420 Sansom St., 215/386-9224, www.whitedog.com
HOURS: Mon. 11:30 A.M.-10 P.M.,
Tues.-Thurs. 11:30 A.M.-midnight,
Sat. 10:30 A.M.-midnight, Sun. 10:30 A.M.-10 P.M.

The success of this one-of-a-kind Philly gem tucked into three adjacent Victorian brownstones can be credited to longtime community activist Judy Wicks, who opened the restaurant in 1983 and went on to prove that progressive and socially conscious business models can work. Her goal was not based purely on profit maximizing, but also on maintaining a positive relationship with the environment and the community—which unfortunately remains a novel concept in the business world today. Local farmers deliver organic, humanely treated, hormone- and pesticide-free ingredients each week, so the menu changes regularly with the seasons, and an advanced composting system in the backyard helps reduce and efficiently dispose of the restaurant's waste. Wicks sold the restaurant in 2009, but she remains involved with the new management, which is committed to upholding the original mission. Best of all, the modern American dishes are made with fresh, organic, local ingredients and you can taste the difference. Visit for lunch, dinner, or weekend brunch, or have drinks and some of the best burgers in town at the bar. Check the website to find out more about the many events at the restaurant.

Northern Liberties Map 7

Northern Liberties has plenty of restaurants, gastropubs, and BYOBs, and most of them are all within a few-block radius. In general, the prices are lower, the vibe more laid-back, and the scene more bohemian than in trendy nearby Old City. This is the place to go for a great meal to start a night of bar-hopping.

INDIAN
❸ TIFFIN ❸

710 W. Girard Ave., 215/922-1297, www.tiffin.com
HOURS: Mon.-Fri. 11:30 A.M.-10 P.M.,
Sat.-Sun. noon-10 P.M.

What started as a takeout and delivery service expanded into a small sit-down restaurant due to popular demand for delicious, affordable Indian food. The menu is filled with classic dishes along with a few more creative specials offered daily. The flavors hit right on the mark each time. Delivery service is available in most areas of the city, including Center City, Old City, Northern Liberties, Washington Square, University City, Fishtown, Queen Village, Bella Vista, Temple University campus, and Fairmount, and the service area is always expanding. Three different meal packages are offered for delivery every weekday, and at least one package is vegetarian. Best of all, the packages, called "tiffins," cost only $7.50 (vegetarian) or $8.50 (meat) each. Options change daily and are always reliably good, but you have to place an order by 10 A.M. for lunch delivery and by 2 P.M. for dinner. Place an order online or by phone, or just go to eat in or take out from the full menu anytime. Thanks to another location in Mt. Airy (7105 Emlen St., 215/242-3656), most of Northwest Philadelphia can now enjoy Tiffin as well.

JEWISH AND SOUTHERN
HONEY'S SIT 'N EAT ❸

800 N. 4th St., 215/925-1150,
www.honeys-restaurant.com
HOURS: Mon.-Fri. 8 A.M.-10 P.M., Sat. 8 A.M.-9:30 P.M.,
Sun. 8 A.M.-4:30 P.M.

This bustling café blends hearty, down-home flavors of Southern/Jewish comfort food. Breakfast is served all day, drawing the big crowds for the challah French toast, Frisbee-sized pancakes, and homemade biscuits and gravy. But while it was breakfast that made Honey's famous, lunch and dinner are also delicious. Don't overlook the long list of specials, which may include fried green tomatoes, lobster macaroni and cheese, and an assortment of vegetarian and vegan options. Dine alfresco if you can snag a table and save room for dessert if at all possible—it won't be. Much to the delight of neighbors (myself included), a second outpost at 21st and South was scheduled to open in 2011.

NEW AMERICAN
NORTH THIRD ❸

801 N. 3rd St., 215/413-3666, www.norththird.com
HOURS: Mon.-Tues. 5 P.M.-midnight, Wed.-Fri.
5 P.M.-1 A.M., Sat. 10 A.M.-3:30 P.M. and 5 P.M.-1 A.M.,
Sun. 10 A.M.-3:30 P.M. and 5 P.M.-midnight; bar open
daily until 2 A.M.

One of the best gastropubs in town, every square inch of the dimly lit bar and restaurant is covered with conversation pieces, from tribal masks and oil paintings by local artists to artifacts. The restaurant is supportive of all types of artists, and Tuesday nights become a mini-theater when people bring in their own short films (under 15 minutes) on VHS or DVD to show and discuss. Classic, perfectly prepared bar fare like burgers, wings, and fish and chips shares space on the menu with salmon, baby-back ribs, and a perfect pulled pork sandwich. With good cocktails and a solid beer list, you can't go wrong whether stopping in for a drink or a meal.

STANDARD TAP ❸

2nd and Poplar Sts., 215/238-0630,
www.standardtap.com
HOURS: Mon.-Fri. 4 P.M.-2 A.M., Sat.-Sun. 11 A.M.-3 A.M.
and 4 P.M.-2 A.M.

One of the most popular bar/restaurants not just in Northern Liberties, Standard Tap is where many a night out in No Libs begins and/or ends. Both floors of the large, converted corner house are filled with tables and booths in various rooms and cozy nooks. Regulars and newcomers come to enjoy the great beer selection (including many local brews), upscale but affordable bar food, and the cool but unpretentious vibe. The burgers and fries are some of the city's best. Check out the chalkboard wall menus to see what other sandwiches, salads, and entrées are offered on any given night, and visit the website to find out about the many goings-on at this neighborhood gathering place.

SPANISH
BAR FERDINAND 💲💲

1030 N. 2nd St., 215/923-1313, www.barferdinand.com
HOURS: Sun.-Mon. 5-11 P.M., Tues.-Thurs.
5 P.M.-midnight, Fri.-Sat. 5 P.M.-1 A.M.

Liberties Walk is a pedestrian path that is home to a sprinkling of appealing eateries and shops, including this authentic tapas bar. Choose the quieter, more romantic dining areas with tables and booths, or the fun, sociable bar—especially happening on weekends. Owner and longtime No Libs local Owen Kamihara emphasizes the importance of the authentic tapas experience, so feel free to come for dinner or just have a

EAT AT A BAR

A relatively new breed of bars that many are referring to as "gastropubs" have become a mainstay in the Philly dining scene, all the more popular since the ban on smoking in bars passed in 2007. At gastropubs the food is at least as big a draw as the drinks – as opposed to places where chicken fingers and wings are par for the course and jalapeño poppers are gourmet cuisine. Serving everything from lobster spring rolls to seared tuna to colorful salads, gastropubs are generally affordable, casual places to eat and drink, and they are many locals' choice for dinner on an average night. Many of these spots do still serve the classic bar food like burgers – but those burgers are likely to be stuffed with Roquefort cheese or topped with truffles and served on a gourmet roll. And you will usually be able to choose a salad to accompany it in lieu of fries, but if you do opt for fries, they just may be sweet-potato fries, or they may come with a bourbon-mayo dipping sauce instead of ketchup. You get the idea; these places serve great food and are a worthwhile stop whether for a meal or just a

few drinks. Most of them also feature a nice variety of unique beers to match the meal. Some of the best are: **Johnny Brenda's, Standard Tap,** and **North Third** in Northern Liberties; **Eulogy Belgian Tavern** and **The Plough and the Stars** in Old City; **Nodding Head Brewery, Monk's Café, Good Dog,** and **Sidecar Bar & Grille** in Center City; and **Devil's Den** and **Royal Tavern** in South Philly.

Standard Tap

© CHRISTOPHER WOODS

few bites while you drink, as is customary in Spain. Hot and cold tapas range from tiny bites to larger portions and cost $4–14; they include olives, oysters, cured meats and cheeses, and interesting configurations of empanadas and skewers. An excellent selection of Spanish wine is available by glass or bottle, along with sangria, beers, and specialty cocktails.

Chestnut Hill and Manayunk

Map 8

The majority of restaurants in Northwest Philadelphia are located on or near Germantown Avenue in Chestnut Hill or on Main Street in Manayunk—bustling business strips in otherwise residential neighborhoods. Both areas also have excellent cafés and gourmet markets, including the Chestnut Hill just behind the Chestnut Hill hotel. The nearby neighborhoods of Mt. Airy, East Falls, and Roxborough also have a few neighborhood gems.

CHESTNUT HILL
Asian
OSAKA JAPANESE RESTAURANT $$$

8605 Germantown Ave., 215/242-5900, www.osakapa.com

HOURS: Mon.-Thurs. 11:30 A.M.-2:30 P.M. and 5-10 P.M., Fri.-Sat. 11:30 A.M.-2:30 P.M. and 5-11 P.M., Sun. 4-9 P.M.

A contemporary Japanese restaurant with a full sushi bar, Osaka is a Chestnut Hill favorite for a night on the town. Don't let the traditional decor complete with *tatami* room fool you; the kitchen turns out modern Asian fusion dishes and inventive specialty rolls using only the freshest ingredients. Cocktails, including those made with sake, are strong and delicious.

Cheesesteaks and Sandwiches
McNALLY'S TAVERN $

8634 Germantown Ave., 215/247-9736, www.mcnallystavern.com

HOURS: Mon.-Sat. 11 A.M.-11 P.M., Sun. noon-8 P.M.

Just when you thought you couldn't get any more artery-clogging than the cheesesteak, along comes the Schmitter. In addition to beef, onions, and extra cheese, the Schmitter comes with tomatoes, salami, and a special secret mayonnaise-y sauce. The sandwich has become a widely known Philly phenomenon that is now also sold at Citizens Bank Park during Phillies' games, but this is where it all began. McNally's also offer plenty of less intimidating house specialties, soups, salads, and good-old regular cheesesteaks and hoagies, which suddenly seem healthy next to the Schmitter. A casual spot in the refined Chestnut Hill neighborhood, it has a long history. An early incarnation of the restaurant was established in 1921 by Rose McNally to provide lunch for the trolley operators, including her husband, who drove outside on Germantown Avenue. Her greatgranddaughters operate the business today out of the same house the family bought to accommodate the growing business in 1927.

MANAYUNK
Cajun and American
BAYOU BAR & GRILL $

4245 Main St., 215/482-2560, www.thebayoubar.com

HOURS: Mon.-Thurs. 4 P.M.-2 A.M., Fri. noon-2 A.M., Sat.-Sun. 11 A.M.-2 A.M.

With most items under $10, the Bayou is an affordable place to eat among some of its more pricey neighbors on Main Street, with a lively atmosphere. Cajun and Creole classics like gumbo, jambalaya, and Creole chili are served along with standard pub fare like burgers, appetizers, and award-winning buffalo wings. The hard-shell crabs are a big hit. In existence since 1993, it's a local favorite that draws a regular crowd for dining and an even more regular crowd for the bar scene. A friendly atmosphere, nightly drink and happy hour specials, football games, and a covered outdoor deck when the weather is nice are just some of the highlights. In search of more upscale Cajun-inspired cuisine? Check out **Bourbon Blue** (215/508-3660, www .bourbonblue.com) at Main and Rector Streets.

RESTAURANTS

New American
JAKE'S AND COOPER'S
WINE BAR ⑤⑤⑤

4365 Main St., 215/483-0444,
www.jakesrestaurant.com

HOURS: Jake's: Mon.-Thurs. 5:30-9:30 P.M., Fri.
5:30-10:30 P.M., Sat. 5-10:30 P.M., Sun. 10:30 A.M.-3 P.M.
and 5-9 P.M.; Cooper's: Sun.-Thurs. 11:30 A.M.-10 P.M.,
Fri. and Sat. 11:30 A.M.-11 P.M.

The only truly fine-dining restaurant in
Manayunk is Jake's. In existence since 1987,
Jake's serves upscale modern American cuisine
in an elegant setting. It has earned the coveted
four stars from *Mobil Travel Guide* and high
praises from *Zagat, Gourmet, Wine Spectator,*
and the *Philadelphia Inquirer,* among others over
its long history. In 2008, Chef Cooper opened
the adjoining Cooper's Brick Oven Wine Bar.
Offering a more casual and more affordable
alternative to Jake's, Cooper's serves gourmet
pizza with seasonal toppings, small plates, and a
few traditional favorites from Jake's in a modern
space with an open kitchen.

MANAYUNK BREWERY
AND RESTAURANT ⑤⑤

4120 Main St., 215/482-8220,
www.manayunkbrewery.com

HOURS: Mon.-Thurs. 11 A.M.-10 P.M., Fri.-Sat. 11 A.M.-11 P.M.,
Sun. 1-9 P.M.; late-night menu served Mon.-Thurs. until
11 P.M., Fri.-Sat. until 1:30 A.M., Sun. until 10 P.M.

A former textile factory, the restaurant and
brewery is now a staple of Manayunk's Main
Street. In addition to their classic menu offerings, there is also a sushi bar, stone pizza
oven, and a rotisserie. From burgers to crab
cakes to raw tuna, there is something for every
taste and budget on the extensive menu. Sushi
fiends be warned; there is no sushi on Monday.
Several different bars offer a large selection of
beer, wine, and drinks, including the popular
in-house brews. It has one of the nicest and
largest alfresco dining areas in the city, so be
sure to sit on the back deck overlooking the
Schuylkill River if you visit when the weather is
nice. There are often events and live entertainment, including a live jazz brunch on Sundays,
10:30 A.M.–2:30 P.M.

Pizza
THE COUCH TOMATO CAFÉ ⑤

102 Rector St., 215/483-2233,
www.thecouchtomato.com

HOURS: Daily 11 A.M.-10 P.M.

University of Delaware graduates promise
quick service of "Manayunk cuisine without
the Manayunk prices" at their cozy, laid-back
café. In addition to the extravagantly topped
20-inch gourmet pizzas cooked to perfection
over pizza stones, they offer salads, soups,
wraps, calzones, and desserts. Indoor and outdoor seating are available, but convenient curb-
side pickup and a wide delivery make takeout
a popular option.

Greater Philadelphia   Map 9

The following are a select number of restaurants that fall outside the major neighborhoods
outlined in this book. Within the Philadelphia
city limits but not in the central neighborhoods, they are included because they are well
worth the short trip.

CHEESESTEAKS
AND SANDWICHES
CHUBBY'S STEAKS ⑤

5826 Henry Ave., 215/487-2575

HOURS: Thurs. 11 A.M.-1 A.M., Fri.-Sat. 11 A.M.-2 A.M.,
Sun. 11 A.M.-11 P.M.

This seemingly unimpressive sandwich stop is
regarded as one of the best in the city, making the trip to Roxborough in Northwest
Philadelphia well worth it. With steaks this
filling, side dishes won't be necessary, but fries
(mmm, cheese fries) or onion rings are a good
addition if you've got a big appetite. Have a beer
with your cheesesteak at the bar or in the back
booths, or grab a six-pack to go. Just across the

street, you'll see **Dalessandro's** (600 Wendover St. at Henry Ave., 215/428-5407), another local favorite. Like the Pat's-and-Geno's rivalry in South Philly, locals have their favorite on this Roxborough corner. I prefer Chubby's.

JOHN'S ROAST PORK $

14 E. Snyder Ave., 215/463-1951,
www.johnsroastpork.com
HOURS: Mon.-Fri. 6:45 A.M.-3 P.M.

Pat's and Geno's get all the publicity, followed by Jim's, but ask a real Philly eater who serves the best sandwich in town and your answer very well may be John's. On the same South Philadelphia corner since 1930, John's is a no-frills joint, with little more than a counter and an outdoor table for accommodations. The cheesesteaks—greasy, oozing cheese on perfect rolls—are simply delicious. The roast pork sandwiches, it should go without saying, are also exceptional. John's closes by midafternoon, so get there early if you want to taste some of the best sandwiches in Philadelphia.

NEW AMERICAN
VALLEY GREEN INN $$$

Valley Green Rd. at Wissahickon, 215/247-1730,
www.valleygreeninn.com
HOURS: Mon.-Thurs. noon-4 P.M. and 5-9 P.M.,
Fri. noon-4 P.M. and 5-10 P.M., Sat. 11 A.M.-4 P.M. and
5-10 P.M., Sun. 10 A.M.-3 P.M. and 5-9 P.M.

While Fairmount Park is most popular for hiking, biking, or visiting historic homes, there is one more reason to go—a totally unique dining experience in the middle of Wissahickon Park. The elegant Valley Green Inn draws crowds as a destination in itself. Built in 1850, the building once served as the Valley Green Hotel but has since been converted

into a restaurant. The menu changes seasonally with classic offerings like New Zealand rack of lamb alongside modern dishes like lobster spring rolls. Sunday brunch is popular, and the perfect time to take in the idyllic setting along the creek surrounded by towering trees. With no other houses in sight, you'll feel like you're visiting a remote colonial-era farmhouse. The interior matches the feel, with period furnishings and unfinished hardwood floors. Additional seating on the wooden front porch is some of the best alfresco dining around when the weather is nice.

PIZZA
⟨ Tacconelli's Pizzeria $

2604 E. Somerset St., 215/425-4983,
www.tacconellispizzeria.com
HOURS: Wed.-Thurs. 4:30-9:30 P.M., Fri.-Sat. 4-10 P.M.,
Sun. 4-9 P.M.

Giovanni Tacconelli came to Philly in 1918 and with the help of some friends built a massive 20-square-foot brick oven. For many years, he used it just for baking bread, until the 1940s when he started using it to make pizza. Now, five generations later, Tacconelli's ultra-thin-crust pies—still baked in that same hand-crafted oven—remain a Philly tradition. People travel from all over the city and beyond to the Port Richmond neighborhood, which is not by any stretch a typical stop on the tourist or even local dining circuit. The cash-only BYOB offers a variety of toppings, and in addition to the excellent tomato sauce, white pizza is a popular choice. You have to call a day ahead to reserve your dough; if you show up unannounced, you could wait over an hour and they may run out. Grab a seat near the oven and watch the expert pizza makers whip out pizzas almost as quickly as you can eat them.

NIGHTLIFE

Nightlife in Philly spans the cheesy, swank, hip, and divey, along with everything in between. And while there is no shortage of upscale martini spots and velvet-lined lounges, Philly is by and large a casual city, where many locals can be found hanging out at the corner bar on an average night. Neighborhood bars can reveal much about local culture, and usually won't cost you more than $3 for a Yuengling lager or a beer from Philadelphia Brewing Co., the local brews of choice. Gamers can find heated karaoke competitions, team trivia games (known locally as Quizzo), or pool tournaments throughout the city. And there is plenty of high-quality bar food, so when deciding where to eat dinner, bars should be considered, especially since the smoking ban in bars passed in 2007.

Though there are countless exceptions, the busiest nightlife scenes can loosely be classified by area. Trendy Old City bars and clubs tend to cater to a young, decked-out, bar-hopping crowd, including many youngsters from New Jersey looking for a night on the town and perhaps a hookup. The somewhat more sophisticated lounges and bars around Rittenhouse are hopping for happy hour since this is also where most of the skyscrapers are located, but the area gets a bit quieter late-night. South Street has a mix but generally a grungier feel, with pool tables and pitchers of beer. Northern Liberties has been known as the hip, artsy part of town, but has fast become the destination of choice for youngsters of all types for its great concentration of bars, clubs, and concert venues. East Passyunk Avenue in South Philly is also

HIGHLIGHTS

LOOK FOR ◖ TO FIND RECOMMENDED NIGHTLIFE.

◖ **Best Dive Bar:** More than just a dive bar, **Bob & Barbara's** is a local institution. The $3 special – a shot of whiskey and a can of PBR – can't be beat, and unique weekly events attract a diverse clientele (page 116).

◖ **Best Quizzo Game:** In a city where competitive bar sports are all the rage, there is no shortage of intense Quizzo (team trivia) games. **Fergie's** – with big prizes and fierce competition – is the best (page 117).

◖ **Best Bar to Catch a Live Show:** More than just a bar serving great food and craft beer, **Johnny Brenda's** offers an intimate 2nd-floor performance space that is acoustically superb (page 119).

◖ **Best Bar Burger:** Philly's own Iron Chef, Jose Garces, serves up perfect juicy Angus burgers along with more than 80 varieties of whiskey at **Village Whiskey** (page 123).

◖ **Best Karaoke:** A Chinatown gem, **Yakitori Boy** has public and private karaoke rooms where you can croon the night away while sipping Sapporo and snacking on sushi (page 123).

◖ **Best Dance Club, Beer Garden, and Diner in One:** One of the best dance clubs in Northern Liberties, **Silk City** is also home to an adjoining upscale diner and an outdoor beer garden (page 125).

◖ **Best Gay Nightlife: Woody's,** the center of gay nightlife in Philly for nearly 30 years, boasts a variety of spaces and themed nights (page xx). The alley behind it is home to **Sisters,** the only club in town specifically devoted to lesbians, complete with a lively upstairs dance floor (page 126).

◖ **Best Place to Drink Like a Mobster:** The delicious, strong drinks at **Franklin Mortgage & Investment Co.** don't come cheap, but you'll feel like Al Capone at this hidden speakeasy that pays homage to the Prohibition era (page 131).

◖ **Best Wine Bar:** The food, microbrews, and, of course, the wine are spectacular at **Tria.** With two Center City locations, you're never far from delicious cheese and a perfect Cab (page 132).

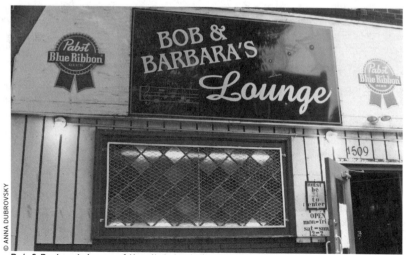

© ANNA DUBROVSKY

Bob & Barbara's is one of the city's best dive bars.

NIGHTLIFE

increasingly popular as a nightlife destination for locals and anyone else in the know.

Fans of live music will be happy to know that every major and minor act comes through Philly, and on any given night—especially on weekends—you can find national headliners, up-and-comers, and open-mike stages in diverse venues across the city. From intimate clubs to hipster bars to acoustically superb stages, Philly has the perfect stage for every act.

Most bars and clubs in Philly close at 2 A.M. sharp, and most don't have a dress code. That said, there is always a major concert, DJ, or late-night party happening somewhere around town; just ask a friendly local, or check out the weekly papers, *PW* and *City Paper,* for extensive listings of nightlife events as well as good happy hours about town. Happy hour specials abound across the city, usually 5–7 P.M. on weekdays but with some bars offering late-night or early afternoon specials as well.

And last, in 2010, after years of debate, Philadelphia opened its first-ever full-scale casino in Fishtown. Just a short drive (or shuttle bus ride) from Center City, now gamblers can get their fix at Sugarhouse Casino.

Bars

THE BARS

2013 Walnut St., 215/569-9585
HOURS: Daily 10 A.M.–2 A.M.
COST: No cover
Map 3

In a sea of Irish pub imposters, The Bards is the real thing. Any Guinness aficionado (except for the ones who swear by The Plough and the Stars in Old City) will tell you that this is the best place in Philly to grab a pint of the dark stuff. Outfitted in an Irish literary theme, The Bards is a good place to read or write while you sip a pint and feast on fish-and-chips on a quiet afternoon in the middle of the week. Weekend nights, including live traditional Irish music on Sunday evenings, and Quizzo nights (Thurs. 10 P.M.) tend to get a bit rowdier. Sometimes The Bards even turns a little more Greek than Irish when the Penn frat boys cross the river to play darts and blast Bon Jovi and Journey on the electronic jukebox.

BOB & BARBARA'S

1509 South St., 215/545-4511
HOURS: Mon.-Fri. 3 P.M.–2 A.M., Sat.-Sun. noon-2 A.M.
COST: No cover
Map 3

While others try so hard, B & B's is simply cool without having to try. The Crowd Pleasers, a distinguished jazz band of mature men decked in tuxes, plays on weekends, so despite the dirt-cheap prices and dirty floors, the place has an air of class. The relaxed vibe and varied events draw a diverse crowd. Order the "special," a shot of whiskey and a can of Pabst Blue Ribbon for the irresistible price of $3; even if you think you don't like PBR, you'll find yourself craving one after a few minutes surrounded by wall-to-wall vintage posters advertising it. On any given night you'll find a diverse crowd there for various events, including Ping Pong and bingo tournaments, a drag show, and even a competitive drunken spelling bee (I once came in second to a guy who had "Born to Spell" tattooed on the inside of his lip.) Stop at **Tritone** (1508 South St., www.tritonebar.com) across the street for more good vibes, decent bar food, a live music stage, and the same irresistible "special." Cash only.

CAVANAUGH'S

119 S. 39th St., 215/386-4889,
www.cavanaughsrestaurant.com
HOURS: Daily 11 A.M.–2 A.M.
COST: No cover
Map 6

Cavanaugh's is University City's premier sports bar. Hosting a rowdy crowd for professional and college games—especially when the Eagles or one of the "Big 5" local college basketball games

ORDER A LAGER

Yuengling lager, that is. In Philly – in most of Pennsylvania, in fact – lager is synonymous with the Yuengling brand. The first Yuengling beer was brewed in 1829 in Pottsville, Pennsylvania, making the brewery America's oldest. While the brewery makes other beers, including a porter, the traditional golden lager is the most popular. Considered better than other domestic brews at about the same price, it is many locals' drink of choice. So if you want to fit in, sidle up to the bar and order a "lager." The minute you say "Yuengling lager," it's obvious you're not from around here.

are on—it is a good place to be part of the action if you're into that scene. Food and drink specials abound, catering to the light-walleted college crowd. The local favorite, College Night, draws coeds by the masses for 75-cent drinks and free pizza. Although at Cavanaugh's, every night is really college night.

DEVIL'S DEN

1148 S. 11th St., 215/339-0855,
www.devilsdenphilly.com
HOURS: Daily 11 A.M.-2 A.M.
COST: No cover
Map 5

This cozy gastropub has an insanely long list of draft and bottle beers to choose from— I mean like, insane. You'll find pretty much any domestic or imported beer your heart desires; try a generously portioned flight of four if you can't choose just one. You'll find offerings like oysters and mussels in a variety of sauces, alongside standard bar fare like burgers and pulled pork sandwiches. Lots of wood, low lighting, and a fireplace make for a pleasant atmosphere. While weekends get busy, this is still a place where you can enjoy conversation without shouting across the table. Stop for beers, brunch, snacks or a full dinner. Happy hour (Mon.–Fri. 5–7 P.M.) offers half-priced drafts and tapas.

DIRTY FRANK'S

347 S. 13th St., 215/732-5010,
www.myspace.com/dirtyfranksbar
HOURS: Daily 11 A.M.-2 A.M.
COST: No cover
Map 2

Dirty Frank's is a total and complete dive, not one of those pseudo-dives that is hip and dive-y in an intentional way, but a real, true dive. The bartenders are aloof; the beer is cheap, and the crowd is very, very down-to-earth. The booths are torn; the walls are covered in graffiti; and the bathrooms—well, just avoid them if you can. But if you're looking for a place to sit in a booth and kick a few back without going broke, this is a perfectly good place to do so. The only touch of class is the mural, courtesy of the Mural Arts Program, on the outside of the building, consisting of famous Franks, including Frankie Avalon, Aretha Franklin, Franklin Delano Roosevelt, Frank Zappa, Frankenstein, St. Francis of Assisi, and Frank Sinatra.

EULOGY BELGIAN TAVERN

136 Chestnut St., 215/413-1918, www.eulogybar.com
HOURS: Mon.-Wed. 5 P.M.-2 A.M.,
Thurs.-Sun. 11 A.M.-2 A.M.
COST: No cover
Map 1

Just three blocks from Independence Hall, this two-story row-house bar immediately feels like home. But with over 300 international and domestic craft-brewed bottled beers and over 20 on draft, it's just that much better than your fridge full of Bud. Try a pint of Eulogy's Busty Blonde, brewed in Belgium exclusively for Eulogy, and don't miss the highlight of the stellar pub fare, the Belgian *frietjes* served with a delicious dipping sauce. In typical Old City form, it's packed on weekend nights, and getting a seat can be very difficult.

◖ FERGIE'S

1214 Sansom St., 215/928-8118, www.fergies.com
HOURS: Mon.-Sat. 11 A.M.-2 A.M., Sun. 5 P.M.-2 A.M.
COST: No cover
Map 2

Fergie's Irish bar has the attitude of a

NIGHTLIFE

NIGHTLIFE

© CHRISTOPHER WOODS

Fergie's Pub serves great burgers.

neighborhood dive bar with zero pretentiousness, even though it's in the heart of Center City and offers a much nicer setting and far better food and beer. You'll find entertainment and events on most nights, including live music and the popular Open Mike Night (Mon. at 9 P.M.) which draws a regular, talented crowd. But the busiest nights of all are often Tuesday and Thursday, when you can go upstairs to play or watch the most competitive Quizzo game in the city. Regulars come early to reserve their favorite tables; come by at least 8 P.M. for the 9 P.M. game and bring your smartest friends. It's free to play and first-place winner gets a $50 credit off the bill, and $25 off the tab for second place.

GIGI

319 Market St., 215/574-8880, www.gigiphilly.com
HOURS: Daily 10 A.M.–2 A.M.
COST: No cover
Map 1

Gigi has a large outdoor patio and sidewalk seating, and with its proximity to the major

attractions of Old City, it makes a great stop for a snack or drinks in the middle of a long, hard day of sightseeing. The menu offers a variety of tasty small plates with international influences, and the bar offers plenty of beer, wine, sangria, and an extensive list of signature cocktails. On weekdays 5–7 P.M., those normally $10–15 cocktails are half priced, along with $5 tapas and wine, $4 imported beers and well drinks, and $3 bottles of beer.

GOOD DOG

224 S. 15th St., 215/985-9600, www.gooddogbar.com
HOURS: Daily 11:30 A.M.–2 A.M.
COST: No cover
Map 3

This unassuming bar in the heart of Center City has the feel of a casual neighborhood spot. Featuring a canine-themed decor, it's popular with locals for its great food, great location, and great vibe, and is sometimes short on seating. If you can't score a booth downstairs or a table upstairs during high-traffic times, pull up a seat at the bar and order one of the many regionally brewed beers on draft, or head up to the 3rd floor for standing room only. Many people come for the Good Dog signature burger stuffed with Roquefort cheese (voted one of the best burgers in Philly by the premier local food critic) and a side of mixed traditional and sweet potato fries. Food is served until 1 A.M.

GRACE TAVERN

2229 Grays Ferry Ave., 215/893-9580,
www.gracetavern.com
HOURS: Daily 11:30 A.M.–2 A.M.
COST: No cover
Map 3

This small, unassuming bar on the edge of Center City South was one of the neighborhood's best-kept secrets until one of the major weekly papers, *PW,* named it the #1 bar in Philadelphia. Soon, bar-goers from across the city were coming out to enjoy what neighbors have known all along. Pressed tin ceiling and walls and an elegant old-fashioned mirrored bar bring a touch of class to this chill neighborhood spot. The menu is small but mighty, offering a variety of burgers that come with your choice of delicious fries or (almost) equally delicious spicy green beans, along with a few salads, sandwiches, and jambalaya.

C JOHNNY BRENDA'S

1201 N. Frankford Ave., 215/739-9684,
www.johnnybrendas.com
HOURS: Daily 11 A.M.–2 A.M.
COST: Bar and restaurant no cover; stage and dance areas cover varies by event
Map 7

Charmingly rustic, this Fishtown staple serves surprisingly excellent seafood, including oysters on the half shell and exclusively local craft beer. But it's most notable for the intimate 2nd-floor concert venue that was handcrafted from a converted flophouse. The performance space boasts spectacular sound quality and a bar and balcony worthy of a much larger arena. The venue hosts local and international bands and even the occasional private party, which—thanks to its size and setting—is essentially what every concert at Johnny Brenda's feels like.

KHYBER PASS PUB

56 S. 2nd St., 215/238-5888, www.khyberpasspub.com
HOURS: Daily 11 A.M.–2 A.M.
COST: No cover
Map 1

The owners of the South Philly favorite Royal Tavern bought this formerly down-and-dirty bar/live music venue in early 2011. The main bar area is still a great place to grab a quick beer, but the live stage area has been transformed into a dining room. The tasty menu features bar food with a southern flair, including a good dose of barbecue and a variety of daily specials. In a sea of trendier Old City offerings that draw people for the scene, the Khyber Pass promises good food and a solid beer menu in a chill setting.

KUNG FU NECKTIE

1248 N. Front St., 215/291-4919,
www.kungfunecktie.com
HOURS: Daily 5 P.M.–2 A.M.
COST: Varies
Map 7

Under the elevated train, on a blank strip of Front Street, sits this cool kid clubhouse. The former dump was artfully salvaged, with an interior

NIGHTLIFE

© G. WIDMAN FOR GPTMC

Johnny Brenda's is a popular Fishtown bar, restaurant, and live music venue.

that's as eccentric as the name would imply. The classic mahogany back bar is adorned with kooky knickknacks, and the old-fashioned jukebox is loaded with punk rock records. The bar has a small stage outfitted with a top-notch sound system and hosts a variety of acts, from bands to comedy shows and DJ nights, almost every night of the week. Check the website for the calendar.

LAS VEGAS LOUNGE

704 Chestnut St., 215/592-9533,
www.lasvegaslounge.com
HOURS: Mon.-Sat. 11 A.M.-2 A.M., Sun. 4 P.M.-2 A.M.
COST: No cover
Map 1

Despite its fancy name and worn-out red pleather booths, the Las Vegas Lounge is definitely more of a cheap neighborhood bar than a chic lounge. Those wanting to get away from the trendier Old City spots can venture a few blocks west to this local hangout. Nightly drink specials offer reduced prices on the already cheap drinks. The large space has plenty of seating, pool tables, and a Ms. Pac-Man game. Food consists mostly of typical greasy bar apps and sandwiches, which goes down nicely with that 20-ounce draft beer that is the norm for most patrons at LVL, as it's affectionately termed.

McGLINCHEY'S

259 S. 15th St., 215/735-1259
HOURS: Mon.-Sat. 10:30 A.M.-2 A.M., Sun.
11:30 A.M.-2 A.M.
COST: No cover
Map 3

Somewhat of an urban enigma, this quintessential dive bar is in the heart of the Center City action. Waitresses are charmingly informal and prices are dirt cheap, especially for pitchers of domestic draft classics like Yuengling, Yards, and Rolling Rock, with Guinness not much more. The bar is dark, dingy, and lined with booths. You can order a hot dog with all the fixin's, listen to the rock 'n' roll–packed jukebox, or play Ms. Pac-Man at an old-school sit-down-style game. It's one of the few places in town where you can still smoke, so be prepared to leave smelling like you did even if you don't.

NEW DECK TAVERN

3408 Sansom St., 215/386-4800,
www.newdecktavern.com
HOURS: Daily 11 A.M.-2 A.M.
COST: No cover
Map 6

Always bustling, New Deck Tavern is a worthwhile stop on the University City circuit even if you're not a college student. The Irish ivy-covered pub has been delighting not just students but the entire U City community for over two decades. Large portions of tasty bar food and a good selection of beer are served inside or outside on the patio. Quizzo, live acoustic music sessions, and karaoke are regular events.

NODDING HEAD BREWERY

1516 Sansom St., 2nd fl., 215/569-9525,
www.noddinghead.com
HOURS: Mon.-Sat. 11:30 A.M.-2 A.M., Sun. 11 A.M.-2 A.M.
COST: No cover
Map 3

A medal-winning microbrewery, Nodding Head provides the thirsty with eight of its own delicious beers along with a excellent selection of foreign brews. An English-style pub, it turns a bit rowdy during soccer games and heated Sunday-night Quizzo tournaments but at other times is a chill spot for dinner and conversation. An extensive bobble-head collection (get it—Nodding Head?) greets patrons at the entrance to the dark-wood bar area lined with wooden booths; a side room offers a quieter atmosphere. The menu offers far-flung variety with high-quality bar fare that is reasonably priced. The same burgers, fries, and mussels served at the popular nearby Monk's (of the same owners) can be enjoyed here with a much shorter wait.

PLOUGH AND THE STARS

123 Chestnut St., 215/733-0300, www.ploughstars.com
HOURS: Mon.-Fri. 11:30 A.M.-2 A.M.,
Sat.-Sun. 10:30 A.M.-2 A.M.
COST: No cover
Map 1

This high-ceilinged restaurant/bar has an elegant appearance with a casual vibe. By day, it's is a respectable place to grab a nice sit-down lunch on the main floor or on the balcony of the high-ceilinged space. By night, it lives up to its prime Old City location and hosts some of the loudest partying and excessive drinking in town. Though ostensibly Irish, the Plough's menu has a decidedly contemporary flair, with a seasonal menu and a fairly extensive wine and drinks list alongside the traditional shepherd's pie and fish-and-chips. Serving lunch, dinner, and weekend brunch, it also has a good bar menu available until midnight except on Saturdays. It is also home to what many claim to be the best pint of Guinness in the city. The traditional Irish music session on Sundays 5–9 P.M. welcomes all to bring an instrument and join in the fun.

PUB AND KITCHEN

1946 Lombard St., 215/545-0350,
http://thepubandkitchen.com
HOURS: Mon.-Fri. 4 P.M.-2 A.M., Sat.-Sun. 11 A.M.-4 P.M.
COST: No cover
Map 3

Just a few blocks from Rittenhouse Square sits one of the best gastropubs in town. Just be careful not to miss the cream-colored brick building on the corner of 20th and Lombard with a black pabbit (half pig/half rabbit) painted on the front; there is no sign outside, adding to the allure. While it's most definitely a bar, with its lively scene and a good showing for watching sporting events on the big-screen TVs behind the bar, to come and not try the food would be a real shame. The menu is small, but nothing on it disappoints, from staples like the Windsor burger and the pulled pork sandwich to more expensive but always delicious entrées that change seasonally and use only the freshest, usually local, ingredients. Save room for dessert; you won't regret it.

PUB ON PASSYUNK EAST (POPE)

1501 East Passyunk Ave., 215/755-5125,
www.pubonpassyunkeast.com
HOURS: Daily 11 A.M.-2 A.M.
COST: No cover
Map 5

Located in the heart of charming Passyunk

Square, the Pub on Passyunk East (P.O.P.E. for those in the know) is the quintessential corner bar, with dark lighting, stained glass, and an old-fashioned juke box. The crowd is an eclectic mix of old and young South Philadelphians and youngsters from all over the city who come for the great atmosphere. The food menu is basic (stick with simple items like chicken wings or pierogies), but the beer menu is extraordinary. Beer geeks will have a field day here, as fancy beers like Hitachino Nest from Japan are often priced below the norm.

RESURRECTION ALE HOUSE

2425 Grays Ferry Ave., 215/735-2202,
www.resurrectionalehouse.com
HOURS: Mon.-Fri. noon-2 A.M., Sat.-Sun. 11 A.M.-2 A.M.
COST: No cover
Map 3

On an up-and-coming stretch just south of Center City and across the South Street Bridge from University City, the split-level bar Resurrection Ale House brings life to this otherwise desolate corner. With a strong craft beer selection, good lunch, dinner, and weekend brunch menus, and friendly owners and servers, it has fast become a neighborhood staple. Their fried chicken was named one of the 10 best in the country by Bon Appetit magazine; twice fried with a spiced honey drizzle—you can't go wrong.

ROYAL TAVERN

937 E. Passyunk Ave., 215/389-6694,
www.royaltavern.com
HOURS: Mon.-Fri. 11:30 A.M.-2 A.M.,
Sat.-Sun. 10 A.M.-2 A.M.
COST: No cover
Map 5

A gorgeous antique wooden bar is the centerpiece of this great neighborhood bar in the Bella Vista neighborhood just a few blocks from the Italian Market. The converted row home is usually filled with regulars chatting and drinking at the bar or dining at small tables. There is a solid beer selection as well as tasty, reasonably priced salads, sandwiches, and entrées. While some people come just to drink, the majority come to eat as well.

NIGHTLIFE

SIDECAR BAR & GRILLE

2201 Christian St., 215/732-3429,
www.thesidecarbar.com

HOURS: Mon.-Fri. 3 P.M.-2 A.M.,
Sat.-Sun. 10:30 A.M.-2 A.M.

COST: No cover

Map 3

Sidecar is a mecca of good food, drink, and fun in an otherwise mostly residential neighborhood. Partly for that reason, but also because it is a really great bar with good vibes, excellent food, and a well-chosen beer list, it is always busy. It's small, but when the weather is nice, the outdoor tables on two sides nearby double the available seating. Specials throughout the week include weekday happy hour (4–7 P.M.) with excellent prices on some of the appetizers and discounts on beer and drinks. The kitchen is open until 1:30 A.M. every night, which is unusual in a town where it's hard to come by anything other than cheesesteaks past 11 P.M.

SUGAR MOM'S

225 Church St., 215/925-8219,
www.myspace.com/sugarmoms

HOURS: Wed.-Sat. noon-2 A.M.

COST: No cover

Map 1

Affordable bars are much harder to come by in swanky Old City than in the rest of the city, but Sugar Mom's fits the bill. Offering dirt-cheap drinks, pool tables, and debauchery, the basement space is filled with a casual crowd as well as a few of the fancier Old City bar-hoppers who've spent all their money at nearby establishments and need one last nightcap. A few retired bumper cars on the floor provide additional seating for the drunken masses. Typical fried bar fare and pitchers of beer are served, and there are often some ridiculously cheap specials on any given night.

TATTOOED MOM

530 South St., 215/238-9880

HOURS: Daily noon-2 A.M.

COST: No cover

Map 5

This South Street gem's cheap prices and casual,

wall art on the second floor of
Tattooed Mom

grungy atmosphere make it a popular hangout. The 1st floor is painted an odd shade of green, and has strange sculptures perched just outside its windows, but it could be considered upscale compared to what you'll see when you venture up the stairs. The funky second floor walls are covered in graffiti from floor to ceiling, and two pool tables occupy the entire front room. Farther back is a bar and still farther is a room with a variety of seating, including a few bumper cars. Standard pub fare—poppers and mozzarella sticks—is available on both floors.

TEN STONE

2063 South St., 215/735-9939, www.tenstone.com

HOURS: Mon.-Sat. 11:30 A.M.-2 A.M., Sun. 10 A.M.-2 A.M.

COST: No cover

Map 3

Just on the edge of Center City, Ten Stone is a popular spot in this rapidly growing stretch of South Street, with both neighbors and students from University City just across the South Street Bridge. Wooden booths line the warm orange walls and a full wooden bar sits at the center of the main room. It's a bit on the pricey side for a neighborhood hangout, but that doesn't seem to stop it from filling up. A side room offers a pool table and darts game, and the outside tables are popular when the weather is nice.

VILLAGE WHISKEY

118 S. 20th St., 215/665-1088, www.villagewhiskey.com
HOURS: Sun.-Mon. 11:30 A.M.-11 P.M., Tues.-Thurs. 11:30 A.M.-midnight, Fri.-Sat. 11:30 A.M.-1 A.M.
COST: No cover
Map 3

Take Philly's top chef and America's latest Iron Chef Jose Garces, a tiny space, no reservations accepted, and what many consider the best burgers in the city, and you'll understand why there is always a wait at Village Whiskey. The only Garces spot that is more bar than restaurant, and that does not specialize in Latin cuisine, this is based around one of his other loves—whiskey. When you finally get a table, choose from more than 80 different whiskeys served neat or on the rocks or one of the delicious cocktails. Reminiscent of a classic American speakeasy, the food menu is small, but there's no reason to consider anything other than a perfect, juicy Angus burger with your choice of toppings like Roquefort cheese, caramelized onions, a fried egg, or truffled mushrooms, all extra—meaning that $11 burger may cost $20 when you're done with it. The ultimate is the Whiskey King burger ($24), served with blue cheese, applewood-smoked bacon, and a heaping portion of foie gras. And if you're going that far, don't forget to order the duck fat fries with that. Yum.

YAKITORI BOY

211 N. 11th St., 215/923-8088,
www.yakitoriboy-japas.com
HOURS: Daily 5 p.m.-2 a.m.
COST: No cover
Map 2

In the scattered abyss of karaoke nights around the city, you can count on Yakitori Boy as a place to work out those pipes publicly seven days a week. In the heart of Chinatown, the sleek Japanese restaurant and sushi bar is

NIGHTLIFE

© JULIA GAVIN

Yakitori Boy has private and public karaoke rooms, along with Japanese food and a full bar.

popular for dinner, a snack, or drinks, but karaoke is the major draw. For the exhibitionist, there is a large communal room where you'll have to wait your turn, and for the shyer singer or perhaps the microphone hog there are private rooms of varying sizes that can be rented by the hour. Channel your favorite rock star as you belt out tunes in the soundproof booth while efficient servers appear at the push of a button, serving up Sapporo, sushi, champagne, or whatever your heart desires. It's almost too good to be true, at least until the bill comes; you'll be having so much fun crooning, it's easy to rack up a high tab here.

Dance Clubs

THE BARBARY

951 Frankford Ave., 215/634-7400,
http://thebrbry.blogspot.com
HOURS: Daily 9 P.M.-2 A.M.
COST: Varies by event
Map 7

The Barbary is a nonstop party seven days a week. Like a hipster church, complete with cathartic spasms and speaking in tongues, this is either your idea of heaven or hell. At once divey and cozy, often sweaty and sticky, the club hosts varied weekly and monthly DJ dance parties, from indie rock to hip-hop to '80s, karaoke on Sundays, and occasional live acts. The Barbary has one of the best photo booths in the city and some of the worst bathrooms. You can periodically escape the heat from the dance floor upstairs at Barbarella, which has a relaxed pub atmosphere and serves inexpensive comfort food like mac-and-cheese balls, in case you're starting to feel a little too tipsy.

FLUID

613 S. 4th St., 215/629-3686, www.fluidnightclub.com
HOURS: Vary, usually 9 P.M.-2 A.M., closed Tues.
COST: Varies by event, usually $3-10, only after 10 or 11 P.M.
Map 5

Since it opened in 1997, Fluid has become a staple of the underground music scene. Its diverse DJ lineup includes electronica, funk, house, soul, trip-hop, trance, progressive, drum and bass, jungle, break beat, hip-hop, rock, punk, and everything in between. Regular DJs include Philadelphia's own ?uestlove of the Roots, along with many other top national and international guests. The cave-like 2nd-floor space is dark enough to get lost in anonymous dancing for hours, but just light enough to check out the other fine dancers. Coming early can often avoid a cover charge, and there are often drink specials offered before midnight.

L'ETAGE

624 S. 6th St., 215/592-0656,
www.creperie-beaumonde.com
HOURS: Tues.-Thurs. and Sun. 7:30 P.M.-1 A.M., Fri.-Sat. 7 P.M.-2 A.M.
COST: Varies by event, Fri.-Sat. $5 after 10 P.M.
Map 5

Just off South Street above the delicious crêperie Beau Monde lies a decadent little dance club that regularly packs the house. The French-themed lounge has a beautiful dark-wood bar, comfy leather banquettes, and a cozy dance floor that gets packed on weekends. Nightly entertainment includes everything from DJs to cabarets and story slams to movies. Check the website to see the calendar. On weekend nights, you can rely on danceable tunes and a full house; come before 10 P.M. to avoid the $5 cover.

700 CLUB

700 N. 2nd St., 215/413-3181, www.the700.org
HOURS: Daily 3:30 P.M.-2 A.M.
COST: No cover
Map 7

On other days, the 700 Club is just a neighborhood hangout, but on Thursday–Saturday nights after 10 P.M., the 2nd floor becomes a sweaty free-for-all as the DJ spins hip-hop, indie rock, and '80s for the mostly 20-something crowd. It looks and feels like Grandma's house—complete with old, musty furniture and a pseudo-kitchenette as a bar, but the lights are low enough to hide the stains on the upholstery and to encourage you to dance like no one is watching. The 700 Club takes you back to the days of high school parties when your parents were out of town and drinking was an exhilarating, illicit event. Best of all, there is never a cover and drinks are reasonably priced. This is also a great place to catch local and international soccer games on the telly.

SHAMPOO

417 N. 8th St., 215/922-7500,
www.shampoonline.com
HOURS: Wed.-Sun. 9 P.M.-2 A.M.
COST: Varies
Map 7

One of the last behemoth clubs in the Philly scene, Shampoo has succeeded by being many things to many different people, depending on the night. The cavernous warehouse features a multitude of rooms of various sizes, so hip-hop heads, reggaeton rovers, pop lovers, and dance drones can peacefully coexist. Check the website to see what is going on any particular night—from goth nights to gay nights—and note that the dress code is "club fashionable"— whatever that means.

◖ SILK CITY

435 Spring Garden St., 215/592-8838,
www.silkcityphilly.com
HOURS: Bar and diner daily 4 P.M.-2 A.M., lounge usually 10 P.M.-2 A.M.
COST: Varies, usually $3-7 for club, no cover for diner
Map 7

Part diner and part dance club, Silk City is your one-stop shop for Saturday night. Formerly a truck stop called DeeDee's Diner, a hole-in-the-wall serving cheap booze and beer out of questionable taps, Silk City is now one of the most popular party spots in the city. One side is

NIGHTLIFE

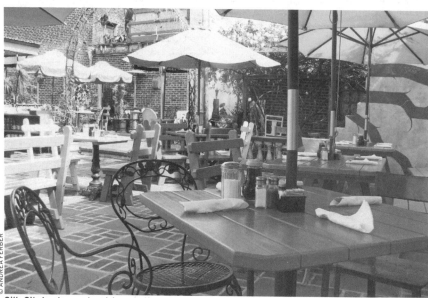

© ANDREA FERBER

Silk City's pleasant outdoor patio

a snazzy diner and bar serving gussied-up food that goes beyond standard diner fare. The adjoining club/lounge hosts popular DJs and live acts, and a Saturday night dance party is always packed. The outdoor beer garden is a lovely place to knock a few back on a nice summer night.

Gay and Lesbian

Many claim that the gay scene in Philly is third only to New York and San Fran and perhaps ties with Chicago in its offerings. Best of all, they are all within a few blocks of each other in Washington Square West (the "Gayborhood") in the heart of Center City, so head out that way and you will quickly find more in addition to those listed here.

THE BIKE STOP

206 S. Quince St., 215/627-1662, www.thebikestop.com
HOURS: Mon.-Fri. 4 P.M.-2 A.M., Sat.-Sun. 2 P.M.-2 A.M.
COST: No cover
Map 2

Philly's leather bar for nearly three decades is a chill neighborhood watering hole where you can gather with friends and enjoy cheap pitchers—and the occasional spanking. Depending on the night, patrons might see sitcom reruns on the flat-panel TVs or watch a leather-clad man getting whipped on stage; it's the luck of the draw. The little-used 3rd floor offers a small dance floor, but it's the downstairs Pit Stop room (Wed., Fri., and Sat. 10 P.M.-2 A.M.) that draws a crowd for its underwear-only Wednesdays and cruise-y weekend nights. Beer and alcohol specials abound throughout the week.

Q LOUNGE

1234 Locust St., 215/732-1800, http://qphilly.com
HOURS: Tues.-Wed. 5 P.M.-midnight,
Thurs.-Sat. 5 P.M.-2 A.M., Sun. 11 A.M.-6 P.M.
COST: Usually no cover or $5 for a coupon to be used for a drink
Map 2

For those seeking a little luxe in their nightlife, Q offers a sumptuously appointed interior of leather couches, metal mesh drapery, and red tinted lamps. It draws a mixed crowd of gay men and lesbians, with some straights tossed in for color, who all enjoy its strong cocktails, creative appetizers and entrées, and upbeat music. Q is particularly well known for its "Werq" Wednesdays, starring New York drag queen Mimi Imfurst and music by local drag queen Salotta Tee.

◀ SISTERS

1320 Chancellor St., 215/735-0705,
www.sistersnightclub.com
HOURS: Tues.-Sat. 5 P.M.-2 A.M., Sun. noon-2 A.M.,
usually closed Mon.
COST: Varies but usually no cover Sun., Tues.,
and Wed., $5 or $10 Thurs., $6 Fri. and Sat.
Map 2

Sisters, Philadelphia's only dedicated lesbian bar, is tucked away in the alley behind Woody's. The bartenders know how to keep the liquor flowing on both floors of the large two-level space. Tables off the main bar offer a place to sit and chat, while the upstairs has a rowdier dance-club atmosphere. Thursday (9:30–11:30 P.M.) offers what is possibly Philadelphia's most economical invitation for public drunkenness, where a $10 cover gets you eight (yes, eight!) draft beer or well drink tickets, a buffet, karaoke, and dancing. While the wait for drinks can be long, and they are served in small plastic cups that you can knock back in a few sips, it is still an unbeatable deal. You can also spend $2 for bottled beer or $3 for top-shelf. Either way, and gay or straight, this is one of the most happening dance floors in the city on Thursday night. (Cover drops to $5 when the special ends at 11:30 P.M.)

TAVERN ON CAMAC
243 S. Camac St., 215/545-0900,
www.tavernoncamac.com
HOURS: 4 P.M.-2 A.M.
COST: No cover
Map 2

Tavern on Camac is an "only in Philly" type of place. The popular historic tavern is an old-fashioned piano bar with nightly live entertainment. Meanwhile, head upstairs to **Ascend** for one of the city's best dance floors on weekends along with nightly entertainment during the week, including karaoke and game shows (daily 9 P.M.-2 A.M.). Patrons of all ages switch between high-energy house music and melodic show tunes several times throughout the night. If you're hungry, just head downstairs from the Tavern to the New American restaurant **Terra** (215/545-1102, www.terrapa.com). Eat, then relax with an after-dinner cocktail and piano tunes, and then dance the night away, all in one historic building on Camac Street.

UNCLES
1220 Locust St., 215/546-6660
HOURS: Daily 11 A.M.-2 A.M.
COST: No cover
Map 2

Despite the common perception, which can be partly attributed to its name, a good number of younger guys and even the rare girl frequent Uncles in additional to the more, ahem, mature gay men. The friendly neighborhood bar has a decent jukebox and welcoming bartenders, and the crowd typically includes businessmen, old friends, and the occasional college student. On warmer days, the large picture windows are open to the street for great people-watching. And if you happen to be a young, cute guy,

there are often a few "uncles" willing to buy you a few drinks.

VOYEUR
1221 St. James St., 215/735-5772,
www.voyeurnightclub.com
HOURS: Fri.-Sat. 9 P.M.-3:20 A.M., weeknights vary, call or check website
COST: Varies
Map 2

This is the only club in the Gayborhood that stays open after hours, so while the main floor is often sparsely populated for most of the night, it picks up around 2 A.M. for another hour and a half of dancing and debauchery (some of which purportedly happens in the bathroom stalls). It has a large mezzanine that offers amazing wraparound views of the main floor below, and the more intimate Pink Lounge is the place for karaoke, bingo, and Quizzo. The $2 "pink drinks" served nightly from 9 to 11 P.M. ensure that patrons are both exhausted and hungover the next day.

WOODY'S
202 S. 13th St., 215/545-1893, www.woodysbar.com
HOURS: Daily 11 A.M.-2 A.M.
COST: $10 Thurs.-Sat.
Map 2

Woody's is the epicenter of gay nightlife in Philadelphia. The huge venue has half a dozen bars spread out over two floors, an upstairs dance floor, and a restaurant on the street level. The decor is nothing to write home about—think early-'80s dive with flourishes of ski lodge—but the bartenders are friendly and they have a heavy hand with the booze. Monday is karaoke night, Wednesday is College Night (those over 18 can enter), Thursday offers Latin and top 40, and on weekends, you'll find wall-to-wall men on the prowl with a few women thrown in for good measure rocking out and making out to house and top 40.

NIGHTLIFE

Live Music

In addition to the venues listed, many of the bars in this chapter offer live music on select nights of the week.

ELECTRIC FACTORY

421 N. 7th St., 215/627-1332, www.electricfactory.info
HOURS: Vary by event
COST: Varies by event
`Map 7`

Founded in 1968 and housed in a converted electric factory, this archetypal Philly venue has two floors, each equipped with a full bar and seating area, ensuring ample visibility and elbow room from every section. With a performance roster ranging from mainstream radio's premier rock bands to the newest hip-hop crazes, the Factory has become a rite of passage for bands graduating from the smaller local venues and the fans willing to follow them.

FILLMORE AT THE TLA

334 South St., 215/922-1011, www.livenation.com
HOURS: Vary by event
COST: Varies by event
`Map 5`

Formerly the Theater of Living Arts, this South Street staple provides an intimate setting for performances by bands ranging from the independent to the infamous. Often an alternative-rock showcase, the venue has hosted many of today's most beloved indie darlings. Patrons can enjoy a great view from anywhere inside with two floors of space and plenty of room to dance. The newly renovated decor promises a trip down memory lane with walls adorned with vintage concert posters.

FIRST UNITARIAN CHURCH

2125 Chestnut St., 215/821-7575,
www.r5productions.com
HOURS: Vary by event
COST: Varies by event
`Map 3`

One of the flagship venues for R5 Productions, this Unitarian church has become a renowned house of a different kind of worship for the local punk rock scene. Many of independent rock music's best up-and-coming acts make their Philly debuts in the church's small basement. A small stage offers an intimate perspective that larger venues don't allow, while the loud acts and hyped attendees create an atmosphere worthy of a much larger arena. No alcohol is served, so this is always an all-ages venue.

NORTH STAR BAR

2639 Poplar St., 215/787-0488,
http://northstarbar.com
HOURS: Daily 5 P.M.–2 A.M.
COST: Varies by event, no cover downstairs bar
`Map 4`

Just four long blocks from the Philadelphia Museum of Art, the North Star Bar offers a full bar menu and pool tables in the front area, but is cherished for its eclectic lineup of reasonably priced live shows several nights a week. It's nothing to look at from the outside, but the stage area offers great acoustics and a 2nd-story balcony that practically overhangs the stage. Catching a cab after the show can be tough at this somewhat isolated corner in the Fairmount neighborhood; ask the bartenders to call one for you.

ROTUNDA

4014 Walnut St., 215/573-3234, www.therotunda.org
HOURS: Vary
COST: Varies but most events free
`Map 6`

Straddling the fuzzy line where University City becomes the grittier part of West Philly, the Rotunda offers an excellent reason to cross over. An old church transformed into a community and artistic space now hosts live music and events, including rock, jazz, hip-hop, theater, spoken word, film, DJs, panels, art installations, flea markets, and much more. The alcohol- and smoke-free venue welcomes all ages and, best of all, most events are free. Audiences are diverse but tend towards the

PHILLY'S MUSIC ROOTS

Philly-born chart-toppers like Pink, Eve, and Will Smith are familiar names to anyone breathing, but Philadelphia's diverse musical history goes well beyond that. Classical composers like Alexander Reinagle, Rayner Taylor, and Susannah Haswell Rowson made their names in the 18th century, while the 19th century was given over to English opera, religious orchestrals, and gospel. In the 20th century, Philly was at the center of the national musical consciousness with vibrant jazz musicians like John Coltrane, Dizzy Gillespie, Eddie Lang, and Joe Venuti.

In the 1950s, Dick Clark took center stage with *American Bandstand,* drawing attention to local acts like Bobby Rydell and Frankie Avalon as well as the nascent phenomenon known as rock 'n' roll. The '60s and '70s were most notably marked by contributions of African American musicians, including girl groups like Brenda & the Tabulations, Barbara Mason,

Claudine Clarke, and the (Patti) LaBelle Sisters. As they fired up the charts, the production team of Gamble and Huff created "The Sound of Philadelphia." TSOP, for short, is a rich, funk-driven sound created with large ensembles of string and horn instruments – a break from the blues-oriented sound of earlier rhythm and blues. The TSOP studio, Philadelphia International Records, still stands at Broad and Spruce Streets.

More-recent Philly musicians include Boyz II Men, Lisa Lopes (the "crazy one" in TLC), Eve, Beanie Sigal, the Roots, Jill Scott, Jedi Mind Tricks, and Musiq Soulchild. Local DJ and producer Diplo is a star of the electronic music world, while Dieselboy is one of the most popular drum and bass producers in the world. The music scene today is as alive as it has ever been; there is a stage and an audience for everyone from the little guys to Beyoncé here in Philly.

eager undergrad and activist types. Many attendees enjoy drinks at one of the nearby bars before stumbling in for a free show.

STARLIGHT BALLROOM

460 N. 9th St., 215/769-1530
HOURS: Vary by event
COST: Varies by event
Map 7

A frequent host to R5 Productions' shows, the Starlight Ballroom has expanded beyond its dance-club roots to become a formidable live music venue. The dancehall layout makes for a perfect forum for smaller acts with loyal followings. There are tables, bars, and concessions available for patrons occasionally coming off the dance floor for air. As more bands and audiences discover it, the Ballroom could very well eclipse the neighboring Electric Factory as the area's premier concert spot.

TOWER THEATER

19 S. 69th St., Upper Darby, 610/352-2887,
www.tower-theatre.com

HOURS: Vary by event
COST: Varies by event
Map 9

Built a year before the Great Depression, the Tower retains its classic, lavish decor while hosting some of music's most prestigious modern-day acts. The seated venue consists of an orchestra, loge, and two balconies, making it one of the area's largest venues. The lineup of performers is even bigger, as the theater has evolved from its days as a vaudeville mainstay into the perfect forum for intimate acts as well as larger arena-worthy acts.

TROCADERO THEATRE

1003 Arch St., 215/922-6888, www.thetroc.com
HOURS: Vary by event
COST: Varies by event
Map 2

A landmark on the outskirts of Chinatown, this former burlesque theater is one of the city's busiest and most versatile venues. The main roster most frequently consists of up-and-coming punk rockers, metal enthusiasts, and the

THE BEST IN INDIE MUSIC: R5 PRODUCTIONS

Born in 1996, R5 is a local promotion company named for the SEPTA regional rail that connects the Main Line to Center City. Founded by Ardmore native Sean Agnew with the express purpose of bringing back quality indie rock to a city that was often skipped over by touring bands due to lack of suitable venues, the idea was to give audiences big shows in small spaces for a more intimate live music experience. With no alcohol served and generally low prices, the shows cater to all ages, but especially the younger set. R5 has hosted many of today's best names in indie music at a variety of small-but-mighty venues, including the staple, **The First Unitarian Church;** bars including the **Barbary** and **Johnny Brenda's;** and dance halls like **Starlight Ballroom.**

Agnew's baby has become synonymous with Philadelphia's independent music scene. Punk and indie crowds no longer need to travel to New York or D.C. to see their favorite acts play, nor do they have to pay double admission price to see old favorites play larger, overcrowded clubs and arenas. Likewise, bands can come to Philly and play to the whole audience and not just the people in the front row. And the fact that many of them come at all, as opposed to a decade ago, can be gratefully attributed to R5. Agnew's philosophy is "for the kids, by the kids," and no self-respecting music lover in Philly would have it any other way. Check out www.r5productions.com for lineup and venue information.

occasional indie-rock stalwart courtesy of R5 Productions, while the "Balcony Bar" on the 2nd floor provides the pre-gaming and after-parties with DJs and a smaller yet just as mighty stage. On Monday nights, the venue even doubles as a movie theater, showing both newish releases and cult classics to a packed house.

WORLD CAFÉ LIVE

3025 Walnut St., 215/222-1400,
www.worldcafelive.com
HOURS: Mon.-Fri. 11 A.M.-2 A.M., Sat.-Sun. 5 P.M.-2 A.M.
COST: Varies by event
Map 6

World Café Live represents another big step in making University City worth the trip across the river from Center City. Two truly lovely performance spaces, Upstairs Live and Downstairs Live, have been carved out of an old 40,000-square-foot Art Deco factory building, hosting independent, contemporary, and folk artists several nights a week. The venue's diverse performance lineup isn't the only draw; it also serves delicious food and drinks. Also housed in the building are the studios for WXPN, the noncommercial radio station whose nationally syndicated *World Café*

program gave the venue its name. Come for a show, a meal, or happy hour for discounted drinks and food, weeknights 5–7 P.M.

World Café Live in University City is a live music venue and home to radio station WXPN.

© KARRIE GAVIN

Lounges

BLEU MARTINI

24 S. 2nd St., 215/940-7900,
www.bleumartinionline.com
HOURS: Daily 4 P.M.-2 A.M.
COST: $10 Fri. and Sat. after 9 P.M., otherwise no cover
Map 1

One of several swanky (some might say cheesy) lounges in the heart of Old City, Bleu Martini specializes in—you guessed it—martinis, offering more than 30 different ones. You can have anything from the classic to a fruity, alcoholic dessert in a glass. The food menu is a fusion of Asian, American, and French cuisine, including elaborate sushi creations, and everything is pricey. There is music nightly, with a small dance floor that gets packed on weekends. A VIP lounge and waitress-only table service are available if you're willing to pay the steep price. Ladies, be prepared to be hit on—sometimes by men old enough to be your father. This strip is filled with this type of establishment, so if you're into this scene, or out for a bachelor/bachelorette party, get dressed to the nines and head out to 2nd Street in Old City.

FRANKLIN MORTGAGE & INVESTMENT CO.

112 S. 18th St., 267/467-3277, www.thefranklinbar.com
HOURS: Mon.-Sat. 5 P.M.-2 A.M., Sun. 7 P.M.-2 A.M.
COST: No cover
Map 3

Blink and you'll miss this clandestine but classy speakeasy. The doors to the basement barroom are pitch black and the subtle signage doesn't exactly scream "saloon," but once inside and finally seated you'll feel like a mobster. According to the bar's website, in the 1920s the Franklin Mortgage & Investment Co. served as the front for the largest alcohol ring in the country, an operation dwarfing even that of Al Capone. This swank, sexy space pays authentic homage to pre-Prohibition era barrooms with artful, delicious, strong cocktails. That delicious drink made with only the freshest ingredients will cost you about $14, but you're

not just paying for the drink; you're paying for the ambience. Only as many patrons as there are seats may enter at a time, so the bad news is there is often a long wait, especially on weekends, but the good news is you'll also never wait in line for the restroom, fight for the bartender's attention, or feel a sweaty guy breathing down your neck pressed up against the bar.

32°

16 S. 2nd St., 215/627-3132, www.32lounge.com
HOURS: Wed.-Sat. 9 P.M.-2 A.M.
COST: No cover
Map 1

This lounge (32 degrees when you say it aloud) is a lavish, trendy place where people come to see and be seen. The ultimate in nightlife excess, it features a dimly lit interior, bottles highlighted on elaborately lighted display cases, and liquor lockers for regulars. A well-coiffed waitstaff serves an impressive choice of imported and domestic liquors and a selection of interesting cocktails, and clubby, pulsating music, usually hip-hop, rocks the house. European-style bottle service is available for those with more money than they know what to do with, making this a popular spot with ballers and hip-hoppers in town. Close to the Ben Franklin and Walt Whitman Bridges, and just a few blocks from the PATCO train to Jersey, it is popular with New Jersey youngsters looking for a hot club scene.

WALNUT ROOM

1709 Walnut St., 2nd floor, 215/751-0201,
www.walnutroomredux.com
HOURS: Tues.-Sun. 9 P.M.-2 A.M.
COST: After 10 P.M. only, $5 Wed., $10 Fri.-Sat., no cover Tues. or Thurs.
Map 3

Walnut Room is a stylish, low-lit lounge with a sleek minimalist look compared to the neon and lights of many of the Old City clubs and lounges. It serves a diverse clientele, and you'll

ROLL OF THE DICE: SUGARHOUSE CASINO

Philadelphia's first and only casino opened in September 2010 after years of intense debate among neighbors, developers, and city officials. Before, gamblers went to the nearby suburb of Bensalem to Parx Casino and Racetrack or drove about an hour into New Jersey to Atlantic City. Now, card and slot junkies can get their fix right on the Delaware waterfront in the Fishtown neighborhood just a short drive from Center City. Only time will tell whether Sugarhouse is ultimately good or bad for the city. Most likely it will be good for some and very bad for others: good for the occasional visitor and bad for those who spend their paychecks here on a weekly basis, good for those employed here and perhaps not so good for neighbors.

But alas, Sugarhouse is here to stay, so if you're the gambling type, go check it out and see for yourself. It's a little out of the way but not far from Northern Liberties and easily accessible by car (with free parking), public transportation, or the Sugar Express, a free shuttle serving Center City, South Philly, and even Northeast Philly (check website for stops and times). The casino has about 1,600 slots, 40 table games, and several dining and drinking options, including the Refinery, serving bar food and drinks overlooking the water. While the shiny, new casino is a pleasant enough space, unlike Atlantic City (with its shows, shops, and restaurants), the only real reason to go is to gamble, so if that's your thing, by all means, hop on the Sugar Express and have a ball (1001 N. Delaware Ave., 877/477-3715, www.sugarhousecasino.com, open 24 hours, must be over 21 to enter).

find punks chatting with trendies while young professionals take shots with hip-hop ballers. They all come for the danceable music in this 2nd-floor space in the heart of Rittenhouse Row. The DJs and type of music vary by night (hip-hop is generally a good bet), so call or check the website to see what is on the agenda. Weekends are generally packed dance parties. The delicious cocktails can get pricey and the bottle service is a tad frivolous, but overall, Walnut Room is a good place for serious dancing in a small bar/lounge rather than a massive nightclub. And the late-night happy hour 9–11 P.M. each night offers $3 beer, $4 wine, and $5 cocktails and champagne. Downstairs and run by the same people, Alfa serves up food and cocktails in a more typical bar setting, popular with the happy hour crowd.

Wine Bars

◖ TRIA
123 S. 18th St., 215/972-8742, www.triacafe.com
HOURS: Daily noon–1 A.M.
COST: No cover
Map 3

The three stars at Tria are wine, cheese, and beer. Whether you prefer a bold Cabernet, a full-bodied Riesling, an earthy Raclette, or a buttery Nevat, the long wine list leaves nothing to be desired, but a selection of microbrewed beers from around the world offers an alternative if you prefer. Artisan cheeses, cured meats, bruschetta, salads, and sandwiches are offered, and while it's possible to order a relatively simple chicken sandwich, only food virgins should leave without sampling the numerous other sensuous delights. A cheese tasting, paired with exotic accompaniments, is an essential part of the experience. There is a second Tria in Center City East (Map 2, 1137 Spruce St., 215/629-9200), and as of 2010, University City has its own **Biba Wine Bar** (Map 6, 3131 Walnut St., 215/222-2422), by the same folks.

© JULIA GAVIN

Tria offers an excellent wine and craft beer selection to go with their delicious food.

VINTAGE

129 S. 13th St., 215/922-3095,
www.vintage-philadelphia.com

HOURS: Mon.-Thurs. 4 P.M.-2 A.M., Fri.-Sat. noon-2 A.M.

COST: No cover

Map 2

The wine menu changes regularly, but an excellent selection of at least 60 wines by the glass and around 20 by the bottle are available at this French bistro and wine bar. With most glasses $5–8 and some bottles in the $30 range, it's cheaper than you'd pay for a glass of lesser wine at most bars. An appealing atmosphere, large windows, and high ceilings attract wine and food lovers who come for a mix of classic and creative French dishes.

ARTS AND LEISURE

From world-class museums, theaters, and art galleries to practically every type of recreation imaginable, there are abundant arts and leisure opportunities in Philadelphia. While there is plenty to do throughout the year, the city kicks into turbo gear during spring and summer with a multitude of festivals and musical and cultural events, and this is the best time to take advantage of the city's wealth of outdoor recreation.

There are museums devoted to practically every slice of Philadelphia's rich history and diverse culture, from world-class art, science, and history museums to museums honoring different ethnic groups. The very latest is the National Museum of Jewish American History, which opened in 2010 in the heart of Independence Park. The Benjamin Franklin Parkway, dubbed the Museum District, is home to some of the biggest and best, including the Philadelphia Museum of Art, the Rodin Museum, Academy of Natural Sciences, and the Franklin Institute, soon to be joined by the Barnes Museum when it relocates from its suburban home to Center City (slated for 2012). The multitude of art galleries large and small range from traditional to cutting-edge, and ongoing events and open houses like First Fridays make them accessible to everyone.

The Avenue of the Arts, the section of Broad Street that extends south from City Hall, is home to most of the city's first-run theater and classical concert venues, from the grand old Academy of Music to the stunningly modern Kimmel Center. Additional concert venues are spread throughout the city, ranging from the

HIGHLIGHTS

LOOK FOR 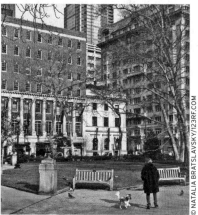 TO FIND RECOMMENDED ARTS AND ACTIVITIES.

◖ **Newest Major Museum:** The **National Museum of American Jewish History** opened its ultramodern doors in the heart of Independence Park in 2010. Celebrating 350 years of Jewish history in America, it is the largest museum of its kind in the world (page 140).

◖ **Most Interactive Museum:** The **Franklin Institute** science museum showcases the best scientific advancements in history. The interactive museum is a giant playground for adults and children alike (page 142).

◖ **Best Kids' Museum:** The hands-on exhibits at the sprawling **Please Touch Museum** are so much fun that kids won't realize they're learning. The museum has much more to offer than ever before since its 2008 move to Memorial Hall, a National Historic Landmark built for the 1876 World's Fair in Fairmount Park (page 143).

◖ **Best Concert Halls:** It's a tie. The **Academy of Music,** built in 1857, and the **Kimmel Center,** built in 2001, are Philly's most esteemed, world-class venues. The two superstars of the Avenue of the Arts represent the best of historic and modern architecture (page 147).

◖ **Best Art House Cinema:** Between the three Ritz movie houses run by **Landmark Theatres** in Old City, you can always find that foreign, indie, or artsy movie you've been dying to see. While you won't find stadium seating or the glitz of the mainstream theaters, each theater offers excellent titles in comfortable spaces with great concession stands (page 149).

◖ **Best Festival:** Usually held during the first two weeks of September, the **Philadelphia Live Arts Festival and Philly Fringe** presents cutting-edge theater, dance, music, and other events. There is no limit to the quantity and diversity of events, since the "fringe" element means any artist can self-produce and become part of the festivities. For a more mainstream option, **Wawa Welcome America Festival** offers a full 11 days of patriotic activities, including free concerts and fireworks in honor of

the July 4 holiday in the city where it all began (page 152).

◖ **Best City Park:** **Rittenhouse Square** is the crown jewel of the ritzy Rittenhouse neighborhood in Center City West. The beautifully landscaped park occupies a prime piece of real estate amid many of the best restaurants and shops in the city, making it a favorite resting place for locals and visitors alike (page 155).

◖ **Best Walking, Jogging, and Biking Trail:** The **Schuylkill River Trail** winds around both sides of the river. The easily accessible and popular 8.4-mile paved stretch known as "the loop" extends out behind the Art Museum. Those wanting a longer ride can continue all the way to Valley Forge and beyond (page 157).

◖ **Best Place to Get Away from it All:** In the northwest section of the city, **Wissahickon Park** offers 1,800 acres of towering trees and scenic trails. It's easy to get lost in the woods and completely forget you're in the city (page 157).

◖ **Best Bowling Alley:** If you've never thought of bowling as particularly hip, then you've never been to **North Bowl.** This popular Northern Liberties spot offers a late-night lounge along with two levels of lanes (page 160).

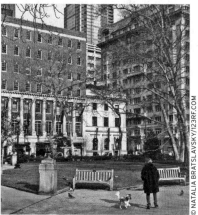

Rittenhouse Square

ARTS AND LEISURE

Fairmount Park is the largest urban municipal park system in the world.

huge Wells Fargo Center, hosting the top national acts, to casual, open-air stadiums like the Mann Center for the Performing Arts in Fairmount Park.

Outdoors types will be thrilled to discover that Philadelphia is home to Fairmount Park, the largest urban municipal park system in the world, offering endless recreational opportunities, hundreds of miles of hiking, biking, and jogging trails, and water sports. In fact, gardens, arboretums, dog parks, playgrounds, and sports fields are abundant throughout the city, and they often double as venues for events, markets, and festivals in spring and summer.

Sports fans should try to catch at least one professional game while in town. In addition to the four major long-standing professional teams—the Eagles (football), Phillies (baseball), Flyers (hockey), and 76ers (basketball)—the city gained a professional soccer team, the Union, in 2010, which quickly gained a strong fan base. Win or lose, there is simply no city more impassioned and committed to its teams than Philadelphia, with an even greater vigor than ever since the long losing streak was broken with the Phillies' World Series win in 2008. An example of just how seriously this city takes its sports is that former Philadelphia mayor, then Pennsylvania governor, Ed Rendell, hosts the Eagles post-game show every Sunday, which he did even while he was in office. Rooting for—and talking trash about—our teams brings the city together, perhaps more than anything else.

The Arts

Check the free weekly papers *PW* and *City Paper* for listings of special events at the numerous museums, theaters, galleries, and concert venues. Also, note that the Philadelphia Museum of Art is listed in the *Sights* chapter rather than here, because it is an iconic sight to behold both inside and out.

MUSEUMS
Art
BARNES FOUNDATION
300 N. Latches Ln., Merion, 610/667-0290, www.barnesfoundation.org
HOURS: Sept.-May Thurs.-Sun. 9:30 A.M.-5 P.M., Jun.-Aug. Wed.-Fri. 9:30 A.M.-5 P.M.
COST: $15
`Map 9`

Eccentric art collector Albert C. Barnes probably never could have imagined his little art collection would cause such trouble. His legacy, the Barnes Foundation, is an awesome multibillion-dollar collection of Impressionist and Expressionist works by Cézanne, Gauguin, El Greco, Goya, Manet, Matisse, Modigliani, Monet, Picasso, Renoir, and Van Gogh, along with impressive African sculptures and much, much more. Cosseted away at Barnes's former estate in the Philadelphia suburbs of Merion since the 1920s, the collection was embroiled in a lengthy battle over whether to move to a more accessible Center City location. Some of the same suburban neighbors who complained about visitor traffic fought for it to stay once they realized they might lose it, while Philadelphia city officials have longed to acquire it for the city for the revenue and tourism it will attract.

Well, after much debate, it was finally decided in court that the museum will relocate to the Benjamin Franklin Parkway and 21st Street. It will take up residence along the Museum District corridor that is home to many of Philadelphia's other top museums, including the Philadelphia Museum of Art, the Franklin Institute, Academy of Natural Sciences, and the Rodin Museum, with a projected opening of 2012. At the time of printing, construction was well under way on the new space, and the design team is committed to recreating a space in line with its original home as much as possible. Some of the collections were still available for viewing in Merion while others are being preserved and prepared for the big move.

Visitors should call or check online to see where to go, but whether it's still in the 'burbs or in the city, all art lovers should make it a point to see this world-class collection. Merion has limited visiting hours, and reservations are recommended at least a month in advance for preferred dates and times, but hopefully when it's in Philadelphia you'll be able to walk right in as you can with other museums, which is one of the many reasons many people wanted it to move. Anyone interested in learning more about the battle over the Barnes can watch *Art of the Steal,* an interesting documentary about the collection and Albert Barnes himself, a fascinating man who made a fortune on a medical invention and spent most of it creating one of the world's best collections of art.

INSTITUTE OF CONTEMPORARY ART
118 S. 36th St., 215/898-7108, www.icaphila.org
HOURS: Wed. 11 A.M.-8 P.M., Thurs.-Fri. 11 A.M.-6 P.M., Sat.-Sun. 11 A.M.-5 P.M.
COST: Free
`Map 6`

One day, the lay public will understand the difference between modern, postmodern, and contemporary art, but until then, the Institute of Contemporary Art is keeping its name direct and to the point. The ICA, nestled away on Penn's campus in University City, hosts exhibitions, commissions works, produces publications, and holds educational programs. Hopefully, those classes will be able to explain why a gallery showing Rothko would never put up a piece by Duchamp.

PENNSYLVANIA ACADEMY OF THE FINE ARTS

118 N. Broad St., 215/972-7600, www.pafa.org

HOURS: Tues.-Sat. 10 A.M.-5 P.M., Sun. 11 A.M.-5 P.M.

COST: Permanent collection $10 adult, $8 senior, student, and youth (13-18), free child 12 and under; special exhibitions (including permanent collection) $15 adult, $12 senior, students, and youth (13-18), free child 12 and under

Map 2

Having recently celebrated its 200th anniversary—take that, Guggenheim!—the Pennsylvania Academy of the Fine Arts is the oldest art school and museum in the country. Inside the National Historic Landmark building, holdings include paintings and other artworks by many of the masters, including Cecilia Beaux, William Merritt Chase, Frank Duveneck, Thomas Eakins, Winslow Homer, Childe Hassam, and Edmund Tarbell. Eakins was also a controversial and paradigm-shifting director of PAFA. Now, the academy he led is one of the most prestigious art schools in America—a must-see for any art lover. Guided tours are included with admission (Tues.,

Thurs., and Fri. at 11:30 A.M. and 12:30 P.M.; Wed., Sat., and Sun. at 1 and 2 P.M.). The **Morris Gallery** exhibitions on the ground floor are free.

RODIN MUSEUM

22nd St. and Benjamin Franklin Pkwy., 215/568-6026, www.rodinmuseum.org

HOURS: Tues.-Sun. 10 A.M.-5 P.M.

COST: $5 donation suggested

Map 4

Many will recognize Auguste Rodin's famous sculpture *The Thinker*, which welcomes visitors into the museum dedicated entirely to the French artist's work. Walk past the garden and fountain to see many of his other masterpieces, including *The Gates of Hell* framing the main entrance of the impressive building. Wander through the high-ceilinged, marble-floored rooms and you'll be amazed by the endless true-to-life sculptures of the human body—he was especially skilled at and obsessed with creating human hands—that Rodin created. Exhibiting one of the largest Rodin collections in the world, the small but lovely

The Thinker, by August Rodin, welcomes visitors to the Rodin Museum.

© KARRIE GAVIN

museum provides an in-depth look at not only his work but also his thought processes and his life. Some of his original tools, early sketches, and journals are on display.

History and Culture
AFRICAN AMERICAN MUSEUM IN PHILADELPHIA

701 Arch St., 215/574-0380, www.aampmuseum.org
HOURS: Tues.-Sat. 10 A.M.-5 P.M., Sun. noon-5 P.M.
COST: $10 adult, $8 senior, student, child (4-12)
Map 1

Founded in 1976 in honor of the bicentennial celebration, the African American Museum in Philadelphia was the first museum in a major U.S. city dedicated to celebrating African American culture and history. The museum holds over 750,000 objects, including arts, artifacts, clothing, furniture, weapons, documents, photographs, records, and diaries highlighting the African diaspora, African American history in Philadelphia, and the contemporary achievements of African Americans. With frequent additions of permanent and rotating exhibits, the museum also hosts a variety of lectures and educational programming.

AMERICAN SWEDISH HISTORY MUSEUM

1900 Pattison Ave., 215/389-1776,
www.americanswedish.org
HOURS: Tues.-Fri. 10 A.M.-4 P.M., Sat.-Sun. noon-4 P.M.
COST: $6 adult, $5 senior and student,
free child under 12
Map 9

Swedish colonists settled in the Delaware Valley in the mid-1600s—long before William Penn arrived—and this museum aims to preserve their history. The nation's oldest Swedish museum, it was founded in 1926 on the 150th anniversary of the drafting of the Declaration of Independence. Built on land given to colonist Sven Skute by Sweden's Queen Christina in 1653, the building was modeled after a 17th-century Swedish manor. Numerous artifacts fill the galleries showcasing the history of the colonists, including collections of early Swedish furniture and handmade peasant dolls. Other exhibits honor famous Swedes such as author Carl Sandberg, inventor/

seaman John Ericsson, and Alfred Nobel, who invented dynamite and established the Nobel Prize. Located a bit out of the way in deep South Philly, it's worth a trip for history buffs or anyone interested in Swedish culture.

FIREMAN'S HALL MUSEUM

147 N. 2nd St., 215/923-1438, www.firemanshall.org
HOURS: Tues.-Sat. 10 A.M.-4:30 P.M., 10 A.M.-9 P.M. first Friday of month
COST: Free
Map 1

Benjamin Franklin had the unprecedented idea of starting a fire insurance company in Philadelphia in the 1730s; he is just one of many people and advancements honored at the Fireman's Hall Museum, which is operated by the Philadelphia Fire Department. Housed in a restored 1902 firehouse, the museum pays tribute to the brave men and women who fight fire and risked their lives for public safety. The collection of firefighting history and memorabilia includes an array of axes, hoses, tools, fire trucks, and parade badges dating as far back as the 1800s.

INDEPENDENCE SEAPORT MUSEUM

Penn's Landing, 211 South Columbus Blvd.,
215/413-8655, www.phillyseaport.org
HOURS: Daily 10 A.M.-5 P.M.
COST: $12 adult, $10 senior, $7 child 3-12, student, military; free Sun. 10 A.M.-noon
Map 1

Independence Seaport Museum explores the city's rich maritime history in a fitting location on Penn's Landing, overlooking the Delaware River. The exhibits "Bound for Philadelphia" and "Coming to America" highlight the city's immigration history and its importance in the growth of the nation's population, while exploring the hardships and hazards often faced by immigrants who crossed the Atlantic in search of a new life. Enjoy the excellent views of the Delaware River throughout many of the exhibit spaces, making it easy to imagine the people landing on that very shore in centuries past. Exhibits about small crafts, industrial shipping, and deep-diving technology add a modern aspect to the museum. While you're

ARTS AND LEISURE

here, you can explore the USS *Olympia,* which served as a flagship in the Spanish-American War, and the USS *Becuna,* a World War II submarine. Both National Historic Landmarks are open during museum hours, and on the first Saturday of each month (noon–4 P.M.) get a behind-the-scenes guided tour of the ship, including areas normally closed to the public.

MUMMERS MUSEUM

1100 S. 2nd St., 215/336-3050,
www.mummersmuseum.com
HOURS: May-Sept. Wed., Fri. and Sat.
9:30 A.M.-4:30 P.M. and Thurs. 9:30 A.M.-9:30 P.M.;
Oct.-Apr. Wed.-Sat. 9:30 A.M.-4:30 P.M.
COST: $3.50 adult, $2.50 child under 12, senior, and student
Map 5

"What is a mummer?" you may ask. He or she is a lavishly costumed, dancing, marching, instrument-playing, feather-and-sequin-covered Philadelphian who brings the city's unique brand of celebration to fever pitch. The purest example of Philadelphia's spirit, the mummers celebrate every occasion, but none more so than the New Year, which they usher in with a parade on Broad Street. If you haven't seen a mummers parade before, it is a sight not to be missed. While the earliest mummers date back to ancient Egypt, the tradition of mummers in Philadelphia began in the late 17th century and has held strong every since. The joyous group is passionate and proud, and their traditions have become an important part of Philadelphia's history. The Mummers Museum in South Philadelphia pays homage to their unique history.

NATIONAL LIBERTY MUSEUM

321 Chestnut St., 215/925-2800,
www.libertymuseum.org
HOURS: Mon.-Sat. 10 A.M.-5 P.M., Sun. noon-6 P.M., closed Mon. except in summer
COST: $7 adult, $6 senior, $5 student, $2 child 5-17, $15 family
Map 1

Just two blocks from the Liberty Bell and Independence Hall, the National Liberty

Museum celebrates the profound accomplishment of creating a free society. The museum's varied galleries explore topics of heroism, freedom, diversity, faith, and more, and pay homage to people who have contributed to the creation of a free country. The fine art gallery features an array of sculptures, paintings, and an impressive collection of delicate glass works that explore the idea of the beauty and fragility of freedom. Galleries include "Coming to America, Heroes from Around the World," and "Heroes of 9/11 Memorial."

◖ NATIONAL MUSEUM OF AMERICAN JEWISH HISTORY

101 S. Independence Mall East, 215/923-3811,
www.nmajh.org
HOURS: Tues.-Fri. 10 A.M.-5 P.M.,
Sat.-Sun. 10 A.M.-5:30 P.M., closed for major U.S. and Jewish holidays
COST: $12 adult, $11 senior, military, and youth (13-21), free 12 and under
Map 1

The world's largest museum showcasing

© JULIA GAVIN

The National Museum of American Jewish History opened in 2010 directly across from the Liberty Bell.

American Jewish history opened in the heart of Philadelphia's Independence Mall in 2010. The new museum is an outgrowth of a modest museum just around the corner. Showcasing a small collection of artifacts, the former museum has shared space with the historic Congregation Mikveh Israel, one of the nation's first organized Jewish congregations, since 1976. The new museum is a strikingly modern, five-story, 100,000 square-foot building with an all-glass facade symbolizing accessibility, the open nature of America, and the fragility of democracy. An eight-foot-tall continuously burning flame visible from the street represents the permanence and endurance of Jews in America and American freedom in general. The museum celebrates 350 years of Jewish history in America through more than 10,000 artifacts, permanent and rotating exhibits, and interactive displays. While the focus of several other museums, most notably the United States Holocaust Memorial Museum in Washington, D.C., is on the Jewish experience before coming to America and the oppression and genocide of Jews, this museum is about the accomplishments, struggles, and experiences of Jews here in America. Beginning with the first permanent Jewish settlement in 1654 and continuing through to the present day, the museum tells diverse stories of Jews in America.

PHILADELPHIA HISTORY MUSEUM
15 S. 7th St., 215/685-4830,
www.philadelphiahistory.org
HOURS: Call ahead
COST: Call ahead
Map 1

This Greek Revival building on the edge of Old City originally housed the Franklin Institute until it was relocated to its current large space on the Benjamin Franklin Parkway. A. Atwater Kent purchased the space to create a museum that would honor Philadelphia's history. Formerly called the Atwater Kent Museum, it was slated to reopen in 2011 as the Philadelphia History Museum after renovations. The museum showcases local inventions in manufacturing and technology, toys

and tools from the colonial era, and local artwork. While not as widely appreciated as many of the major Old City sights, this museum is a must for those who want an in-depth look at Philadelphia's past, and is expected to gain more attention after its reopening.

POLISH AMERICAN CULTURAL CENTER AND MUSEUM
308 Walnut St., 215/922-1700,
www.polishamericancenter.org
HOURS: Jan.-Apr. Mon.-Fri. 10 A.M.-4 P.M.,
May-Dec. Mon.-Sat. 10 A.M.-4 P.M.
COST: Free
Map 1

This small museum in the heart of Old City honors Polish culture and heritage and celebrates the contributions of its citizens to the United States and the world. The center was founded in February 1981 and offers a small display of memorabilia and biographical materials about famous Poles, including religious leader John Cardinal Krol, Revolutionary War heroes Thaddeus Kosciuszko and Casimir Pulaski, composers Fryderyk Chopin and Ignacy Jan Paderewski, and scientists Marie Curie and Nicholas Copernicus. There is a prominent display on Pope John Paul II. Exhibits highlight Polish traditions that immigrants brought to the states, including *pisanki* (painted Easter eggs) and decorative wooden plates.

UNIVERSITY MUSEUM OF ARCHAEOLOGY AND ANTHROPOLOGY
3260 South St., 215/898-4000, www.penn.museum
HOURS: Tues. and Thurs.-Sun. 10 A.M.-5 P.M., Wed. 10 A.M.-8 P.M.
COST: $10 adult, $7 senior, $6 student and child (6-17), free child under 6 and Penn staff and students
Map 6

A paradise for the Indiana Jones at heart, the University of Pennsylvania's museum houses a magnificent chest of archaeological treasures. It opened in 1899 and today contains more than 100 unique displays and one million artifacts representing practically every corner of history and prehistory. Trace the earliest *Homo sapiens'* routes as you walk the long artifact-lined corridors and wander through rooms that offer glimpses into centuries and civilizations past. Decipher North America's earliest hieroglyphics in the Mesoamerica Exhibit; walk before the enormous sphinx at the Palace of the Pharaoh Merenptah; and advance through the technology, art, politics, and religion of the Etruscans, Greeks, Canaanites, and Romans.

Science
ACADEMY OF NATURAL SCIENCES

1900 Benjamin Franklin Pkwy., 215/299-1000, www.ansp.org
HOURS: Mon.-Fri. 10 A.M.-4:30 P.M., Sat.-Sun. 10 A.M.-5 P.M.
COST: $12 adult (over 13), $10 child (3-12), senior, military, and student, free under 3, additional fee for special exhibits
Map 4

A skeleton replica of a 42-foot-long, 7.5-ton *Tyrannosaurus rex* smiling with razor-sharp teeth greets guests upon entering the Academy of Natural Sciences. From dinosaurs to apes to tigers, the exhibits take visitors through evolutionary history from the Mesozoic era to present day, capturing animal life across the planet in glass-enclosed, realistic-looking habitat displays. Children love to take part in real archaeological digs and to see the live animal exhibits.

◖ FRANKLIN INSTITUTE

222 N. 20th St., 215/448-1200, www2.fi.edu
HOURS: Daily 9:30 A.M.-5 P.M.
COST: $15.50 adult, $14.50 senior and military, $12 child (4-11), free under 4, additional fee for IMAX or Franklin Theater and other special exhibits
Map 4

Scientist and inventor Benjamin Franklin would be proud of the impressive museum named for him and dedicated to one of the major focuses of his life work—expanding knowledge of the universe through science. A larger-than-life statue of Ben welcomes guests into the grand high-ceilinged lobby. The large museum showcases many of Franklin's own inventions along with countless technological and scientific advances through history

© K. CIAPPA FOR GPTMC

Franklin Institute, named for Benjamin Franklin, is a world-class science museum.

with interactive exhibits that are often as interesting and educational for adults as they are for children. Visitors can explore the engine room of a real 19th-century locomotive, walk through a massive replica of the human heart, and take in the vast expanse of the cosmos in the "Space Command" exhibit. The institute hosts the world's best traveling science exhibits in addition to ever-expanding permanent displays. A planetarium show is included with the price of admission. One of the best surround-style IMAX theaters in the country and a 3-D theater (the Franklin Theater) round out the museum's diverse offerings, and admission can be added to a museum ticket or purchased for a separate fee if visited individually.

MUTTER MUSEUM

19 S. 22nd St., 267/563-3737, www.collphyphil.org
HOURS: Daily 10 A.M.-5 P.M.
COST: $14 adult, $10 child (6-17), military, senior, and student, free 5 and under
Map 3

Gross or cool? The Mutter Museum, a fascinating showcase of medical oddities founded in 1858 by the College of Physicians of Philadelphia, is a little bit of both. Exhibits include a wall of real eyeballs, President Grover Cleveland's tumor, the tallest skeleton in the country, and the world's largest colon. Impressive portraits and other artworks by famous Philadelphia artists Thomas Eakins and John Singer Sargent are on display alongside body parts in jars. With such a weird array of science and medicine guests are bound to learn something—if they can stomach it.

PLEASE TOUCH MUSEUM

4231 N. Concourse Dr., 215/581-3181, www.pleasetouchmuseum.org
HOURS: Mon.-Sat. 9 A.M.-5 P.M., Sun. 11 A.M.-5 P.M.
COST: $15 adult and child, free child under 1
Map 8

This 38,000-square-foot playground is a kid's dream come true, and with an emphasis on learning, development, and encouraging imagination through play, it's a place parents can feel great about taking kids. With a name like Please Touch, it's obvious the museum is meant to be enjoyed hands-on; children can dress up in costumes, operate flying machines, drive a SEPTA bus, and much, much more. There is so much to do that some locals take their kids on a near-weekly basis. The museum has been a favorite for families since it opened in Center City in 1976, but since it moved to its much larger and impressive current space in 2008, it is truly a world-class kids' museum. While kids won't care, parents should note that the building, Memorial Hall, is a National Historic Landmark that was built for the World's Fair in 1876 but left abandoned for many years in between; it is wonderful to see the fantastic space put to such great use.

GALLERIES

Art galleries can be found all over the city selling and showcasing items that range from reasonably priced to limited-edition nationally known pieces. The galleries around Rittenhouse tend to be at the high end while Northern Liberties and Chinatown are home to more independent artists and co-ops, and Old City has the greatest concentration of galleries of all kinds. Listings here are a small sampling of what is available, but there are way too many to even begin to scratch the surface. Visit www.phillygalleryguide.com for many more listings. The following are free unless otherwise noted.

CLAY STUDIO

139 N. 2nd St., 215/925-3453, www.theclaystudio.org
HOURS: Tues.-Sat. 11 A.M.-7 P.M., Sun. noon-6 P.M.
Map 1

For more than 30 years, the Clay Studio has been a veritable fixture in Philadelphia's urban art community. As you walk down the hallway leading to the gallery, which features funky mosaic tile work by local artist-celeb Isaiah Zagar (of the Magic Gardens), you'll know you're in for a treat. The gallery displays juried solo exhibits, work from local emerging ceramists, and artists from its highly competitive studio-run residency and fellowship programs. The Clay Studio offers a little something for every taste, ranging from functional vessels like coffee mugs and vases to more conceptual work like sculptures and installations.

FABRIC WORKSHOP AND MUSEUM

1214 Arch St., 215/568-8888, www.fabricworkshop.org
HOURS: Mon.-Fri. 10 A.M.-6 P.M., Sat.-Sun. noon-5 P.M.
COST: $3 adult, free under 12
Map 2

The only nonprofit arts organization of its kind in the United States, the Fabric Workshop and Museum is devoted to creating new work in new materials. The museum and shop is a successful collaboration between emerging and famous artists experimenting with a multitude of unfamiliar media—often, but not solely, fabric. Founded in 1977, the museum displays permanent and rotating exhibits. Located in a former industrial building near the Convention Center, it contains three exhibition galleries, a video lounge, a shop, and artist studios. Just down the street, the **New Temporary Contemporary** (1222 Arch St.) offers additional exhibition space.

FLEISHER ART MEMORIAL

719 Catharine St., 215/922-3456, www.fleisher.org
HOURS: Mon.-Fri. 11 A.M.-5 P.M., Sat. 10 A.M.-3 P.M.
Map 5

This Bella Vista neighborhood gem is home to a small rotating gallery of drawings, paintings, sculpture, and photography by mostly local artists, but perhaps the coolest thing about Fleisher is low-priced or free classes offered on an ongoing basis. You heard that right—free! This is a great opportunity for everyone from beginners to advanced artists to hone their skills in a supportive and affordable environment. Advanced workshops and classes, including photography, sculpture, art history, and drawing and painting, are offered for very reasonable fees.

F.U.E.L. COLLECTION

249 Arch St., 215/592-8400,
www.phillyartgalleries.com/gallery_fuel.htm
HOURS: Tues.-Fri. 11 A.M.-7 P.M., Sat.-Sun. noon-4 P.M.
Map 1

F.U.E.L. is an acronym for Fostering Undergraduate Exposure on Location. The mission of this progressive gallery is to "expose the unexposed, promote the next generation of artists, encourage creative collaboration, and aid the launch of successful artistic careers by creating a truly unique and singular forum for the display of art." F.U.E.L. is more than just a gallery displaying interesting and diverse up-and-coming artists' work; it is also a community haven and support system for budding artists. As such, the work does not fall into any specific genre, but the gallery offers a wide variety of interesting and affordable pieces. On a side note, before it was F.U.E.L. the building was once a bank and was later home to "seven

---

ART FOR ALL: FIRST FRIDAYS

First Friday has become the most popular ongoing event in the city since its start in 1991. On the first Friday evening of each month, art galleries throughout the city open their doors to the public for free, some with the added allure of free wine, beer, snacks, and even music, creating a festive atmosphere. The galleries feature practically every form of art, including painting, drawing, photography, designer furniture, crafts, glass, and more, which range from traditional to truly off-beat. While some of it is relatively affordable for purchase, many people go out just to look. Most galleries are open 5-9 P.M.

While the nexus of the action is in Old City between Market and Vine and Front and 3rd Streets (visit www.oldcityarts.org for more information), additional events are springing up with increasing frequency in other areas of the city, especially in the artist enclaves of Northern Liberties and Fishtown. In addition, some of those galleries hold open houses on **Second Thursdays,** distinguishing themselves from the more mainstream First Friday. **Crane Arts** (1400 N. American St., 215/232-3203, www.cranearts.com), home to artist studios and a gallery space, holds ongoing Second Thursday events.

strangers, picked to live in a house and have their lives taped . . ." (Yes, you got it; this was the house used for MTV's *The Real World*.)

SNYDERMAN-WORKS GALLERIES

303 Cherry St., 215/238-9576,
www.snyderman-works.com
HOURS: Tues.-Sat. 10 A.M.-6 P.M.
Map 1

In an expansive 6,000-square-foot space in Old City, this popular gallery is considered by some to be a must-see on the national art circuit. Formerly two different complementary galleries, The Snyderman and the Works, they are now commingled. Among other things, the gallery showcases the continually evolving areas of studio furniture and sculptural glass, and hosted one of the first exhibits of Dale Chihuly's renowned botanical glass work and architect Robert Venturi's furniture designs for Knoll. It is also dedicated to ceramics, jewelry, textiles, and fiber. Stark white walls, two-story rooms, and delicate work atop a series of pillars offer a lovely setting for intricate handiwork in a variety of materials.

SPACE 1026

1026 Arch St., 2nd fl., 215/574-7630,
www.space1026.com
HOURS: No official hours
Map 2

This well-known collaborative art space/gallery hosts quirky events and sometimes also doubles as a venue for indie bands, performances, and film screenings. Occupying two floors of space used by a community of local artists and art enthusiasts, it often displays work that has roots in pop surrealism and comic books, and specializes in screen printing. Unique shows such as a flipbook festival are not uncommon. There are no official hours, but you can stop by anytime and ring the bell or call ahead to make sure someone is there to let you in.

VOX POPULI AND KHMER GALLERY

319 N. 11th St.; Vox, 3rd fl., 215/238-1236,
www.voxpopuligallery.org; Khmer, basement,
215/922-5600, www.khmerartgallery.com
HOURS: Vox Wed.-Sun. noon-6 P.M.;
Khmer Wed., Fri., and Sat. 11 A.M.-4 P.M.
Map 7

These two unique galleries are not related other than by nature of being housed in the same large warehouse just north of Chinatown. Vox Populi hosts contemporary exhibitions, including experimental film, cutting-edge installations, and a wide range of work mostly by Philadelphia-based artists. It is also hosts numerous indie and experimental musical performances, and has a sophisticated feel while remaining a true DIY artist collective.

Khmer, in the basement level, features original and reproduction Cambodian sculpture, artwork, jewelry, and photography. Many of the pieces are massive and way out of the price range of mere civilians—try upwards of $50,000 for a marble garden statue—but some of the jewelry and small artwork is more affordable, and the space is fun to wander through even if you're not looking to furnish a massive Asian-themed restaurant or estate.

THEATER
ADRIENNE THEATRE

2030 Sansom St., 215/568-8077,
www.adriennelive.org
Map 3

Just a quick walk from Rittenhouse Square, but worlds away from the big theater houses on the Avenue of the Arts, the Adrienne Theatre offers an intimate space for small theater companies. Actually, it offers three different spaces of varying sizes. Named for theater professional Adrienne Neye, the theater hosts resident companies, including ComedySportz, an interactive improv comedy show. The largest resident company is the socially minded InterAct Theatre, whose mission is to produce plays that explore the cultural, social, and political issues of the day. The intention is admirable, so we'll look the other way if InterAct's sometimes heavy-handed productions are a touch didactic. Still, when good, these shows hit a real nerve, whether they're examining America's appetite for war, complex racial questions, or the role of the outsider in society. One thing's certain:

ARTS AND LEISURE

You'll find works here that broach topics no other company will touch, and the mission is admirable and necessary.

ARDEN THEATRE COMPANY
40 N. 2nd St., 215/922-1122, www.ardentheatre.org
Map 1

When it moved from Center City to Old City in 1995, the Arden Theatre helped reinvigorate what was then still an old industrial neighborhood on the verge of transformation. Since 1988, Arden has been producing top-quality productions of plays, musicals, and children's shows. On its 360-seat main stage and 175-seat blackbox, shows range from reinterpretations of Shakespeare and Shaw to works by emerging playwrights.

FORREST THEATRE
1114 Walnut St., 215/923-1515, www.forrest-theatre.com
Map 2

Built in the late 1920s by the Shubert organization and named for legendary 19th-century actor Edwin Forrest, the Forrest Theatre hosts traveling musicals, comedies, and dramas. With most first-run Broadway fare setting up shop at the nearby Academy of Music, it is frequently empty, which is unfortunate since the building is lovely. If you get a chance to see a show in this historic theater, you will not be disappointed.

NEW FREEDOM THEATRE
1346 N. Broad St., 215/765-2793,
www.freedomtheatre.org
Map 7

Most of the action on the Avenue of the Arts goes on below Market Street, while Freedom Theatre struggles to keep North Broad Street hopping. The oldest African American theater in Pennsylvania, Freedom has in the past showcased fine plays based on African American stories, like Toni Morrison's *The Bluest Eye*. Its operations today consist primarily of conducting theater and dance classes for kids and adults, with some performances conducted through the Performing Arts Training Program.

PAINTED BRIDE ART CENTER
230 Vine St., 215/925-9914, www.paintedbride.org
Map 1

The Painted Bride Art Center was founded in 1969, and it moved from South Street to Old City in 1982—long before the former warehouse neighborhood was the hot spot it is today. Stepping past the colorful mirror-and-tile mosaic exterior, you'll enter a large gallery space showcasing the works of daring young artists. The theater features dance, world music, performance, jazz, and more, plus many socially conscious or political works with a focus on advocacy for excluded communities. The Bride features local faves and international stars, and is responsible for Philadelphia's longest-running jazz series.

PHILADELPHIA THEATRE COMPANY AND SUZANNE ROBERTS THEATRE
480 S. Broad St., 215/985-0420,
www.phillytheatreco.org
Map 2

The first of several eager young theater companies to take 1970s Philly by storm, the Philadelphia Theatre Company has evolved into one of the most respected arts organizations in the region. Not content to merely rehash classics or safely import successful traveling shows, it has held over 100 world and Philadelphia premieres by playwrights including Terrance McNally, Christopher Durang, and Naomi Wallace. But the plays aren't the only new and exciting thing for the company; after a long residency at the small Plays & Players Theater in the Rittenhouse neighborhood, in 2007 the company moved into its stunning new home, named the Suzanne Roberts Theatre for its benefactor. The $25 million 370-seat theater occupies a deserved location among the city's top theaters on the Avenue of the Arts.

WALNUT STREET THEATRE
825 Walnut St., 215/574-3550,
www.walnutstreettheatre.org
Map 2

The official State Theater of Pennsylvania is

the Walnut Street Theatre, the oldest continually operating theater in the English-speaking world. It opened in 1809 as a circus house but is now known for more high-minded productions. Luminaries who have graced its stage include Edwin Booth, Marlon Brando, Henry and Jane Fonda, Audrey Hepburn, and Sidney Poitier. Besides the 1,000-plus-seat main theater, it also holds Studios 3 and 5, smaller houses for second-stage productions and rentals to outside theater companies.

WILMA THEATER

265 S. Broad St., 215/546-7824, www.wilmatheater.org
Map 2

We may never get to see David Mamet in drag, but the Wilma Theater is named after Shakespeare's fictional female alter-ego. Since the early 1970s, the company has been staging daring, tradition-defying productions of new plays and classics, including works by Tom Stoppard, Sophocles, Arthur Miller, Tennessee Williams, Bertolt Brecht, and yes, Mamet. Even in its beautiful and spacious home on the Avenue of the Arts, it hasn't lost the intimate feeling that makes small theaters so appealing.

CONCERT VENUES

☾ ACADEMY OF MUSIC

Broad and Locust Sts., 215/893-1999,
www.academyofmusic.org
Map 2

Nobly dubbed "The Grand Old Lady of Broad Street," the Academy of Music has been a proud institution since 1857. It is the oldest grand opera house in the United States still functioning as an opera house today. The regal Renaissance theater is adorned with wood carvings, ceiling murals, and a massive crystal chandelier hanging elegantly overhead. Home to the Opera Company of Philadelphia and the Pennsylvania Ballet, the Academy of Music is no stranger to the most gifted musicians that come through the city. Over the years it has hosted Igor Stravinsky, Richard Strauss, Pyotr Tchaikovsky, Joan Sutherland, and a myriad of other world-renowned artists and composers.

CURTIS INSTITUTE OF MUSIC

1726 Locust St., 215/893-5252, www.curtis.edu
Map 3

One of the most prestigious music conservatories in the world occupies an equally prestigious spot in the heart of Rittenhouse Square. While its foremost goal is teaching gifted students classical music, it was founded on the philosophy of learning by doing. Performances include operas; orchestra, solo, and chamber music recitals; and a family concert series. While some performances are held at other nearby theaters, many are held on-site at Field Concert Hall. Prices vary greatly, but more than 100 student concerts are free and open to the public. They are generally held Monday, Wednesday, and Friday at 8 P.M., but call the student hotline (215/893-5261) to confirm.

☾ KIMMEL CENTER

260 S. Broad St., 215/790-5800,
www.kimmelcenter.org
Map 2

The Kimmel Center opened its doors in 2001 and provided the city with a venue that easily deserves the bold label of "world-class." Architect Rafael Viñoly and acoustics company Artec Consultants combined efforts in creating this magnificent crown jewel of the Avenue of the Arts. With two posh theaters, imported exotic wood finishes, and a soaring vaulted glass ceiling rising 150 feet above the lobby, the Kimmel is breathtaking. Its resident companies include the renowned Philadelphia Orchestra, the Chamber Orchestra of Philadelphia, and the Philadelphia Chamber Music Society, but it's much more than just a venue for "ladies who lunch." The Kimmel is also home to local dance company PhilaDanco and a pop orchestra, Peter Nero and the Philly Pops. It also is the venue for many of the biggest name concerts that come through Philadelphia with shows spanning every musical genre, along with many free concerts. Performances are held in the innovative music halls, offering incredible acoustics and aesthetics. The expansive Verizon Hall seats over 2,500 on its red velvet chairs, and the more intimate Perelman

Kimmel Center on the Avenue of the Arts

Theater holds 650. Before or after a performance, you can stroll through the Dorrance H. Hamilton Roof Garden to enjoy the great views. If you can't come for a show, come and take the free hour-long tour of the venue, offered daily at the information desk at 1 P.M.

MANN CENTER FOR THE PERFORMING ARTS
5201 Parkside Ave., 215/893-1999,
www.manncenter.org
Map 8

Located in leafy Fairmount Park, the Mann provides a large open-air venue for a diverse range of performances. Originally a summer home for the Philadelphia Orchestra, today the Mann hosts instrumental music, jazz, opera, pop, dance, drumming, and ballet. It has also hosted many big-name pop and rock musicians, although most of the very biggest names now perform at the larger Susquehanna Bank Center in Camden instead. It holds up to 4,000 under the pavilion and up to 10,000 on the lawn and terrace. On nice summer nights, bring a picnic and come for an orchestra performance.

WELLS FARGO CENTER
3601 S. Broad St., 800/298-4200,
www.wellsfargocenterphilly.com
Map 9

Philly provides venues aplenty for all kinds of spectator activities, but for major music acts, and professional basketball and hockey, only the Wells Fargo Center will do. The state-of-the-art indoor arena has changed owners and names several times since it opened, but in 2010, it became the Wells Fargo Center, owned by Comcast-Spectacor. It hosts at least 250 events a year with room for more than 20,000 and very few if any bad seats in the house. It is home to the Philadelphia Flyers, the 76ers, the Soul (indoor football), and the Wings (lacrosse), and Billy Joel, Madonna, Ray Charles, KISS, and just about everyone else you can think of has performed here. Any huge names that are not performing here are probably playing at the Susquehanna Bank Center in Camden, New Jersey.

CINEMA
INTERNATIONAL HOUSE
3701 Chestnut St., 866/468-7619, www.ihousephilly.org

Map 6

Possibly the strangest and coolest dorm ever, International House is home to over 400 international students studying at area colleges and universities. It's also a nexus of cultural and artistic programming for University City and Philly as a whole. I-House offers an extensive and jaw-droppingly diverse series of film screenings, art shows, installations, live music, food festivals, dance performances, speakers, and more. The auditorium has a large projection screen, and while not quite up to par with a typical movie theater as far as quality, this place is much cooler than anything typical, and you'll see movies here that you won't see anywhere else.

◖ LANDMARK THEATRES
Ritz 5 (214 Walnut St.), Ritz at the Bourse
(400 Ranstead St.), and Ritz East (125 S. 2nd St.),
215/925-7900, www.landmarktheatres.com

Map 1

When Philadelphians want to see movies that don't feature loud explosions, foolish gags, or flashy nudity, they usually head to one of the Ritz movie houses in Old City. A total of 12 screens are spread out over the three different Ritz theaters, all offering clean, enjoyable places to watch high-quality films. Concessions include the standards—Jujubes and Raisinets—along with more upscale offerings that vary by theater but may include Toblerone and Lindt chocolates, yogurt-covered pretzels, coffee, and tea. The art-house chain was acquired by Landmark Theatres, but theaters maintain the Ritz name along with its mix of independent, international, and all-around good artsy-fartsy programming. There is a parking lot at the Bourse and Ritz East; have your ticket validated at any of the theaters for a reduced rate.

RAVE MOTION PICTURES
UNIVERSITY CITY 6
4012 Walnut St., 215/386-0869,
www.ravemotionpictures.com

Map 6

This theater (formerly the Bridge: Cinema de Lux until 2010) opened its doors in University

The Ritz at the Bourse is one of several Ritz movie theaters in Old City.

© JULIA GAVIN

ARTS AND LEISURE

City in 2002, making many local movie-goers very happy. No longer did we have to brave sticky floors and the stinky bathrooms of Riverview or drive to a mega-mall in the suburbs or Cherry Hill, New Jersey, to see a first-run blockbuster. The clean, spacious theater offers plush stadium seating, a specialty coffee bar, and a bar and lounge. Located near plenty of dining options, it's a convenient spot for a dinner-and-a-movie date.

UNITED ARTISTS RIVERVIEW STADIUM 17
1400 S. Columbus Blvd., 215/755-2353
`Map 5`

You can count on the Riverview to run all the top blockbusters in this large, adequate, but unremarkable and sometimes not entirely well-kempt megaplex. You certainly won't be getting the Ritz experience, but if you need to catch the latest natural disaster summer blockbuster, this is your place.

Festivals and Events

Philly has a variety of festivals and special events throughout the year, the majority in spring and summer and to celebrate major holidays. The winter holiday is kicked off with a Thanksgiving Day parade, and soon after, signs of Christmas light up Center City. The last hurrah of the year is the New Year's Eve fireworks display. Here is a sampling of some of the best and biggest annual events, but be sure to visit www.visitphilly.com/events, www.phillyfunguide.org, and the festivals' individual websites for more comprehensive listings and exact dates. The weekly newspapers *City Paper* and *PW* are also invaluable event resources.

WINTER
WING BOWL
Wells Fargo Center, 800/298-4200, www.610wip.com

Fans of chicken wings, drinking, and scantily clad women will find their own strange heaven at this popular event. The Wing Bowl was founded by AM radio staple WIP 610 as a promotion to compensate for the Philadelphia Eagles' losing ways. The city needed something to get excited about since the team kept losing, and somehow the Wing Bowl has partially lived up to that strange expectation, garnering much local fanaticism in its own right. It's traditionally held the Friday before the Super Bowl at the Wells Fargo Center, and

crowds form outside well before dawn, enjoying beer and wings for breakfast. Over 150 contestants compete in the wing-eating contest, and more than 20,000 attend to watch the intensely competitive gorge-fest. Tickets are required and the event often sells out within 24 hours.

SPRING
DAD VAIL REGATTA
Schuylkill River along Kelly Dr., 215/542-1443, www.dadvail.org

Over 100 universities from North America participate in this rowing classic on the Schuylkill in early May. One of the nation's oldest student athletic events, the Dad Vail Regatta brings thousands of students and families to Philadelphia each year, while hordes of locals and visitors come out for the festivities. The 6,000-foot race winds along the Schuylkill River; the best seats are at the Grand Stand finish line beyond Boathouse Row coming from the Art Museum. The packed bleachers afford a great view and the atmosphere is bustling with cheering onlookers.

EQUALITY FORUM
Various locations in the Gayborhood, 215/732-3378, www.equalityforum.org

It's fitting that Equality Forum, the country's largest gay-lesbian-bisexual-transgendered civil rights organization, hails from the city where American democracy began. What began as weekend-long PrideFest Philadelphia in 1993 is now a full week of programs, panels, screenings, and social events around the city in late April/early May. It is capped off by SundayOUT, which is certainly Philly's, but also one of the country's largest and most fabulous gay pride events. During its off-season, the Equality Forum organization keeps busy by producing gay-themed documentaries, advocating for same-sex marriage, and lobbying Fortune 500 corporations for nondiscrimination policies and domestic-partner benefits.

ITALIAN MARKET FESTIVAL

9th St. btwn. Fitzwater and Federal Sts.,
www.9thstreetitalianmarketfestival.com

The Italian Market has a festive atmosphere on any Saturday afternoon, but on one weekend each May, it closes to car traffic and an all-out party ensues. As if the market wasn't tempting enough with its delicious smells and tastes, vendors set up shop outside their businesses with foods that are simply irresistible. Stroll and shop, sample goodies along the way, and don't miss the stage featuring live music and chef demonstrations.

PENN RELAYS

235 S. 33rd St., Franklin Field, 215/898-6151,
www.thepennrelays.com

Penn Relays dates back more than 100 years, making it the oldest recognized relay meet in the world. Each year in late April, massive crowds come to the University of Pennsylvania's Franklin Field to watch the world's top track athletes compete. The highlight and most popular event is the USA vs. World races on Saturday. In addition to the action on the field, there is a carnival atmosphere around the entire campus with food, crafts, and entertainment.

RITTENHOUSE ROW FESTIVAL

Walnut St. btwn. Broad and 19th Sts.,
www.rittenhouserow.org

Center City celebrates spring in style on the first Saturday of May, rain or shine. Vendors set up in and around Rittenhouse Square and several blocks of Walnut Street, which is closed to car traffic. Enjoy samples of five-star dining at great prices in front of the restaurants along with other special offers from many local businesses. There is music and people galore, and when the weather is nice, the event is that much better.

SUBARU CHERRY BLOSSOM FESTIVAL

Various locations, 215/790-3810, www.jasgp.org/sakura

Named for *sakura,* the pretty pink cherry blossoms that come out in March and early April and hold deep significance in Japanese culture, this festival welcomes spring with several weeks of events around the city. Watch taiko drumming or martial arts demonstrations, learn to make origami or sushi, or take part in a traditional tea ceremony. Sakura Sunday is the highlight—this festival at the Japanese House and Gardens in Fairmount Park takes place towards the end of the festival in early April. Even if you miss the organized events, be sure to take a moment to take in the cherry blossoms throughout the city, especially in Fairmount Park.

SUMMER
CONCERTS IN THE PARK

Rittenhouse Square, 18th and Walnut Sts.,
www.philadelphiaweekly.com

On a series of summer Wednesdays, usually during the month of August, *Philadelphia Weekly* sponsors concerts in Rittenhouse Square. Everyone comes out with blankets, food, and drinks to sit on the grass and listen to live music, usually from 7 to 9 P.M. The acts are varied and generally good, but often take second stage to the socializing happening around them.

ODUNDE AFRICAN AMERICAN STREET FESTIVAL

23rd and South Sts.

The Odunde Street Festival takes place the second weekend in June in one of Philadelphia's oldest, historically African American neighborhoods in Center City South. In existence for more than 30 years, it has become a three-day event filled with festivities and cultural events, culminating with a large street festival on Sunday featuring African music, food, and crafts. Around the same time, mid-June, there are often other events throughout the city in honor of Juneteenth, the holiday that celebrates the official end to slavery.

PRO CYCLING TOUR
Kelly Dr. and other locations,
www.procyclingtour.com

Known locally as the Bike Race, one of the biggest sporting events in the United States is, for most Philadelphians, just another excuse to party. On a Saturday in June, cyclists complete 10 laps of a scenic 14.4-mile circuit, passing over the Benjamin Franklin Parkway, Kelly Drive, through Fairmount Park, and up the infamously steep Manayunk Wall. Watch from the Benjamin Franklin Parkway, the steps of the Philadelphia Museum of Art, Main Street in Manayunk, or near the Manayunk Wall. Many neighborhood households along the route hold parties on their front porches to cheer the athletes on and drink the day away.

◖ WAWA WELCOME AMERICA FESTIVAL
Various locations, www.welcomeamerica.com

It's fitting that Independence Day is a huge deal in the city where it all began. The 11-day festival is filled with fun, family-friendly concerts, museum events, outdoor screenings, street festivals, fireworks, discounts at many businesses, and a big parade, concert, and fireworks on the Benjamin Franklin Parkway, which has featured Hall and Oates, Elton John, the Roots, and the Goo Goo Dolls among other stars. While some locals try to escape the mayhem and the heat by heading to the Jersey shore, others embrace the revelry and join the throngs of tourists in the action.

FALL
FILM FESTIVALS
Various theaters, 267/253-3599,
www.filmadelphia.org

Film lovers should take advantage of the **Philadelphia Film Festival** in October, the spring preview in April, or its midsummer sibling, the **Philadelphia International Gay and Lesbian Film Festival** (267/765-9800, www.qfest.com). Both festivals are huge affairs with hundreds of screenings across multiple venues, guest stars, VIP meet-and-greets, and of course, loads of parties and events.

◖ PHILADELPHIA LIVE ARTS FESTIVAL AND PHILLY FRINGE
Various locations, 215/413-1318, www.livearts-fringe.org

There's a lot to love about the Philadelphia Live Arts Festival and Philly Fringe. The early fall extravaganza is a tribute to theater, dance, music, spoken word, and other arts and performance mediums. The Live Arts part is developed by festival organizers, bringing the best performers from around the world to Philly. However, it's the Fringe part that gets really wild, since anyone with a venue and a dream can include a show in the program. And yes, "venue" occasionally means the sidewalk. It's a thrilling and unpredictable artistic ride, and the no-cover fringe cabaret promises good times, and often hungover mornings, for all involved. Visit the website for details and to learn about some year-round events organized by the organization.

TERROR BEHIND THE WALLS AT EASTERN STATE PENITENTIARY
2124 Fairmount Ave., 800/745-3000,
www.easternstate.org/halloween
COST: $20-30 depending on day
Map 4

The place is creepy enough on a regular tour, but every October, the former prison hosts Philadelphia's most frightening tradition. Eastern State Penitentiary's haunted-house tour lets guests walk through long, shadowy

© SVETLANA SEWELL/123RF.COM

In October the tour of the Eastern State Penitentiary is even more frightening than usual.

corridors and past dark, (seemingly) empty cells. Enhanced by realistic cosmetics, deformed and decaying monsters are everywhere and eager to greet you. Tours begin at 7 P.M. every night and continue every 30 minutes.

Be warned: There is often a line around the block to get into this popular event. Ask about the more subdued "Family Night," which offers a somewhat less terrifying alternative for the easily frightened and younger crowds.

Recreation

Most of the city's recreational opportunities take place in Fairmount Park. In addition to the large areas of the park that straddle the Schuylkill River—East and West Parks—it also encompasses 63 distinct neighborhood parks and gardens, and hundreds of miles of hiking, biking, and jogging trails, including the popular Schuylkill River Bike Path. Those in search of less-trafficked areas head to the Wissahickon in the northwest section of the city or to one of the many nearby suburban parks and nature reserves. Beyond the endless recreational opportunities on

land, Philadelphia's two major rivers—the Delaware and Schuylkill—offer water enthusiasts a place to enjoy kayaking, rowing, boating, and water tours. Visit Philadelphia Parks & Recreation (www.phila.gov/recreation) for more information about all things outdoors.

PARKS AND GARDENS

You're never far from a park bench to sit on and take a break to read your newspaper (or Moon guidebook) anywhere in Philadelphia. Several impressive arboretums, children's playgrounds,

ARTS AND LEISURE

and historic gardens can also be found. The majority of Philadelphia's parks and gardens are part of the Fairmount Park system, even those that are not physically connected to the major park areas.

BARTRAM'S GARDEN

54th St. and Lindbergh Blvd., 215/729-5281, www.bartramsgarden.org

HOURS: Garden daily 10 A.M.–5 P.M.; tours of house and garden May-Oct. Fri.-Sun. 10:30 A.M.-4:30 P.M.

COST: Gardens free; tours $10 adult, $8 senior and student, free 12 and under

Map 9

The nation's first botanical garden is alive and well in Southwest Philadelphia. Founded in 1728 by John Bartram, a devout Quaker, the gardens and adjacent Bartram family home are both National Historic Landmarks. The 44 acres straddling the Schuylkill River feature native plants and flower gardens, ancient trees, a water garden, and a river trail. The oldest gingko tree in the country and the *Franklinia alatamaha*, a tree named for John Bartram's friend Benjamin Franklin, are just two of the notable flora you can find here. Explore the garden on your own or take a 45-minute guided tour of both the home and garden. History, science, and nature programs are also often offered. On summer weekends, you can get there via the **Schuylkill Banks River Tour** (888/748-7455, www.schuylkillbanks.org, $25 adult, $20 students and children 12 and under). The scenic guided boat tours depart from the Schuylkill River Bike Path and include a guided tour of Bartram's Gardens—a lovely 2.5-hour trip.

CLARK PARK

4400 Baltimore Ave., 215/555-8186, www.clarkpark.info

Map 6

Established in 1895, this nine-acre park in West Philadelphia is a treasured community asset offering lots of green space for picnics and sports and serves as a venue for many community gatherings. There are plenty of pleasant places to sit and relax on any given day, and a host of events

and concerts bring people in hordes. They come for fresh, affordable, produce at the **farmers market** (May–Thanksgiving Sat. 10 A.M.–2 P.M., June–Thanksgiving Thurs. 3–7 P.M., rest of the year Sat. 10 A.M.–1 P.M.). The Uhuru Solidarity Movement runs a monthly **Flea Market** on Saturdays (Apr.–Oct.) offering food, antiques, crafts ,and more (call 215/387-0919 for dates). Check out the Gettysburg Stone (a large Civil War battlefield monolith) and a life-size bronze statue of Charles Dickens and Little Nell from his novel *The Old Curiosity Shop*—a literary celebration is held in the park each February to honor Dickens's birthday.

FAIRMOUNT PARK

Multiple entrances, 215/683-0200, www.fairmountpark.org

Map 8

One of the best things about Philadelphia, Fairmount Park is considered the largest urban municipal park in the world, covering more than 9,200 acres. Not to brag, but for a little perspective, New York's Central Park is only 843 acres. The largest continuous sections of the park are East and West Fairmount Parks, which straddle the Schuylkill River. In addition, the Wissahickon in the northwest section of the city and Pennypack Park in the northeast section of the city are huge areas that are technically part of Fairmount Park but usually referred to by their own individual names. The entire park system encompasses 63 distinct neighborhood parks and gardens, including hundreds of miles of hiking, biking, and jogging trails, including the popular Schuylkill River Bike Path, as well as the central city squares Franklin Square, Logan Square, Rittenhouse Square, and Washington Square. Pretty much every patch of green in the city is technically part of Fairmount Park, but when people refer to it, they are usually referring to one of the large swaths on either side of the Schuylkill River that extend out behind the Art Museum into Northwest Philadelphia. Most recreational opportunities in the city take place in Fairmount Park, and the city's website is a great resource for all that it has to offer.

MORRIS ARBORETUM

100 E. Northwestern Ave., 215/247-5777,
www.upenn.edu/arboretum

HOURS: Apr.-Oct. Mon.-Fri. 10 A.M.-4 P.M.,
Sat.-Sun. 10 A.M.-5 P.M., Thurs. in summer until 8:30 P.M.;
Nov.-Mar. daily 10 A.M.-4 P.M.

COST: $14 adult, $12 senior, $7 student, active military,
or child 3-17, free child under 3 and PennCard holders

`Map 8`

Morris Arboretum is a lovely 92-acre beautifully landscaped Victorian garden, complete
with streams and sculptures, featuring more
than 2,500 types of plants. In the late 1800s,
"Compton" was the summer estate of wealthy
Quakers John and Lydia Morris, brother and
sister. They built a lovely plant and sculpture
collection on the grounds and hoped to one
day add a school and laboratory of horticulture and botany. This dream was ultimately
realized after their time, when in 1932 the
University of Pennsylvania transformed the
site into the Morris Arboretum. An interdisci-
plinary resource center, it is the official arboretum of the Commonwealth of Pennsylvania,
listed on the National Register of Historic
Places. There is an on-site café as well as frequent special exhibits and events.

PHILADELPHIA
HORTICULTURE CENTER

100 N. Horticultural Dr. (and Montgomery Ave.),
215/685-0096, www.fairmountpark.org/HortCenter.asp

HOURS: Display house daily 9 A.M.-3 P.M.; grounds
Nov.-Mar. daily 8 A.M.-5 P.M., Apr.-Oct. daily 8 A.M.-6 P.M.

COST: Free

`Map 8`

Fairmount Park's Horticulture Center includes an arboretum that dates to 1876, an
expansive greenhouse built for the bicentennial celebration in 1976, and more than 20
acres of lush landscape. Paths wind through
gardens, also home to a butterfly garden, a
large reflecting pool, and various sculptures
of poets, musicians, and animals. The inside
display area contains colorful tropical plants,
flowers, perennials, herbs, everlastings, and
rare trees. Picnic areas are available on the
grounds.

◖ RITTENHOUSE SQUARE

Btwn. 18th and 19th Sts. and Walnut and Locust Sts.

`Map 3`

When the weather is nice, it can be difficult to
find a bench in Rittenhouse Square, especially
during lunchtime. In fact, the pretty tree-lined
park in the swankiest part of town is pretty
hoppin' throughout the year, yet it somehow
remains a peaceful respite from the Center City
bustle—right in the middle of it all. A convenient break from skyscrapers and upscale shops
just beyond its perimeter, the square is filled
with suits on lunch break, families, dogs, artists, musicians, and a few homeless people as
well. Rittenhouse was called Southwest Square
until 1825, when it was renamed for famous
Philadelphia astronomer and clockmaker
David Rittenhouse (1732–1796), descendant
of William Rittenhouse of paper-mill fame.
Architect Paul Cret, also responsible for the
Benjamin Franklin Parkway and many of its
buildings, designed the entrances, the central
plaza, stone railings, the pool, and the fountain
in 1913. If you can't snag a bench, there is usually space to sit along the walls surrounding the
center fountain—great for people-watching—
and many people bring a blanket and set up on
the grass with a picnic lunch.

ROSE GARDEN AND
MAGNOLIA GARDEN

Locust St. btwn. 4th and 5th Sts.

`Map 1`

While touring the sights of Old City and
Society Hill, take a minute to stop and smell
the roses. A cobblestone path leads through
the Rose Garden, a tribute to the signers of
the Declaration of Independence and the
Constitution planted by the Daughters of the
American Revolution, a volunteer women's service organization dedicated to promoting pa-
triotism and preserving American history. The
buds peak in June. Just across the street, the
smaller Magnolia Garden was built in honor
of George Washington, who apparently loved
the magnolia tree. The 13 magnolia trees bor-
dering the garden represent the 13 original
colonies.

ARTS AND LEISURE

SHOFUSO JAPANESE HOUSE AND GARDENS

Landsdowne and Horticultural Drives, 215/878-5097, www.shofuso.com

HOURS: May–Oct. Tues.-Fri. 10 A.M.-4 P.M., Sat.-Sun. 11 A.M.-5 P.M.

COST: $6 adult, $3 student, child, or senior, free under 3

Map 8

In 1876, the Japanese Bazaar and Garden came to this area for the Centennial Exposition. While the site has changed shape several times, there has been some form of Japanese landscaping on this spot, now part of the Horticultural Center, ever since. Shofuso was designed by Junzo Yoshimura in 1954 for the Museum of Modern Art in New York to introduce Americans to Japanese design. It was relocated and reassembled here in Fairmount Park in 1958 as a gift from Japan. The authentic replica offers a glimpse into the life of a 17th-century wealthy Japanese scholar, high-ranking priest, or member of the upper class. Enjoy the tranquil setting, observe the symmetrical architecture, take part in a traditional tea ceremony, and learn about the history and culture of an authentic Japanese house. Tours of 30–45 minutes are offered based on staff availability.

SMITH: THE KIDS' PLAY PLACE IN THE PARK

33rd and Oxford Sts., East Fairmount Park, 215/765-4325, http://smithkidsplayplace.org

HOURS: Playground (children 10 and under) Apr.-Oct. Tues.-Sun. 10 A.M.-4 P.M., extended hours to 7 P.M. weekends late June-Aug.; playhouse (children 5 and under) year-round Tues.-Sun. 10 A.M.-4 P.M.

COST: Free

Map 8

Wealthy Philadelphians Richard and Sarah Smith wanted to create a safe, free place for children to play, so they opened one in Fairmount Park in 1899. While it has gone through several renovations since its opening, their original vision is still alive and well more than a century later. The 6.5-acre park and 24,000-square-foot playhouse offer a unique, fun, and educational play space for children 10 and under. The highlight is the giant enclosed wooden slide; built in 1905, it is large enough to accommodate about 10 kids across at a time. There is plenty for kids to play with inside the unique toy-filled mansion, and the most recent renovations and additions have made this historic play space better than ever before.

WASHINGTON SQUARE PARK

Btwn. Walnut and Locust Sts. and 6th and 7th Sts.

Map 1

A quieter counterpart to Rittenhouse Square, Washington Square serves a similar purpose for the Old City and Society Hill neighborhoods it straddles. The leafy respite is a place to sit and eat, read, or just take a break from it all amid a bustling urban area. Originally called Southeast Square when it was founded in 1682, it was renamed as a tribute to George Washington in 1825. Used as a burial ground for troops during the Revolutionary War and for victims of the yellow fever epidemics that followed, it wasn't until the surrounding neighborhoods developed that the square transformed into its current shape. In 1952, a major renovation included the creation of a monument to the soldiers and sailors of the Revolutionary War. Designed by architect G. Edwin Brumbaugh, the *Tomb of the Unknown Soldier* occupies an area near the center, serving as a memorial for the soldiers buried below. A constant flame burns to honor them.

HIKING, BIKING, AND JOGGING TRAILS

With more than 215 miles of scenic trails winding through Fairmount Park, there is a place for everyone to jog, hike, blade, bike, or ride horses. Paths range from paved to rocky terrain, flat to steep, and crowded to desolate. Some trails are only open to hikers or bikers, so be aware of the markers. You can grab a map of Fairmount Park at the visitor center or visit www.fairmountpark.org/trailsintro.asp for more information. Valley Forge, Fort

Washington, and Ridley Creek offer additional trails just outside the city.

PENNYPACK PARK

8500 Pine Rd., 215/281-7664, www.pennypackpark.com

Map 9

This 1,395-acre portion of Fairmount Park in Northeast Philadelphia is underutilized, but restoration projects over the past decade are finally bringing it to the attention of residents and visitors. Pennypack, named after the Lenni Lenape Indian word for slow-moving water, follows Pennypack Creek southeast for nine miles from Montgomery County to the Delaware River. Miles of paved and unpaved trails offer hikers, bikers, and horseback riders a variety of paths for recreation. Visit the website for a schedule of the free summer concert series held on select Wednesday evenings, featuring mostly tributes to big-name entertainers like the Beatles and Elvis. The on-site Pennypack Environmental Center offers programs at nearby Fox Chase Farm, a city-owned 112-acre working livestock farm.

(SCHUYLKILL RIVER TRAIL

Many access points along the Schuylkill River throughout Philadelphia and beyond, 215/683-0200, www.schuylkillrivertrail.com

Map 3

The city's most popular trail continues well beyond the city and into surrounding counties. When all the paving is complete, it is projected to be about 130 miles long. It follows the Schuylkill River from Center City and connects with Valley Forge National Park, which offers many additional trails. Whether you want a short ride or an all-day outing, there is a section of this trail to suit most needs. It is mostly flat and paved. It consists of several Fairmount Park trails and the Manayunk Canal Tow Path, so terrain varies somewhat along the way, but is constantly improving and expanding to connect an even greater area. The trail can be accessed in Center City via stairs or ramps on Market, Chestnut, or Walnut Street, or on the street level on Locust Street or just behind the

Art Museum. The busiest portion is the River Drive Recreational Loop, commonly referred to as "the loop." This 8.4-mile paved stretch begins and ends near the Art Museum, winds around both sides of the river, and crosses the East Falls Bridge. Exercise caution when walking or riding here, especially with children or on weekends, as it gets very crowded on nice days. **Lloyd Hall** (1 Boathouse Row), the first boathouse behind the Art Museum, has a café, bathrooms, and bicycles and inline skates available to rent by the hour on weekends April–October.

(WISSAHICKON PARK

Multiple access points, main entrance Valley Green Rd. near Wissahickon

Map 8

Those seeking an escape will be thrilled to learn that dense forests, lush greens, and a gentle creek exist within the city limits. The part of Fairmount Park that occupies the northwest section of Philadelphia is known as "the Wissahickon." It surrounds

© R. KENNEDY FOR GPTMC

The Wissahickon is a lovely part of Fairmount Park in the Northwest section of the city.

Wissahickon Creek, which runs through the park for seven miles. There are around 57 miles of trails snaking through the park and the Wissahickon Gorge—crossing bridges, climbing high ridges, and offering ample views. Some are rugged and hilly and others are flat with gravel. The Friends of the Wissahickon organization publishes a detailed map, available at its office in Chestnut Hill (8708 Germantown Ave., 215/247-0417, www.fow.org) and online. It includes roads, trails, buildings, bridges, dams, and statues, and is well worth it for anyone looking for an in-depth exploration of the park. Easy access and parking can be found near Forbidden Drive, the 11-mile well-traversed gravel stretch. There are no restrooms along the trails, so use the public restrooms at the entrance near the Valley Green Inn restaurant and parking area. There are multiple entry points throughout the neighborhoods of Mt. Airy, Roxborough, and Chestnut Hill.

Bike Rentals and Repairs

Bicycling is an excellent way to see the city, eliminating the problems of parking, traffic, and waiting for and spending money on public transportation. And since Center City is mostly flat, it's an easy ride. There is an increasing network of bike-friendly streets with wide bike-only lanes; for your safety and comfort, use these routes whenever possible, as Philly drivers can be a bit stingy about sharing the road. A map of routes can be found at the Independence Visitor Center or http://phillymap.com. The bike rental shops listed here are all conveniently located on or near the Schuylkill River Path, the most popular biking trail in the city. Credit card and photo ID are generally required for rentals. **The Bicycle Club of Philadelphia** (www.phillybikeclub. org) is also a great resource for bike enthusiasts. Founded in 1979, the club sponsors recreational cycling activities open to the public for a small fee and promotes bicyclists' rights and safe biking practices.

DETOURS

22 N. 3rd St., 267/324-5408,
http://detourstouring.com
HOURS: Tues.-Sun. 8 A.M.-5 P.M.
COST: 4 hours $29, 6 hours $35, all day $45
Map 1

In addition to bicycle rentals, Detours also offers guided bike, Segway, and running tours for varying fees. There are two routes to choose from: The Blue route goes through Independence Park, while the Orange route ventures to the Art Museum and the Schuylkill River Trail. The office is conveniently located in the heart of Old City.

FAIRMOUNT BICYCLES

2015 Fairmount Ave., 267/507-9370,
www.fairmountbicycles.com
HOURS: Tues.-Fri. 11 A.M.-6 P.M., Sat.-Sun. 10 A.M.-6 P.M.
COST: $18 half day, $30 full day, $120 week
Map 4

A full-service bike shop relatively new to the Fairmount neighborhood, Fairmount Bicycles sells new and refurbished bikes. Not too far from the Schuylkill Trail and very close to Eastern State Penitentiary, it offers hybrid bikes with racks for rent at prices a bit lower than others.

HUMAN ZOOM

4159 Main St., Manayunk, 215/487-7433,
www.humanzoom.com
HOURS: Mon., Tues., Thurs., and Fri. 11 A.M.-7 P.M., Wed. 11 A.M.-8 P.M., Sat. 10 A.M.-6 P.M., Sun. 11 A.M.-4 P.M.
COST: Hybrids $8 an hour, $30 daily (24 hours), $50 weekend (48 hours), $100 weekly; road bikes $80 up to 48 hours
Map 8

A seller of top-quality bikes, Human Zoom also has rentals and is the only place in the city that offers road bikes in addition to hybrids. It's close to the Schuylkill River Trail in Manayunk, making it convenient for anyone staying in Manayunk and wanting to spend a day on the path or ride into Center City. No reservations are accepted for hybrids—it's first-come, first-served.

LLOYD HALL BIKE SHACK

1 Boathouse Row, 215/568-6002,
http://breakawaybikes.com
HOURS: Apr.-Oct. Sat. 10 A.M.-6 P.M., Sun. 10 A.M.-4 P.M.
COST: $10/hour, $50/day
Map 4

Breakaway Bikes is a full-service bike store (1923 Chestnut St.) in Center City West that has teamed up with Fairmount Park to offer a convenient way to rent bikes to ride along the Schuylkill River Trail. Located at the hut near Lloyd Hall, the first boathouse just behind the Art Museum, bikes and inline skates are available for rent. The price includes helmet, pads, and locks.

NEIGHBORHOOD BIKE WORKS

3916 Locust Walk (Penn's campus btwn. Walnut and Locust Sts. near 40th St.), 215/386-0316,
www.neighborhoodbikeworks.org
HOURS: Call ahead
COST: Varies
Map 6

Neighborhood Bike Works is a very cool and unique nonprofit whose mission is "to create educational, recreational, and career-building opportunities for youth through bicycling in the Philadelphia area, and to promote cycling as an environment-friendly, healthy form of transportation." Among many youth and adult programs, the University City location offers free repairs and classes. It's known as "the bike church" because it is located in the basement of St. Mary's Church, and visiting is literally and figuratively an underground experience. The warehouse offers used and salvaged bike parts at a minimal price—normally ranging just $1–10—and there is no service charge since you do the work yourself. The veteran volunteer bike mechanics that facilitate the repairs are sometimes understaffed. Stick it out and have patience; they are always willing to help. They can even assist you in building a custom bike from scratch. The nonprofit has expanded in recent years and now has locations in North Philly, South Philly, Haddington, and Norristown, although the bike church in University City remains one of a kind.

PHILADELPHIA BIKE TOURS

Location varies, 215/514-3124 or 866/667-3395,
www.philadelphiabiketour.com
HOURS: Vary; weekends only
COST: Bike rental $57/day, $68 guided tour; moped rental $87/day, $56 guided tour

Bikes and mopeds are available for rental and can be delivered directly to your hotel. Or you can take a guided two-hour moped tour, three-hour bike tour, or customized tour of your choosing for a group of four or more. Tour stops may include the Italian Market, Independence Square, the Edgar Allan Poe House, Water Works, and the Philadelphia Museum of Art, among other sites, and the pace is relaxed, allowing time to stop and take in the attractions. Call 24 hours in advance to book. Tours are generally offered on weekends only, but weekday tours can sometimes be arranged with advance notice.

OTHER RECREATION
Bowling
LUCKY STRIKE LANES

1336 Chestnut St., 215/545-2471,
www.bowlluckystrike.com
HOURS: Sun. noon-midnight, Mon.-Thurs. 11:30 A.M.-midnight, Fri. 11:30 A.M.-2 A.M., Sat. noon-2 A.M.
COST: $5.95-$7.95 per game, or $45-75 per hour, depending on day and time, $4.25 shoe rental
Map 2

Lucky Strike Lanes is the Beverly Hills of bowling, bringing a slice of Los Angeles—where the swank chain originated—to Philadelphia. You'll pay a high price for the surprisingly good cuisine, modern technology, and posh clubby scene. The concept is based on the circa-1960 Hollywood Star Lanes, so there is a faux-vintage element to the decor. A strictly enforced dress code forbids sweats, jerseys, headgear, construction boots, sleeveless or "excessively baggy T-shirts," making Lucky Strikes the most exclusive—okay, only exclusive—alley in town. The 24 lanes can get crowded on Friday and Saturday nights, but many come in just for the scene or to play pool on one of the six tables. Reservations are accepted to rent lanes by the hour but not to pay per game. You must be 21 to enter after 9 P.M., and food and drink specials are available during happy hour (Mon.–Fri. 5–7 P.M. and Sat.–Sun. 6–8 P.M.).

🎳 NORTH BOWL

909 N. 2nd St., 215/238-2695,
www.northbowlphilly.com
HOURS: Mon.-Fri. 5 P.M.-2 A.M., Sat.-Sun. noon-2 A.M.
COST: $3.95-$5.95 depending on day and time,
$3 shoe rental
`Map 7`

In a former mechanics garage, North Bowl's 21,000 square feet of space spread over two floors. It's a popular pre- or post-bar-hopping hangout in Northern Liberties. People come as much to hang out in the stylish yet comfortable setting as they do for the lanes. The restaurant serves much better food than you'd expect at a bowling alley, and pool tables and games offer additional entertainment. Happy hour specials (Mon.–Fri. 5–7 P.M.) promise discounts on bowling, food, and drinks and a lively after-work scene. There is often a wait for lanes on weekends, so call ahead to reserve, or snag a seat on one of the leather benches while you wait. You have to be over 21 to enter after 9 P.M.

STRIKES BOWLING LOUNGE

4040 Locust St., 215/387-BOWL,
www.strikesbowlinglounge.com
HOURS: Mon.-Fri. 3 P.M.-2 A.M., Sat.-Sun. 10 A.M.-2 A.M.
COST: $3-5 depending on day and time, $3 shoe rental
`Map 6`

Strikes Bowling Lounge in University City offers bowling, billiards, and beverages to its mostly collegiate crowd. With a lively atmosphere on weekends and decent bar food to snack on between frames, it's easy to spend an entire night here. Lanes, food, and drinks can add up to a fat bill at the end of the night, but daily drink specials, happy hours, and lane discounts for students help keep prices in check. A student ID will save you $2 per game, and the best deal is on Sunday and Monday nights

7 P.M.–2 A.M., when you pay $10 admission to bowl as much as you want.

Fitness Centers

There are plenty of local and international chain fitness clubs with multiple locations all over the city, including Bally's, Sweat, Philadelphia Sports Club, and an extensive network of YMCAs that differ in amenities and cost but tend to be cheaper than private clubs. The two gyms listed here were included because they are unique offerings in a sea of well-equipped, if sometimes pricey, easy-to-find chain establishments.

RITTENHOUSE FITNESS CLUB

2002 Rittenhouse Sq., 215/985-4095, www.ritfit.com
HOURS: Mon.-Thurs. 6 A.M.-10 P.M., Fri. 6 A.M.-8 P.M.,
Sat.-Sun. 9 A.M.-5 P.M.
COST: $479/year, $35/month with $99 initial fee,
$10 day pass, discounts for students and couples
`Map 3`

Despite the ritzy association with the name "Rittenhouse," this no-frills health club is one of the best deals in town. It has all the standard equipment but lacks some of the lavish amenities and high prices of other Center City gyms. Many members have been coming forever, so it's a place where everybody knows your name but no one is likely to hit on you while you exercise. All the standard classes are held, including yoga, pilates, aerobics, spinning, and the new favorite, zumba.

12TH STREET GYM

204 S. 12th St., 215/985-4092, www.12streetgym.com
HOURS: Mon.-Thurs. 5:30 A.M.-11 P.M., Fri.
5:30 A.M.-10 P.M., Sat. 8 A.M.-8 P.M., Sun. 8 A.M.-7 P.M.
COST: $39/month with year commitment, $49/month
no commitment
`Map 2`

Located in the heart of the Gayborhood, the facility is one the largest in the city, with a 22-station strength training circuit, cardio machines galore, a roof deck, pool, sauna, juice bar, and full-size basketball and racquetball courts. More than 60 weekly group fitness classes include old standbys like cardio, abs, yoga, and pilates, along with tae-bo, mixed martial arts, and fun dance classes like hip-hop and zumba. A membership is one of the better deals among the first-rate gyms, but a one-day pass costs $20. Many members also frequent the **Soleil Tanning Center** next door; it's owned by the gym but you don't have to be a gym member to use it.

Frisbee Golf
SEDGELEY WOODS DISC GOLF COURSE
East Park, 33rd and Oxford Sts.,
www.fairmountpark.org/discgolf.asp
Map 8

Established in 1977, the second-oldest disc golf course in the country occupies a lovely setting in East Fairmount Park. As its name implies, the sport is a combination of Frisbee (the only

THE PAST AND FUTURE OF LOCAL SKATE CULTURE

Philly has long been a hot spot for skateboarding. For many years, skaters from New York, Boston, Los Angeles, and even overseas made the journey to Philadelphia's landmark **Love Park** (officially JFK Plaza). They came to thrash on its ramps, ledges, and stairs in a prime setting smack in the center of urban Philadelphia. Featured in practically every skate magazine there is and frequented by many pro and semi-pro skaters, Love Park was internationally recognized, and Philly was even chosen to host the 2001-2002 ESPN X Games as a result.

And then the city government stepped in and ruined everything. In response to damage complaints and other alleged nuisances, one of Philadelphia's major recreational assets and one of the things that made it so popular with youth came to an end. Despite many protests, the city closed Love Park to skaters in 2002 so that the suits on lunch breaks could eat in peace.

Since then, the skaters have been relegated to the only remaining large-scale skateboarding area in the city, **FDR Park.** Located on Pattison Avenue and Tuscany Drives at the park's south end, it's within walking (or rolling) distance to the Broad Street Subway Line. Philly's skate culture lives on in the shade of the raised highway, I-95, above. Fishbowls, ramps, innovative skate structures, and a 30-foot half pipe make this skate park perfectly nice, but the location leaves something to be desired. It's completely separate from the rest of the city, unlike prominent Love Park.

There is (hopefully) a happy ending to this story. Plans are underway for a brand-new,

better-than-ever skate park in another outstanding location. The proposed **Paine's Park** has found a 2.5-acre home on a picturesque stretch along the Schuylkill River next to the Art Museum. The designs incorporate interesting skate-friendly surfaces with art and green space, in the hopes that it will attract the general public to share the space with the skateboarders. Momentum is building, funds are being raised, and while at the time of printing, more funds were needed before breaking ground, the city is (hopefully) getting closer to having the world-class skate park that skaters have been waiting for since the loss of Love.

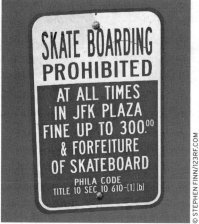

The penalty for skateboarding at Love Park (JFK Plaza) is steep.

equipment used) and golf (the object is to hit specific targets in the fewest number of attempts). Considered a great course by disc golf aficionados, the woods provide many natural obstacles. The course and parking are free and open to the public, but it's BYOD—bring your own discs.

Ice-Skating
BLUE CROSS RIVER RINK
AT PENN'S LANDING

Market St. and Columbus Blvd., 215/925-7465, www.riverrink.com

HOURS: Nov.-Feb. Mon.-Thurs. 6–9 P.M., Fri. 6 P.M.–1 A.M., Sat. 12:30 P.M.–1 A.M., Sun. 12:30–9 P.M., extended hours between Christmas and New Year's Eve

COST: $8 admission, $9 Fri. and Sat. nights, $3 rental, $10 parking

Map 1

When the temperature drops, the city and the Ben Franklin Bridge become a scenic backdrop for skaters gliding on the outdoor Blue Cross River Rink. Straddling the Delaware River at

the Blue Cross River Rink with the Ben Franklin Bridge beyond

Penn's Landing, the River Rink is a nice way to spend a winter day with kids or on a date. Most skating sessions run for two hours, which is enough time to skate, but plan ahead so you don't arrive in the middle of a session. Holiday parties, New Year's Eve countdowns, and St. Valentine's soirees are just a few of the special events that take place throughout the season.

UNIVERSITY OF PENNSYLVANIA ARENA

3130 Walnut St., 215/898-1923, www.business-services. upenn.edu/icerink

HOURS: Sept.-Mar. Mon., Wed., and Fri. noon–1:30 P.M., Sat. 5:45–7:15 P.M., Sun. 1:30–3 P.M.,

COST: $5 weekday, $7 weekend, $3 rental

Map 6

An impressive donation by the University of Pennsylvania's Class of 1923 funded this facility. Built in 1972, it is located in University City just across the Walnut Street Bridge from Center City. Frequented by Penn students and home to collegiate events for more than 30 years, ice hockey, figure skating, and speed games are common practice at the rink. The arena boasts 18,000 square feet of skating surface, six locker rooms, and 2,900 seats, and is open to the public for skating when other events are not taking place. It is also home to the Philly Roller Girls, a women's roller derby club.

WISSAHICKON ICE SKATING RINK

550 W. Willow Grove Ave., 215/247-1759, www.wissskating.com

HOURS: Public skate Friday 8:30–10:30 P.M., classes, teams, and leagues other times

COST: $9 admission, $3 rental, $1 guest card for nonmembers

Map 8

Chestnut Hill's indoor year-round ice rink is popular with families and with pre-teens looking for a fun night out on a weekend. It's also home to youth and adult hockey leagues, skating lessons, figure skating, and a pro-skating club. Many people on the ice are members, but the general public is also welcome. Session times vary by season, but the rink is open to the public Friday evenings year-round.

Yoga and Meditation
DHYANA YOGA
1611 Walnut St., Center City West, 215/496-0770, www.dhyana-yoga.com

Map 3

What started as a lovely little studio founded by an inspiring yoga instructor, Dhyana, has expanded to include locations in Old City, University City, and even the 'burbs of Ardmore and nearby Haddonfield, New Jersey. Classes are offered in a wide variety of styles, including Vinyasa, Kundalini, and Anusara, and include beginner and advanced options. If the additional studios are anything like the original, you can count on top-notch classes taught by inspiring instructors. Check the website for the frequent workshop offerings. A single class costs $15 with packages offered for repeat yogis. Additional studios are located at 68 N. 2nd Street, Old City, and 3945 Chestnut Street, University City.

WAKE UP YOGA
2329 Parrish St., Museum District, 215/235-1228, www.wakeupyoga.com

Map 4

Wake Up's original Vinyasa studio is in Fairmount; they later opened the U City and the South Philly location. Each studio offers several 90-minute classes a day varying in level of difficulty, but all levels are welcome to any class. Wake Up emphasizes the physical, spiritual, and philosophical aspects of yoga as much if not more than the physical workout and seeks to provide a nurturing, supportive atmosphere for students. Most single classes cost $14, but some are offered at the bargain price of $7. Additional studios are located at 4916 Baltimore Avenue, University City, and 1839 E. Passyunk Avenue, South Philadelphia.

Spectator Sports

In addition to the four major long-standing professional teams—the Eagles, Phillies, Flyers, and 76ers—the city gained a professional soccer team, the Union, in 2010, which quickly gained its own strong (sometimes maniacal) fan base. Philly has several minor league teams that play entertaining if somewhat less emotionally charged games at lower prices, and is home to an unparalleled five college basketball teams in the Big 5: Temple, University of Pennsylvania, St. Joe's, Villanova, and LaSalle. Penn's arena, the Palestra, has a storied history, and while somewhat run-down, it remains a favorite place for b-ball enthusiasts to watch a game.

BASEBALL
PHILLIES
Citizens Bank Park, 1 Citizens Bank Way, 215/463-1000, www.phillies.com

Map 9

The Phillies turned Philadelphia sports culture on its head with their World Series win in 2008. The championship-clinching strikeout

© KARRIE GAVIN

Citizens Bank Park is home to the Philadelphia Phillies.

© KARRIE GAVIN

Philadelphia Phillies fans watch the 2008 World Series celebration.

unleashed a wild celebration throughout the region, which culminated in a euphoric parade down Broad Street, a shared moment of joy for multiple generations of Philadelphians, sports fans and non-sports fans alike. It was the first championship of any major Philadelphia team in 25 years, forcing locals to reassess our perennial loser mentality.

The Phillies ended the decade with four consecutive National League East division titles and back-to-back World Series appearances in 2008 and 2009. Their success, coupled with their high-profile roster and magnetic ballpark, has made baseball as much of a local obsession as football. Excitement and interest in the ballclub are at an all-time high, and the Phillies now do what only a few years ago seemed impossible: They expect to win. And usually, they do.

Not so long ago a much different reality existed. Prior to their World Series title in 2008, no team had lost more games for more years and in more torturous ways and circumstances than the Philadelphia Phillies. The oldest pro team in the city, the Phillies had been instilling cynicism into the hearts of baseball fans since 1883, and had won a grand total of one championship—the World Series of 1980. In 2007, they lost their 10,000th game, setting a record for most losses of any professional team in any sport in American history.

While hardly a storied franchise for most of its history, many superb ballplayers have worn the Phillies uniform, even before 2008. The Whiz Kids of 1950 and the ragamuffin squad of 1993 gave the city thrilling rides to the World Series before losing—both remain etched in the memories of fans. The 1964 team was 6.5 games in front with just 12 games to play when they lost 10 in a row and missed the playoffs, becoming forever one of the gold standards for choking in baseball.

Citizens Bank Park opened in 2004, replacing the cavernous relic of Veterans Stadium. While many die-hard fans were resistant to the change, the bright, clean, modern stadium has been a big hit with fans and a major marketing tool for the franchise. Always a great spectator sport with its unique rhythm and laidback atmosphere, baseball in Philadelphia is, now more than ever, a fun day or night out. Crowds are a mix of families, couples, college kids, and rowdy fanatics, all united in cheering the Phillies toward victory.

It should also be noted that the Phillies Fanatic is hands-down the greatest mascot in all of sports. He alone is worth the price of admission. Tickets, relative to other professional sports, are affordable at around $20–65, but they are much harder to come by than they used to be, so you'll have to plan ahead. And, although it's illegal, it's also not uncommon to encounter scalpers selling tickets outside on game day.

PHILLY PHANATICS

The stereotype of Philadelphia sports fans is that they are a boorish, negative collection of boo-birds who revel in their collective misery when their teams aren't winning titles. And while I can't completely dispute this stereotype, it isn't the full picture. The unique passion for sports in Philadelphia means that all of our major sports have a fan base that is ravenous, persistent, and incredibly loyal. Being a Philadelphia sports fan means expecting to lose but watching anyway – year after year. It means getting pumped every season and saying to each other "this is the year," and at the end of the season when the team loses, shaking our heads and saying "that's Philly for you."

The signature call of the Philly fan is the much used, oft-discussed, and never ambiguous boo. Booing is done in nearly every city in America, but in Philly, booing is an act of protest, a fight for inclusion into the happenings on the field or court – our own way of participating. People boo for good reasons, like when a referee makes a bad call, and for poor ones, like a fan answering a question wrong during a time-out game. In the equal opportunity nature of booing, kids get booed when they drop a foul ball, cheerleaders get booed if they don't dance well, officials get booed, coaches get booed, and players, obviously, get booed.

But the boos are merely a small chapter in a complex relationship between the fans and the teams. As tough as the city is on its teams, a good team will always be supported by big crowds in Philadelphia – especially a good team that plays hard and has character. For all these reasons, Philadelphia is one of the few true sports towns in the country. And just remember, the relationship between the teams and the fans is like a family: You can insult your own family all you want, but if somebody else does, watch out. So if you're not from around here, be careful, especially if you're here to cheer for someone else in our arenas. Check out a game and see for yourself what a Philly crowd is all about.

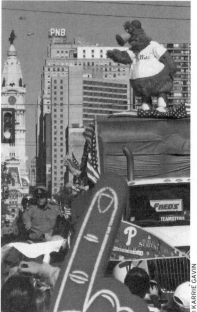

© KARRIE GAVIN

Phillies phanatics during the 2008 Phillies World Series parade

BASKETBALL
76ERS
Wells Fargo Center, 3601 S. Broad St., 800/298-4200, www.nba.com/sixers

Map 9

Providing the city with countless highlights, lowlights, and players of legendary and infamous status, the 76ers, or the "Sixers," has been Philadelphia's pro basketball team since 1963. Despite the team's rich history and pedigree of the franchise, recent struggles have led to small crowds and diminished expectations.

The Sixers began the decade as a championship-caliber team led by a dynamic superstar(Allen Iverson) and a legendary coach (Larry Brown), but have since struggled mightily to regain an identity and strong fan base. Following the NBA Finals appearance in 2001, the team has gone through numerous players, coaches, and rebuilding plans, all with the same result: mediocrity.

The immediate future of the team is important, because without significant progress on the court (and in the win column), the Sixers risk falling even further behind the other teams in the city in terms of popularity and visibility. The once-proud franchise brought back former player Doug Collins to instill some passion and leadership to a young group of players as they seek to turn from an afterthought to a contender.

It wasn't always this way. Beginning in the 1960s with Wilt Chamberlain, the Sixers have always boasted star power if not always a stellar record. The fortunes of the franchise have coincided with the comings and goings of some of the greatest superstars in NBA history, including Julius "Dr. J" Erving, Moses Malone, Charles Barkley, and Allen Iverson. Unfortunately for Sixers fans, most of these stars were ultimately traded away in bad deals for the team.

Among the enduring legacies of the Sixers are the championship titles, the fierce and often personal battles waged against division rival Boston in the 1960s–1990s, the fast-breaking teams of Dr. J. and George McGinnis in the mid to late '70s, the sustained excellence of the team from the late '70s–mid-'80s, the explosiveness and candor of Charles Barkley, and the singular talent and heart of Allen Iverson—who in 2001 led the team to its first finals appearance since 1983. The all-time low was the 9–73 record in 1972–1973, which to this day remains the record for fewest wins in a season by a professional basketball team.

Games are played at the Wells Fargo Center. The crowd at a Sixers game is the most diverse in age and ethnicity of any of the pro teams, and on a good night, it is an electrifying experience. Tickets are generally not difficult to get and range from as low as $10 to well over $100, available online or at the stadium.

BOXING
THE LEGENDARY BLUE HORIZON
1314 N. Broad St., 215/763-0500, www.legendarybluehorizon.com

Map 7

The nation's oldest boxing ring operating today, the Legendary Blue Horizon is well known in the boxing world as one of the last remaining old-school boxing venues in the country. The building dates to 1865, but it wasn't until 1961 that it became a boxing venue. It has earned the "legendary" in its title by housing some of the greatest fights in history. It has become a landmark center for training, education, and community participation, and the best boxers and teachers from the city and beyond train, fight, and teach here throughout the year. Come out for "fight night" to see the purest showcase of boxing available today. The Blue Horizon has been voted the "#1 Boxing Venue in the World" by *Ring* magazine and the "last boxing venue in the country" by *Sports Illustrated*.

FOOTBALL
EAGLES
Lincoln Financial Field, 1 Lincoln Financial Field Way, www.philadelphiaeagles.com

Map 9

In a crowded and passionate sports town, no team draws more attention than the Eagles. The combination of being a perennial contender, the national obsession with football, and Philly's general obsession with the game, has positioned the Eagles as the number one sports draw in the city and surrounding area—a standing that shows no sign of changing soon. Even with the Phillies' recent success there remains a uniquely feverish connection between the town and the football team, though the popularity of the club far outpaces the championship output of the franchise.

The Eagles are still looking for their first Super Bowl Championship (before the Super Bowl existed, they won the Championship in 1960), a quest that riles the fan base into a fever every autumn, and so far has left them heartbroken every January. When Andy Reid became head coach in 1998, the team was following a depressing 3–13 season. What has taken place since is the franchise's most consistently competitive streak in 50 years. The Reid era continues as of 2011 despite the team trading away longtime star and polarizing local figure Donovan McNabb in 2010 and taking on an even more polarizing Michael Vick (for anyone who doesn't follow the news, that's the guy who served time for running a brutal dog-fighting ring) as the new starting quarterback.

Despite competitive and exciting teams, frequent trips to the playoffs, and a roster stocked with high-profile names, the lack of a Super Bowl trophy looms large over the team and the city. Nothing short of a championship will satisfy the embattled Eagles fans, who with each passing year become more vociferous and cranky, turning Lincoln Financial Field into a notorious cauldron of noise, emotion, and the occasional drunken brawl. The party inside the stadium is an extension of the tailgate scene that begins early on Sundays and continues until kickoff. And beyond the stadium scene, football and Sunday go hand-in-hand in Philadelphia, as the Eagles' faithful use the entire day to drink and yell away the previous week of work and responsibility.

Possessing a bad reputation that is not entirely unwarranted, Eagles' fans don't often waste a chance to yell at opposing teams and their fans, and sometimes even each other, in and outside of the stadium. Be warned: If you show up at a game wearing a jersey of the other team, you *will* catch heat and may be putting yourself at real risk.

Eagles tickets have become the most expensive and elusive in the city, with a long and implacable waiting list. Individual tickets go on sale before the season's start and get snapped up in a matter of minutes. The best bet for tickets is at the team website (www.philadelphiaeagles.com), or on eBay or Craigslist (www.craigslist.org), but either way you will pay hundreds of dollars to see a game. Scalpers sell tickets at the stadium in exchange for a high price and the risk of arrest for the illegal purchase.

SOUL

Wells Fargo Center, 3601 S. Broad St., 888/744-5235, www.philadelphiasoul.com

Map 9

Named for the distinct sounds of soul music that originated in Philly, the Philadelphia Soul is the city's team in the Arena Football League. Under the direction of New Jersey–born rock star Jon Bon Jovi, who founded the team in 2004, Soul games are family-friendly events at the Wells Fargo Center. With alcohol-free seating zones and games and activities for children, fans can get close to the action. The season begins in March, and ticket packages are available. This version of Philly football is a far cry from the Eagles, but with low-end tickets available for as little as $13, it offers an affordable alternative to satisfy a football fix.

HOCKEY
FLYERS

Wells Fargo Center, 3601 S. Broad St., http://flyers.nhl.com

Map 9

The Orange and Black. The Broad Street Bullies. The Philadelphia Flyers, the youngest of the professional teams in Philly, lack for nothing when it comes to owning a secure place in the mythology of the sports scene. With some of the most loyal and fervent fans in the city, Flyers hockey has always meant big hits, wild punches, and sold-out stadiums.

LEGENDARY SPORTS FIGURES

Philadelphia has been home to some of the most legendary sports figures of all time. Remembering them is a bittersweet endeavor, since the teams have generally seen less than their share of success considering how many superstars have played in Philly. (Perhaps that is why the most famous Philadelphia sports figure of all is a fictional character – Rocky Balboa, a gritty fighter who never fell short against all odds.) But any true sports fan should read on to understand the impact that some of the most colorful athletes of all time had on the game – and the city.

BASKETBALL

Wilt Chamberlain was the towering center who grew up in West Philly and played for the Philadelphia Warriors and the 76ers. Combining size, strength, and agility, Wilt destroyed opponents and records. His impressive credits include 100 points in a game, 55 rebounds in a single contest, and averaging 50 points a game for an entire season, and his off-court records include his famous claim of going to bed with 20,000 women.

Julius "Dr. J" Erving, a showman who joined the 76ers in 1976 and rejuvenated the sport, had a massive afro and debonair goatee,

Wilt Chamberlain (right) in 1966

along with an in-your-face elegance that brought style and flair to the NBA. His ability to float in the air created the standard by which all high-flyers – from Michael Jordan to Vince Carter – are judged today. One of the most popular players in franchise history, he led the 1983 team to a world championship, cementing his iconic status forever.

Charles Barkley was considered short (at 6'6") and fat (sometimes topping 300 lb.) when he entered the NBA in 1984. With explosive strength and intensity, he became the face of the franchise when Dr. J retired in 1986. Arguably the greatest pure rebounder of his era, he became the shortest player to lead the league in rebounds in 1987. His emotions and relationship with fans and media were tumultuous, but today he is remembered for his honesty and self-deprecating humor, remaining hugely popular in Philly.

A six-foot shooting guard who threw his body around like a football player, **Allen Iverson** was the number one overall pick in the 1996 draft when he came to Philly. His astonishing scoring ability was matched by his passion and willingness to play through injury. This, along with his frenetic style, endeared him to fans and carried him through numerous off-court distractions and tabloid headlines. There was never a dull moment with A.I., and while many bristled at his contempt for authority, the city was mesmerized by his toughness and electric abilities. He played every game like it was his last – a favorite line of his – and for that he'll always be loved. Despite a hopeful but ultimately disappointing return to Philly for part of the 2009–2010 season, which ended abruptly due to injury and personal struggles, Iverson is the Sixers' most recent superstar and will always have a place in fans' hearts.

FOOTBALL

Chuck Bednarik, known as "Concrete Charlie," was a linebacker and center for the Eagles in the 1950s and '60s. One of the last "two-way" players, Bednarik had mangled hands and a nasty attitude that fans loved. He is fondly remembered as the face of the only championship team in Eagles history, the 1960 NFL Champions (pre-Super Bowl, which came into existence in 1966).

Dick Vermeil was the coach of the 1980 Eagles team that went to the Super Bowl – the team's first title game since 1960. The team played above expectations for a coach known for his intensity and 20-hour days. A high point for the team was a victory over its hated rival, the Dallas Cowboys – a team that otherwise had its way with the Eagles throughout the 1970s. Unfortunately, the Eagles were routed by an Oakland Raiders team that spent nights out on Bourbon Street while the Eagles studied plays in their hotel rooms to no avail.

Reggie White, who played for the Eagles 1985-1992, is arguably the best defensive lineman in team history. With legendary strength, he routinely tossed huge offensive linemen out the way en route to the quarterback. A devout Christian and ordained minister, "the Minister of Defense" was a rare combination of athlete and leader who headed one of the best defenses in NFL history.

HOCKEY

Ask anyone about the Flyers and they're sure to mention **Bobby Clarke.** Captain of the Stanley Cup-winning teams of 1973-1974 and 1974-1975, "Clarkie" embodied the blood-and-guts effort of the hockey team and the town. A diabetic, he was never even supposed to play hockey, but his work ethic and talent were an unstoppable combination.

Bernie Parent was the goalie of those Stanley Cup-winning teams, and many knowledgeable fans agree he was the biggest part of those championships. Arguably the best goalie of his era, his record for most games won in a single season was not broken by any goalie until 2007.

Eric Lindros came to the NHL as highly touted as any player in history, and the Flyers landed him after a bitter legal proceeding with the New York Rangers. Despite his talent, his time with the team was marked by injury, bitter disputes, and, disappointingly, no Stanley Cup. He was tagged the next Wayne Gretzky or Mario Lemieux, perhaps unfairly, and he never delivered.

BASEBALL

Richie Ashburn, one of the few men around town who could pull off the nickname "Whitey," was beloved in Philadelphia, first as the center fielder for the Phillies in the 1950s and later as a radio commentator. His understated style and easy humor connected with fans, and he was adopted as a native son. His signature line, "Hard to believe, Harry," (directed to his radio partner, Harry Kalas, also a local hero), often followed a goofy blooper or awkward moment for the Phillies.

Perhaps the greatest third baseman of all time, **Mike Schmidt** played his entire career with the Phils. The cornerstone of the team that won the only World Championship in franchise history in 1980, he made it look easy with great power at the plate and superior glove work at the hot corner. Despite his talent, he had a perplexingly embattled relationship with the home crowd and often heard boos. He has since become more appreciated, and a statue of him is featured prominently outside Citizens Bank Park.

Hall of Fame pitcher **Steve Carlton** was responsible as much as anyone for leading the Phils to the 1980 World Series Championship. Known as "Lefty" for obvious reasons, he was virtually unhittable during his prime in the mid-1970s and early 1980s. Known for his surly nature, he refused to speak to reporters and was not subtle in discouraging the team manager or catcher from "disturbing" him on the mound. He also was known for his large wine collection.

It's perhaps too soon to know who will go down in history from the **2008 Phillies' World Series Championship Team,,** so the entire team has made the list for now. In a 4-1 series victory over the Tampa Bay Rays, the win rocked the city and forced Philly fans to redefine themselves as winners and find something new to complain about besides their decades-long losing streak. The team was overflowing with talent and personality (sure, all the winning didn't hurt either in making us love them), but I'd be remiss not to mention Jimmy Rollins (J-Roll), Chase Utley, Ryan Howard, Shane Victorino, Jason Werth, Cole Hamels, or General Manager Charlie Manuel, the sweet, bumbling old man who can barely string a sentence together for press conferences but clearly kicks butt when it comes to leading a team to a championship win.

Created in 1967 as part of hockey's expansion, the Flyers have been a perennial contender year in and year out, coming close many times but still looking for their first championship since winning back-to-back Stanley Cups in 1973–1974 and 1974–1975. They came heartbreakingly close in 2010 with a Stanley Cup run that ended in overtime of Game 6.

The bruising style and reputation they developed in the early '70s, which earned them the "Bullies" nickname, made the Flyers local heroes in Philly and one of the most hated teams in the league. The championship teams and their players forged a strong connection to the city that remains strong and partially accounts for their intense and loyal following. Fans still clamor for the style of play that was successful in the '70s, and often a crunching check or violent confrontation between two enforcers gets the Philly crowd more juiced than a nice pass or a pretty goal. Hockey tends to takes a back seat to the other three major sports in terms of its overall impact on the city, but when the Flyers are doing well, additional fans come out in droves.

Tickets can be purchased online at the team website and at the stadium. Even during down years the Flyers remain a tough ticket to nab—and an expensive one, with tickets starting around $70 and reaching upwards of $150 for the best seats.

HORSE RACING
PARX RACING
3001 Street Rd., Bensalem, 215/639-9000, www.parxracing.com
Map 9

Live thoroughbred racing and a casino draw visitors to Bensalem, about a 10-minute ride from Center City just outside of Northeast Philadelphia. Watch and bet from inside the Pennsylvania Derby Room or take a picnic lunch and enjoy the grounds when the weather is nice. Gates usually open at 11 A.M. Friday–Tuesday year-round, although the schedule changes from time to time, so call or check

the website. First race of the day starts around 12:30 P.M.

LACROSSE
WINGS
Wells Fargo Center, 3601 S. Broad St., 215/389-9464, www.wingslax.com
Map 9

Lacrosse fans will find a rowdy crowd in the Wells Fargo Center when the Philadelphia Wings take to the turf. With constant chants, inescapable heckling, and the team's unofficial anthem, Guns & Roses' "Welcome to the Jungle," playing at every game, it's difficult to leave without a hoarse throat. The season begins in January, with NLS playoffs following in the spring.

SOCCER
UNION
PPL Park, 1 Stadium Dr., Chester, PA, 877/218-6466, www.philadelphiaunion.com
Map 9

In 2010 Philadelphia welcomed professional men's soccer to its already fully stocked sports scene when the Philadelphia Union became the 16th team in the MLS. The Union immediately attracted a dedicated fan base of soccer enthusiasts that seems to be growing. The most loyal of all of those fans call themselves the Sons of Ben (Franklin, that is), who petitioned the MLS in 2007 to bring a team to Philly in the first place. As obsessed with their team as the guys who paint their faces green for Eagles games, the Sons of Ben make themselves known at every game. Whether or not soccer grows into an impact professional sport in the region is yet to be seen, but the high-energy games are certainly worth checking out. The attractive stadium, PPL Park in Chester, was built just for the Union as part of an effort to revitalize the waterfront in an otherwise rundown area. Just outside of Philadelphia, it's is an easy drive or can be accessed via SEPTA's Wilmington/Newark regional rail line and a free shuttle from the station to the stadium.

SHOPS

There was a time when the most fashionable Philadelphians regularly made the two-hour trip to New York for their serious shopping needs. Fortunately, as with most things in Philadelphia, the shopping scene has come into its own, especially in the past decade. The major shopping districts have expanded while unique, independent shops have sprung up in neighborhoods throughout the city. With no shortage of boutiques, vintage shops, specialty stores, and all the chain stores you'd hope to find in a major metropolitan area, you can find everything your consumer heart desires in Philadelphia.

Center City is the nexus of the shopping world, with the bulk of stores concentrated on or near Walnut and Chestnut Streets west of Broad, also called Rittenhouse Row. Old City, South Street, Washington Square West, and Northern Liberties are also home to large concentrations of shops, and the three shopping rows—Jewelers Row, Fabric Row, and Antique Row—offer unparalleled selections of their respective specialties. Several indoor urban shopping malls—the Gallery, Liberty One, the Shops at the Bellevue and the Comcast Center—offer a range of standard and high-end chain stores. Chinatown sells all things Asian, and Reading Terminal Market and the Italian Market are tops for kitchenware, gourmet treats, and other specialty items. Chestnut Hill and Manayunk offer a small-town shopping atmosphere just a short drive from Center City, while the big-box stores on Delaware Avenue and several nearby malls round out the options.

Weekends are bustling in the major shopping areas, and the heart of Center City is pretty

© DUROSS & LANGEL

HIGHLIGHTS

LOOK FOR ◖ TO FIND RECOMMENDED SHOPS.

◖ **Best Independent Bookstore:** The small, inconspicuous **Joseph Fox Bookshop** offers an excellent selection of titles, with a friendly, helpful staff that can help you find your next favorite (page 177).

◖ **Best Vinyl Selection:** The **Philadelphia Record Exchange** is a must for all record lovers. Three full floors in a row house just off South Street are stocked with rock, jazz, soul, punk, R&B, and more (page 178).

◖ **Best Sports Gear:** For more than a century, **Mitchell & Ness** has been providing quality sporting gear to Philadelphia teams and

© JOEL KATZ/COURTESY JOSEPH FOX BOOKSHOP

Joseph Fox Bookshop

locals. Today, it draws huge crowds from far beyond the city for its classic throwback jerseys, with online orders from around the globe for people who can't make it to Philly (page 180).

◖ **Best Shoe Store: Benjamin Lovell Shoes** proves that you don't have to sacrifice comfort for style. Offering men's and women's shoes in three different locations, the store carries the top brands in the world of high-comfort shoes (page 183).

◖ **Best Place to Get a Handmade Messenger Bag: R.E. Load Baggage, Inc.** is the place to go for durable custom-designed bags. This grassroots company is 100 percent Philly (page 187).

◖ **Best Gift Shop: Verde** offers a wide array of accessories and home and gift items, including gourmet chocolates, T-shirts, bags, mugs, and baby clothes, all bearing iconic yet hip Philly images. (page 188).

◖ **Best Outdoor Shopping: The Piazza at Schmidts** is Northern Liberties very own European-style plaza. It's lined with boutiques, galleries, and unique shops; the best time to visit is for the market on weekends, when vendors set up their wares outside (page 190).

◖ **Best Bath and Body Shop: Duross & Langel** offers soaps and all sorts of body, face, and hair lotions as well as potions in every delicious scent you can imagine. Made using natural ingredients crafted on location, the items at this independent shop are lower-priced than at most of the upscale cosmetic chains (page 192).

◖ **Best Place to Take a Break: Terme Di Aroma** offers a calm, soothing haven in the heart of bustling Old City. Take a break from sightseeing and get pampered with an aromatherapy massage or facial (page 194).

much always bustling. Most Center City shops are open seven days a week, but in some neighborhoods, many shops are closed on Monday. Some stores in Center City stay open a few hours later on Wednesday evening. And remember, there is no sales tax on clothing in Pennsylvania, so take full advantage if you're looking for any big-ticket items like that hot leather jacket you've had your eye on for so long.

SHOPPING DISTRICTS

All of these districts are great starting points for shopping. Characterized by their own distinctive styles and atmospheres and home to a large concentration of stores, they make pleasant areas to stroll whether you're stocking up on gifts and souvenirs, buying a whole new wardrobe for yourself, or just window shopping.

CHESTNUT HILL

Germantown Ave. between Abington Ave. and Evergreen Ave.

`Map 8`

Germantown Avenue in Chestnut Hill is just "the Avenue" to locals of the upscale neighborhood in Northwest Philadelphia. The only business district in an otherwise residential area, it feels like a small-town Main Street with its attractive storefronts, Victorian lampposts, cobblestone streets, and shoppers who stop to chat with one another. While selections are varied, you can find a good dose of antiques, upscale home goods, several art galleries, spas, and clothing and jewelry shops. More people from the surrounding neighborhoods and suburbs than from Center City frequent these shops, although a few of the unique art, antiques, and furniture stores draw the downtown sect as well.

EAST PASSYUNK AVENUE

East Passyunk Ave. between Federal and Tasker Sts.

`Map 5`

This stretch of East Passyunk Avenue in South Philly has gone through a major Renaissance in the past decade. Home to several centuries-old mom-and-pop shops that help it maintain its Old World character, the area has exploded with gourmet markets and coffee

shops, boutique and vintage clothing and jewelry shops, garden supplies, and much more. A young, vibrant community has moved in, joining many of the families that have been rooted here for generations, and businesses keep springing up to meet their needs.

MANAYUNK

Main St. between Green Ln. and Shurs Ln.

`Map 8`

Formerly a run-down mill town, Manayunk has transformed into one of the city's major business districts in the past few decades. Straddling the Schuylkill River a short drive from Center City, the shops are concentrated on Main Street and include both upscale and vintage boutiques, jewelry, accessories, stylish eyeglasses, and independent music and art galleries. Main Street also claims to hold the largest concentration of furniture and home-goods stores on one street on the entire East Coast.

MIDTOWN VILLAGE

13th St. between Market and Spruce Sts.

`Map 2`

While Center City west of Broad Street, or the Rittenhouse area, is usually considered the center of downtown shopping because it is home to the major chain stores, the area east of Broad is also a shopper's paradise. While the name Midtown Village has not fully caught on yet with locals, there is no disputing that this area, roughly bordered by Market and Spruce Streets from Broad to 11th, is a bustling shopping district, and it keeps getting better. Shops, mostly unique boutiques and specialty stores, are concentrated on 13th Street, which is also home to plenty of restaurants and bars. Nearby or overlapping with Antique Row, Washington Square West, and the Gayborhood, the area offers diverse shopping opportunities.

OLD CITY

3rd St. between Chestnut and Race Sts.

`Map 1`

Old City is not only home to the city's largest concentration of historic attractions; it is also a shopper's paradise, where tourists and locals alike flock for cool clothing boutiques and art galleries, with the largest concentration of boutiques on 3rd Street north of Market Street. Whether you're looking for books and music, vintage jeans, or furniture that doubles as artwork, Old City has it all. With great restaurants, bars, coffee shops, and an attractive, manageable several square blocks to navigate, it is also one of the most pleasant shopping areas. The best time to shop for art is during the first Friday of each month, when galleries open their doors to the public to display and sell their wares.

RITTENHOUSE ROW
Walnut St. between Broad and 18th Sts.
Map 3

If you have a deep wallet and a love of shopping, you'll find paradise in the sophisticated

ROWS AND ROWS

In addition to the varied neighborhood and downtown shopping districts, Philadelphia is home to Antique Row, Fabric Row, and Jewelers' Row, each offering unparalleled selections of their respective specialties and a one-of-a-kind shopping experience. Like most things in Philly, each of these "rows" has its own unique history.

ANTIQUE ROW
The tree-lined stretch of Pine Street concentrated between 9th and Broad Streets is a treasure trove of antiques stores and boutiques known as Antique Row. But the oldest continuously operating antiques district in the entire country has continually evolved, so while there are at least 15 antiques stores remain today, the area represents a diverse mix of the old and the new. It is now also home to a wide variety of furniture, home accessories, jewelry, stained glass, clothing, and collectibles stores just steps from one another on Pine Street. Shops range from **Kohn and Kohn** (1112 Pine St., 215/923-0432, www.kohnandkohnantiques.com), established in 1932, specializing in antique furniture, glass, and collectibles, to fully modern shops to those offering a mix of antique and modern items, like **Halloween** (1329 Pine St., 215/732-7711), an impressive jewelry shop packed tight with a mix of vintage and estate pieces and unique modern and handcrafted gems. Antique Row is also part of the Washington Square West neighborhood, straddling the Midtown Village shopping district, so there are plenty of additional stores of all kinds along the nearby streets to the north, especially along 13th Street – home to everything from books, records, and cosmetics to gay-themed specialty stores.

FABRIC ROW
At the turn of the 20th century, scores of Jewish immigrants settled in the southern outskirts of Center City – now South Philadelphia. The many skilled tailors and seamstresses among them were often forced to take jobs in sweatshops creating fine clothes for the upper class. Many sold goods in pushcarts on several blocks of South 4th Street below South Street; some eventually opened their own shops, and the area became known as Fabric Row (http://fabricrow.com). What remains is a vibrant and eclectic (if a bit rundown on the outside) community of fabric shops, along with a sprinkling of clothing and shoe boutiques, a gourmet market, and a café. While the stores appear mostly the same on the outside and it is hard to know where to start, many locals have their favorites. For creating clothing or home wares, **Kincus Fabrics** (754 S. 4th St., 215/923-8836) has a vast selection of cotton, spandex, Lycra, rayon, silk, draperies, and faux fur; **Marmelstein's** (760 S. 4th St., 215/925-9862) offers a comprehensive selection of decorative trimmings and drapery hardware; and the basement of **Maxie's Daughter** (724 S. 4th St., 215/829-2226) offers a veritable fabric history of Philadelphia, with vintage textiles that haven't seen the light of day for the better half of a century. If you don't work with fabric already, the fabulous finds just may inspire you to sew your own curtains or reupholster that old, comfy chair.

Rittenhouse Square area. The abundance of retail opportunities is unparalleled, with unique boutiques and high-end luxury chain stores concentrated on Walnut and Chestnut Streets west of Broad Street and the surrounding blocks. Several indoor urban malls—the Shops at Liberty Place, the Shops at the Bellevue, and the Shops at the Comcast Center—are packed with additional mainstream and high-end retailers. In fact, all the chain staples can be found in this area, including Gap, J. Crew, Victoria's Secret, Ann Taylor, Borders, Zara, H&M, Loehmann's, and American Apparel, along with the somewhat harder-to-find chains like Puma, Lucky Jeans, Kiehl's, Barney's Co-op, and Sephora, and high-end chains like Kenneth Cole, Brooks Brothers, BCBG, Tiffany, Nicole Miller, and Williams-Sonoma. The latest major chain to call

JEWELERS' ROW

Get your bling on, on Jewelers' Row – the oldest and second-largest (after New York) diamond district in the country. Concentrated on a brick-paved stretch of Sansom Street between 7th and 8th Streets and continuing along 8th Street between Chestnut and Walnut Streets, Jewelers' Row is home to more than 300 jewelry specialists, retailers, wholesalers, craftspeople, and traders, offering a staggering variety of diamonds, precious and semiprecious stones, platinum, pearls, watches, and more. The sky is the limit on prices, but with so much competition in such a small area, good deals can often be found. Retailers include large stores like **Steven** **Singer Jewelers** (739 Walnut St., 215/627-3242) and smaller ones like **I. Gansky & Co.** (718 Sansom St., 215/922-0505), with many more that be found at www.philadelphiajewelersrow.com.

The row was established as a center for jewelers in the years 1860-1880, but its historical significance dates back even further. Originally named Carstairs Row for builder and architect Thomas Carstairs, the row was home to 22 look-alike dwellings built 1799-1820 and considered the first row homes in the country. They provided affordable housing and initiated a widespread housing trend that remains prevalent throughout downtown Philadelphia and much of the country today.

© KARRIE GAVIN

Jewelers' Row is home to an array of jewelry shops as well as the nation's first row homes.

Rittenhouse home is a long-awaited Apple Store in 2010, raising the status of the Philadelphia shopping scene yet again to a level befitting one of the largest cities in the country.

SOUTH STREET
South St. between Front and 8th Sts.
Map 5

Concentrated primarily on the blocks and side streets between Front and 8th Streets, South Street offers an eclectic mix of several hundred shops. Most are independently owned and cater to a diverse mix of people. Head shops, tattoo parlors, hip-hop clothing stores, independent record stores, whimsical home and gift shops,

and kinky lingerie and sex shops coexist on the street. From the ridiculously comfortable options at Benjamin Lovell Shoes to the cheap and trendy fashions at Bare Feet to athletic wear at Reebok and Foot Locker, South Street is also the place for shoes of all kinds. Venture deeper into South Philadelphia to visit the **Italian Market** on 9th Street between Christian Street and Washington Avenue for gourmet specialty stores and treats. Still deeper south, the ever-growing **East Passyunk Avenue** business district, extending south from Dickinson Street, offers an eclectic mix of boutiques, gourmet groceries, old-school South Philly clothing shops, and much more.

Books and Music

While there is nothing wrong with a place where you can buy the bestsellers or the greatest top 40 hits (Borders and Barnes & Noble in Center City), you should also take advantage of Philly's underground book and music scene at some of these unique gems. If you don't, they just may not be here much longer.

BOOKS
BOOK TRADER
7 N. 2nd St., 215/925-0511
HOURS: Daily 10 A.M.–10 P.M.
Map 1

This one-of-a-kind Old City bookstore has a laid-back staff and a even more laid-back vibe. While the store is cluttered, it is cluttered with great used books at reasonable used-book prices, so we can't complain. The perfect place to relax and hunt for great reading material, it's the antithesis of the overpriced, squeaky-clean chains taking over the world, so enjoy while it lasts. In addition to used books galore, you can find used DVDs, VHS tapes, and vinyl records, and there is a comfy couch on the 2nd-floor reading area with a view of historic Christ Church across the street, so you can feel free to stay awhile.

BRICKBAT BOOKS
709 S. 4th St., 215/592-1207,
http://brickbatbooks.blogspot.com
HOURS: Tues.-Sat. 11 A.M.-7 P.M., Sun. 11 A.M.-6 P.M.
Map 5

A new and used bookstore on Fabric Row in

© JEREMY ERIC TENENBAUM

a poetry reading at Brickbat Books

© JOEL KATZ/COURTESY JOSEPH FOX BOOKSHOP

Joseph Fox Bookshop has been serving Philadelphia's literary community since 1951.

South Philly, Brickbat is cozy and homey with its soft music and pleasant lighting. With a substantive collection of literary fiction, mysteries, children's books, attractive art and photography tomes, and limited edition collectibles, there is something for everyone to buy or just peruse. They also buy used books and host readings and events.

GIOVANNI'S ROOM

345 S. 12th St., 215/923-2960, www.giovannisroom.com
HOURS: Mon.-Sat. 11:30 A.M.-7 P.M., Sun. 1-7 P.M.
Map 2

Founded in 1973 and originally located on South Street, Giovanni's Room has become a mainstay on its prime corner location in the heart of the Gayborhood. One of the largest bookstores in the world that specializes in gay, lesbian, bisexual, and transgender literature, the store contains enough rainbow paraphernalia to stock a *Queer as Folk* reunion tour, in addition to shelves stocked with queer-oriented novels, magazines, videos, calendars, self-help books, travel guides, and art books. It hosts speakers and readings, and serves as a de facto community resource center. The enthusiastic staff can help you find what you need and will track down hard-to-find titles if they're not in stock.

JOSEPH FOX BOOKSHOP

1724 Sansom St., 215/563-4184, www.foxbookshop.com
HOURS: Mon.-Sat. 9:30 A.M.-6 P.M., Wed. until 7 P.M.
Map 3

It's cramped. It's overcrowded with books. It's in the basement. There's no Internet and no coffee. And those are just some of the reasons we love it. Established in 1951, Joseph Fox Bookshop has always been independently owned and operated by passionate lovers of the written word. Committed to supporting and showcasing talented local authors, it may not have every book, but it has a carefully chosen selection of what the owners consider to be the best, and additional items can be special ordered. Take a step back in time to when having quality at your fingertips mattered more than having everything at your fingertips.

ROBIN'S BOOKSTORE

110A S. 13th St., 215/735-9600,
www.robinsbookstore.com

HOURS: Mon.-Thurs. 11 A.M.-7 P.M., Fri.-Sat. 11 A.M.-8 P.M.

Map 2

The oldest independent bookstore in Philadelphia, Robin's opened in 1936 and has seen several locations and incarnations in its long history. With hundreds of author readings through the years from greats like Sonia Sanchez, Walter Mosley, and Maya Angelou, the history of this liberal and counter-cultural literary outpost is palpable. The 2nd floor is filled with used books and magazines, and is connected to the Moonstone Arts Center, which is a nonprofit arm responsible for events and readings, including a poetry series, discussion groups, and multimedia performances.

MUSIC

AKA MUSIC

27 N. 2nd St., 215/922-3855,
www.facebook.com/pages/aka-music

HOURS: Mon.-Thurs. 11 A.M.-8 P.M., Fri.-Sat. 11 A.M.-9 P.M.,
Sun. 11 A.M.-6 P.M.

Map 1

The musical times, they are a-changin'. Luckily for old-school music enthusiasts, AKA is a welcome aberration in the age of digital downloads. Catering mostly to the indie rock crowd, the large, bright, meticulously organized warehouse space is stocked with rare originals and reissues, as well as many current titles. Can't find what you're looking for? The incredibly fine-tuned ears of the savant-like staff will be glad to turn you on to a similar artist you've probably never heard of. They also buy used vinyl if it happens to be something they want and don't already have.

HIDEAWAY MUSIC

8612 Germantown Ave., 215/248-4434,
http://hideawaymusic.org

HOURS: Mon.-Sat. 10 A.M.-6 P.M., Sun. 11 A.M.-5 P.M.

Map 8

Chestnut Hill's independent music store is a popular local stop for its excellent selection of DVDs, LPs, vintage concert posters, rock 'n' roll memorabilia, and new and used CDs. The CD selection offers contemporary and classic selections, and the vinyl collection is dominated by good old rock 'n' roll. The friendly staff in the small shop will be glad to help you find that Stones album you somehow lost track of over the years.

MAIN STREET MUSIC

4444 Main St., 215/487-7732,
www.mainstreetmusicpa.com

HOURS: Mon.-Thurs. 11 A.M.-7 P.M., Fri.-Sat. 11 A.M.-9 P.M.,
Sun. noon-6 P.M.

Map 8

The only record store in Manayunk, this independent-music mainstay has a faithful following. Listen to new and used CDs at listening stations, and if you like what you hear, buy or trade for some of your own old music. For a small space, it's well stocked with plenty of indie, local bands, new releases, and random oldies of whatever other people traded. The helpful and well-versed staff will order anything you want at no extra charge. They also host intimate live acts in the store; check the website for details and upcoming events.

◖ PHILADELPHIA RECORD EXCHANGE

618 S. 5th St., 215/925-7892, www.philarecx.com

HOURS: Daily noon-8 P.M.

Map 5

The Philadelphia Record Exchange is a vinyl lover's dream, with the largest selection in the city. Unless you're being watched over by a higher power, you're not likely to find a sought-after hidden classic amid the stacks, since music diehards and DJs regularly troll the shelves. But if your taste is eclectic and you have the time to browse, you'll probably get lucky and find a few gems. Record Exchange also buys music, but they are choosy and at times a bit snobby, so go in with a thick skin if you're looking to sell your childhood memories.

REPO RECORDS

538 South St., 215/627-3775, www.reporecords.com

HOURS: Mon.-Thurs. and Sun. noon-9 P.M., Fri.-Sat.
11 A.M.-11 P.M.

Map 5

Specializing in punk/hard-core and dance/

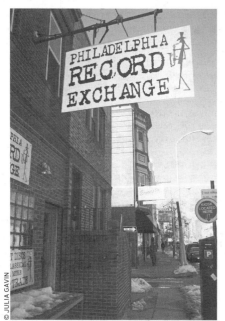

© JULIA GAVIN

Philadelphia Record Exchange offers a large selection of new and used vinyl.

electronic, this South Street record store has a wealth of new and used records and CDs, boxed sets, imports, hard-to-find indie singles, and B-sides. Out-of-print finds from the U.K. and beyond can also be found here. The downstairs is home to plenty of seven-inch vinyl, used CDs, and bargain bins with dirt-cheap offerings.

SOUND OF MARKET STREET (JAZSOUND)

15 S. 11th St., 2nd floor, 215/925-3150, www.jazsound.com
HOURS: Mon.-Sat. 9:30 A.M.-7 P.M.

Map 2

With more than 80,000 titles in stock, Sound of Market is Philadelphia's largest independent music store, boasting one of the most extensive selections of R&B, jazz, and gospel on the East Coast. The wide array of genres represented includes old-school and current rap and hip-hop, disco, dance, reggae, funk, doo-wop, Afro-Cuban, big band/swing, country, electronic, experimental, and folk. The large space is packed with music, spanning the 2nd and 3rd floors of the building.

Clothing, Accessories, and Shoes

With so many independently owned boutiques and shops in Philadelphia, many owners stock the shelves with a little bit of all of their favorites, so there is often crossover between stores offering clothes, shoes, accessories, home, and gift items. Many offer items for both men and women, and in some cases children as well. To help point you in the right direction more quickly, they are grouped here into what they are best known for, but keep in mind that these categories are not strictly bound.

CHILDREN'S STORES

ALI'S WAGON

2017 Fairmount Ave., 215/787-0611, www.aliswagon.com

HOURS: Tues.-Fri. 11 A.M.-6 P.M., Sat. 11 A.M.-5 P.M., Sun. noon-5 P.M.

Map 4

Quality kids' clothing (often organic) and toys are available at this Fairmount neighborhood store at prices more reasonable than some of the high-end Rittenhouse Row boutiques. In addition to cool children's stuff, you can find unique housewares, bath and body items, gifts, and accessories. But the most distinctive aspect of this husband-and-wife-run gem is the Parenting Center, which hosts parenting workshops to bring families together to learn and play at reasonable (sometimes even free!) prices.

BORN YESTERDAY

1901 Walnut St., 215/568-6556,
http://bornyesterdaykids.com
HOURS: Mon.-Sat. 10 A.M.-6 P.M., Sun. noon-5 P.M.
Map 3

If adults ask for Walnut Street designer shops for the latest fashions, then why wouldn't babies cry for the same? High-fashion, European-style clothing lines the aisles at this Rittenhouse destination, in sizes up to 8 for boys and 10 for girls. Born Yesterday carries the newest designs and latest trends in infant clothing as well, so your newborn can be posh before crawling. Modern and vintage toys are available for babies up to about two years.

CHILDREN'S BOUTIQUE

1702 Walnut St., 215/732-2661,
www.echildrensboutique.com
HOURS: Mon.-Sat. 10 A.M.-6 P.M., Sun. noon-5 P.M.
Map 3

In business since 1966, the family-owned store carries all the big brand names, including Lacoste, Polo Ralph Lauren, Amiana, and Joan Calabrese, as well as special designs available only here. Domestic and European designs for children of all ages are on hand, along with shoes, toys, gifts, and select items for infants. The Children's Boutique offers plenty of formal clothing for children, and orders can be placed online. Warning: It's expensive.

MEN'S CLOTHING AND ACCESSORIES

BOYD'S

1818 Chestnut St., 215/564-9000,
www.boydsphila.com
HOURS: Mon.-Sat. 9:30 A.M.-6 P.M., Wed. until 8 P.M.,
Sun. noon-5 P.M.
Map 3

Finely tailored men's slacks, dress shirts, jackets, and suits are the specialty of this world-class retailer. The climate is set by extravagant marble and mahogany fixtures, while a bountiful array of doting salespeople help you navigate through the fine European import fabrics. Browse the ready-to-wear sportswear and

formal attire by luxury-lifestyle purveyors like Hugo Boss, Burberry, Ferragamo, Gucci, and Zegna. A smaller selection of women's wear can also be found, with highlights including coveted designers Badgley Mischka, Narciso Rodriguez, Piazza Sempione, and Zac Posen. Stop at the in-store café for a shot of espresso or, even better, a martini in between fittings, or if you're not fully loaded, just stroll through the store to see how the other half lives.

I. GOLDBERG

1300 Chestnut St., 215/925-9393, www.igoco.com
HOURS: Mon.-Sat. 9 A.M.-5:45 P.M., Fri. until 6:45 P.M.
Map 2

You won't be awarded the purple heart for shopping at I. Goldberg, the Philadelphia Army Navy store that outfits the rugged urban soldier, but you will be awarded some fashion brownie points. Stocked with standard surplus gear like wool pea coats, bright-orange hunting vests, and water canteens, along with brands like Carhartt, Timberland, Levi's, Wrangler, North Face, and Dickies, these clothes, shoes, and accessories are designed to get you ready for the trenches, but they also make good understated-yet-stylish city wear.

MITCHELL & NESS

1201 Chestnut St., 866/879-6485,
www.mitchellandness.com
HOURS: Mon.-Sat. 10 A.M.-7 P.M., Sun. 11 A.M.-6 P.M.
Map 2

If sportswear-makers are allowed to have a storied history, then Mitchell & Ness is the stuff of legends. Starting out in a modest downtown storefront in 1904, the two-person outfitter started crafting and retailing tennis racquets, golf clubs, and other items before moving on to specialize in team uniforms. The Phillies, Athletics (pre-Oakland, of course), and Eagles all wore their clothes. Flash forward to the present, when the team jersey has become a high-priced fashion item, and Mitchell & Ness is the supplier of choice for urban and suburban high-schoolers, middle-aged men recapturing their youth, hip-hop heads, and ballers. A destination shop, it is a must for anyone interested in classic sports gear. It moved down Chestnut Street to a larger, more modern space that is more appropriate for its status. It's so popular with a national and even international crowd that a branch opened in Japan in 2007. Items can also be ordered by phone or through the website.

WOMEN'S CLOTHING AND ACCESSORIES

ANTHROPOLOGIE

1801 Walnut St., 215/568-2114, www.anthropologie.com
HOURS: Mon.-Sat. 10 A.M.-8 P.M., Sun. 11 A.M.-6 P.M.

`Map 3`

This wildly successful international chain began right here in Philly. Founded by the same clothiers behind the even more wildly successful chain Urban Outfitters, this is its more sophisticated, higher-quality, pricier big sister. The three-story historic Rittenhouse Square mansion is filled with pretty, feminine, well-made clothes and accessories. Be prepared to shell out big bucks for embellished cotton sundresses in the summer and cozy, intricately detailed woolens in the frostier months. Home goods and an ample sale rack fill the lower level.

JOAN SHEPP

1616 Walnut St., 215/735-2666, www.joanshepp.com
HOURS: Mon.-Sat. 10 A.M.-6 P.M., Wed. until 8 P.M., Sun. noon-5 P.M.

`Map 3`

Joan Shepp keeps the ladies of Rittenhouse in the business of high fashion, and the wealthiest, most fashionable ladies of Rittenhouse repay the debt by keeping Joan Shepp in business. This lofty, high-ceilinged store boasts classic wardrobe staples and trendy accents from design houses like Marni, Dries Van Noten, and Yohji Yamamoto. And no silhouette would be complete without a pair of Louboutin or Miu Miu pumps from their drop-dead-gorgeous shoe selection. If you've got cash to burn and appreciate high fashion, go now.

KNIT WIT

1718 Walnut St., 215/564-4760, www.knitwitonline.com
HOURS: Mon.-Sat. 10 A.M.-6 P.M., Wed. until 8 P.M., Sun. noon-5 P.M.

`Map 3`

Chic formal dresses and basic separates line the racks of this upscale retailer. Find the latest pieces from the collections of famous designers like Alexis Bittar, Helmut Lang, or Chan Luu, to name just a few. Pick up a supple leather handbag by Romy Gold or a beaded clutch by Moyna, or snag a hot new pair of Elizabeth and James pumps or Diane von Furstenberg boots for a night on the town.

PETULIA'S FOLLY

1710 Sansom St., 215/569-1344, www.petuliasfolly.com
HOURS: Mon.-Sat. 10 A.M.-6 P.M., Wed. until 7 P.M., Sun. noon-5 P.M.

`Map 3`

In architecture, a folly is an ornate and embellished building created to publicly communicate artistic vision and self-expression. In fashion and home accents, Petulia's Folly is the stylish equivalent. With a bevy of high-end but exceptionally unique jewelry, handbags, candles, throw pillows, women's clothing, and shoes, it would be a criminal folly to overlook this one-of-a-kind boutique. If you're on a budget, regular sales mean you can finally pick up the designer duds you've been coveting all season.

PLAGE TAHITI

128 S. 17th St., 215/569-9139, www.knitwitonline.com
HOURS: Mon.-Sat. 10 A.M.-6 P.M., Wed. until 7 P.M.

`Map 3`

It's no surprise that this selective women's clothing and accessories boutique is a frequent winner of the "Best of Philly" award from *Philadelphia* magazine. Conjured up by the owners of the longstanding Philly fashion hub Knit Wit, Plage Tahiti is a little bit funkier and a little bit less pricey (just a little) sister store just around the corner. It's best known for its colorful bikinis and well-made summer fashions, and the 2nd floor will appease the more budget-conscious with major discounts throughout the year, especially at the end of the season.

THIRD STREET HABIT

153 N. 3rd St., 215/925-5455,
www.thirdstreethabit.com
HOURS: Mon.-Sat. 11 A.M.-7 P.M., Sun. noon-6 P.M.
Map 1

Most habits are easy to acquire and tough to break; Third Street Habit is no exception to this rule. The hip clothing and accessories boutique has received much praise since it opened in 2004, including being named one of the top 10 boutiques in the U.S. by *Lucky* magazine. Denim, retooled vintage, and unique accessories are among the fantastic items lining the walls, and the knowledgeable, friendly staff are happy to help you pick out items that complement your style. Sorry wallets; there's a new habit in town, and it isn't cheap.

THREE SIRENS

134 N. 3rd St., 215/925-3548, www.threesirens.com
HOURS: Sun.-Mon. noon-5 P.M., Tues.-Sat. 11 A.M.-7 P.M.
Map 1

If the mythical three sirens had been outfitted by the Philly boutique bearing the same name, Odysseus would have been a goner. Crooning on sharp rocks all day long necessitates functional fashion, and Three Sirens has got your body covered. Luxuriate in comfy cottons, designer denims, and silk sundresses, and top it off with the perfect Rebecca Minkoff handbag to complete the look. Thanks to relatively reasonable price points for a quality boutique, you don't have to have epic pockets to dress like a deity.

TOPSTITCH BOUTIQUE

54 N. 3rd St., 215/238-8877,
www.topstitchboutique.com
HOURS: Tues.-Sat. 11 A.M.-7 P.M., Sun. noon-5 P.M.
Map 1

Prepare to be dazzled by a wide array of hand-picked vintage and original pieces, many made by local designers. The racks are filled with pretty but edgy clothes, and while many come for the stylish duds, perhaps even more come for the jewelry. Nature-inspired feathered earrings, dainty one-of-a-kind brooches, and rings made from a variety of materials are among the many unique designs. Monthly trunk shows display the work of local artists. From cool combat boots to sexy stilettos, you can also find shoes here to complete most looks.

URBAN OUTFITTERS

1627 Walnut St., 215/569-3131,
www.urbanoutfitters.com
HOURS: Mon.-Sat. 10 A.M.-9 P.M., Sun. 11 A.M.-8 P.M.
Map 3

Back in 1970, the first of numerous Urban Outfitters to follow opened its doors in a small house on the University of Pennsylvania's campus. With the free-love climate of the '60s not far behind, and whiffs of the disco days of the '70s breezing in, the urban artsy bohemian set embraced the avant-garde retailer with open suede-fringed arms. Today, the funky fashion housed in this multimillion-dollar international chain retailer still draws some of its clientele from its original roots, and much of its inspiration from the urban hipster crowd. The beautiful Center City warehouse-like store pays homage to the original dream with retro frocks, vintage-flavored housewares, and ironic T-shirts on four floors. By nature of its large scale, it is no longer quite as cool as it was at the outset, yet the stylish and comfy clothes at this Philadelphia original still attract youngsters in hordes. There is another store in the heart of University City (110 S. 36th St.), which is fitting, as this is the neighborhood where it all began.

VAGABOND

37 N. 3rd St., 215/671-0737,
www.vagabondboutique.com
HOURS: Mon.-Sat. 11 A.M.-7 P.M., Sun. 11 A.M.-5 P.M.
Map 1

A boutique and yarn shop boutique that has remained popular since it opened in 2001, Vagabond's large, minimalist space houses the perfect combination of fabulous vintage frocks and ultra-stylish, sleek, and contemporary designs—many from local designers. Check out the back room for yarn, children's clothing, accessories, housewares, and monthly art exhibits. And don't be fooled by the name—while your pants certainly won't be threadbare, your pockets may be after shopping here. Clothes are definitely chic, but certainly not cheap.

SHOES

◖ BENJAMIN LOVELL SHOES

119 S. 18th St., 215/564-4655,
www.benjaminlovellshoes.com

HOURS: Mon.-Sat. 10 A.M.-7 P.M., Sun. noon-5 P.M.
`Map 3`

"Style never felt so good" is the motto at Benjamin Lovell, a small, mostly local chain that stocks its shelves with a diverse range of casual and dressier footwear for men and women. The well-established brands sold include Mephisto, Ecco, Naot, and Dansko—the unifying theme for inclusion at Benjamin Lovell being comfort. Prices are somewhat high, but worth every penny for the quality and durability you are buying. The Rittenhouse location has a large regular and a small discount selection, while the South Street branch (318 South St., 215/238-1969, Mon.–Thurs. 11 A.M.–8 P.M., Fri.–Sat. 11 A.M.–9 P.M., Sun. 11 A.M.–6 P.M.) is much smaller overall, but has a larger bargain section in the back, where prices are dramatically slashed at the end of each season. There's also a Manayunk outpost (4305 Main St., 215/487-3747, Mon.–Sat. 11 A.M.–7 P.M., Sun. noon–6 P.M.).

HEAD START SHOES

126 S. 17th St., 215/567-3247, www.headstartshoes.com
HOURS: Mon.-Sat. 10 A.M.-7 P.M., Sun. 11 A.M.-6 P.M.
`Map 3`

The shoes at Head Start are the stuff of folklore and fantasy. If it buckles, snaps, zips, clips, or is covered in studs, you'll find it here. Owner George Patti travels to Italy twice a year to select the unique women's styles, including gravity-defying heels and kinky cowboy boots. Find balance on a pair of Dries Van Noten platform wedges, or walk a straight line with a pair of Via Spiga Mary Janes. All the while you'll be

Benjamin Lovell Shoes, with several locations in the city, offers stylish and comfortable shoes.

getting a head start on the season's most distinctive styles.

UBIQ

1509 Walnut St., 215/988-0194, www.ubiqlife.com
HOURS: Mon.-Sat. 11 A.M.-8 P.M., Sun. noon-6 P.M.
Map 3

A Philadelphia flagship of this selective chain, Ubiq positions itself as sneaker and clothing purveyor, art gallery, and all around urban-youth lifestyle destination. Walk (or skate) up the ramp on the 1st floor and you'll find yourself in sneaker and designer-T heaven. Upstairs, you'll discover a gallery to the left and a sneaker boutique to the right. Popular brands include Jordan's, Vans, Palladium, Converse, The Hundreds, and Original Fake. There is another outpost in the Gallery at 10th and Market Streets.

VINTAGE AND THRIFT

BUFFALO EXCHANGE

1713 Chestnut St., 215/557-9850,
www.buffaloexchange.com
HOURS: Mon.-Sat. 10 A.M.-8 P.M., Sun. noon-6 P.M.
Map 3

This nationwide consignment thrift store aims to reuse and recycle one-of-a-kind fashions. Supply and demand dictates the ever-changing stock, which usually consists of higher-end vintage, designer basics, evening wear, shoes, and accessories. With most items in excellent condition, you won't look like you just rolled out of the thrift store after shopping here, but your wallet will feel a bit like you did. You can bring in your former-favorite clothing and accessories to sell, although the buyers are discriminating, so don't bother unless your old duds are in great shape and still likely to be stylish in someone's mind.

LOST & FOUND

133 N. 3rd St., 215/928-1311
HOURS: Mon.-Thurs. 11:30 A.M.-7 P.M., Fri.-Sat.
11 A.M.-7 P.M., Sun. noon-6 P.M.
Map 1

Thrifters and fashion-forward females rejoice!

There is a holy ground where reasonably priced, girly vintage duds and modern ultra-femme dresses, funky shoes, and colorful accessories exist together in peaceful harmony. Fun men's and women's tees and hip shoes line the walls in this small, unassuming Old City treasure with a perfect name and a super-friendly staff.

PHILADELPHIA AIDS THRIFT

514 Bainbridge St., 215/922-3186,
www.phillyaidsthrift.blogspot.com
HOURS: Mon.-Thurs. 11 A.M.-8 P.M., Fri.-Sat. 11 A.M.-9 P.M.,
Sun. 11 A.M.-7 P.M.
Map 5

Philadelphia AIDS Thrift (aka PAT) follows the "one man's trash is another's treasure" model. Bring in the wares you no longer need and AIDS Thrift will sell them for you, with a significant portion of the proceeds going to local AIDS/HIV organizations. This eclectic and eccentric spot has everything from used toasters to movie posters, instructional workout videos, children's toys, lampshades, and winter coats. You might have to dig around a bit to uncover the true gems, but rest assured you'll find them if you have the patience.

SUGARCUBE

124 N. 3rd St., 215/238-0825, www.sugarcube.us
HOURS: Mon.-Sat. noon-7 P.M., Sun. noon-5 P.M.
Map 1

Sugarcube has a great mix of precious vintage clothing and of-the-moment designs from local and national designers. It's stocked with feminine and fashionable dresses and tops and a small but excellent selection of jeans; the prices are often high but worth it for the unique, quality styles. The shoe selection has won a "Best of Philly" award and the handbags and accessories, like everything else, are carefully chosen. Best of all, the changing room at Sugarcube is housed in an old bank vault, making you feel very secure and a little spooked while trying on your cool new clothes.

Gift and Specialty

GOURMET TREATS
GROCERY
101 S. 13th St., 215/922-5252, www.grocery13.com
HOURS: Mon.-Fri. 8 A.M.-8:30 P.M., Sat. 11 A.M.-7 P.M.
Map 2

Half café and half specialty upscale food market, Grocery has something for everyone, whether you need an on-the-go lunch, snack, or sweet, or to find a gift for a foodie friend. Owners Marcie Turney and Valerie Safran sell several of the restaurant's specialties in the store. Flavored oils, spreads, and tea are offered along with a small but excellent supply of kitchenwares.

NAKED CHOCOLATE CAFÉ
1317 Walnut St., 215/735-7310,
www.nakedchocolatecafe.com
HOURS: Mon.-Thurs. 10 A.M.-11 P.M., Fri.-Sat.
10 A.M.-11:30 P.M., Sun. 11 A.M.-9 P.M.
Map 2

The sumptuous Naked Chocolate Café is an excellent way to expand your waistline and

© JAMES J. KELLY/WWW.FLICKR.COM/PHOTOS/6261956@N00

Naked Chocolate Café

lighten your wallet. A chocolate lover's dream, the café offers endless varieties of chocolates, truffles, and baked and confectionery treats, mostly made on-premises. One of the most popular items is drinking chocolate like you've never imagined: hot, thick, impossibly rich, and spiced with flavors like chili powder and cinnamon. Enjoy the decadent sugar fix while picking up a few gifts for the chocolate lover in your life. The café has two other outposts offering many of the same delicious treats under the name **Artisserie Chocolate Café:** One is in Center City West (31 S. 18th St., 215/564-3860) and the other in University City (3421 Walnut St., 215/222-3710).

PREMIUM STEAP
111 S. 18th St., 215/568-2920, www.premiumsteap.com
HOURS: Mon.-Fri. 10 A.M.-5:30 P.M., Sat. 10 A.M.-6 P.M.
Map 3

Premium Steap invites you to become a loose-tea connoisseur with its long walls of shiny and mysterious canisters filled with tea from around the globe. In addition to the tea itself, the store offers a host of cool teapots, cups, mugs, canisters, strainers, and all things tea. The owner knows her tea and, if she isn't too busy, can be helpful in recommending a choice for specific ailments or tastes.

INTERNATIONAL WARES
GARLAND OF LETTERS
527 South St., 215/923-5946
HOURS: Mon.-Thurs. noon-9 P.M., Fri. noon-9:30 P.M., Sat. 11 A.M.-9:30 P.M., Sun. noon-8 P.M.
Map 5

When Mother Earth and Father Sky get busy, they rely on incense from the Garland of Letters to set the mood. Philly's leading purveyor of books on mysticism, philosophy, Eastern religion, nature worship, holistic healing, self-improvement, massage, and more offers a soothing escape from the bustle of South Street. With an assortment of lotions, oils, music, art, home accessories, crystals, and, of course, incense, the atmosphere is somewhat New Age-y, but in the best possible way. If you need to pick up a book on the meanings of various henna tattoos, recordings of Vedic chanting, or a Tantric sex guide, this is the place.

TEN THOUSAND VILLAGES
1122 Walnut St., 215/574-2008,
www.tenthousandvillages.com
HOURS: Mon.-Sat. 10 A.M.-7 P.M., Sun. noon-5 P.M.
Map 2

It takes a village, or in this case, ten thousand, to raise a handicrafts store totally dedicated to the support of fair trade and child labor laws in the developing world. This unique chain has outposts scattered throughout the United States, offering items ranging from textiles, baskets, and jewelry to musical instruments, ceramics, and handmade soaps—crafted by artists from every corner of the globe. With a portion of the proceeds benefiting the economic vitality of these artisan communities, you and your newly purchased Bangladeshi recycled tote can shop guilt-free. You can also check out the outpost in Chestnut Hill (8331 Germantown Ave., 215/242-3040, Mon.–Sat. 10 A.M.–6 P.M., Wed. until 8 P.M., Sun. noon–5 P.M.), carrying many of the same as well as some unique items.

SPECIALTY SHOPS
AIA BOOKSTORE AND DESIGN CENTER
1218 Arch St., 215/569-3188, www.aiabookstore.com
HOURS: Mon.-Sat. 10 A.M.-6 P.M., Sun. noon-5 P.M.
Map 2

What began in 1976 as a resource and information center for the American Institute of Architects (AIA) attending a convention in Philadelphia has grown into much more. Architecture and design buffs will continue to find endless items of interest throughout the varied selection, while there is also plenty for the layperson to enjoy as well. The books (many ideal for a coffee table) cover a wide range of home and design topics along with collecting, tasting, urban studies, politics, and more. Plenty of quirky gifts and housewares are also available, including lighting, jewelry, puzzles, and cute baby clothes and toys. This is the store where

you can find a gift for that person that already has everything—particularly if that person has a penchant for art or design. A unique collection of greeting cards and screen-printed note cards is available for anti-Hallmark types.

APPLE STORE
1607 Walnut St., 215/861-6400,
www.apple.com/retail/walnutstreet
HOURS: Mon.-Thurs. and Sat. 10 A.M.-8 P.M., Fri. 10 A.M.-9 P.M., Sun. 11 A.M.-6 P.M.
Map 3

In 2010, Philly finally got a long-awaited Apple Store. We used to go to Cherry Hill or King of Prussia Mall for all of our Mac-related needs, but now we only have to stroll to Walnut Street in the heart of Rittenhouse Row. The store is big, bright, and bustling, as any Apple Store should be. We like it.

ART STAR
623 N. 2nd St., 215/238-1557, www.artstarphilly.com
HOURS: Tues.-Sat. 11 A.M.-7 P.M., Sun. noon-6 P.M.
Map 7

This quirky little Northern Liberties boutique/gallery is committed to providing local budding artists an opportunity to be seen and hopefully make a buck. One-of-a-kind and limited-edition ceramics, prints, clothing, dolls, and jewelry are sold on consignment. Exhibitions rotate every six weeks and range from cartoon paintings to unusual stuffed animals and other household items. Named "the city's first cutting-edge craft shop" by *Philadelphia* magazine, Art Star offers an eclectic mix that reflects the diverse Northern Liberties arts community.

HELLO WORLD
1007 Pine St., 215/545-7060, www.shophelloworld.com
HOURS: Wed.-Fri. 11 A.M.-6 P.M., Sat.-Sun. 11 A.M.-5 P.M.
Map 2

While the items found at Hello World's Rittenhouse and Antique Row locations vary somewhat, both maintain the same standard of quirky and high-end gift and houseware excellence. Retro barkcloth and Bakelite bangles dress the windows, while sleek Chadwick door- and placemats keep the floors and tables

Philly's long-awaited Apple Store is now open on Walnut Street.

clean. Save the trip to the flea market and scoop up one of owner and textile designer J. Lamancuso's hand-picked vintage lamps, tables, and chairs. Although the shop offers mostly new designs, there is also a small selection of carefully chosen second-hand items. The diverse offerings include pillows, jewelry, handbags, clocks, and cute T-shirts for babies. The second location is in the Rittenhouse area (257 S. 20th St., 215/545-5207, Mon. noon–7 P.M., Tues.–Fri. 11 A.M.–7 P.M., Sat.– Sun. 11 A.M.–5 P.M.).

◖ R.E. LOAD BAGGAGE, INC.

608 North 2nd St., 215/625-2987, www.reloadbags.com

HOURS: Tues.-Fri. 11 A.M.–6 P.M., Sat. by appt.

`Map 7`

Former bike messengers Roland and Ellie (the R. and E. in the company name) founded this one-of-a-kind local company in 1998 on their quest to create the perfect messenger bag. Using only the highest-quality materials, R.E. Load Baggage carefully constructs messenger and courier bags, backpacks, and just about any other type of bag that holds stuff. The best part is, each bag is custom-designed and made by hand to reflect the needs and desires of the lucky owner-to-be. Specialized orders can be placed in the store, online, or over the phone, or you can choose from a small ready-made selection. The bags are pricey (upwards of $250), but they are made to last a lifetime, or close anyway. Each has its own special flair chosen by you, so you're not just paying for a bag— you're paying for an extension of your personality to wear over your shoulder. R.E. Load bags are also sold at select retail stores throughout the country, mostly in bike shops.

SCARLETT ALLEY

241 Race St., 215/592-7898, www.scarlettalley.com

HOURS: Mon.-Fri. 11 A.M.–7 P.M., Sat. 10 A.M.–6 P.M., Sun. noon–5 P.M.

`Map 1`

Founded by mother-and-daughter Mary Kay and Liz Scarlett, this is the place to go for beauty and spa products, home accents, jewelry, housewares, and gifts, with a wide selection for babies and kids. Wander to the back to unearth a sweet collection of lingerie, pajamas, and slippers cozy enough to make you never want to leave the house again. Many of its products have been featured in magazines, including *Oprah* and *Lucky*. An annex called Scarlett Bride offers everything for brides-to-be outside of the dress.

VIA BICYCLE

606 S. 9th St., 215/627-3370, www.bikeville.com
HOURS: Tues. and Thurs.-Sat. 10 A.M.-5 P.M., Wed. 1-9 P.M.
Map 5

The self-proclaimed "most interesting bike shop in the world," Via Bicycle is an excellent resource for buying and selling used and vintage bikes and for low-cost repairs. The shop itself is a sight to be seen with its authentic vintage decor filled with bikes and accessories. Road bikes, beach cruisers, classics, basics, and rare one-of-a-kind bikes are available for sale. You can also stop by to fill up your tires outside next to the signature yellow benches where

locals do a little fine-tuning. The mechanics are knowledgeable and friendly, prices are average, and if you have a special vintage bike that needs a repair, this is the place.

❰ VERDE

108 S. 13th St., 215/546-8700, www.verdephiladelphia.com
HOURS: Mon.-Sat. 11 A.M.-8 P.M., Sun. noon-6 P.M.
Map 2

Verde was named "Best of Philly" in 2010 for Hostess Gifts and as a One-Stop Shop by *Philadelphia* magazine, and it offers delicious chocolates that have been featured in *The New York Times Magazine*; it seems there is no one that does not love Verde. A perfect addition to the Marcie Turney and Valerie Safran empire along 13th Street, Verde does it all, from flower arrangements to sparkly jewelry to unique Philly gifts and souvenirs that are tasteful not tacky. Among the many perfect gifts you will find here are the nine-piece handcrafted chocolates, each stamped with iconic Philly images, or any of the T-shirts or adorable baby onesies from the *We Heart Philly* line.

Home Furnishings and Accents

ANASTACIA'S ANTIQUES

617 Bainbridge St., 215/928-9111
HOURS: Thurs.-Sat. noon-6:30 P.M., Sun. noon-5 P.M.
Map 5

Victorian and early-American collectibles and practical pieces fill this antique furniture and accessory store. Get lost in the maze of ornate mirrors and unique pieces and be sure to save time to get lost in the fantastic Bakelite bangles and Lucite-adorned clutches in the vintage jewelry cases. The staff's open and friendly vibe will make you feel right at home while they help you find the next piece to fit your personal collection—and your personal budget. Prices are reasonable, and if you live nearby, large items can be delivered to your home.

MATTHEW IZZO

151 N. 3rd St., 215/829-0606, www.matthewizzo.com
HOURS: Mon.-Sat. 11 A.M.-7 P.M., Sun. noon-4 P.M.
Map 1

A trailblazer in the Philly fashion and design scene, Matthew Izzo began as a successful high-end clothing boutique on Antique Row especially popular for its cool yet sophisticated men's fashion. He then moved into chic, minimalist housewares and furniture, along with art. Now in a larger Old City space, you can find coveted furniture and housewares from Jonathan Adler, Umbra, MoMA Design, and Italian kitchen-accessory favorite Alessi along with a selective line of men's and women's clothing from hard-to-find labels like Cheap Monday and Nice Collective, for the complete Matthew Izzo experience all in one stop.

OPEN HOUSE

107 S. 13th St., 215/922-1415, www.openhouseliving.com
HOURS: Mon.-Sat. 11 A.M.-8 P.M., Sun. noon-6 P.M.
`Map 2`

How to furnish the contemporary urban living space? Open House has found simple and functional answers that come in the shape of sleek end tables and colorful home accessories. City-dwellers can rejoice at the selection of space-conserving items, including stools, side tables, hanging light fixtures, and glass storage jars of all sizes. Soft bedding, decorative rugs, minimalist kitchenwares, bath and body items, and adorable baby clothes and toys round out the eclectic mix.

SCARLET FIORELLA

113 S. 13th St., 215/922-1955, www.scarletfiorella.com
HOURS: Mon.-Sat. 11 A.M.-7 P.M., Sun. noon-5 P.M.
`Map 2`

Scarlet Fiorella is named after the owner's daughter, and its specialty is custom antique furnishings, but it carries much more. Upon entering, you'll notice plenty of eye-catching housewares and bath and body products. Adorable and sometimes ironic children's T-shirts, shoes, and accessories also find shelter among the adult offerings, while magnificent vintage chandeliers provide the ideal lighting to showcase the lovely hodgepodge.

WEST ELM

1330 Chestnut St., 215/731-0184, www.westelm.com
HOURS: Mon.-Sat. 10 A.M.-8 P.M., Sun. 11 A.M.-6 P.M.
`Map 2`

Minimalist designs and colorful palettes are what you'll find at West Elm, the nationwide home furnishings store with furniture so well-made and unique you'll forget it's a chain store. Prices are comparable to the Crate & Barrels of the world, but with an emphasis on more modern, youthful, and spare decor. Many of the textiles appeal to a simple, breezy "Far East meets beach house" sensibility, while the lighting and wall fixtures echo a sleeker *Metropolitan Home* aesthetic. The large warehouse-like showroom space displays wares in color-coded sections.

© CHRISTOPHER WOODS

West Elm on Chestnut Street

Malls, Department Stores, and Shopping Centers

In addition to these malls and shopping centers, which are notable for their size, content, or location, several additional standard suburban malls are located just outside the city. Plymouth Meeting Mall, Willow Grove Mall, and the Cherry Hill Mall (in nearby New Jersey) offer department stores, chain stores, food courts, and movie theaters.

FRANKLIN MILLS OUTLET MALL

1455 Franklin Mills Circle, I-95 and Woodhaven Dr., 215/613-2222, www.simon.com/mall
HOURS: Mon.-Sat. 10 A.M.-9:30 P.M., Sun. 11 A.M.-7 P.M.
Map 9

There aren't too many reasons for visitors to travel to the far corner of Northeast Philadelphia, but Franklin Mills is a good one. The Garden of Eden to the devout discount shopper, the sprawling one-story mall is home to a plethora of outlet stores. Most of the major chains are represented, including Gap, Banana Republic, J. Crew, and Ann Taylor, along with higher-end manufacturers like Off Fifth (Saks Fifth Avenue), Polo, Ralph Lauren, and Last Call Neiman Marcus—all selling wares at sinfully low prices. With over 200 shops, seven themed restaurants, a 14-screen movie theater, and a bowling alley to choose from, you'll want to set the entire day aside for your trip; you'll need it.

GALLERY AT MARKET EAST

Market St. between 9th and 12th Sts., www.thegalleryatmarketeast.com
HOURS: Mon.-Thurs. 10 A.M.-7 P.M., Fri. 10 A.M.-8 P.M., Sat. 10 A.M.-7 P.M., Sun. noon-5 P.M.
Map 2

For those who enjoy the suburban convenience of mall shopping and the vitality of urban life, Philly offers the Gallery at Market East. Stretching out over three blocks above its eponymous Market East train station, it holds over 170 stores on four levels, a food court, gym, and even a fish market. Unlike the Shops at Liberty Place, a smaller indoor

mall with somewhat more upscale offerings, both the shops and the clientele at Gallery at Market East better reflect the racial and economic diversity of the city. In addition to the typical mall chains like Foot Locker and Old Navy, it has a Kmart and a Burlington Coat Factory, and vendor booths selling spray-painted T-shirts, watches, jewelry, cell phone paraphernalia, and edible treats. While often crowded and loud, it's is a perfectly convenient place to shop. And with the regional rail line underneath the mall, it's easy to make a quick getaway from the urban bustle.

MACY'S

1300 Market St., 215/241-9000, www.macys.com
HOURS: Mon.-Sat. 10 A.M.-8 P.M., Sun. 11 A.M.-7 P.M.
Map 2

If you've seen one Macy's, you've seen 'em all, right? Wrong! This Macy's is housed in a building that was formerly home to Wanamaker's, considered North America's first full-fledged department store. Lord & Taylor's followed in this historic location and was replaced by Macy's in August of 2006. Designed to resemble Paris's Les Halles, the grand building comes complete with marble floors, elegant columns, and gold details around a grand central atrium. It also boasts one of the world's largest playable pipe organs and a 2,500-pound bronze eagle statue from the 1904 St. Louis World's Fair. A light-and-music show of the *Nutcracker* plays hourly in the central atrium during the holiday season; the old Philadelphia tradition has survived the changing of the store's ownership, drawing crowds each year. Be sure to peek inside even if you don't need to buy anything.

◖ THE PIAZZA AT SCHMIDTS

N. 2nd St. and Germantown Ave., 215/467-4603, www.atthepiazza.com
HOURS: Vary by store
Map 7

The crown jewel of Northern Liberties, the Piazza at Schmidts is an open-air landscaped

THE KING OF CONSUMERISM

The largest shopping mall in the entire country based on retail space, second only to Minnesota's Mall of America based on total size, the King of Prussia Mall is a shining beacon of materialism less than a half hour's drive from Center City Philadelphia. Just a few miles from Valley Forge National Historical Park, the world-famous destination mall easily attracts far more visitors than the historic site. Known to locals simply as "K.O.P," the mall boasts more than 400 stores and 2.8 million square feet of retail space. It has two distinct sections; the Plaza opened in 1963 as an open-air shopping mall, which has since been enclosed, and the Court was added in 1981.

In addition to all the standard stores you can imagine, there are dozens of high-end national and international upscale boutique shops and department stores, including Bloomingdale's, Nordstrom, Neiman Marcus, Versace, Hugo Boss, Donna Karan, Hermes, Thomas Pink, and much more. It's almost too much to tackle, but with three food courts and over 40 restaurants, there are plenty of places to stop for a break and to refuel. If you're not scared away yet, check it out for yourself; just be sure to leave the Jimmy Choos at home and wear your walking shoes on any trip to K.O.P. (Rte. 202 at Mall Blvd., 610/265-5727, www.kingofprussiamall.com, Mon.-Sat. 10 A.M.-9 P.M., Sun. 11 A.M.-6 P.M.).

shows, farmers markets, and musical festivals. It is already popular but will no doubt continue to grow as the cultural center for Northern Liberties and Fishtown. Saturdays and Sundays (noon–7 P.M.) are great days to visit, when the Market at the Piazza brings vendors selling arts, crafts, clothing, antiques, vintage goods, and more, in addition to all the permanent shops. The enterprising developers responsible for the Piazza also opened the nearby Shops at Schmidts in 2011; the massive retail space brought a much-needed supermarket to the neighborhood, meaning neighbors really can have it all within a few square blocks.

THE SHOPS AT LIBERTY PLACE

1625 Chestnut St., 215/851-9055,
www.shopsatliberty.com
HOURS: Mon.-Sat. 9:30 A.M.-7 P.M., Sun. noon-6 P.M.
Map 3

Somewhere between the over-the-top elegance of the Shops at the Bellevue and the down-and-sometimes-a-little-dirty Gallery at Market East, the Shops at Liberty Place offer yet another indoor urban mall experience. The central atrium is covered by a domed-glass ceiling, offering a bright and open shopping space. Shops surround the center and extend out along several hallways on two floors. Above it, the skyscraper has endless floors of offices, making the food court a popular stop for the downtown business set at lunchtime. You'll find chain clothing stores, including Express, J. Crew, and Victoria's Secret; health and beauty brands Aveda, Bath & Body Works, and The Body Shop; shoe stores Easy Spirit, Aldo, and Florsheim Shoes, along with many other standard and higher-end shops.

THE SHOPS AT THE BELLEVUE

200 S. Broad St., 215/875-8350,
www.bellevuephiladelphia.com
HOURS: Mon.-Sat. 10 A.M.-6 P.M., Wed. until 8 P.M.,
Sun. varies by store
Map 3

Luxury seeps through the gold-and-marble atrium of this small shopping center in the heart of Center City's Avenue of the Arts. The

plaza the size of a large city block. Lined with boutiques, galleries, restaurants, bars, offices, apartments, and artist studios, it was built to mimic European city squares. Born in 2008, the young structure is still forming its identity, and has been host to some unfortunate revolving door retail spaces along with stronger ones. The square holds a 40-by-20-foot high-definition screen that draws friendly crowds for sporting events and movie screenings, and it hosts frequent free events, including trunk high-end stores make sense, considering the mall is part of the Bellevue, one of the city's finest hotels, housed in a 1904 Beaux Arts building. If your wallet is fat, stop at Nicole Miller for that last-minute cocktail dress and Tiffany & Co. for new jewels to go with it. Visit the third-largest Polo Ralph Lauren store in the world, Williams-Sonoma for delectable treats and kitchenwares, or Teuscher Chocolates of Switzerland to satisfy your most decadent chocolate craving, and be sure to stop at Vigant for high-end luggage to transport your new wares home. There is a lower-level food court and a Starbucks on the main level.

Spa, Bath, and Beauty

BALANCE HEALTH CENTER
112 S. 20th St., 215/751-0344,
www.balancehealthcenter.com
HOURS: Daily 9 A.M.-7 P.M.
Map 3

A true health center, as its name reveals, rather than your typical spa, this isn't a place to go to look better, but a place you go to *feel* better. Rooted in holistic health principles, the spa works with each client to develop personalized feel-better strategies. Offering an array of services to soothe or heal the mind, body, and spirit, Balance offers massage, acupuncture, chiropractic care, hypnotherapy, nutrition counseling, and yoga classes. Traditional Chinese medicine and Ayurveda, a treatment approach rooted in India, are also offered.

BLUEMERCURY APOTHECARY AND SPA
1707 Walnut St., 215/569-3100, www.bluemercury.com
HOURS: Mon.-Sat. 10 A.M.-7 P.M., Sun. noon-6 P.M.
Map 3

Many of the women you'll see walking around Rittenhouse Square require a certain beauty quotient that can't be unearthed at the local drugstore. Enter Bluemercury. As a purveyor of luxury makeup, lotions, and potions, this upscale apothecary stocks all of the top brands, including Bobbi Brown, Bliss, NARS, and more. Picture slipping into a luscious Fresh "Sugar" bath, your senses soothed by the scent of the Tocca candles burning all around, followed by a dollop of skin-quenching Laura Mercier Tarte au Citron body lotion. With expert staff and pricey but decadent spa and beauty treatments, including facials, wraps, massage, and waxing, Bluemercury goes the extra mile to give the Rittenhouse elite the full pampering experience.

BODY KLINIC
2012 Walnut St., 215/563-8888,
http://salon-philadelphia.com
HOURS: Mon.-Fri. 10:30 A.M.-9 P.M., Sat. 10 A.M.-6 P.M., Sun. 10:30 A.M.-6 P.M.
Map 3

This small spa provides a wide array of spa services, including massage, reflexology, wraps, scrubs, nail and makeup services, waxing, electrolysis, and more. Facials range from gentle refreshers to microdermabrasion, peels, and acne- and anti-aging treatments. While there isn't a lot of room for lounging in the small single floor of the converted row house, it offers good, reasonably priced services. Check the website for monthly specials and coupons, often offering steep discounts on select treatments.

◖ DUROSS & LANGEL
117 S. 13th St., 215/592-7627,
www.durossandlangel.com
HOURS: Mon.-Sat. 11 A.M.-7 P.M., Sun. noon-5 P.M.
Map 2

If smelling deliciously fragrant were your job, you could expect a promotion after a visit to this bath-and-body-product sanctuary. The big hunks of natural, organic handmade soaps in mouthwateringly sweet scents along with more subtle fragrances look good enough to eat. Candles made from natural soy wax and essential oils are equally refreshing, in scents of

Duross & Langel's products are made using fair-trade ingredients.

tangerine, Moroccan cedar, and lemon sugar, and the emollient face and body washes are gentle enough for the most sensitive skin types. Hair products are also top-notch, and the ultra-moisturizing lip balm is simply divine. The local company is committed to using natural products, fair-trade policies for its raw materials, and gift packages of 100 percent recycled paper. Sign up for one of their workshops, offered on the third Sunday of most months, to learn how to whip up your own lotions, scrubs, and soaps.

KIEHL'S

1737 Walnut St., 215/636-9936, www.kiehls.com
HOURS: Mon.-Sat. 10 A.M.-7 P.M., Sun. noon-6 P.M.
Map 3

From its 1851 start as a apothecary specializing in homeopathic remedies in New York's Lower East side, Kiehl's has spread its old-fashioned corrugated-tin ceilings and highly organized shelves all over the world, including to this prime Rittenhouse Square location. Soothing natural and classically fragrant formulas paired

with an unending dedication to customer satisfaction (check out all of the free samples) are what set this hair-and-skin-product haven apart. The unadorned packaging (and maybe also the steep prices) create what could just be a well-marketed illusion that the products provide real medicinal value, or perhaps they actually do. In either case, most products do work remarkably well, and smell terrific.

RESCUE RITTENHOUSE SPA

255 S. 17th St., 215/772-2766,
www.rescuerittenhousespa.com
HOURS: Mon.-Fri. 9 A.M.-8 P.M., Sat. 9 A.M.-7 P.M.
Map 3

"Beautiful skin is a matter of choice, not chance," says Danuta Mieloch, owner and founder of Rescue Rittenhouse Spa. When you step off the elevator onto the 2nd floor of this Center City office building, you'll enter a tranquil 4,000-square-foot lounge with minimalist, soothing decor that will put you in the mood for relaxation. Mieloch and her talented staff have won numerous awards for their treatments, most notably their famous transformative facials, including peels, micro-current, and microdermabrasion. They also offer excellent massage, nail services, waxing, and makeup application and an array of high-end products.

SALON L'ETOILE & SPA

4360 Main St., Manayunk, 215/483-2500,
http://manayunk.salonletoile.com
HOURS: Sun. 10 A.M.–4 P.M., Mon., Tues., and Thurs.
10 A.M.–8 P.M., Wed. 8:30 A.M.–8 P.M., Fri. 9 A.M.–6 P.M.,
Sat. 8 A.M.–5 P.M.
Map 8

Well worth the short drive from Center City, the salon offers excellent hair, nails, and waxing in a beautiful old building with huge windows overlooking Main Street in the heart of Manayunk. It's a lovely multi-level oasis where you can go to get pretty and to get pampered. Upstairs is a serene spa offering massage, body treatments, and facials, while the downstairs is a bright, high-energy salon. The friendly, talented beauticians and therapists are happy to help you choose the perfect treatment or the best haircut for you. Reflexology, a treatment utilizing pressure points on your feet, can be experienced alone or added on to another treatment; try it out, it's divine.

◖ TERME DI AROMA

32 N. 3rd St., 215/829-9769, www.termediaroma.com
HOURS: Tues. noon–8:30 P.M., Wed.-Fri.
11 A.M.–8:30 P.M., Sat. 10 A.M.–7 P.M., Sun. 10 A.M.–4 P.M.
Map 1

This delightful Old City spa specializes in aromatherapy massage, wraps, and facials in an atmosphere that is sweet-smelling bliss. Soothing sounds, scents, and relaxing lighting surround you from the moment you enter the lobby. Have a cup of tea or juice and read a magazine in the cozy lounge before or in between treatments. Essential oils are chosen based on your preferences and what you hope to gain from your treatment—be it renewal and relaxation or headache and tension release. The facials are mostly gentle and relaxing, designed so you'll enjoy the process as much as the outcome, and the massages are simply divine. Prenatal, shiatsu, Reiki, reflexology, and thai yoga massage are offered in addition to aromatherapy and deep tissue, and prices are reasonable, considering the high quality of services and atmosphere and the prime Old City location.

TOPPERS SPA AND SALON

117 S. 19th St., 215/496-9966,
http://toppersspa.site.dejazzd.com
HOURS: Tues. and Thurs. 10 A.M.–7:30 P.M.,
Wed. 10 A.M.–8:30 P.M., Fri. 10 A.M.–6:30 P.M.,
Sat. 9 A.M.–6:30 P.M., Sun. 10 A.M.–4:30 P.M.
Map 3

In the heart of Rittenhouse Square, you'll find a spa and salon offering a diversity of spaces and services spread over its five floors. The 1st and 2nd floor offer an upscale hair and nail salon that belies the more soothing atmosphere waiting on the uppermost levels. A cozy Victorian-styled sitting area and changing room, along with private massage treatment rooms, make up the 3rd floor, while the 5th-floor atrium offers the most unique setting of all with its greenhouse-like ceiling. In addition to treatment areas, the lounge area is filled with umbrellas, chaises, and cabanas, offering an island-y vibe that will make you forget you're in the middle of the city. In addition to the Rittenhouse Square location, this semi-local chain has outlets in Devon and Bucks County, Pennsylvania, as well as Marlton, New Jersey, and Dover, Delaware.

HOTELS

Along with all the standard chain hotels you'd expect in a major city, Philadelphia offers plenty of independent and boutique hotels, bed-and-breakfasts, and two youth hostels. In addition, many of the chain hotels have taken up residence in unique, historic buildings, offering way more character than their big, boring names might suggest. Whether you're working with an unlimited expense account or you can barely scrape together change for a cheesesteak, there is a place for you to lay your head in Philly.

The bulk of hotels are located in Center City—convenient considering this is where most visitors spend the majority of their time. You won't be more than a 10-minute drive or about a 30-minute walk from the city's major sights, dining, and nightlife anywhere

in Center City. If money is no object, stay at one of Philadelphia's drop-dead gorgeous, world-class hotels: the Four Seasons, the Ritz-Carlton, the Park Hyatt at the Bellevue, or the independent, award-winning Rittenhouse Hotel. And if you can't afford to stay in one of these luxury hotels, at least stop in to check out the elegant lobbies, eat or drink at one of their swank restaurants or bars—or to use their fancy bathrooms. Or check out the newest hotels to open in Philadelphia: the Hotel Palomar, Le Méridien, or the Independent, each offering a brand-new look in distinctive settings.

At the other end of the spectrum, budget travelers have several options, including the Apple Hostel in Old City, the Chamounix Mansion hostel in Fairmount Park, and the International House in University City. In the

© CHRISTOPHER WOODS

HIGHLIGHTS

LOOK FOR TO FIND RECOMMENDED HOTELS.

Best Place to Make Friends: The closest thing Philly has to a European-style hostel, **Apple Hostels of Philadelphia** offers budget accommodations in the heart of Old City to its mostly international clientele (page 198).

Most Distinctive Bed-and-Breakfast: At **Madame Saito Bed & Breakfast** near South Street, the multi-talented innkeeper cooks Japanese, Thai, and French cuisine and teaches sushi-making out of the attached restaurant. Come for the affordable digs but don't leave without trying Madame's sushi (page 199).

Most Colonial Digs: Two of Benjamin Franklin's contemporaries owned impressive homes in late-18th-century Philadelphia that have been converted to bed-and-breakfasts named in their honor. Immerse yourself in colonial history at the **Thomas Bond House Bed and Breakfast** (page 201) in Old City or the **Morris House Hotel** in nearby Society Hill (page 200).

Best Hotel Lobby: Even if you can't afford to blow a week's salary to stay at **The Ritz-Carlton of Philadelphia,** be sure to stop in to see the elegant domed lobby. Enjoy tea, lunch, or drinks in the grand space, or just sneak a peek (page 203).

Most Environmentally Friendly: The **Hotel Palomar** opened in 2009 in the heart of Rittenhouse Row. Philadelphia's first LEED Gold Certified hotel, it has received the highest awards for its eco-friendly design (page 204).

Best Place to See Stars: The ultra-elegant, independent **Rittenhouse Hotel** is popular with celebs who visit Philly or stay long-term while filming movies. It's easy to see why, considering its plush amenities and prime location overlooking Rittenhouse Square (page 205).

Cheapest Way to Sleep in a Historic Mansion: Just because you're traveling on a budget doesn't mean you can't do it in style. The **Chamounix Mansion** hostel, a converted 18th-century mansion in Fairmount Park, offers private and dorm-style accommodations at the lowest rates in town (page 208).

Rittenhouse Hotel

© G.WIDMAN FOR GPTMC

PRICE KEY

💲 Less than $150 per night
💲💲 $150-250 per night
💲💲💲 More than $250 per night

midrange, there are plenty of chain and independent hotels, bed-and-breakfasts, and rooms in private homes.

It is wise to reserve a room well in advance when visiting at peak times, namely summer and during festivals and holidays. Independence Day is a huge event in Philadelphia, so if you plan to be here for the weeklong festivities, you'd better have a friend in town, a huge wad of money, or a reservation.

CHOOSING A HOTEL

Old City is the place to be if you're visiting primarily to experience the historic attractions in and around Independence National Historical Park, but with few exceptions, it is expensive. It is jam-packed with families in summertime, but isn't quite as crowded—or pricey—during other times of the year. If you can't find a room in Old City, anywhere in Center City is convenient for visiting the historic area as well as the museums of the Benjamin Franklin Parkway and the rest of downtown Philadelphia.

Bed-and-breakfasts can be found scattered throughout Center City, especially in and around Washington Square West, Society Hill, and University City. Wash West is a great, centrally located place for anyone to stay, but is especially popular with gay visitors since it is the center of the city's gay culture. Rooms in the area fill well in advance during the annual Equality Forum in May.

The Museum District is lovely during the day when the museums are open, but can be a bit desolate at night; home to mostly chain hotels, it is also very close to Center City. University City just across the Schuylkill River is a bit less expensive while still close to Center City. Home to University of Pennsylvania and Drexel University, this area can be a good

choice for students with its bustling college scene and affordable bars and restaurants. And for a quieter stay, near Fairmount Park and historic Germantown but farther from the city's main attractions, Chestnut Hill offers several options near its main business district.

Since chain hotels are so easily found with a few clicks of a mouse, the majority of this chapter is devoted to the lesser-known, unique Philadelphia establishments. Chains are, however, included when there are limited options in a particular area or in some cases because the chains are in historic buildings that are too beautiful or the location is simply too convenient to leave out. In addition to Center City, you'll find plenty of chain hotels near the airport, including the Philadelphia Airport Marriott, directly connected to the airport. There is also a Holiday Inn near the stadium—convenient for those attending events at the sports arenas.

All rates listed are based on double occupancy in summer (high season). Most hotels offer parking at a daily cost on-site or in a nearby lot, usually for around $20 a day. The

SAVE WITH THE PHILLY OVERNIGHT HOTEL PACKAGE

The Philly Overnight Hotel Package is available through the Independence Visitor Center's website (www.visitphilly.com). It will buy you two nights accommodations with free parking for both nights (a $75-plus value at some Center City hotels) and a free gift when you check in. Additional promotions are sometimes included, like tickets to attractions and exhibits, so it's always worth checking the website for details when planning your visit. The deal is available seven days a week for any two-consecutive-night stay; the site connects with a Travelocity search so you can select from participating hotels. Most local hotels participate.

Official Visitor Site for Greater Philadelphia (www.visitphilly.com) is another excellent resource for additional listings, descriptions, reservations, and discounts, including the **Philly Overnight Hotel Package,** which includes hotel accommodations for two nights, free parking, and a gift and coupon book upon check-in. **Bed and Breakfast Connections of Philadelphia** (800/448-3619, www.bnbphiladelphia.com) has additional offerings if you're looking for something cozy and unique.

Old City and Society Hill   Map 1

If you're visiting for the historical attractions of Independence National Historical Park, Old City is the ideal place to stay. The area is also great for shopping, dining, entertainment, and nightlife and is also one of the prettiest areas of the city. With the exception of Apple Hostels and a few of the midrange chains, this is an expensive area and rooms tend to fill quickly, especially in summer. Society Hill is Old City's neighbor to the south, offering proximity to the main historic attractions in a somewhat quieter, more residential setting. The waterfront Hyatt Regency at Penn's Landing and the Sheraton Society Hill are both fully equipped chain hotels in excellent locations. Several character-filled bed-and-breakfasts provide nearby alternatives at lower prices.

APPEL'S SOCIETY HILL BED & BREAKFAST 🅢🅢
414 Spruce St., 215/925-5460

The modern decor of the rooms at this small, four-room bed-and-breakfast is a contrast to the historic building dating from 1805. Offering a quieter alternative to the bustle of Old City in nearby Society Hill, with rooms including an extended continental breakfast starting at $135 a night, this is a great deal in a pleasant area. It often fills even though the owners do not advertise, so be sure to book in advance, especially in summertime. Each of the basic bedrooms has private bath, air-conditioning, and wireless Internet, and a minimum two-night stay is required. Saturday and Sunday check-in is discouraged but can be arranged for longer stays.

🌙 APPLE HOSTELS OF PHILADELPHIA 🅢
32 S. Bank St., 215/922-0222, www.bankstreethostel.com

Formerly Bank Street Hostel, the only Center City Philadelphia hostel came under new ownership in 2008. This is a good thing. Now renamed Apple, the hostel was upgraded in the process and even voted second best hostel in the U.S. by Hostelworld.com. Perhaps the best change of all is that there is no longer a curfew, which is a great thing considering the prime location in the heart of Old City. On a quiet street but just steps from the historic attractions, restaurants, and nightlife, this is the place to stay for budget-conscious travelers. The vibe is friendly, laid-back, young, and communal, so if you're not any of those things, this probably isn't the place for you. But if you don't mind dorm-style beds or shared bathrooms, and perhaps are looking to make new friends, this is the place for you. It's an excellent—and pretty much the only—budget option in Old City; high season (summertime) rates are $35–38 for a dorm bed, with a few private and semi-private rooms available for $79–94. Weekly rates and other specials can be found online, and booking online will save you $2 a night. Students receive a $2 discount per night, and non–Hostelling International members pay an extra $3 a night. It caters to students and international travelers; locals are not allowed to stay—in fact, ID proving that you live outside of a 100-mile radius is required. Linens and towels are provided, and a communal kitchen, dining area, and lounge with foosball table and Wii are available. Free Internet

© JULIA GAVIN

Apple Hostels is Philly's only European-style youth hostel.

access, lockers (bring your own padlock), and laundry are available. Tours and other communal events sometimes offered, including an open-mike night on Fridays. Check-in is at 2 P.M. and checkout is 11 A.M., but bags can be stored until 8 P.M., and you are free to use the common areas and Internet after you check out. All guests must be 18 or older, or accompanied by guardian.

BEST WESTERN INDEPENDENCE PARK HOTEL $$

235 Chestnut St., 215/922-4443, www.independenceparkinn.com

You'd never guess that this building—listed on the National Register of Historic Places—is part of the Best Western chain. Combining modern hotel amenities with plenty of character, the comfortable high-ceilinged guest rooms ($180–260) are decked out in Victorian-era furnishings. It's in a prime spot among Old City's most popular restaurants and bars and just across the street from Independence National Historical Park; prices at this popular hotel are considerably higher on weekends in summertime than at other times, but be sure to check the website for discounts, including AAA, military, extended stay, and advance booking. A complimentary continental breakfast with a make-your-own-waffle station is included.

COMFORT INN DOWNTOWN-HISTORIC AREA $$

100 N. Columbus Blvd., 215/627-7900, www.comfortinn.com

The Penn's Landing location and reasonable prices ($130–190) are the primary draws for this basic 10-story, 185-room chain. While the hotel is on a stretch of highway, the attractions of Old City and Society Hill are all within a short walk, and complimentary van service will take you to Old City and Center City. The hotel is clean and offers standard amenities, including wireless Internet, a bar, a small exercise room, laundry service, an airport shuttle, and a parking lot ($23/day), and a microwave and refrigerator can rented for $10 a day. A continental breakfast is included. Request a room on an upper floor facing the river for a view of the Benjamin Franklin Bridge.

HOLIDAY INN HISTORIC DISTRICT $$

400 Arch St., 215/923-8660, www.holidayinn.com

There are modern, renovated rooms ($170–220) in this eight-story Holiday Inn. The central Old City location is ideal for touring Independence Park. You can find all the standard amenities, like a fitness center, restaurant, and bar, but best amenity of all has to be the rooftop pool, which offers much-needed relief from the summer heat and makes it a great place to stay with kids. Parking costs $22 a day, but once you're there, you can leave the car and walk, cab, or take a bus all over the city.

◀ MADAME SAITO BED & BREAKFAST $

124 Lombard St., 215/922-2515, http://sushi.madamesaito.com

Trilingual Madame Saito, the self-proclaimed "queen of sushi," does it all out of two adjoined Society Hill row homes a block north of South

HOTELS

STAY AWHILE

Relocating to Philly temporarily or permanently? You have a few good options for lodging while you make the transition. For budget travelers, the **International House** in University City is available to students or faculty with valid IDs from any academic institution; stay for a night, a week, a month, a semester, or the entire school year at a reasonable price.

Catering primarily to business travelers staying for a week or more, **AKA Rittenhouse Square** on 18th and Walnut Streets, directly on Rittenhouse Square, and **Windsor Suites** (a bit less luxurious and a bit less expensive), on the Benjamin Franklin Parkway, both offer fully equipped apartments close to the Center City business district. For everyone else, bed-and-breakfasts or rooms in a private home are often the best bet, offering homey accommodations across a wide range of prices. Many owners encourage long-term visitors with reduced rates for stays of a week or more, and even steeper discounts for stays of a month or more.

Try **Madame Saito Bed & Breakfast** for standard rooms at very low rates, or **Bella Vista Bed & Breakfast, Clinton Street Bed & Breakfast,** or **La Reserve Center City Bed & Breakfast** for fully equipped studios with kitchenettes. Visit online or call **Bed and Breakfast Connections of Philadelphia** (800/448-3619, www.bnb-philadelphia.com) for plenty of additional options in neighborhoods across the city. And even if the site doesn't mention discounts for long-term stays, be sure to ask the owner and shop around for rates; since most are privately owned, there is usually wiggle room. Many of the small bed-and-breakfasts are actually just homes in which the owner rents out a few rooms as an additional source of income, so they are often amenable to longer-term residents. And, of course, there is always **Craigslist** (www.craigslist.org), the ultimate site for finding sublets, temporary, permanent, and shared housing, and pretty much any other unique arrangement you can imagine.

Street. In addition to running a five-room bed-and-breakfast, she operates an attached restaurant and catering business specializing in Japanese, French, and Thai cuisine (not fusion, which Madame does not like, just all three cuisines separately). She also teaches ballroom dancing and sushi-making classes in her spare time and is a fascinating woman worth meeting whether you stay here, take a class with her, or come in for dinner. A comfortable private room with one or two double beds ranges $80–120 in summer and a bit lower other times of the year, with discounts available for stays of a week or more. For an additional fee of $10–12, you can enjoy a traditional Japanese breakfast cooked by the fabulous Madame herself.

◖ MORRIS HOUSE HOTEL ⑤⑤
225 S. 8th St., 215/922-2446,
www.morrishousehotel.com

The perfect balance of colonial charm and modern amenities, the Morris House Hotel offers period furnishings and wireless Internet. Built in 1787, this three-story bed-and-breakfast was home to the prominent Morris family for generations. The National Historic Landmark has been beautifully restored; the 15 guest rooms vary in size and price, with doubles starting at $179, suites starting at $199, and extended luxury suites at $249 with the presidential loft quite as high as $349 on weekends. Rooms in the new addition next door are attractive and comfortable but quite modern, so if it's colonial ambience you're after, be sure to request a room in the original building. A delicious continental breakfast and afternoon tea are included, and when the weather is nice, you can eat breakfast outside in the pretty walled garden.

OMNI HOTEL AT INDEPENDENCE PARK ⑤⑤
401 Chestnut St., 215/925-0000, www.omnihotels.com

Ranked #1 Business Hotel in Philadelphia by *Travel + Leisure*, the Omni's prime location in the heart of the historic district also makes it popular with tourists and visitors of all kinds. At this AAA four-diamond luxury hotel, rooms start around $229 a night, but deals can sometimes be found on the website or other search engines, as well as AAA and advance purchase discounts. Boasting European-style luxury, the 150 large rooms offer every standard amenity, along with great views of Independence National Historical Park. The elegant on-site Azalea restaurant serves modern American cuisine for breakfast, lunch, and dinner, and the on-site bar offers a sophisticated lounge atmosphere. Unwind in the heated indoor pool or enjoy a massage or facial at the Lux Spa.

PENN'S VIEW HOTEL $$

14 N. Front St., 215/922-6600 or 800/331-7634,
www.pennsviewhotel.com

This elegant medium-sized boutique hotel in the heart of Old City is family-owned and operated, and it shows in the level of service provided. Built in 1828, the building has been a shipping warehouse, hardware store, and a coffeehouse in its long history, and is on the National Register of Historic Places. The Italian-born Sena family (which also owns a local favorite restaurant, La Famiglia) purchased and renovated the hotel in 1989, and opened Ristorante Panorama and Il Bar on-site. Rooms ($180–299) have a touch of European elegance with large mirrors and armoires, and some have unique designs like exposed brick walls. Some of the rooms are

equipped with whirlpool tubs, marble fireplaces, and views of the Delaware River. Continental breakfast is included.

THOMAS BOND HOUSE BED AND BREAKFAST $$

129 S. 2nd St., 215/923-8523,
www.winston-salem-inn.com/philadelphia

This charming bed-and-breakfast is in the heart of Independence National Historical Park, adjacent to Welcome Park, where William Penn's home once stood. It has 12 guest rooms, including two large suites with full-size sofa beds, working fireplaces, and whirlpool tubs. Built in 1769, the Georgian-style home was named for its first owner, Thomas Bond, acclaimed surgeon and friend of Ben Franklin, who was a regular guest at the home. With period furnishings and personal touches, including books, games, complimentary sherry, and fresh-baked cookies, a stay here feels like visiting the home of a colonial-era friend. Most rooms are $125–155 with the two suites costing $190 and two smaller rooms for $105. Continental breakfast is served on weekdays, and a full breakfast is included on weekends. Complimentary wine and cheese is served nightly, and all the restaurants of Old City are steps away, including historic City Tavern just across the street.

HOTELS

Center City East

Map 2

Broad Street divides Center City into East and West. Center City East is home to the convention center, Chinatown, and Washington Square West (also called the Gayborhood). Smack dab in the center of the city, it makes it a great base for exploring the historic attractions of Old City as well as shopping in Rittenhouse and seeing the museums of the Benjamin Franklin Parkway. There are plenty of chain hotels on and near Market Street that cater to the Convention Center crowds, including the Wyndham, Hilton Garden Inn, Holiday Inn, and the Marriott. Bed-and-

breakfasts can be found near Antique Row in Washington Square, along with a few independent, midrange, midsize hotels nearby. If it's gay culture you're after, Uncle's Upstairs Inn and the Alexander Inn are two excellent choices.

ALEXANDER INN $

12th and Spruce Sts., 215/923-3535,
www.alexanderinn.com

Popular with gay travelers, this boutique hotel in the heart of Washington Square West neighborhood is a good deal with double rooms starting at $129 including a continental breakfast buffet. Comfortable rooms, a prime location, and friendly staff make the 48-room hotel a popular choice for returning visitors. The Deco style is a bit outdated, a throwback to cruise ships, but while a little cheesy it's not totally over the top. Some of the rooms are very small, so request a larger one when available. A 24-hour fruit and snack table is available for returning late-night revelers or those in search of a midday snack, and a 24-hour fitness room is there for anyone looking to squeeze in a quick workout.

CLINTON STREET
BED & BREAKFAST 💲💲

1024 Clinton St., 215/802-1334,
http://1024clintonstreetbb.com/bb

This charming bed-and-breakfast occupies a historic 1836 Federal-style town house on a tree-lined, primarily residential street near Antique Row. Seven spacious suites ($129–219 a night) each have their own unique character, and all of them come complete with private baths, kitchens, sitting areas, and Internet access, and most have a fireplace. The emerald suite is the largest, making it ideal for extended stays. Innkeeper Kathleen Rabun provides the makings for a do-it-yourself breakfast (coffee, juice, eggs, bread plate, and more) in your suite so you can eat at your own pace without leaving your room.

THE INDEPENDENT HOTEL 💲💲

1234 Locust St., 215/772-1440,
www.theindependenthotel.com

This 24-room boutique hotel opened in a prime location in the heart of Midtown Village in 2008. Occupying a restored Georgian Revival building listed on the National Register of Historic Places, the elegant lobby features a 30-foot hand-painted mural, indicative of many personal touches of character to come. The rooms are spacious and the tin-ceilinged bathrooms and hardwood floors lend a modern, clean look. Each room has its own unique accents, from fireplaces and exposed brick walls to cathedral ceilings, French windows, and lofts, with luxurious linens and attractive furniture to match the distinctive architecture. All rooms have TVs, wireless Internet, refrigerators and microwaves, and some have kitchenettes. High-season rates start at $154, including a light breakfast in the lobby or delivered to your room and a wine and cheese reception on weekdays.

LE MÉRIDIEN 💲💲💲

1421 Arch St., 215/422-8200,
www.LeMeridien.com/Philadelphia

Housed in a 10-story Georgian Revival building that was once a YMCA, Le Méridien opened in 2009. Part of the Starwood Hotels Group, recognized worldwide for the highest service and luxury, it has an air of sophistication and the feel of a unique, independent hotel. Modern, clean, lines featuring black, white, and red colors contrast with the elaborate architectural details of the building. Just steps from the Convention Center and Reading Terminal Market and close enough to walk to both Rittenhouse and Old City, the location is popular for both tourists and business travelers. The 202 rooms start at $399 in the high season with Internet deals sometimes available.

LOEWS HOTEL 💲💲

1200 Market St., 215/627-1200, www.loewshotels.com

The modern, stylish Loews occupies the former PSFS (Philadelphia Savings Fund Society) building, considered the first modern, international-style skyscraper in the country. Designed by George Howe and William Lescaze, it was constructed in 1932, and despite its modern incarnation as a chain hotel today, it retains some original and early details, including Cartier clocks and bank-vault doors. There is a full-service health spa with lap pool, treatment rooms, steam room, and sauna on the 5th floor, and a high-end seafood restaurant and a stylish bar on the first level. The hotel is well-equipped for the business traveler with T1

HOTELS

© JULIA GAVIN

The Ritz-Carlton of Philadelphia on the Avenue of the Arts

cable lines, modem lines, and electronic safes, and its location a block from the Convention Center makes it a popular choice. But it's cool enough to be chosen by many leisure travelers for its host of amenities, stylish decor, and central location a block from Reading Terminal market, smack dab in the middle of Center City. Rates start at $199, though specials and package deals are often available.

◖ THE RITZ-CARLTON OF PHILADELPHIA ❸❸❸
10 Avenue of the Arts, 215/523-8000, www.ritzcarlton.com

In its prime Avenue of the Arts location, the Ritz-Carlton is the epitome of luxury. The five-diamond hotel occupies the historic former Girard/Mellon Bank building, and the lobby—with its domed ceiling, marble floors, and grand columns—is absolutely breathtaking. Each of the 330 guest rooms offers the ultimate in luxury—as they should, with prices starting at $379 a night. The Ritz is home to a state-of-the-art fitness center and the full-service D'Ambra Day Spa & Salon. The 10 Arts Lounge serves cocktails and snacks in a cozy lounge setting, while the 10 Arts Bistro features upscale American cuisine.

UNCLE'S UPSTAIRS INN ❸
1220 Locust St., 215/546-6660

Catering to a predominantly but not exclusively gay clientele, this small bed-and-breakfast occupies a 19th-century row home above a gay bar. It's the heart of the Gayborhood, and most guests begin their nights in the lively downstairs bar, which is a great place to meet fellow travelers and locals. Request a room on an upper floor if you're not an all-night party animal, as rooms directly above the bar tend to be loud until closing at 2 A.M. A basic continental breakfast is provided. There are six rooms starting at $100 per night, with the two larger rooms starting at $125.

Center City West Map 3

Most of the accommodations in Center City West are near Rittenhouse Square, a lovely area in the heart of the downtown shopping district and an easy walk to the Benjamin Franklin Parkway museums. A popular and pricey part of town, it offers high-end chain hotels along with a few midrange hotels and bed-and-breakfasts.

HOTEL PALOMAR ⓢⓢⓢ
117 S. 17th St., 215/563-5006,
www.hotelpalomar-philadelphia.com

This LEED Gold Certified luxury boutique hotel in the Rittenhouse shopping district opened in 2009, and is the first of its kind to receive the ultimate eco-friendly certification in the city. Part of the Kimpton Hotel Group, known for its reuse of historic buildings, the hotel's tagline is "Art in Motion." Each of its hotels has a theme or a story, and this one pays homage to the arts in all their constantly changing forms with a variety of original artwork placed throughout the hotel's common spaces, including the lobby, restaurant, and fitness center. Boasting a unique sustainable design, including water and energy efficiency, eco-friendly materials and furnishings, high indoor air quality, the hotel offers 230 rooms and suites designed with neutral earth tones, modern lines, and Art Deco details. A lovely new hotel in a lovely location. Rooms start at $225 in high season, with discounts often available for three nights or more.

LA RESERVE CENTER CITY BED AND BREAKFAST ⓢ
1804 Pine St., 215/735-1137, www.lareservebandb.com

This restored 1850s four-story row house sits on a quiet, residential block in an idyllic location near Rittenhouse Square. There are 12 rooms to choose from, including six fully equipped studio and one-bedroom suites, which are intended for people staying a week or longer. Standard

the Art Deco-style Hotel Palomar

rooms that share a bath with one other room are $80–125; deluxe rooms with private bath are $115–150; and studios and executive suites are $120–175. This is an unbeatable deal for the location, especially for long-term stays with discounts of 10–30 percent depending on length of stay. There are no TVs in the rooms, but a Steinway piano in the parlor and endless activities in nearby Rittenhouse Square keep guests entertained. A continental breakfast is served on weekdays and a full breakfast on weekends and holidays, and homemade cookies and afternoon tea are served daily.

THE LATHAM $

135 S. 17th St., 215/563-7474, www.lathamhotel.com

This 139-room boutique hotel occupies a busy corner on Walnut Street in the heart of the Rittenhouse business district, surrounded by many of the best shops, restaurants, and bars in the city. It's popular with business travelers as well as vacationers, and all the standard hotel amenities are provided in comfortable rooms decked out in attractive, if not entirely authentic, Victorian furnishings. Dating from 1907, the building is listed on the National Register of Historic Places. A friendly doorman dressed in traditional British horseback-riding attire creates an air of European sophistication. High-season doubles start at $229, which isn't terrible considering the prime location.

RITTENHOUSE HOTEL $$$

210 W. Rittenhouse Sq., 215/546-9000, www.rittenhousehotel.com

Oprah Winfrey, Bill Clinton, Mark Wahlberg, and Tom Hanks are just a few of the famous guests who have called the Rittenhouse Hotel home during their stays in Philadelphia—and no wonder, considering the ideal location, luxurious accommodations, and perfectly attentive yet unobtrusive service. Nearly all of the rooms, starting at $215 with larger suites as high as $600 and up, offer a great view of Rittenhouse Square below. The independent luxury hotel is consistently ranked among the top boutique hotels in the world by *Travel + Leisure* magazine and other publications, and

has received the esteemed five diamonds from AAA for two decades. With long-term apartment accommodations available for those with fat wallets, everything you want can be found on-site—an indoor pool, health club, salon, and spa. Dining options include the Smith & Wollensky Grill, a steakhouse; Lacroix, one of the most esteemed fine-dining establishments in the city; and a tea room and garden serving afternoon tea and cocktails.

RITTENHOUSE 1715 $$$

1715 Rittenhouse Square St. (btwn. Locust and Spruce Sts.), 215/546-6500, www.rittenhouse1715.com

You'll be treated to pure elegance and comfort at this 23-room bed-and-breakfast tucked away on a quiet street just off bustling Rittenhouse Square. With standard rooms starting at $249, junior suites at $309, and the crème de la crème—the deluxe, two-level presidential suite—as high as $699, this level of luxury obviously does not come cheaply. But if you've got the cash (or credit) and you're looking for a more intimate alternative to the larger luxury hotels, or you want to splurge for a romantic special occasion like an anniversary, Rittenhouse 1715 cannot be beat. Think plush robes, fireplaces, elegant furniture, dim lighting, plasma TVs, marble baths, and nightly turndown service. A tasty extended continental breakfast is served each morning, and complimentary wine is offered in the drawing room in the evenings.

WESTIN $$$

99 S. 17th St., 215/563-1600, www.starwoodhotels.com

With rooms starting at around $239 a night, this deluxe chain in the heart of the downtown business and shopping district is a top choice for business travelers with expense accounts. With clean lines and soothing colors, both the rooms and common areas are sleek, stylish, and modern. The 294 guest rooms and 19 suites have all the luxury amenities, but the greatest amenity of all has to be the signature Heavenly Bed—it is, quite simply, the most comfortable bed in the world. The hotel is connected to the Shops at Liberty Place with all the Rittenhouse shops just outside your door.

Museum District Map 4

An easy walk to Center City and Fairmount, and just next door to a few of the city's biggest museums, including the Philadelphia Museum of Art and the Franklin Institute, the area is home to primarily chain hotels, including the Sheraton, Embassy Suites, Crowne Plaza, and the impressive Four Seasons. Popular with business travelers, but also a good base for tourists, the area is bustling during the day but a bit quiet at night.

BEST WESTERN CENTER CITY $

501 N. 22nd St., 215/568-8300, www.bestwestern.com

Nothing fancy, the lowest-priced hotel in the area (with rooms starting at $107 when booked two weeks in advance) is a standard chain with 183 guest rooms, free parking, fitness room, gift shop, and an outdoor pool. The decor is a bit outdated, and the outside is an unremarkable block, but it makes a reasonably comfortable and affordable base for exploring, or at least a decent place to crash while you're in town for a few days. There is nothing in the immediate vicinity outside of the on-site sports bar and restaurant, but it's just a short walk from Center City and the Fairmount neighborhood.

FOUR SEASONS $$$

1 Logan Sq., 215/963-1500, www.fourseasons.com/philadelphia

Arguably the city's finest hotel, the Four Seasons has earned five diamonds from AAA and was named one of the top 20 U.S. hotels by *Condé Nast Traveler*. Catering to a wealthy and discriminating clientele, the Four Seasons rarely disappoints, with its elegant lobby, 364 rooms including 96 suites (starting around $395) with every amenity, and state-of-the-art facilities, including a beautiful indoor pool. While this luxury chain has hotels all over the world, each has its own special character. In Philadelphia, the classic design was inspired by the Federal period in early American history. Complimentary town car service is available in Center City, and small pets are allowed. The hotel is also home to the Swann Lounge and the Fountain Restaurant, offering some of the most elegant dining and tea service in the city.

WINDSOR SUITES $

1700 Benjamin Franklin Pkwy., 215/981-5678, www.windsorhotel.com

This 24-story hotel sits directly on the Benjamin Franklin Parkway and is easily recognizable by its curved exterior. Offering spacious apartment-style accommodations and large work stations, it's popular with long-term guests in town for business. But considering the reasonable price for the location (rooms start at approximately $100 per night), it is also a decent option for anyone looking to prepare meals at home and stay near the heart of Center City. A 24-hour fitness facility, free Internet access, a seasonal rooftop pool, and a sundeck are a few of the amenities. Two on-site dining options offer Asian and Mediterranean cuisine.

South Philadelphia   Map 5

Just south of South Street, the Queen Village and Bella Vista neighborhoods are two of the city's most popular areas, with lots of character and plenty of great restaurants. There are no hotels in this part of the city, but a few good, reasonably priced bed-and-breakfasts are available, all within a short walk of Old City. In addition to the excellent one listed here, you can find several more at www.bnb philadelphia.com.

BELLA VISTA BED & BREAKFAST $

752 S. 10th St., 215/238-1270,
www.philadelphiabellavistabnb.com
Just a block from the Italian Market, this converted circa-1860 townhouse has nine rooms and seven suites, with rates $85–135. Rooms vary in size (from small to spacious) and design (from colonial to contemporary), but each has its own charm, filled with artwork, antiques, and eclectic touches. All rooms have satellite TV and DSL, and most have private baths. A continental breakfast with homemade muffins is included in the price. Some have kitchens and separate living areas, and with great deals on long-term stays, they make a great option for long-term visitors or anyone planning to relocate to Philly who wants to feel at home but needs some time to find a place.

HOTELS

University City   Map 6

An affordable alternative to staying in Center City, especially for college students or anyone visiting Penn or Drexel, University City is easily reached via several car and foot bridges. Numerous Victorian bed-and-breakfasts with loads of character offer alternatives to the two chain hotels, the Hilton Inn at Penn and the Sheraton University City. In addition to those listed, there are plenty other great options that can be found at www.bnbphiladelphia.com.

CORNERSTONE BED & BREAKFAST $$

3300 Baring St., 215/387-6065,
www.cornerstonebandb.com
This restored 1865 Victorian mansion has six beautifully appointed rooms ($165–205), including two suites. Located near the campuses of the University of Pennsylvania and Drexel, it offers a nice alternative for visiting parents, professors, or students. Rooms have a mix of antique and contemporary furniture, and include modern amenities like large flat-screen televisions. A full breakfast is served in the dining room on weekends, and continental on weekdays. The wraparound porch is surrounded by a lovely garden, offering a lovely place to sit when the weather is nice.

GABLES $

4520 Chester Ave., 215/662-1918, www.gablesbb.com
Built in 1889 by prominent Philadelphia architect Willis Hale, this restored Victorian mansion is one of the most popular bed-and-breakfasts in West Philadelphia, with 10 rooms available for guests. The innkeepers have created a beautiful and friendly atmosphere with a mix of antique furniture and modern amenities, including air-conditioning, cable television, and wireless Internet. Most rooms, which range $115–185, have private baths, but visit the website for detailed descriptions of each unique space. A computer station, refrigerator, and microwave are available for guest use in the common area, and a full homemade breakfast is served every day. A large wraparound porch—-a classic feature in most large homes in this area—is a great place to meet fellow travelers.

THE HILTON INN AT PENN $$

3600 Sansom St., 215/222-0200,
www.theinnatpenn.com

In the heart of the University of Pennsylvania's campus, this is the most popular hotel for visiting parents, faculty, and guests of the university, and it is as comfortable and high-tech as you'd expect from an Ivy League–affiliated establishment. The AAA four-diamond hotel is managed by Hilton but retains its own character. With 238 rooms, including four suites, prices start at $186 when purchased several weeks in advance. The already attractive rooms were undergoing a multimillion dollar renovation in early 2011, so they should offer even more amenities once complete. The hotel's on-site dining options include an Italian restaurant, Penne, open for lunch and dinner, and the University Club for breakfast, with plenty of additional dining, shopping, and entertainment options just outside the door. Rooms fill early during the beginning and end of the semester and especially during graduation in May.

INTERNATIONAL HOUSE $

3701 Chestnut St., 215/387-5125, www.ihousephilly.org

There is a lot going on inside this large, boxy, bland-looking building on the edge of the University of Pennsylvania's campus. The International House offers basic accommodations for a few days, monthly, or long-term. Rooms are rented to students, prospective students, faculty, or anyone with an academic affiliation (ID is required). Singles ($80), private rooms ($100), and efficiency apartments ($150) are rented on a nightly basis when available, but many residents stay for a month ($930–1,280) or more (price is lower with stays of three months or more). This is where many international students studying at Penn live for a semester or a year, for its affordability, community spirit, and for a host of other programs built in that cater to the international community, including the on-site movie theater showing mostly international films, events and parties, and language and other classes. Note that you don't have to stay here to take advantage of all the great programming.

Fairmount Park and Chestnut Hill   Map 8

There is a youth hostel, Chamounix Mansion, tucked away amidst the trees and trails of Fairmount Park. The location is accessible but a bit out of the way for exploring the major tourist attractions, but the setting is unique and lovely, making a great option for outdoor lovers or anyone on a budget.

Chestnut Hill has one full-service hotel in the heart of the Germantown Avenue business district. It's a lovely part of the city, but about a 25-minute drive from downtown, so you'll want to have a car to do ample exploring from here. It's a great base for visiting the historic attractions of nearby Germantown, Wissahickon Park, and the Manayunk business district. The area is filled with mansions, some of which rent out rooms as bed-and-breakfasts. Visit www.bnbphiladelphia.com for more information.

◖ CHAMOUNIX MANSION $

3250 Chamounix Dr., 215/878-3676 or 800/379-0017, www.philahostel.org

A one-of-a-kind mansion turned youth hostel, Chamounix (pronounced CHAM-ah-nee) occupies a bucolic setting in the heart of Fairmount Park. Originally built as a country home for Philadelphia merchant George Plumstead in 1802, the restored mansion offers clean, air-conditioned dorm accommodations with several private rooms available, at an unbeatable price of $20 for Hostelling International members with valid ID, $23 for nonmembers, and $8 for children 16 and under. A public SEPTA bus runs into the city from a stop a short walk from the hostel, but having a car or bike is useful for greater flexibility and safety, especially at night; there are a few free bikes available for guests. There is

Chestnut Hill Hotel

a 2 A.M. curfew, and alcohol and smoking are not permitted on-site. Included in the common areas is an Internet kiosk, a TV/VCR lounge with a video library, and a recreation room with table tennis, a piano, and foosball. Linens, pillow, and blanket are provided free of charge. A washer, dryer, towels, and lockers are available for a fee. There is a daily lockout 11 A.M.–4:30 P.M. each day.

CHESTNUT HILL HOTEL $$

8229 Germantown Ave., 215/242-5905,
www.chestnuthillhotel.com

Built in 1864, the current building replaced an inn in the same location that dated from 1772. The comfortable 36-room hotel offers modern amenities with antique-looking furnishings that pay homage to its long history, with high-season rates starting at $139. The only full-service hotel in Chestnut Hill, it is an excellent base for exploring the area right in the heart of the business district, which is bustling during the day and relatively quiet at night. The three on-site restaurants happen to be some of the neighborhood's best, but there are a myriad of other options nearby. The AAA three-diamond establishment has hosted its fair share of celebrities, including Kate Hudson, Billie Jean King, and Cuba Gooding Jr.

EXCURSIONS FROM PHILADELPHIA

You'll never run out of things to do in Philadelphia, but if you get the chance to take a day or weekend trip outside of the city, there is much more to see and do within just a short drive. The Brandywine Valley, Bucks County, and Pennsylvania Dutch Country are the most popular nearby destinations, all only 45–90 minutes away by car. While each is unique, you can find charming towns, villages, and farms sprinkled amidst a bucolic landscape in all three. You'll also find cozy bed-and-breakfasts, a diversity of dining options, opportunities for recreation, and shopping galore—from outlets to antiques to fine art to handmade crafts.

While Bucks County and the Brandywine Valley offer museums, gardens, wineries, galleries, and antiques shops, Pennsylvania Dutch Country beckons visitors to experience the lifestyle of our non-electricity-using, horse-and-buggy-riding Amish neighbors amid lush, rolling farmlands.

As you explore, you'll learn about the long, rich history, of each area—many aspects of which are linked with Philadelphia's history. For example, there are several key Revolutionary War sites in the Brandywine Valley and Bucks County, and the reason that the largest Pennsylvania Dutch settlement is near Philadelphia is because persecuted Amish communities came to Pennsylvania from Germany because of William Penn's pledge of religious freedom.

The three excursions detailed in this chapter are some of the best and closest year-round destinations, but there is plenty more to do seasonally in addition to those detailed here.

© WWW.DISCOVERLANCASTERPA.COM/TERRY ROSS

HIGHLIGHTS

LOOK FOR TO FIND RECOMMENDED SIGHTS, ACTIVITIES, DINING, AND LODGING.

Best Place to See the Brandywine Valley in Still Form: The **Brandywine River Museum** displays an impressive collection of American art, including many paintings of the local landscape by world-renowned Andrew Wyeth (page 215).

Best Historic Gardens: With more than 1,000 acres of landscaped gardens, **Longwood Gardens,** another local du Pont family legacy, is one of the best horticultural showcases in the world (page 216).

Best Decorative Arts Collection: One of several local du Pont family estates in the Brandywine Valley, **Winterthur Museum, Garden, and Library** is home to America's most esteemed collection of decorative arts, along with 1,000 lush acres of rolling hills, streams, and gardens to explore (page 221).

Most Charming Town: An artist enclave straddling the Delaware River, **New Hope** offers shops, restaurants, art galleries, antiques, and bed-and-breakfasts for a bustling culture in a small-town setting (page 224).

Best Castle Museums: Fonthill and the Mercer Museum in Doylestown were built by Henry Chapman Mercer, one of Bucks County's most famous sons. Along with Moravian Pottery and Tile Works, the three National Historic Landmarks make up the **Mercer Mile** (page 226).

Best Kids' Theme Park: **Sesame Place,** the world's only theme park based on the Sesame Street television series, is just outside of Philly in Langhorne and it hugely popular with kids (page 227).

Best Way to Cool Off on a Hot Day: Several Bucks County companies offer **water sports on the Delaware River.** For tubing, rafting, canoeing, and kayaking, try Delaware River Tubing Co. on the New Jersey side of the river and Bucks County River Country on the Pennsylvania side (page 228).

Best Market: Lancaster's **Central Market** is reminiscent of Philadelphia's Reading Terminal Market, but with lower prices and even more homemade Amish goods and crafts for sale among its diverse offerings. Originally an outdoor market in the 1730s, it is the oldest continually operating market in the country (page 230).

Most Historic Theater: See a show – at Lancaster's historic **Fulton Theatre,** built in 1852. The intimate venue has seen many a famous actor grace its stage, including most of the Barrymore family, Sarah Bernhardt, W. C. Fields, and Mark Twain (page 231).

© WWW.DISCOVERLANCASTERPA.COM

Central Market in Lancaster

EXCURSIONS

EXCURSIONS FROM PHILADELPHIA

SEE "BUCKS COUNTY" MAP

WATER SPORTS ON THE DELAWARE RIVER

NEW HOPE

Washington Crossing

SESAME PLACE

Penndel

Bristol

Langhorne

Newtown

MERCER MILE

Doylestown

Dublin

PHILADELPHIA

NEW JERSEY

ATLANTIC CITY EXPRESSWAY

NEW JERSEY TURNPIKE

ATLANTIC CITY

10 mi

10 km

SEE "BRANDYWINE VALLEY" MAP

King of Prussia

Valley Forge National Historical Park

Media

WINTERTHUR MUSEUM, GARDEN, AND LIBRARY

BRANDYWINE RIVER MUSEUM

Chadds Ford

Kennett

LONGWOOD GARDENS

West Chester

Brandywine Valley

Kennett Square

Wilmington

DELAWARE

Emmaus

Douglassville

HOPEWELL FURNACE

Birdsboro

Reading

Kutztown

Leesport

Shartlesville

MARYLAND

PENNSYLVANIA

Susquehanna River

RAILROAD MUSEUM OF PENNSYLVANIA

Intercourse

New Holland

Paradise

THE NATIONAL TOY TRAIN MUSEUM

Strasburg

Willow Street

EPHRATA CLOISTER

Ephrata

Adamstown

LANDIS VALLEY MUSEUM

SEE "PENNSYLVANIA DUTCH COUNTRY" MAP

FARM AND BULK STORES

CENTRAL MARKET

Lancaster

FULTON THEATRE

Columbia

Lebanon

Hershey

To Harrisburg

© AVALON TRAVEL

In summertime, follow the stream of locals who head "down the shore"—local vernacular for the New Jersey beach towns. And for lovers of skiing or snowboarding, no winter trip to the area is complete without a trip to the Poconos in northeastern Pennsylvania, or "up the mountains" as some locals say. And of course, New York, Baltimore, and D.C. are all within a three hour or less drive, train, or bus ride. So whether you're just visiting the area or you live here and you're looking for a break from the buzz of the city, be sure to take advantage of the wealth of vastly different areas within your reach.

PLANNING YOUR TIME

Each of these destinations can be experienced in a day trip if that is all the time you have, but an overnight—or even better, a weekend—will make for a more relaxing and in-depth experience. The Brandywine Valley is closest to Philadelphia (around 45 minutes), followed by Bucks County (about an hour) and Pennsylvania Dutch Country (an hour and a half). Since it is the farthest and also the most spread out, Pennsylvania Dutch Country is the destination in which you'll most want to spend at least

a night. The Brandywine Valley and Bucks County are very doable as day trips, although with the great wealth of historic inns in both areas, you'll want to stay overnight if possible.

The best way to travel to any of these areas is by car, although parts of each are accessible by public transportation if you have the patience and no other options. Biking is an excellent option within all three areas when the weather is nice, especially in Bucks County, which is well known for scenic trails and paths. The Brandywine Valley and Pennsylvania Dutch Country are in roughly the same direction, west of Philadelphia, so they may be planned in coordination if you have time to do both.

All are year-round destinations with a climate similar to Philadelphia and plenty to do no matter when you go, but with the summer generally busier. There are a multitude of holiday events during the winter season, but you'll miss out on the outdoor attractions, like hiking or tubing on the Delaware River. As with Philadelphia, the most pleasant time to visit is in the spring or fall when the gardens are in bloom, the foliage is colorful, and temperatures are generally mild and pleasant.

EXCURSIONS

Brandywine Valley

Spanning southeastern Pennsylvania and northern Delaware, the Brandywine Valley is around 30 miles southwest of Philadelphia. Home to charming towns, Revolutionary War sites, museums, wineries, and the impressive Longwood Gardens, its central towns include Chadds Ford, Kennett Square, West Chester, and Wilmington, all of which make a fine base for exploring. The area's most popular attractions include several lavish, historic estates and gardens of generations of various du Ponts, one of the wealthiest and most prominent American families in history. The local landscape has been immortalized by the world renowned painter Andrew Wyeth, and the Brandywine River Museum showcases many of those works.

SIGHTS
Chadds Ford and Kennett Square

Route 1 runs through Chadds Ford and Kennett Square, and the area's main attractions are just a short drive from one another along or near the main road. At the heart of Chadds Ford, at the intersection of Routes 1 and 100, there are about a dozen shops, including boutiques, an art gallery, an inn, and several restaurants. Kennett Square offers plenty of shopping, dining, and entertainment in a small-town setting; be sure to sample some mushrooms while you're in the "mushroom capital of the world."

BRANDYWINE BATTLEFIELD HISTORIC SITE

The largest Revolutionary War battle in the

WINE TRAILS OF THE BRANDYWINE VALLEY AND BUCKS COUNTY

Both the Brandywine Valley and Bucks County are gaining increasing respect as East Coast producers of quality wine, and visiting just one, or several, of the area wineries is a lovely way to spend a day. You'll pass rolling farmlands, quaint towns, antiques shops, restaurants, and historic inns and bed-and-breakfasts as you drive between wineries. Each winery is different in size, style, and varieties of wine produced, and each has its own story. All are relatively small, making for an intimate visit, and many are family-owned and -operated.

Most of the area wineries are part of Brandywine Valley Wine Trail (www.bvwinetrail.com) or the Bucks County Wine Trail (www.buckscountywinetrail.com), and these two websites offer much information and often discounts for visiting more than one. Visit each winery's individual website to learn more about the history, wine, and special events offered throughout the year. Most offer tastings and tours for free or for a small fee. Hours change seasonally, with some only open on weekends, and most have longer summer hours, so call or visit the website before visiting.

BRANDYWINE VALLEY WINE TRAIL

- **Black Walnut Winery:** 3000 Lincoln Highway, Sadsburyville, 610/857-5566, www.blackwalnutwinery.com
- **Chaddsford Winery:** 632 Baltimore Pike, Chadds Ford, 610/388-6221, www.chaddsford.com
- **Kreutz Creek Vineyards:** 553 S. Guernsey Rd., West Grove, 610/869-4412, www.kreutzcreekvineyards.com
- **Paradocx Vineyard:** The Shoppes at Longwood Village, Rte. 1, Kennett Square, 610/444-9003, www.paradocx.com
- **Penns Woods Winery:** 124 Beaver Valley Rd., Chadds Ford, 610/459-0808, www.pennswoodswinery.com
- **Twin Brook Winery:** 5697 Strasburg Rd., Gap, 717/442-4915, www.twinbrookwinery.com

BUCKS COUNTY WINE TRAIL

- **Buckingham Valley Vineyards:** 1521 Rte. 413, Buckingham, 215/794-7188, www.pawine.com
- **Crossing Vineyards & Winery:** 1853 Wrightstown Rd., Washington Crossing, 215/493-6500
- **New Hope Winery:** 6123 Lower York Rd., Rte. 202, New Hope, 215/794-2331, www.newhopewinery.com
- **Peace Valley Winery:** 300 Old Limekiln Rd., Chalfont, 215/249-9058, www.peacevalleywinery.com
- **Rose Bank Winery:** 258 Durham Rd., Newtown, 215/860-5899, www.rosebankwinery.com
- **Rushland Ridge Vineyards:** 2665 Rushland Rd., Rushland, 215/598-0251, www.rushlandridge.com
- **Sand Castle Winery:** 755 River Rd. (Rte. 32), Erwinna, 800/722-9469, www.sandcastlewinery.com
- **Wycombe Vineyards:** 1391 Forest Grove Rd., Furlong, 215/598-9463, www.wycombevineyards.com
- **Unami Ridge Winery:** 2144 Kumry Rd., Quakertown, 215/804-5445, www.unamiridge.com

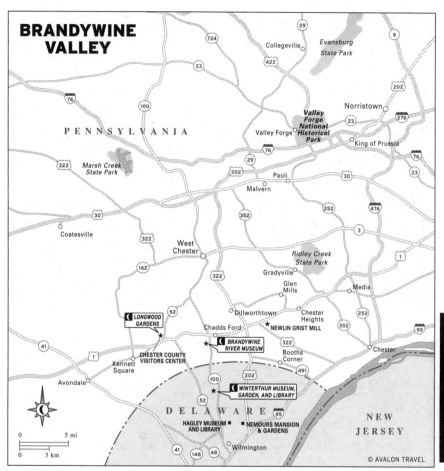

Philadelphia area was fought on this site on September 11, 1777. The British won, the American army lost thousands of soldiers, and the remaining American troops retreated to Valley Forge while the British went on to occupy Philadelphia. Despite this devastating outcome, history buffs will enjoy exploring the grounds and visiting the two restored homes that served as headquarters for George Washington and General Lafayette as they camped here. The **Visitor Center** (1491 Baltimore Pike, 610/459-3342, www.brandywinebattlefield

.org, Apr.–Dec. Thurs.–Sat. 9 A.M.–4 P.M., Sun. noon–4 P.M.) has a small museum containing artifacts, exhibits, and a gift shop and shows a short film about the history of the site. The grounds are free but there is a fee for admission into the museum ($5 adult, $3.50 senior, $2.50 child 13–18, free 12 and under).

◖ BRANDYWINE RIVER MUSEUM

This former 19th-century grist mill (100 Creek Rd., 610/388-2700, www.brandywinemuseum .org, daily 9:30 A.M.–4:30 P.M., $10 adult, $6

© KARRIE GAVIN

The Brandywine Battlefield was a key battle site during the Revolutionary War.

senior, student, and child 6–12, free child under 6) is now a lovely museum of mostly local art. Among more than 3,000 works are a wealth of still-lifes and illustrations from the famous Wyeth family of artists who lived nearby. Andrew, the most famous Wyeth of all, is best known for his moving, realistic portrayals of the Brandywine landscape. As you stroll the galleries, notice the similarities and differences in the works of three generations of Wyeths, including Andrew's father, N. C., and his son Jamie. The Brandywine River can be seen through floor-to-ceiling windows, making it the perfect place to view the works amid the landscape that inspired them. Works of other early American artists are also on display.

◀ LONGWOOD GARDENS

In addition to more than 1,000 acres of lush, beautifully landscaped gardens, there is a sprawling multi-room greenhouse and a museum where you can learn about the early history of the gardens and the families that lived

here, and a restaurant and gift shop/home & garden store. Dating from 1730, the **Peirce-du Pont House** is the oldest building on the grounds; inside a short video plays and several rooms contains exhibits about the history of the estate and gardens. While a wealth of trees were planted on this spot by the Quaker Peirce family, the owners of the land from the early 1700s, much of what exists today can be credited to Pierre S. du Pont, who purchased it in 1906 to save it from destruction. Pierre was great-grandson of Eleuthère Irénée du Pont, a French immigrant who founded the DuPont chemical company when he arrived in the area in 1800. Pierre bought the estate and used it as his weekend residence 1906–1954, during which time he expanded the corporate empire of his family's business and devoted some of his great wealth to the development of Longwood Gardens. New exhibits and expansions have continually taken place since then, but both the Peirce family and Pierre du Pont laid much of the groundwork for the historic gardens that attract so many visitors today (1001 Longwood

© KARRIE GAVIN

Longwood Gardens during the winter holiday season

Rd., Kennett Square, 610/388-1000, www .longwoodgardens.org, $18 adult, $15 senior, $8 student and child, free 4 and under). Like the blooms and the exhibits, the operating hours change seasonally, but the gardens generally open daily at 9 A.M. and close at 5 P.M. January–March, at 6 P.M. during the rest of the year, with extended weekend hours in summer (late May–early Sept. Fri. and Sat. until 10 P.M.) and during the winter holidays (open until 9 P.M. late Nov.–early Jan.). While the blooms in winter are obviously not as plentiful, the holiday decorations, massive Christmas tree display, ice skating performances, and other special events make it a lovely time to visit.

MORE CHADDS FORD SIGHTS

The **Chadds Ford Historical Society** (1736 Creek Rd., 610/388-7376, www.chaddsford history.org, Mon.–Fri. 9 A.M.–2 P.M. year-round, Sat.–Sun. noon–5 P.M. in summer, free) is a nonprofit committed to preserving local history. In addition to a small shop, library, and exhibit room of historic artifacts,

the society preserves the **John Chads House,** built in 1725, and the **Barns-Brinton House,** built in 1714, which are occasionally open for tours and offer a glimpse into the lives of early settlers to the area.

Just down the road is the **Christian C. Sanderson Museum** (1755 Creek Rd., 610/388-6545, www.sandersonmuseum.org, Mar.–Nov. Sat.–Sun. noon–4 P.M., free). Sanderson, born in 1882 in Montgomery County, was an avid collector of early Americana, and his former home contains his 4,000-plus-item collection, including Helen Keller's autograph and Andrew Wyeth's only pastel drawing.

In nearby Glen Mills, the 1704 **Newlin Grist Mill** (Cheyney Rd. and Baltimore Pike, Glen Mills, 610/459-2359, www.newlingristmill.org, office daily 10 A.M.–3 P.M., park daily 9 A.M.–dusk) is the only operating 18th-century grist mill in the Commonwealth of Pennsylvania. The 150-acre park is devoted to the history of the people who lived here and the techniques used to power the mill. The park is free, but there is a $5 admission charged for a tour of the historic buildings, including a blacksmith's shop and a smokehouse. Fishing and picnic grounds are also available.

West Chester and Vicinity

This quaint town has a concentrated area of shops and restaurants along with a few interesting sights. The **Chester County Historical Society** (225 N. High St., 610/692-4800, www.cchs-pa.org, Wed.–Sat. 10 A.M.–5 P.M., $6 adult, $5 senior, $3.50 student and child 6–17, free under 6), with its modest museum, library, and shop, makes a good starting point

---

FORGING A NATION

Valley Forge was a pivotal stop on the road to victory during the Revolutionary War, and **Valley Forge National Historical Park** (1400 Outer Line Dr., King of Prussia, 610/783-1077, www.nps.gov/vafo) offers a glimpse into this period in American history. While no battles were fought here, more than 2,000 American soldiers died from disease during the six months the Continental Army spent here during the brutally cold winter of 1777-1778. General George Washington chose Valley Forge because it was close to Philadelphia, which was occupied by the British army at the time, yet far enough away to be relatively safe from surprise attacks. Lacking adequate clothing, food, and medical supplies, the army persevered against all odds, and trained and came together as the cohesive and powerful army

that went on to defeat the British army and ultimately win the war.

A visit to the park should begin with a stop at the Welcome Center to pick up a map, visit the gift shop, and check out the collection of more than 4,000 exhibits and artifacts. Next, watch the short film shown in the adjacent theater, which provides a visual of the lives of the soldiers at Valley Forge; complete with uplifting music and cannons firing, it's sure to put you in a patriotic mood.

The winding roads and trails of the picturesque 3,600-acre park can be traversed on foot, bike, horseback, or by car. Six miles of pet-friendly, multi-use trails connect the park to Philadelphia and to the Appalachian Trail, and are as popular with locals as they are with visitors, but a car (or guided trolley tour

the Memorial Arch at Valley Forge National Historical Park

© OLIVIER LE QUEINEC/123RF.COM

to the area. The museum contains over 60,000 items celebrating the area's history, including furniture, clothing, and other artifacts, and the galleries showcase permanent and rotating collections. Nearby, the **William Brinton 1704 House and Historic Site** (21 Oakland Rd., 610/399-0913, www.brintonfamily.org,

May–Oct. Sat.–Sun. 1–5 P.M. and by appt., $5 adult, $3 child under 12), a restored home furnished in medieval English style, tells the rich history of its inhabitants, who were some of the early colonists to the area.

For a glimpse into a slice of more recent local history, visit the **American Helicopter**

© ANDREW KAZMIERSKI/123RF.COM

EXCURSIONS

log cabins at Valley Forge National Historical Park

in the summer season) is the best way to see all the historic sites. A free cell phone tour is available by dialing a number at key stops along the Encampment Tour trail, which includes Washington's Headquarters; replicas of the Muhlenberg Brigade huts, where the soldiers lived; the Memorial Arch; and the Washington Memorial Chapel, which also has a used book store, gift shop, and café on the grounds.

Summer is the best time to visit, because the dogwood trees and lush grounds are in bloom, and options for exploring the park abound. In addition to ranger-led walking tours, guided

trolley tours, and bike rentals, Once Upon a Nation (http://historicphiladelphia.org/valley-forge), the same group responsible for the costumed actors in Independence Park, offers special tours and programs, including costumed storytellers, an After Hours tour for a meal with George and Martha Washington, and the Secrets and Spies tour, where kids can be part of the action and learn spy techniques for discovering traitors.

And when you've had your fill of Revolutionary history, you're in luck; the King of Prussia Mall, the largest shopping mall on the East Coast, is only six miles away.

Museum and Education Center (1220 American Blvd., 610/436-9600, www.helicop termuseum.org, Wed.–Sat. 10 A.M.–5 P.M., Sun. noon–5 P.M., $10 adult, $8 senior, $7 child and student, free under 2), the premier museum devoted exclusively to helicopters in the country. Pennsylvania is considered the birthplace of the helicopter, and this museum displays more than 35 civilian and military helicopters, autogiros, and convertaplanes, and artifacts and exhibits spanning from the earliest machines to the latest military technology.

Baldwin's Book Barn (865 Lenape Rd., 610/696-0816, www.bookbarn.com, daily 10 A.M.–6 P.M.) is more than just a rare and used bookstore, and is worth seeing as much for the historic building and grounds as for the fabulous collection of books and antiques inside. The original dairy barn was built in 1822, and has been headquarters for the Baldwin family's used book and collectible business since they moved here in 1946 (the business was around since 1934, but in a different location). The dairy barn has since been converted to a residence, and the large stone barn is now the bookshop, with five floors filled with more than 300,000 used and rare books, manuscripts, maps, paintings, prints, antiques, and collectibles. Exposed wood ceiling beams, cozy reading nooks, and a wood-burning stove create a lovely atmosphere for perusing the books and antiques.

RIDLEY CREEK STATE PARK

Just 16 miles from Center City Philadelphia and about 20 minutes from West Chester in the suburb of Media, Ridley Creek State Park (1023 Sycamore Mills Rd., Media, 610/627-2052, www.friendsofrcsp.org) offers more than 2,600 acres of woodlands and meadows, along with seasonal attractions. There are 12 miles of hiking trails and 5 miles of paved biking trails, along with fishing, horseback riding, camping, cross-country skiing, and tobogganing. A National Historic Landmark, it is also home to the **Colonial Pennsylvania Plantation** (610/566-1725, www.colonialplantation.org, weekends Apr.–Nov., 11 A.M.–5 P.M., $6 adult,

$4 child). At this 300-year-old farming mainstay and small recreated 18th-century village, interpreters in period costume bake bread, mend fences, and card wool. The village aims to recreate the lives of members of the Pratt family, who lived on the Quaker plantation for three generations as early as 1710. Special tours and educational, hands-on workshops are often offered.

WAYNESBOROUGH

Approximately 20 miles from Center City and five miles from Valley Forge in Chester County, Waynesborough (2049 Waynesborough Rd., Paoli, 610/647-1779, www.philalandmarks .org, mid-Mar.–Dec. Thurs.–Sun. 1–3 P.M., $5 adult, $4 student and senior, $3 pp for groups of 10 or more, $12 family, free child 6 and under) was the 18th-century home of Revolutionary War hero General Anthony Wayne. While he was the only commander in chief of the American military that never served as president of the United States, Wayne's contributions to the war were momentous. Nicknamed "Mad Anthony" as a result of his bravery and mercilessness, the national hero led the Pennsylvania Line in the battles of Brandywine and Germantown and survived the Valley Forge encampment. Wayne spent 10 years at Waynesborough, this classic Pennsylvania farm manor house, but left in 1792 when President Washington asked him to serve as major general and commander in chief of the Legions of America. The Georgian-style home was built using stone quarried on the property and has been restored and furnished to reflect the Wayne family's life here over seven generations 1724–1965.

Wilmington and Vicinity

The city of Wilmington, Delaware, and the surrounding area are home to several museums, including the Delaware History Museum, Delaware Center for Contemporary Arts, Natural History Museum, Sports Museum and Hall of Fame, and even the Toy and Miniature Museum. If you have time to do it all, visit the visitor center's website (www

.visitwilmingtonde.com) in downtown Wilmington for more details about the many options. If you only have a day or a weekend, the biggest must-see attractions, detailed here, are some of the estates, homes, and gardens of the du Pont family, which has left its mark all over the area, and the world, with its inventions. A tour of any of their remarkable, lavish estates and gardens is an experience to remember.

HAGLEY MUSEUM AND LIBRARY

The Hagley Museum and Library (200 Hagley Rd., 302/658-2400, www.hagley.org, daily 9:30 A.M.–4:30 P.M., $11 adult, $9 student and senior, $4 child 6–14, free under 6) is part of the 235-acre estate along the Brandywine River belonging to E. I. du Pont, who was responsible for the invention of gunpowder. By 1802, this was home to his mill and the community of workers that operated it, with his own home perched high on a hill overlooking the village and operations. In the three-story museum attached to the visitor center, you can watch a short movie about the du Pont company's many inventions—from gunpowder to pantyhose to countertops—and see exhibits highlighting the history of the family and the site. A bus makes a continuous loop through the sprawling grounds, allowing you to hop on and off and explore, with tour guides posted throughout to explain points of interest. Tours of the du Pont home are offered every half hour with the last tour at 3:30 P.M., except January–mid-March, when there are only two house tours a day, at 10:30 A.M. and 1:30 P.M. The library (open weekdays 8:30–4:30 P.M.) contains research collections and is free and open to the public.

NEMOURS MANSION

For a glimpse into the lavish lives of one of the earliest, wealthiest families in America, take a tour of the spectacular Nemours Mansion (1600 Rockland Rd., 800/651-6912, www .nemoursmansion.org, May–Dec. Tues.–Sat. 9 A.M., noon, and 3 P.M., Sun. noon and 3 P.M., $15, children under 12 not allowed). The

nearly 50,000-square-foot French chateau–style mansion on a 300-acre estate and gardens was built in the early 20th century by industrialist, inventor, and philanthropist Alfred I. du Pont for his second of three wives, Alicia, in the style that she loved. Alfred, son of E. I. du Pont of the gunpowder mills you may have seen at the Hagley Museum Library, followed in his father's footsteps and was involved in over 200 patents, many related to gunpowder. He amassed great wealth through many different inventions and investments, as you will see on a tour of his phenomenal estate and gardens. The operational Alfred I. du Pont Hospital for Children also occupies the grounds, and visitors are allowed to enter by guided tour only. The tours last 2.5–3 hours, so it is probably best that children under 12 are not permitted. Reservations are required and can be made online or by phone on weekdays until 4 P.M. On a tour, you'll watch a short film and then take a bus to explore the formal gardens and lavish mansion. You'll see countless antiques and works of art, including the family's collection of antique cars. You'll also learn about the family's fascinating lives, filled with heartbreak as much as triumph.

◖ WINTERTHUR MUSEUM, GARDEN, AND LIBRARY

Another du Pont family gem, Winterthur (5105 Kennett Pike, 800/448-3883, www.winterthur .org, Tues.–Sun. 10 A.M.–5 P.M., last ticket sold 3:15 P.M. for 3:30 P.M. tour, $18 adult, $16 student and senior, $5 child 2–11, free under 2) was founded and designed by Henry Francis du Pont (1880–1969), an avid antiques collector and horticulturist, with the help of his father, Henry Algernon du Pont, in the spirit of 18th- and 19th-century European country houses. Part of the estate has been converted into a museum displaying the world's largest collection of more than 85,000 decorative and fine arts made or used in America 1630–1860. It's organized into categories including ceramics, glass, furniture, metalwork, paintings and prints, and textiles and needlework, so you can get lost in room after room of American artwork, complemented by pieces from around the world. Henry Francis du Pont added to his original collection until his death in 1969, and Winterthur curators have continued to add new exhibits or artifacts, mostly highlighting local history. Be sure to leave plenty of time to walk or take a trolley ride through the 1,000-acre rolling landscape filled with flowers and streams, including the Enchanted Forest, a three-acre plot complete with a tree house and fairy cottage that is a like a dream come true for kids.

RESTAURANTS
Chadds Ford

Just down the road from the Brandywine River Museum, you'll find upscale cuisine in a stylish yet relaxed setting at **❰ Brandywine Prime** (1617 Baltimore Pike, 610/388-8088, www .brandywineprime.com, Mon.–Sat. 5–10 P.M., Sun. 10 A.M.–2 P.M. and 4–10 P.M.). Serving dinner daily and Sunday brunch, the restaurant's specialty is seafood, perfect cuts of meat, and a fresh oyster bar.

Just next door, **Bistro on the Brandywine** (1623 Baltimore Pike, 610/388-8090, www .bistroonthebrandywine.com, call for hours) offers a somewhat more casual option with French bistro fare, including salads, pizza, crepes, pastas, and gourmet sandwiches, and is open for lunch and dinner. There is a full bar with happy hour specials, as well as the option to BYOB for a $5 corkage fee.

If you're looking for a still more casual breakfast, lunch, or brunch spot, head just across the street to the quintessential greasy-spoon diner **Hank's Place** (Rtes. 1 and 100, 610/388-7061, www.hanks-place.net, Mon. 6 A.M.–4 P.M., Tues.–Sat. 6 A.M.–7 P.M., Sun. 7 A.M.–3 P.M.). The near-constant line out the door speaks volumes about its popularity. Once you taste the packed omelettes, blueberry pancakes, and the Pennsylvania favorite, scrapple, you'll know why. While breakfast is certainly the star, you can also get plenty of cheap, tasty soups, salads, and sandwiches if you go for lunch.

For an elegant and traditional afternoon tea service ($14.25 pp) or just a cup of tea or coffee and a light meal or snack visit **The**

SpecialTeas Tea Room and Gift Shop (100 Ridge Rd., Chadds Ford, 610/358-2320, www .specialteastearoom.com, Mon. noon–3 P.M., Tues.–Sat. 11 A.M.–4 P.M.), owned by two sisters. All the pastries, including the delicious scones, are made by one of the owners. The shop is part of **Old Ridge Village**, which includes stores selling jewelry, crafts, and quilts, along with several restaurants.

West Chester

In West Chester, **Gilmore's** (133 E. Gay St., 610/431-2800, www.gilmoresrestaurant.com, Tues.–Sat. 5:30–8:30 P.M.) is an enormously popular upscale French BYOB in the heart of town. Chef Gilmore (longtime chef at Philly's famous Le Bec-Fin) serves up French cuisine with a modern flair out of an elegant yet comfortable 18th-century townhouse. Be sure to make reservations, as it is one of the area's most acclaimed restaurants.

Or you can head off the main drag about four miles to **Four Dogs Tavern** (1300 W. Strasburg Rd., Marshallton, 610/692-4367, www.thefour dogstavern.com, Mon.–Wed. 11:30 A.M.–10 P.M., Thurs.–Sat. 11:30 A.M.–11 P.M., Sun. 11 A.M.–10 P.M.) for delicious and reasonably priced salads, burgers, and dinner entrées in an upbeat atmosphere. The bar stays open until midnight on weekdays and 1 A.M. on weekends, and there is usually live entertainment on Thurs.–Sun. nights. Nab a seat on the outdoor patio when the weather is warm.

Wilmington

Moro (1307 N. Scott St., 302/777-1800, www .mororestaurant.net, Tues.–Sat. 5–11 P.M.) is a popular Wilmington restaurant serving cuisine described as inspired rustic Italian. The menu changes often to utilize the freshest ingredients available, and from the antipasti to the lamb chops the presentation is stellar, and the wine list is extensive.

HOTELS

There are countless charming inns and bed-and-breakfasts in the area, but one of the very best is the **❰ Inn at Montchanin** (Rte.

100 and Kirk Rd., Montchanin, Delaware, 302/888-2133, www.montchanin.com). Ideally situated for visiting Winterthur, Nemours, and Hagley museums and estates, the award-winning inn was once actually part of the du Ponts' Winterthur estate. Today, it offers every modern convenience in elegant yet cozy rooms and suites. The village-like setting with various buildings amid winding pathways offers loads of character, along with a spa and fitness center, and its own fine-dining restaurant, **Krazy Kat's,** offering quality, creative cuisine for breakfast, lunch, and dinner. The 28 rooms and suites start around $200 a night with suites starting around $300 a night and special packages sometimes offered online. Among its numerous accolades, it has been named "the world's best hotel for under $250" by *Travel + Leisure* magazine.

(Sweetwater Farm Bed & Breakfast (50 Sweetwater Rd., Glen Mills, 610/459-4711, www.sweetwaterfarmbb.com) offers a more bucolic experience, even though it's just a short drive from the sights of Chadds Ford—and that's exactly the point. Remote country roads lead to the sprawling 50-acre estate, circa 1734, and once you're there, there isn't another property in sight. There are seven rooms in the main house and seven additional private cottages just outside. The decor is country farmhouse with plenty of modern amenities, including refrigerators, fireplaces, and oversized whirlpool tubs in some of the rooms. The main house has comfortable sitting and reading areas, a pool table, and a dining room where gourmet breakfast is served each morning. There is also a pool for use in the warmer months and a barn complete with horses. It's owned by the nephew of Grace Kelly; pictures of the Kelly family, as well as the cast and crew of M. Night Shyamalan's *The Village* (who stayed here while filming) are on display in the main lounge. Rates start at $170 on weekdays and $190 on weekends in summer.

The Brandywine River Hotel (1609 Baltimore Pike, 610/388-1200, www.brandywineriverhotel.com) offers a convenient resting place from which to explore the many nearby sights. It's a typical hotel as opposed to the area's bed-and-breakfasts, but it's a nice one with

EXCURSIONS

© KARRIE GAVIN

the sprawling farm and grounds of the Sweetwater Farm Bed & Breakfast all the standard modern amenities, and weekend rates in summer start at just $139 per night, with king rooms with fireplace and Jacuzzi for $199. Complimentary extended continental breakfast and afternoon tea are included.

INFORMATION

Several visitor centers in the area operate useful websites with loads of information about things to do and where to stay. If you're looking for more in-depth information about the area or want to find specific events or special offers, call or visit the websites of the Delaware County's **Brandywine Conference and Visitors Bureau** (800/343-3983, www.brandywinecvb.org) or the **Chester County Conference and Visitors Bureau** (800/566/0109, www.brandywinevalley.com), or visit the conveniently located **Chester Count Visitors Center** (300 Greenwood Rd., Kennett Sq., 800/228-9933) adjacent to Longwood Gardens. For additional bed-and-breakfasts, the **Brandywine Valley Bed and Breakfast** site (www.bvbb.com) offers information and online booking.

GETTING THERE AND AROUND

The Brandywine Valley is about 30 miles southwest of Philadelphia and easily accessible via major interstate routes I-95 and I-476, by U.S. routes 30 and 322, and the Pennsylvania and New Jersey Turnpikes. The major roads running through the area are Routes 202, 1, 100, and 52. A car is the best way to get around, since attractions are spread out, driving on the country roads is pleasant, and parking is abundant. If that isn't an option, **SEPTA** (215/580-7800, www.septa.org) provides limited bus and regional rail service from Philadelphia to West Chester and some nearby areas. **SCCOOT** (Southern Chester County Organization on Transportation, 877/612-1359, www.tmacc.org) connects with some SEPTA routes and offers service between West Chester, Chadds Ford, Kennett Square, and several other locales. **DART** (800/652-DART, www.dartfirststate.com) offers local service in and around Wilmington, Delaware.

Bucks County

Only about 35 miles north of Philadelphia, Bucks County offers a unique blend of rural countryside filled with farms, creeks, and covered bridges, along with a bustling, modern arts, cultural, and dining scene. Local towns of interest include New Hope, Lambertville, Doylestown, and Lahaska, all within a short drive from one another along Route 202, and all offering small-town charm with much to see and do. Doylestown has a few wonderful museums that are well worth a visit, and if you are traveling with kids, a visit to Sesame Place in nearby Langhorne is always a hit.

SIGHTS
New Hope

Situated along the Delaware River, the town of New Hope is easily the most popular destination in Bucks County, drawing loads of visitors from Philadelphia, New York, and well beyond. New Hope, with its rich history and strong artistic roots, is home to charming shops, restaurants, and art galleries in a small-town setting. The action centers on Bridge Street, which connects New Hope with Lambertville, New Jersey, an equally charming town, across a picturesque auto/foot bridge, as well as Union Street in Lambertville and Main Street in both towns. The best way to experience the towns is just to meander around, stopping in shops and galleries and for a bite to eat. While there are specific highlights, the real experience is just in wandering the pretty, lively streets.

In addition to exploring on foot, another great way to see the area (very popular with kids) is to take one of the hourly excursions on the **New Hope and Ivyland Railroad** (32 W. Bridge St., 215/862-2332, www.newhoperailroad.com,

To SR 412
Point Pleasant
32
611
413
Dublin
To the Pearl
S Buck House
313
Doylestown
202
263
611
263
PENNSYLVANIA
RICE'S MARKET
PEDDLER'S VILLAGE
AND PENN'S PURCHASE
Lahaska
202
MERCER MILE
232
313
413
Tyler
State Park
332
Churchville
0   2.5 mi
0   2.5 km
276
309
611
232
532
1
PHILADELPHIA
95
NEW HOPE
Lambertville
Delaware
SCENIC
INN AT BOWMAN'S HILL
WASHINGTON CROSSING
HISTORIC PARK
Washington
Crossing
313
332
532
Newtown
95
413
Wrightstown
BUCKS COUNTY
CONFERENCE AND
VISITOR CENTER
NEW JERSEY
202
31
532
DRIVE
WATER SPORTS ON
THE DELAWARE RIVER
95
River
32
TRENTON
Morrisville
1
1
HISTORIC
FALLSINGTON
SESAME PLACE
13
PENNSBURY
MANOR
130
Bristol
276
413
95
© AVALON TRAVEL
Langhorne
Penndel

$17.50 adult, $15.50 child 2–11, $3.50 under 2). Pulled by a steam locomotive, the ride is about an hour from New Hope to Lahaska and back, and runs daily in summer and on weekends in winter.

Doylestown Museums

Another charming town and cultural center, Doylestown is also home to several impressive museums. Three of them, all National Historic Landmarks, celebrate the life, work, and collections of Henry Chapman Mercer within a short distance of one another in what has become known as Mercer Mile. Another is dedicated to another Doylestown native, James A. Michener, and displays an impressive collection of artwork.

JAMES A. MICHENER ART MUSEUM

The Michener Museum (138 S. Pine St., 215/340-9800, www.michenermuseum .org, Tues.–Fri. 10 A.M.–4:30 P.M., Sat. 10 A.M.–5 P.M., Sun. noon–5 P.M., $10 adult, $9 senior, $7.50 college student, $4 youth 6–18, free under 6) is named for the famous Doylestown local and Pulitzer Prize–winning author, philanthropist, and teacher. It displays a collection of 20th-century American art and sculpture, including a world-class collection of Pennsylvania Impressionism. Occupying the former Bucks County Prison, the nonprofit cultural institution is dedicated to preserving, interpreting, and exhibiting the art and heritage of Bucks County. Don't miss the backyard sculpture garden, set up in a lovely outdoor

© KARRIE GAVIN

An auto and foot bridge connects New Hope, Pennsylvania with Lambertville, New Jersey.

EXCURSIONS

setting in honor of the local landscape that has inspired many artists.

MERCER MILE

Henry Mercer (1856–1930) was an archaeologist, writer, anthropologist, ceramist, scholar, antiquarian, and collector who spent his life in this area. Among his many accomplishments, he designed three distinct poured concrete structures that make up the Mercer Mile. His castle-like home, now **Fonthill Museum** (525 E. Court St., 215/348-9461, www.fonthill museum.org, Mon.–Sat. 10 A.M.–5 P.M., Sun. noon–5 P.M., guided tour only, last tour 4 P.M., reservations advised, $10 adult, $9 senior, $4 youth 5–17), was built 1908–1912 and modeled after a 13th-century Rhenish castle. It is a mix of medieval, Gothic, and Byzantine styles and constructed of poured reinforced concrete. The ornate, mazelike interior contains 32 stairways and 44 rooms, each in a different shape. Mercer's collections of books, prints, and Victorian engravings are on display, and the ceilings and walls are embedded with handcrafted tiles made in Mercer's kilns.

For a more in-depth look at Mercer's famous

tiles, produced during the American Arts and Crafts movement, stroll over to the **Moravian Pottery and Tile Works** (130 Swamp Rd., 215/345-6722, www.mptw.go.to, daily 10 A.M.–4:45 P.M., $4.50 adult, $3.50 senior, $2.50 youth 7–17). The working history museum continues to produce tiles and mosaics in a similar manner to Mercer's original works. Tours of the 1912 factory are offered every half hour and consist of a 17-minute video and a self-guided walk where you can see original installations and displays about the production of the beautiful tiles.

In 1916, Mercer built another six-story concrete castle nearby, now home to the **Mercer Museum and Library** (84 S. Pine St., 215/345-0210, www.mercermuseum.org, Mon.–Sat. 10 A.M.–5 P.M., Sun. noon–5 P.M., $9 adult, $8 senior, $5 youth 5–17, free under 5). The impressive structure is filled with themed rooms containing Mercer's collection of tools, folk art, and articles from early America. Mercer collected more than 40,000 items in all, fearing that the advance of industrialization would wipe out original tools. His mission was to preserve evidence of America's early productivity, when everything was made by hand. If you plan to visit both Fonthill and the Mercer Museum, purchase the Mercer Experience ticket for reduced admission to both (adult $17, youth 5–17 $8).

More Bucks County Sights
HISTORIC FALLSINGTON

Described as "the village that time forgot," Historic Fallsington (4 Yardley Ave., Fallsington, 215/295-6567, www.historicfallsington.org, Tues.–Sat. 10:30 A.M.–3:30 P.M. mid-May–mid-Oct., and by appt. only Tues.–Fri. mid-Oct.–mid-May, tours $6 adult, $5 senior, $3 child, free under 5) is a 300-year-old preserved Quaker village on the National Register of Historic Places. It evolved around a central Quaker meeting house built in 1690, and includes nearly 90 outlying structures of mostly simple design. You can wander around the village on your own, but to enter some of the structures and get a feel for the way of life on the village, take a guided tour. The site really comes alive during special events, so check the website for the calendar.

PENNSBURY MANOR

Pennsbury Manor (400 Pennsbury Memorial Rd., Morrisville, 215/946-0400, www.pennsburymanor.org, summer Tues.–Sat. 9 A.M.–5 P.M., Sun. noon–5 P.M., call in other seasons, $7 adult, $6 senior, $4 child 3–11, $3 grounds pass) was William Penn's personal estate. Penn preferred the tranquility of country living to more crowded urban dwellings, and at the peaceful 43-acre Pennsbury Manor, it is easy to see why. At the recreated 17th-century country manor and farm, visitors can tour the manor house, brew house, workman's cottage, smokehouse, blacksmith shop, and barn, and see farm animals, including oxen, horses, and sheep. Guided tours make it easy to imagine life on the working colonial farm, which has been beautifully restored to look as it did in Penn's time.

◖ SESAME PLACE

Sesame Place (100 Sesame Rd., Langhorne, 215/752-7070, www.sesameplace.com) is the only theme park in the world based on the popular television series *Sesame Street.* Catering to children ages 2–13, it offers amusements, a three-story netted jungle gym, live stage shows, and 14-plus-acre water park. Costumed Sesame Street characters wander around and interact with kids. Because most attractions are outside, the park is only open May–October. It opens daily at 10 A.M. and closes anywhere from 5 to 9 P.M. depending on the day and time of year. An all-day pass costs $55.99 for adults and children, $50.99 senior (over 55), $52.99 AAA member, and free for children under 2.

WASHINGTON CROSSING HISTORIC PARK

This historic site and nature area (1112 River Rd., 215/493-4076, www.ushistory.org/washingtoncrossing, always open for self-guided tours, guided tours Fri.–Sun. 10 A.M.–4 P.M. seasonally, call for prices) commemorates the spot where General George Washington and his troops crossed the Delaware River on Christmas night in 1776, which was considered a pivotal moment in the Revolutionary War. The troops marched on to win a battle at Trenton, which paved the way for the subsequent victories that would lead to defeat of the British army and, hence, the forming of the U.S. as an independent nation. The visitors center was temporarily closed pending renovations at the time of this printing, but a modular unit is set up at the intersection of Routes 32 and 532, where you can stop to get oriented to the park. Don't miss the 125-foot-tall Bowman's Hill Tower, built in 1931 to commemorate Washington and his army. Climb to the top for a beautiful panoramic view (open early Apr.–late Nov. Tues.–Sun. 10 A.M.–4 P.M.).

RESTAURANTS

In a town packed with excellent restaurants, it's hard to have a bad meal. Here are a few fine choices.

◖ **Marsha Brown** (15 S. Main St., New Hope, 215/862-7044, www.marshabrownrestaurant.com, Mon.–Thurs. 5–10 P.M., Fri.

EXCURSIONS

5–11 P.M., Sat. 4:30–11 P.M., Sun. 4:30– 9:30 P.M.) occupies a large former church. More than 125 years old, the stone structure features many stunning original details and furnishings. Despite the stylish, bustling atmosphere, it is easy to imagine its former incarnation, especially on the 2nd floor, with its two-story cathedral ceilings, original woodwork, large stained-glass windows, and a step-up dining area where services were once led. Louisiana-bred owner Marsha Brown's sophisticated New Orleans–inspired menu features upscale versions of classics like jambalaya and inventive new creations using the best cuts of meat and fresh seafood, including an ample raw bar. A happening downstairs bar serves a variety of cocktails.

Mother's Wine Bar and Restaurant (34 N. Main St., New Hope, 215/862-5857, www.mothersnewhope.com, Mon.–Fri. 11:30 A.M.–9 P.M., Sat.–Sun. opens at 10 A.M., closing varies) has been a popular local spot for more than 30 years, despite several changes in ownership. The casual, affordable restaurant and full bar has a friendly atmosphere, and the food ranges from hearty sandwiches and salads for lunch to fresh meat, fish, and pasta dinner entrées to a classic weekend brunch, with alfresco dining available.

Lambertville Station (11 Bridge St., Lambertville, 609/397-8300, www.lambert villestation.com, Mon.–Thurs. 11:30 A.M.– 9:30 P.M., Fri.–Sat. 11:30 A.M.–11 P.M., Sun. 10:30 A.M.–9:30 P.M.) occupies a restored former train station with tracks lining one side of the restaurant. Just across the bridge from New Hope, it is a local favorite for breakfast, lunch, and dinner, serving excellent New American cuisine. Lunch is casual with alfresco dining that's great for people-watching while dinner offers a more upscale environment. It is attached to the popular **Inn at Lambertville Station,** where rooms are decked out in antiques in themes of different cities from around the world—some offering lovely river views.

RECREATION
Water Sports on the Delaware River

Tubing, rafting, canoeing, or kayaking along the Delaware River is a lovely way to spend a hot summer day. The Delaware River moves at an average speed of 1.5 miles per hour, is about

The Inn at Lambertville Station overlooks the Delaware River.

five feet deep, and usually near 80 degrees in summer. There aren't many rapids in the area, so be prepared for more of a lazy, gentle float than an adrenaline-pumping journey. There are two excellent options following similar routes; the **Delaware River Tubing Co.** (2998 Daniel Bray Hwy., Frenchtown, New Jersey, 908/996-5386, www.delawarerivertubing.com) departs on the New Jersey side of the river, and **Bucks County River Country** (2 Walters Ln., Point Pleasant, 215/297-5000, www.rivercountry .net) departs from the Pennsylvania side. The Delaware River Tubing Co.'s packages include a meal plan good for food at the Hot Dog Man stand on the way, for hot dogs, burgers, chips, candy, and drinks, although the hot dog man does not discriminate; if you go with the other company, you can still buy food from him a la carte.

SHOPS

One of the biggest draws to Bucks County is the shopping. New Hope and Lambertville have shops galore lining Main Street in both towns, Union Street in Lambertville, and Bridge Street, which traverses both towns. Shops include antiques, art galleries, and collectibles, along with contemporary clothing, furniture, and home accessories.

Just outside of New Hope in Lahaska, **Peddler's Village** (U.S. 202 and Rte. 263, 215/794-4000, www.peddlersvillage.com) is a local favorite, with around 75 shops connected by brick walkways spread over a quaint 42-acre village, where you can also stay overnight in the **Golden Plough Inn** and keep kids entertained on the Grand Carousel and in a children's play area, **Giggleberry Fair.**

Just across the street from Peddler's Village, **Penn's Purchase Factory Outlet Stores** (5860 York Rd. at U.S. 202, www.pennspur chase.com) offers more than 40 name-brand shops with discount prices.

Rice's Market (1850 River Rd., Solebury, 215/297-5993, www.ricesmarket.com, Wed., Sat., and Sun. 6 A.M.–4 P.M.) is a 30-acre open-air market selling antiques, collectibles, new and used clothing, and gourmet treats.

The **Golden Nugget Antique Market** (1850 River Rd., 609/397-0811, www.gnmarket.com, Wed. and weekends 6 A.M.–4 P.M.) is a 40-year-old indoor/outdoor market. Sunday, the busiest day, often has as many as 400 vendors selling a wide variety of antiques, crafts, and more.

HOTELS

There are so many great bed-and-breakfasts in Bucks County that choosing one can be difficult. One of the most luxurious is about 2.5 miles from the center of town. The ◖ **Inn at Bowman's Hill** (518 Lurgan Rd., New Hope, 215/862-8090, www.theinnatbowmanshill .com) has just four romantic rooms and two extended suites on a private five-acre estate. The inn was voted one of the "top 10 luxury B&Bs/inns in the world" by *Tripadvisor.com* in 2010, among many other accolades. When the weather is warm, a pool offers a lovely place to swim, and when it's colder, the in-room fireplaces and in-room and outdoor whirlpool tubs offer luxurious warmth. A gourmet breakfast is included in the rate, and in-room massage is available for a fee. With rooms and suites $355–575 per night, a stay does not come cheap, but for a romantic getaway or special occasion, there is no better place.

The Lambertville House (32 Bridge St., Lambertville, 609/397-0200, www.lambert villehouse.com), located in the heart of Lambertville just steps from the bridge into New Hope, has 26 rooms offering every modern amenity. Most rooms have in-room fireplaces, some have oversized whirlpool tubs, and all have ultra-comfy beds. Listed on the National Register of Historic Places, it was built in 1812, and has provided rest to Presidents Andrew Johnson and Ulysses S. Grant among other notable guests on their travels between New York and Philadelphia. Have a drink on the pretty front porch of the cozy bar **Left Bank Libations,** perfect for people-watching. Rates including breakfast start at $200 and go as high as $330 for the best room in the attached Carriage House.

Hotel du Village (2535 River Rd., New Hope, 215/862-9911, www.hotelduvillage.com)

is a unique, affordable alternative about a mile outside New Hope. There are 20 rooms on the grounds of what was formerly a prep school for young girls and boys. A cozy, upscale French restaurant is on-site. Rates range $130–155 with continental breakfast included.

The **Doylestown Inn** (18 W. State St., 215/345-6610, www.doylestowninn.com), on a central corner in the heart of town, was built in 1902 but has been updated for a modern look with plenty of amenities. The 11 comfortable rooms, all on the 3rd floor of the historic building, have jetted tubs, and some have fireplaces. A bar offers a nice place to grab a drink or snack. Rates range $170–230 in high season.

There are campgrounds nearby; **Tinicum Park** (901 E. Bridgetown Pike, Langhorne, 215/348-6114, $20/day) is a popular one for camping, hiking and other outdoor activities.

INFORMATION
The **Bucks County Conference and Visitors Bureau** (800/836-2825, www.buckscountycvb .org) offers loads of information about the area's attractions, lodging, dining, and downloadable maps.

GETTING THERE AND AROUND
About 30 miles north of Philadelphia, Bucks County is easily accessible by I-95, Routes 1 and 13, and the Pennsylvania Turnpike. **Amtrak's** regional rail lines travel through Bucks County with stops in Trenton, New Jersey, and other nearby locations (800/872-7245, www.amtrak .org). **SEPTA** (215/580-7800, www.septa .org) has regional rail lines throughout Bucks County with stops in Doylestown and Trenton. Once in Bucks County, it is possible to get between major points on public transportation, but most people prefer to drive or bike, which is essential for getting to some of the more off-the-beaten-path sights. If you plan on staying in New Hope or Lambertville, you can get here on public transportation, and once here most attractions are within an easy walk, but a car is best for exploring outside of these towns.

Pennsylvania Dutch Country

As the largest Amish and Mennonite settlement in the world, Pennsylvania Dutch Country's people and culture are the primary tourist draw, so plenty of attractions have been created to allow visitors a glimpse into their unique way of life. It can be difficult to sift through the tourist traps and find more legitimate cultural experiences, so it always helps to ask a local, like a friendly innkeeper, to point you in the right direction. Taking a horse-and-buggy ride with an Amish or Mennonite guide is a good way to have your questions answered and take in the lovely landscape. And while the Amish are the primary draw, the area also offers more contemporary attractions like theaters, dining, and antiques. The city of Lancaster makes a good base for exploring, or if you prefer a more quintessential small-town experience, check out the quaint towns of Lititz, Ephrata, Bird-in-Hand, Adamstown, Paradise, Strasburg, or Intercourse.

SIGHTS
City of Lancaster
Quaint and quiet in comparison to Philadelphia, Lancaster is bustling and lively compared to the rest of rural Lancaster County. It also has museums, theater, and attractions that pay homage to the Amish experience while offering the largest concentration of accommodations and dining.

◖ CENTRAL MARKET
The Central Market (23 N. Market St., www .centralmarketlancaster.com, Tues. and Fri. 6 A.M.–4 P.M., Sat. 6 A.M.–2 P.M.) is an excellent place to stop for a bite or shop for locally made goods and food. The red brick building

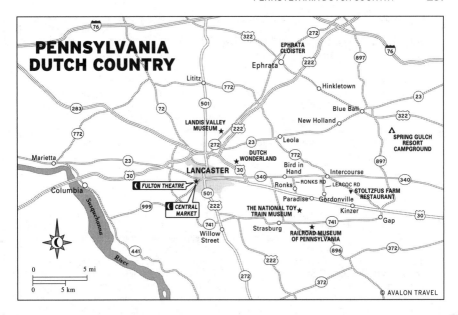

that houses it was built in 1889, but the market's history goes back much further than that; it began as an outdoor market in the 1730s, and is the oldest continually operating market in the country today. Reminiscent of Philadelphia's Reading Terminal Market, but (for obvious reasons) with a greater array of Amish goods and food, it has over 60 stalls, including a variety of fresh produce and meat, fresh-cut flowers, seafood, handcrafted quilts, handmade fudge, baked goods, and international cuisine. Examples of the great prices: A bag of fruit costs around $1, apple fritters are $0.60, and empanadas cost $1.50 each.

◖ FULTON THEATRE

While you're in town, see a show at the historic Fulton Theatre (12 N. Prince St., 717/397-7425, www.thefulton.org) if you get the chance. The Victorian gem, built in 1852, is the oldest continuously operating theater in the country and one of just eight National Historic Landmark theaters. Quality musicals, comedies, and dramas are shown in the elegant venue, which has seen many a famous actor grace its stage, including many Barrymores, Sarah Bernhardt, W. C. Fields, and Mark Twain.

HERITAGE CENTER MUSEUMS AT MARKET SQUARE

Just across the square from the Central Market, you'll find two museums that celebrate local culture. The **Heritage Center Museum** (5 W. King St., 717/299-6440, www.lancaster heritage.com, call for hours, free) is a compact three-story museum committed to preserving local history. With a permanent collection, annual exhibitions, and rotating exhibits, the museum helps makes Pennsylvania Dutch history and culture accessible to all, including kids, with a series of interactive displays.

Walk about three minutes to visit the **Lancaster Quilt & Textile Museum** (37 N. Market St., 717/299-6440, Wed. and Thurs. 10 A.M.–4 P.M., Tues., Fri., and Sat. 9 A.M.–4 P.M., $6 adult, $4 student, free 17 and under), where a collection of gorgeous Amish quilts from the 18th century to the present makes up the majority of the permanent exhibition. If you are able to visit on first

PENNSYLVANIA DUTCH HISTORY AND WAY OF LIFE

The Pennsylvania Dutch (also called Pennsylvania Germans or Pennsylvania Deutsch) are descendants of early German immigrants to Pennsylvania who arrived in droves, mostly before 1800, to escape religious persecution in Europe. Like so many other persecuted groups, they came for William Penn's promise of religious freedom. Today, most speak a variation of their original German language, as well as English, and they are made up of Amish, Mennonite, Lutheran, German Reformed, Moravian, and other groups that share some beliefs while differing in others. While there are other communities living in many parts of the United States and Canada today, the largest settlement is here in Pennsylvania, concentrated in and around Lancaster County.

It is unusual in the United States for the people and culture to be the primary tourist draw, as it is in the area often referred to as Amish Country, but it is no surprise that visitors want to witness a lifestyle so different than their own. Observing the culture, free from modern technology like telephones, computers, and cars, offers a window into a time long past. And while many local Pennsylvania Dutch welcome and have come to rely on the tourist industry for their livelihood, it is important to also be respectful of their privacy; remember that they are real people going about their daily lives. It is important for all visitors to know that among their many unique beliefs, most Pennsylvania Dutch do not believe in having their photograph taken, as they believe it is a sign of vanity.

The many different sects of Pennsylvania Dutch vary from strict followers of the Old Order to more modern groups who have allowed certain aspects of modernity into their lives. Some do not use battery-powered elec-

lush farmlands in Amish Country

© KARRIE GAVIN

© JONATHAN SOUZA/123RF.COM

typical transportation in Amish Country

tronics, while others now use phones or cars. Some do not allow phones in their home but have them in their place of business, as it can be essential to making a living. Each sect has its own rules, ranging from guidelines for dress and hair length to buggy styles and farming techniques. Most Pennsylvania Dutch wear traditional clothing that is simple, unadorned, and made by hand. Jewelry is not worn – not even wedding bands; unmarried men are usually clean-shaven while married men have beards to distinguish them. The Amish are generally averse to anything that could chip away at the family or close-knit community structure, which is of the highest importance. This includes most modern technology as well as education beyond the eighth grade, which they feel can lead to unnecessary egoism and separation. Mennonites hold many of the same beliefs but tend to be somewhat less conservative in dress codes and in the use of technology.

It would take an entire book to delve into the fascinating heritage of the Pennsylvania Dutch and the unique code the different groups live by, but there is no better way to get a glimpse into their unique way of life than to visit the area. You'll learn much through your own observation and through the many museums and sites dedicated to preserving local culture. Most Pennsylvania Dutch tour guides are very open and willing to answer any questions. Many constantly have to reassess their beliefs and choose what to incorporate from the modern world without sacrificing their core values. It is best not to generalize, as every family and sect is different. Times have changed, and continue to change, for the Pennsylvania Dutch, if at a much slower pace than for the rest of the world.

© WWW.DISCOVERLANCASTERPA.COM

The Lancaster Quilt & Textile Museum exhibits a collection of Amish quilts.

Friday (the first Fri. of the month Mar.–Dec., 5–9 P.M.), the museum is free to enter, along with other local galleries.

Nearby Sights
DUTCH WONDERLAND
While there is nothing very "Dutch" about Dutch Wonderland (2249 Lincoln Hwy. E., 866/386-2839, www.dutchwonderland.com, $32.95, free under 2) other than the Dutch Country location, kids don't care about that. The self-proclaimed "kingdom of kids," is a small amusement park with about 40 rides, mini-golf, and live entertainment. Geared towards children 12 and under, it's a pleasant and easy-to-navigate park. Hours vary, but from early June to late August, it is generally open daily 10 A.M.–8:30 P.M., with reduced hours in other seasons.

EPHRATA CLOISTER
The Ephrata Cloister (632 W. Main St., Ephrata, 717/733-6600, www.ephratacloister .org, May–Oct. Mon.–Sat. 9 A.M.–5 P.M., Sun.

noon–5 P.M., Jan.–Feb. closed Mon. and Tues., Mar.–Apr. and Nov.–Dec. closed Mon., $9 adult, $8 senior, $6 youth 3–11, free under 3) was founded in 1732 as the home of a German religious community, one of the first of its kind. Today it is a National Historic Landmark managed by the Pennsylvania Historical and Museum Commission to highlight the history of the people that lived and worshipped here. At its peak, in the 1740s and '50s, about 300 people lived and worked here. The group believed in spiritual rewards and shunned earthly pleasures, including sexual intercourse. The community is known for creating self-composed a cappella music; developing a form of Germanic calligraphy, Frakturschriften; and building a publishing center that included a paper mill, printing office, and book bindery, among other accomplishments. Some parts of the cloister are open for self-guided tours, but to see all of the buildings and to learn more about this interesting group, take a guided tour, included with the price of admission and offered on the hour beginning at 10 A.M. or

1 P.M. depending on the time of year, so call ahead to confirm.

LITITZ FOOD TOURS

In the quaint town of Lititz, you can visit two different historic food institutions. The **Wilbur Chocolate Company's Candy Americana Museum & Store** (48 N. Broad St., 717/626-3249, www.wilburbuds.com, Mon.–Sat. 10 A.M.–5 P.M., free) is open for tours. Get your Willie Wonka fix and learn about the chocolate-making process, try delicious samples, and check out the display of antique candy molds and paraphernalia.

Then for a little salt to go with your sugar, walk over to the **Julius Sturgis Pretzel Bakery** (219 E. Main St., 717/626-4354, www.juliussturgis.com, tours mid-Mar.–Dec. Mon.–Sat. 9:30 A.M.–4:30 P.M., Jan.–mid-Mar. Mon.–Fri. 10:30 A.M.–3:30 P.M., $3 adult, $2 child). It was established in 1861 as America's first commercial pretzel bakery; most of the production has since moved into a larger facility, but you can still tour its original location. You'll learn about the history and symbolism (yes, there is symbolism in the shape of the pretzel) involved in pretzels and you'll even get to twist your own. Stop in the attached store on the way out to pick up an array of pretzels, including the best pretzels of all—chocolate-covered—and other tasty treats.

STRASBURG RAILROAD

Founded in 1832, the Strasburg Railroad (301 Gap Rd., Ronks, 717/687-7522, www.strasburgrailroad.com, seasonal hours, tickets start at $14 adult, $7.50 child 3–11, free under 3) is America's oldest short-line railroad. Visit the historic station to ride the Victorian-style wooden passenger train pulled by a coal-burning steam locomotive. On a 45-minute ride to the town of Paradise and back, you'll pass quintessential scenic rolling Amish farmlands and hear stories about the history of the train, and for an additional fee, you can have lunch onboard. There are several displays and souvenir shops at the station, including one that takes old-fashioned photographs.

Strasburg is home to two more stops you'll want to check out while you're here. Just across

pretzel sculpture outside the Julius Sturgis Pretzel Bakery in Lititz

© KARRIE GAVIN

Ride a steam locomotive at the historic Strasburg Railroad.

the street from the railroad, you can see more historic trains, locomotives, and engines at the **Railroad Museum of Pennsylvania** (300 Gap Rd., Strasburg, 717/687-8628, www.rr museumpa.org, Mon.–Sat. 9 A.M.–5 P.M., Sun. noon–5 P.M., closed Mon. Nov.–Mar., $10 adult, $9 senior, $8 youth 3–11, free under 3). And not far from that, the **National Toy Train Museum** (300 Paradise Ln., Ronks, 717/687-8976, May–Oct. Fri.–Mon. 10 A.M.–5 P.M., Apr. and Nov.–Dec. Sat.–Sun. 10 A.M.–5 P.M., closed Jan.–Mar., $6 adult, $5 senior, $3 child 6–12, free under 6, $15 family), home to a huge collection of toy trains, is especially popular with kids.

WHEATLAND

Wheatland (1120 Marietta Ave., Lancaster, 717/392-8721, www.lancasterhistory.org, Apr.–Oct. Mon.–Sat. 10 A.M.–3 P.M., Nov. Fri.–Sat. 10 A.M.–3 P.M., closed Jan.–Mar., $8.50 adult, $7.50 senior, $6 student, $4 child 6–11, free under 6) was the home of President James Buchanan for 20 years, and it served as Democratic headquarters during the 1856 presidential campaign. Buchanan gave his first campaign address on the front lawn. On a tour, offered hourly, you'll see the restored home and expansive grounds and learn about the era in American history when Buchanan served as president.

WORKING AMISH VILLAGES

The **Amish Farm and House** (2395 Lincoln Hwy. E., Lancaster, 717/394-6185, www .amishfarmandhouse.com, Nov.–Mar. daily 10 A.M.–4 P.M., Apr.–May and Sept.–Oct. daily 9 A.M.–5 P.M., June–Aug. daily 9 A.M.–6 P.M., $8.25 adult, $7.50 senior, $5.25 child 5–11, free under 5) is a replicated traditional Amish village. On a self-guided or guided tour, you can see the working barn, built in 1805, the stone farmhouse and the blacksmith shop, among other structures, and learn about the customs, history, and religion of the Old Order Amish.

The **Landis Valley Museum** (2451 Kissel Hill Rd., 717/569-0401, www.landisvalley museum.org, Mon.–Sat. 9 A.M.–5 P.M., Sun.

© KARRIE GAVIN

one of several small recreated homes at Landis Valley Museum

noon–5 P.M., $12 adult, $10 senior, $8 youth 3–11, free under 3) is another recreated Pennsylvania Dutch village with more than 40 historic structures on 100 acres. The buildings have docents stationed to explain and demonstrate a village at work, including a blacksmith's shop, gun shop, tavern, and homes showing pottery, weaving, cooking, and quilting demonstrations in realistic settings. There are also tours, wagon rides, and a short film that runs in the visitor center explaining the site.

RESTAURANTS

There are plenty of traditional Pennsylvania Dutch restaurants where you'll eat family-style all-you-can-eat meals that are hearty and plentiful, stick-to-your-ribs meat, potatoes, and delicious home-baked bread. Two to try are **Stoltzfus Farm Restaurant** (3716 E. Newport Rd., 717/768-8156, Intercourse, www.stoltzfusmeats.com, Apr.–Oct. Mon.–Sat. 11:30 A.M.–8 P.M., Nov. Fri.–Sat. 11:30 A.M.–8 P.M., closed Dec.–Mar.) or **Plain and Fancy Farm Restaurant** (3121 Old Philadelphia Pike/Rte. 340, Bird-in-Hand, 717/768-4400, www.plainandfancyfarm.com, usually daily 11:30 A.M.–7 P.M., subject to change so call ahead), which offers an all-you-can-eat feast or an à la carte menu, as well as lodging and tours.

Strawberry Hill (128 W. Strawberry St., Lancaster, 717/393-5544, www.strawberryhillrestaurant.com, daily 5–10 P.M.) is a long-time popular Lancaster spot. The old Victorian house on a hill just outside the action of the city has been a hotel, tavern, speakeasy, brothel, corner bar, and steakhouse over time, and since 1986, it has been the Strawberry Hill restaurant. Delicious, creative modern American dishes are served in a cozy, friendly setting, and the extensive wine list with over 1,000 selections has earned the title of "Pennsylvania's top wine destination restaurant" by *Wine Spectator.*

SHOPS

There are plenty of places to shop for authentic Amish goods and foods, which is what most people are looking for when they visit the area. **Kitchen Kettle Village** (3529 Old Philadelphia Pike, Intercourse, 800/732-3528, www.kitchenkettle.com, May–Oct. Mon.–Sat. 9 A.M.–6 P.M., Nov.–Apr. Mon.–Sat. 9 A.M.–5 P.M.) offers a unique shopping experience, with more than 40 shops featuring mostly locally made products, two restaurants, and 17 lovely guest rooms. The quaint village and shopping center has grown out of a canning business that the Burnley family started out of their garage in 1954. Still run by the same family, the village sells Amish and Mennonite canned goods and treats, quilts, ironwork, folk art, pottery, and designer leather among other local crafts and food. Don't miss the Jam & Relish Kitchen, where you can see the products get made and prepared. Lodging starts at $139 per night in summer.

Olde Mill House Shoppes (105 Strasburg Pike, Lancaster, 717/299-0678, www.oldemillhouse.com, hours vary seasonally but usually are Mon.–Sat. 9:30 A.M.–5 P.M. or later) offers more handcrafted home accessories and arts

EXCURSIONS

and crafts from local and national artists, along with all manner of home goods and lighting from national retailers.

Antiques lovers will not want to miss the town of **Adamstown** (just off exit 286 of the Pennsylvania Turnpike, www.antiquescapital .com, hours vary). The self-proclaimed "antiques capital of the U.S." is home to thousands of vendors and dealers of furniture, collectibles, dolls, and all manner of antiques in a concentrated area, mostly along Route 272 just off the turnpike. Check the website for special events.

If you prefer name-brand clothing, jewelry, and shoes at rock-bottom prices, you're also in luck in this area. There is extensive outlet shopping at both **Tanger Outlets** (311 Stanley K. Tanger Blvd., Lancaster, 717/392-7260, www .tangeroutlet.com, Mon.–Sat. 9 A.M.–6 P.M., Sun. 10 A.M.–6 P.M.) and **Rockvale Outlets** (35 S. Willowdale Dr., Lancaster, 717/293-9595, Mon.–Sat. 9:30 A.M.–9 P.M., Sun. 11 A.M.–5 P.M.).

HOTELS

There are many distinctive accommodations in the area, including numerous bed-and-breakfasts. **◖ King's Cottage Bed and Breakfast** (1049 E. King St., Lancaster, 717/397-1017, www.kingscottagebb.com), a distinguished Select Registry Inn, is one of the best. Just a short drive from the heart of the city, the Spanish-style 1913 mansion is a National Historic Landmark offering many modern amenities. Each of the eight luxury rooms has been tastefully decorated with its own special charm; most have fireplaces and some have large whirlpool tubs. The friendly innkeepers, Janis and Ann, know all there is to know about the area, and they are happy to help you plan your visit. Rates range $160–270 with the private carriage house for $295. A delicious homemade gourmet breakfast is included.

For a unique, modern hotel in the heart of the city of Lancaster, try the **Lancaster Arts Hotel** (300 Harrisburg Ave., Lancaster, 717/299-3000, www.lancasterartshotel.com). Housed in a former tobacco warehouse on a bustling corner, this boutique hotel has tons of character, including original brick and stone walls, exposed wood beams, and locally made furniture and artwork. The 1st floor has an art gallery and a restaurant and bar. Rates for the 63 rooms including 16 suites start around $159 in summer.

The **General Sutter Inn** (14 E. Main St., Lititz, 717/626-2115, www.generalsutterinn .com) is a popular spot in the heart of Lititz. Built in 1764, it has been a local institution at the intersection of the two main drags of the town for 250 years. An elegant restaurant and tavern on the 1st floor draws a steady stream of locals, while the rooms decked in Victorian antiques draw overnight guests. Despite a few creaky floorboards and windows, the hotel is clean, comfortable, and in great shape despite its old age. Weekend rates for a queen room start at around $115 per night, and with several connecting rooms and larger apartments, it is a great place for families.

For those who prefer the outdoors, check out the RV and tent campground, **Spring Gulch Resort Campground** (475 Lynch Rd., New Holland, 717/354-3100, www.springgulch .com). Highly rated by camping publications, it has 450 sites over 115 acres, and there are activities and special events planned throughout the year.

INFORMATION AND TOURS

The **Pennsylvania Dutch Visitors Center** (501 Greenfield Rd., 800/723-8824, www .padutchcountry.com, Memorial Day weekend–Oct. Mon.–Sat. 9 A.M.–6 P.M., Sun. 9 A.M.–5 P.M., rest of year daily 10 A.M.–4 P.M.) is an excellent source of information about the area. The website lists attractions, accommodations, dining, shopping, discounts, and more, along with suggested itineraries and a function to create your own itinerary. You can also stop by in person to ask questions, pick up maps, or take the one-hour guided **Amish Farmlands Tour,** which departs from the visitor center daily late May–October and some weekends in November at 10:30 A.M., noon, 1:30 P.M. and 3 P.M.

There are many other walking, buggy, and bus tours to get you oriented to the area and give you an up-close look at Amish life. Led by knowledgeable guides in colonial garb, the **Historic Lancaster Walking Tour** (5 W. King St., 717/392-1776, www.historiclancaster walkingtour.com, departs Apr.–Oct. daily at 1 P.M. and at 10 A.M. Tues., Fri., and Sat.) from the visitor center in the city of Lancaster.

The **Amish Experience** (3121 Old Philadelphia Pike/Rte. 340, Bird-in-Hand, 717/768-3600, ext. 210, www.amishexperience .com) offers tours of an Amish Country Homestead and guided bus tours of the area, which can be combined with other attractions at a discount. They also have an "experiential" theater that features scenes from Amish history recreated with multiple projection screens, special effects, and a three-dimensional set.

The **Mennonite Information Center** (2209 Millstream Rd., Lancaster, 800/858-8320, www.mennoniteinfoctr.com), offers personal tour guides that have Amish or Mennonite heritage and will ride in your car, van, or group tour bus with you while telling you everything you ever wanted to know about local culture. Price varies depending on the number of people, and note that the vehicle is not provided.

There are many different companies and individuals offering buggy rides of the countryside, usually led by an Amish or Mennonite guide. Try **Abe's Buggy Rides** (2596 Old Philadelphia Pike/Rte. 340, Bird-in-Hand, 717/392-1794, www.abesbuggyrides.com). They are not available in winter on Sundays, but that goes for most buggies (too cold in winter) and most authentic Amish guides (because Sunday is a day of worship).

And last, for an exhilarating tour experience, take in the beauty of Pennsylvania Dutch Country from above in a hot-air balloon. The **United States Hot Air Balloon Team** (2737 Old Philadelphia Pike, 800/763-5987, www .ushotairballoon.com) offers flights throughout southeastern Pennsylvania that depart from several locations, including Bird-in-Hand; call for details, prices, and reservations.

GETTING THERE AND AROUND

The heart of Dutch Country is about 65 miles from Philadelphia. It can be reached via I-76 West (Schuylkill Expressway) to U.S. 202 South to U.S. 30 West, or by taking I-76 to the Pennsylvania Turnpike. Since much of the area is wide-open roads and farmland, it is best to have a car for a leisurely tour of the area. However, there is a train that runs from Philadelphia into the city of Lancaster (Amtrak, 800/872-7245, www.amtrak.com), as well as local bus service within Lancaster and nearby towns, including Ephrata and Lititz (Red Rose Transit Authority, 717/397-4246, www.redrosetransit.com).

EXCURSIONS

BACKGROUND

The Setting

GEOGRAPHY

The second-largest city on the East Coast and the sixth-largest in the nation in terms of population, Philadelphia is conveniently located in the middle of the Northeast Corridor. By car, Philadelphia is approximately two hours from New York City and two and a half hours from Washington, D.C. It is an hour's drive from Lancaster County, also known as Amish Country, and an hour from Atlantic City, New Jersey, with the rest of the New Jersey shore points just beyond. The area known as the Greater Philadelphia region consists of five counties in southeastern Pennsylvania (Bucks, Chester, Delaware, Montgomery, and Philadelphia). The four counties in southern New Jersey (Burlington, Camden, Gloucester, and Salem) and New Castle County in Delaware are also sometimes included when referring to the Greater Philadelphia region.

The original city of Philadelphia as outlined by founder William Penn consisted only of the area that is today known as Center City. The rectangular grid occupies approximately two square miles bordered by the Delaware and Schuylkill Rivers to the east and west, Vine Street to the north, and South Street to the south. It wasn't until 1854 that the city

PEACE WALL BY JANE GOLDEN, PHOTO: JACK RAMSDALE/© CITY OF PHILADELPHIA MURAL ARTS PROGRAM

Philadelphia is bordered on the east by the Delaware River.

consolidated and all the boroughs, townships, and districts of the County of Philadelphia were incorporated into the city. Today, the city and county are one and the same, covering approximately 135 square miles. In addition to the neat grid of Center City blocks, the city proper now also includes hills, valleys, winding roads, rivers, creeks, and woodlands.

Water occupies just over 5 percent of the total area of Philadelphia, and parks and woodlands cover around 10 percent of the land area. The lowest point of the city is 10 feet above sea level at the meeting of the Delaware and Schuylkill Rivers in Southwest Philadelphia. The highest point is in Chestnut Hill, at 444 feet above sea level. In addition to the two major rivers, the Delaware and the Schuylkill, smaller bodies of water include the Wissahickon, Cobbs, and Pennypack Creeks.

Covering more than 9,200 acres, Fairmount Park is the largest urban municipal park in the world. The largest continuous sections of the park are East and West Fairmount Parks, on either side of the Schuylkill River,

the Wissahickon Valley Park in the northwest section of the city, and Pennypack Park in the northeast, but the entire park system includes a total of 63 regional and neighborhood parks, including Franklin Square, Logan Square, Rittenhouse Square, and Washington Square. In fact, pretty much every patch of green in the city is technically part of Fairmount Park.

CLIMATE

Philadelphia's four distinct seasons offer very different experiences and activities. Summers can be very hot and humid while winters can be extremely cold, and fall and spring are generally mild and pleasant. While each season offers advantages, you'll need to plan your day and dress accordingly if you visit in one of the more extreme seasons. Average temperatures in July range 67–86°F (20–30°C), but severe heat waves can bring temperatures upwards of 95°F (35°C) with the heat index as high as 110°F (43°C). While this usually lasts only a few days each summer, it is unpleasant to do anything outdoors during a heat wave.

FIVE SQUARES

In one of the earliest examples of thoughtful city planning, William Penn and his surveyor, Thomas Holme, laid out a detailed plan for Philadelphia. Drawn more than 300 years ago, much of it remains in place today. That is because it not only factored in the conditions of the time, but also considered the effects of the growth and expansion that would ultimately occur. The area we now know as Center City was originally the entire city of Philadelphia. Its symmetrical grid of streets between two rivers also contained five strategically placed squares, or parks. There was one at the center of the city and one in each of the four quadrants. Penn recognized the importance of having preserved green spaces to break up the expanses of buildings long before that concept came into vogue. While their names and appearances have changed over time, his five original squares continue to anchor the city and play an important role in Philadelphia today.

Center Square is now the home of City Hall. While it's the only square that is no longer green, it is perhaps the most important one of all. It is home to the main offices of city government, including the mayor's office, and is fittingly located at the geographic center of the city, where its two main thoroughfares, Market Street and Broad Street, intersect. While the current City Hall structure wasn't built until about a century later, it fulfilled Penn's intentions. The city government offices were originally in Old City at the State House (now Independence Hall), but Penn thought they should move when the city grew westward and this became the new center, as he predicted it would. (He was a smart guy.)

The other four well-landscaped squares are primarily spots for rest and relaxation, and each has plenty of green space, park benches, sculptures, and monuments. Originally named for their locations – Southwest, Southeast, Northwest, and Northeast – the squares have all been renamed over time, and today they are, respectively, **Rittenhouse Square, Washington Square, Logan Square,** and **Franklin Square.** Each of these lovely landscaped parks is well worth a visit for a picnic lunch, people-watching, or a photo-op. In addition, Franklin Square underwent a massive makeover in 2006 and is now a popular Old City attraction complete with an old-fashioned carousel and Revolutionary-themed mini-golf course.

the carousel in Franklin Square

Fortunately, most attractions are indoors and air-conditioned. In January, the average temperature is 23–38°F (3–5°C), with occasionally frigid temperatures, severe snowfall, and icing that can make driving dangerous. This is the exception rather than the rule, however, and on most winter days, bundling up in warm clothes will make it possible to get between destinations without too much trouble. The classic northeastern fall is quite beautiful in Philadelphia, complete with leaves changing colors and falling from the trees as the heat of summer gives way to cooler weather, while spring is filled with many perfectly comfortable, pleasant days. Rainfall is moderate with 41 inches annually. Seasonal snowfall varies from a light dusting to the occasional blizzard with an average of 21 inches a year; the snowiest winter ever was 2009–2010, with a whopping 78.7 inches.

History

Philadelphia has one of the oldest and richest histories of any U.S. city, with a wealth of monuments and attractions that keep that history alive. Considered "the birthplace of the nation," Philadelphia is most famous for its central role in the Revolutionary War. Major battles and the drafting of the Declaration of Independence and Constitution took place here, and Philadelphia was the nation's capital for the first 10 years before it moved to D.C.

But while the late 18th century was undeniably one of the most fascinating and most discussed periods in Philadelphia's history, that is only part of the story. Beginning even before William Penn arrived and founded Philadelphia and continuing today, the city's tumultuous and storied history spans more than 300 years. Visiting the city's many historic sights will reveal much, but hardcore history buffs should read *Philadelphia: A 300-Year History* for much more background. In the meantime, here are some of the highlights.

WILLIAM PENN'S VISION

William Penn negotiated to take ownership of the land west of the Delaware from King Charles II of England, as partial payment for a debt the king owed to Penn's deceased father, a wealthy, high-ranking naval officer, admiral, and courtier. The 45,000 square miles that would become Pennsylvania were primarily woodlands, stretching from the Allegheny Mountains to the Delaware River. The king was happy to hand over land that was not of major importance to him, but perhaps even happier to see the rebellious young Quaker and many of his followers leave England.

Quakers were not generally well regarded by proper English society, as their rejection of a hierarchal system clashed with the lavish wealth and strict monarchy of English society and government. William Penn was actually imprisoned several times in England for expressing his religious beliefs and insisting on religious freedom as a moral right. In 1661, Penn was expelled from Oxford for failing to properly honor the Church of England, and shortly thereafter, he became a Quaker, much to the displeasure of his wealthy, traditional family. The young rebel was purportedly beaten by his father, whom he fiercely battled with over matters of religion among other things.

Penn set out to found a society where not only Quakers, but people of all religions, could practice without persecution. This was an unprecedented idea for the colonies of the time and a stark contrast to the Puritanical zeal of the settlers in Boston and New England who longed for stricter religious control over settlers in their communities. Penn began to carry out his "holy experiment" in his new city of Philadelphia when he arrived with his ship, the *Welcome,* one of 23 shiploads of immigrants to arrive in 1682, the first year of Philadelphia's founding.

Penn had hired his cousin William Markam to help him plan "a large Towne or City in the

PHILLY FIRSTS

In addition to being considered the birthplace of the United States of America, Philadelphia claims countless landmark "firsts," among other distinctions in American history. Listed here are just a few of the city's many distinguished accomplishments.

FIRSTS

- 1681: First parks created for the pleasure of people – three of Penn's original squares

- 1690: First paper mill in North America, built near Germantown by William Bradford

- 1685: First almanac: *America's Messenger,* by William Bradford

- 1698: First public school in the American colonies

- 1728: First botanical gardens, by John Bartram on the Schuylkill River

- 1731: First lending library: the Library Company of Philadelphia

- 1736: First voluntary fire squad in the United States (Union Fire Company)

- 1743: First institution devoted to science and philosophy in North America: the American Philosophical Institution

- 1751: First hospital: Pennsylvania Hospital

- 1752: First fire insurance company: Philadelphia Contributionship

- 1776: First reading of the Declaration of Independence

- 1777: First United States flag on record and first Fourth of July celebration

- 1780: First bank (Pennsylvania Bank)

- 1790: First stock exchange (Philadelphia Exchange)

- 1790–1800 First capital of the United States (Philadelphia)

- 1799–1802 First row houses: Carstairs Row (now Jewelers' Row)

- 1802: First public water supply project: Philadelphia Water Works

- 1805: First art museum and art school: Pennsylvania Academy of the Fine Arts

- 1812: First natural history institution: Academy of Natural Sciences

- 1854: First Consolidation Act by a city and its townships, thereby expanding the city's boundaries

- 1874: First zoo

- 1876: First department store: Wanamaker's

- 1920: First Thanksgiving Day Parade

- 1934: First professional football game (for the record, the Philadelphia Eagles beat the Cincinnati Reds, 64-0)

- 1946: First computer (ENIAC), constructed at the University of Pennsylvania

OTHER DISTINCTIONS

- Oldest street in continuous use: Elfreth's Alley (since 1702)

- Most murals (more than 3,000) in any city in the world

- Oldest theater in continuous use in the English-speaking world: Walnut Street Theatre (since 1809)

- Oldest and largest outdoor market: the Italian Market

- Largest landscaped city park: Fairmount Park (9,200 acres)

- Oldest African American newspaper: The Philadelphia Tribune (since 1885)

- Largest masonry building in the world: City Hall

- Longest-running parade: the Mummers New Year's Day Parade, since 1901

© ZU_09/ISTOCK.COM

William Penn envisioned a colony where religious freedom was a core value.

most Convenient place upon the [Delaware] River for health & Navigation." He hoped for a "greene Country Towne, which will never be burnt, and always be wholesome." Penn envisioned a city that bore a closer resemblance to some of the rural towns of England, which he preferred to the overcrowded cities he knew well, such as London, which was more susceptible to disease and fire damage because people lived in such close proximity. Exhibiting one of the first examples of thoughtful city planning in the New World, Penn and his assistants laid out a grid with large lots, wide streets, and space for gardens and orchards, including the five central city parks that remain an important part of life in Philadelphia today. His design served as an example for numerous cities to follow.

THE COLONIAL ERA

Before Penn arrived, the area that would become Philadelphia was inhabited by Native Americans. The Lenni-Lenapes, known as "the Delaware Indians," were the earliest known residents, and many of them were pushed west by the advance of Swedish, Dutch, and English settlers in the early 1600s. In the 1630s and 1640s, the Swedes and Dutch spent approximately 17 years arguing over claims to land along the Delaware River, but the dispute over ownership was never resolved, and the area ultimately fell under British rule.

When Penn arrived, many early settlers were living in caves dug out of the Delaware River banks. Penn made an unprecedented move in attempting to buy, rather than take, their land, aiming to set a new standard for treatment of indigenous peoples. Popular legend has it that Penn made a treaty of friendship with the Lenape chief Tammany under an elm tree at Shackamaxon (the present-day neighborhood of Kensington and home to Penn Treaty Park in memory of the event). The famous painting *Penn's Treaty with the Indians,* by Benjamin West, immortalized the scene, and the giant statue of William Penn atop City Hall was positioned to point to the location of the signing of the treaty. Some historians debate whether the exact event took place, but what it represents—Penn's peaceful relationship with the natives—is well supported. Documents show that Penn wrote to the Indians, asking for peaceful relations and acknowledging the mistakes of previous European settlers, and even learned their language so he wouldn't need a translator.

To attract people to his new colony, Penn advertised for the purchase of large tracts of land at reasonable prices all over Europe. In 1683, there were just a few hundred inhabitants; by 1701, there were around 2,500. The promise of religious freedom and economic opportunity brought not only English, Welsh, German, and Dutch Quakers, but also Huguenots (French Protestants), Mennonites, Amish, Lutherans from Catholic German states, Irish Catholics, and Jews, among others. A group of German Quakers established the first German settlement in America in present-day Germantown.

The vast majority of those first land purchasers settled along the Delaware River, in what is today known as Old City and Society Hill. Despite Penn's hope for westward expansion and plans for large lots surrounded by gardens, nearly all of the lots in that area eventually were subdivided and resold, and smaller alleys were built in between the main streets to accommodate additional homes and people. While Penn's goals were admirable, he had to compete with the reality of a city's natural growth and immigrants from other large cities who were inclined to replicate what they were accustomed to. Until

WHAT'S IN A NAME?

There is an interesting story behind the names of both Pennsylvania (Penn's Woods) and Philadelphia (City of Brotherly Love). Can you guess which one was named by William Penn? If you guessed Pennsylvania, you're wrong. William Penn was given the colony of Pennsylvania by King Charles II of England to repay a debt the king owed to Penn's deceased father, the wealthy, high-ranking naval officer Admiral Penn. The 45,000-square-mile tract of land consisted primarily of woodlands stretching from the Allegheny Mountains to the Delaware River. William Penn wanted to name the colony "Sylvania" after the woods, but the king insisted on adding Penn to the name, in honor of the elder Admiral Penn. William Penn wasn't crazy about the name. The young Billy Penn was part of the Society of Friends, or Quakers, a religious group that denounces excess and self-promotion, and Penn considered it egotistical to name land after oneself. He was embarrassed, knowing that people would assume the colony was named after him, and he was right; many do assume that to this day.

The young William Penn, however, did choose the name for the city that would shape his colony, a name rooted in his own ideals and plan for the city. He set out to found a society where not only Quakers but people of all religions could practice without persecution, an unprecedented idea at the time. Philadelphia was his "holy experiment," and he named it based on the Greek *philos* for "love" and *adelphos* for "brother," which is why Philadelphia is called the City of Brotherly Love.

1704, few people lived west of 4th Street, and it would be many years before they spread west towards the Schuylkill River.

In the spring of 1682, Penn wrote the Frame of Government for Pennsylvania. He consulted with Algernon Sidney and John Locke in drawing out the details; the former complained he was keeping too much power for himself and the latter that he was giving too much to the people. Penn's Frame survived and was studied by Benjamin Franklin, Thomas Paine, and others. Parts of it were used as a model for many state governments to follow, and many of its principles influenced the content of the original United States Constitution, including the call for religious liberty, an assembly elected by the people to make laws, trial by jury, and a penal system designed to reform, not just to punish. In short, Penn was way ahead of his time.

While Penn was largely responsible for the way Philadelphia would eventually develop due to his careful, conscious planning, he barely spent any time here. While certainly a visionary, he was not the best businessman and he ultimately spent much of his life trying to get his finances in order in England. Penn's final significant act before returning to England for good on October 25, 1701, was issuing the Charter of Privileges, also known as the Charter of 1701. It established Philadelphia as a city and gave the mayor, aldermen, and councilmen the authority to issue laws and ordinances and to regulate markets and fairs, and it officially granted the religious freedom that was already practiced. In his later years, Penn actually attempted to sell Pennsylvania back to the English Crown, but in 1712 he had a stroke and could no longer speak. The deal was never made and the colony remained his property, under the control of his mostly ineffective, uninvolved offspring, in the years until the Revolutionary War, when once again, strong leaders would take over the city.

SEEDS OF REVOLUTION

The city prospered in the first half of the 18th century. Streets were paved and gas lights installed, making the streets brighter and safer. Schools and theaters were formed, and by the

BEN FRANKLIN: PHILLY'S FAVORITE SON

When Benjamin Franklin arrived in Philadelphia in October 1723 as a 17-year-old runaway from Boston, no one could have possibly guessed at the significant contributions he would make to the development of the city, the nation, and the world. A man of many talents in his lifetime, Franklin was an author, political theorist, politician, printer, scientist, inventor, civic activist, and diplomat. As a scientist, he is best known for his discoveries and theories regarding electricity, by way of experimenting with lightning and a kite. As a political writer and activist he was one of the major players to fight for and articulate the hopes and meaning of an independent American nation. As a diplomat during the American Revolution, he was largely responsible for securing the support from France that ultimately led to victory.

Among Franklin's many accomplishments in the city of Philadelphia, he established postal routes between Philadelphia, New York, Boston, and several other locations; founded the Union Fire Company to help protect the city from destruction by fire; set up a volunteer group for defense; built two batteries in case the city should be attacked; raised money to build the first hospital in the colonies; and founded the first lending library and the oldest philosophical society. His accomplishments are too great to list, because Franklin was involved in practically every significant accomplishment, decision, and invention that took place in Philadelphia during the most critical time in the city's – and ultimately the nation's – history.

© RITU JETHANI/123RF.COM

1750s, Christ Church and the Pennsylvania State House, now Independence Hall, were built. Philadelphia had developed into a true city, but as it became increasingly established, accomplished, and self-sufficient, a need for change also became evident.

In the 1760s, resentment towards British rule was mounting among many residents. England incurred a large debt during the Seven Years War and attempted to impose unprecedented taxes on the colonies to help pay those debts without the consent of the colonials. The British felt that since the outcome of the war was beneficial to the colonies, they should bear some of the tax burden, but under the Magna Carta, colonies were entitled to a vote on the policies that affected them.

By 1764, the British Parliament was realizing the increasing importance of the colonies and attempted to gain more control. Meanwhile, many colonists were increasingly frustrated that they had no voice in the governmental decisions of a distant ruler and were starting to wonder if their relationship with the crown did them more harm than good. Tensions escalated with the Stamp and Townshend Acts of 1765 and 1767 respectively, in which the British imposed a direct tax on stamps and an import tax on products including lead, paper, paint, glass, and tea. In both cases, colonists revolted and successfully boycotted the importation of British goods until the acts were repealed. The phrase "no taxation without representation" became popular during this time.

After the boycotts, the only remaining food tax imposed by England was on tea—but not for long. In 1773, the famous Boston Tea Party took place in Boston Harbor. The massive protest was a response to the Tea Act, which allowed England to sell tea in the colonies with no import taxes. Revolutionaries broke into a British ship the night before it was scheduled to arrive in Boston and dumped an estimated 90,000 pounds of tea overboard. The radical act of defiance further inspired revolt among colonists along the eastern seaboard.

The British government was outraged and responded by passing five acts that became known to colonists as the Intolerable Acts. While their action was an attempt to regain power and order and scare the colonists into submission, it backfired, inciting the colonies to unite in support of Massachusetts and resolve to not be taken advantage of by England any longer. Benjamin Franklin, who considered himself a loyal British subject until that time, was staunchly against what he called the "capricious English policy."

The tide was quickly turning and there was a call for a general congress of the colonies to meet and discuss the issues. The First Continental Congress was held in September 1774 in Carpenters' Hall in Philadelphia, chosen because it was centrally located. The 55 delegates in attendance represented all the colonies except for Georgia. As a result of the meeting, the Articles of Association, a formal agreement to boycott British goods, was drafted on October 20, 1774. It was wildly successful, and imports from Britain dropped 97 percent the following year, showing that the colonies could be powerful when they banded together. The Congress agreed that if the Intolerable Acts were not repealed, the colonies would cease to provide exports to Britain after a certain date. They also planned for a Second Continental Congress to meet in Philadelphia on May 10, 1775.

REVOLUTIONARY WAR

Most members of the First Continental Congress hoped a commercial boycott would persuade the British government to grant their demands but that the colonies would remain part of the British Empire, but this was not to be. Instead, they were quickly thrust into the Revolutionary War. The king of England declared Massachusetts in a state of rebellion due to its boycott of the Intolerable Acts, and trade was severely restricted throughout New England. Acts of protest, picketing, and even the burning of several British ships took place. On April 19, 1775, British troops advanced at Concord and Lexington in Massachusetts and fired at colonists; this became known as "the shot heard around the world." Word quickly spread, marking the unofficial beginning of the Revolutionary War.

When the Second Continental Congress met as planned in 1775 at the Pennsylvania State House, now Independence Hall, they declared war and formed the Continental Army with George Washington as commander. During the war, this Congress essentially acted as the government of the country-to-be, making all the leadership decisions for the now-united colonies.

In March of 1776, the British began a blockade of the Delaware Bay and moved south through New Jersey. By December, half of Philadelphia's population had fled and the Continental Congress went to Baltimore for fear the city was about to be invaded. But American troops pushed back the British at the Battles of Princeton and Trenton, and most refugees as well as Congress returned to the city. By late spring of 1776, the Americans forced the British to evacuate Boston, and by July all of the British Royal officials had fled and the patriots were ready to declare victory—but the British weren't ready to give up.

DECLARATION OF INDEPENDENCE

Meanwhile, while the war was still raging, a committee including John Adams, Benjamin Franklin, and Thomas Jefferson was assigned to draft a Declaration of Independence. It

© DRBUELLER/ISTOCK.COM

The Liberty Bell summoned citizens to hear the first public reading of the Declaration of Independence on July 8, 1776.

declared that the 13 colonies in North America were "free and independent states" and that "all political connection between them and the State of Great Britain, is and ought to be totally dissolved." The final document that we know today was the result of much debate and multiple drafts, and while it is believed that Adams wrote the bulk of it, Franklin made several key edits. The delegates voted and the document passed in Congress on July 4, 1776. As legend has it, the Liberty Bell sounded to summon citizens to hear the first public reading of this revolutionary document on July 8, 1776.

In September 1777, American troops could no longer hold off the British, who invaded Philadelphia from the south. Washington tried to stop them at the Battle of Brandywine but was driven back. Residents fled into other parts of Pennsylvania and New Jersey, and Congress fled to Lancaster and later to York. British troops went on to claim Philadelphia, abandoned by all residents who had the means to flee, for 10 months.

There was a change of tide when the French Army joined the American cause and gave them the extra help they needed to begin to win battles. After several key victories, the British troops eventually pulled out of Philadelphia on June 18, 1778, to try to defend New York City. American troops began to reoccupy Philadelphia and the Continental Congress returned in early July when the city was no longer under serious threat. The war was essentially won, though it wasn't official until 1783, when the Treaty of Paris recognized U.S. sovereignty.

THE CONSTITUTION

Under the Articles of Confederation, Congress only had power over colonial governments, but not the citizens themselves. After the war ended, this system grew problematic, especially since any change to the Articles of Confederation required a unanimous vote by representatives of all of the colonies. This was nearly impossible since each acted independently and there was often refusal to participate for the common good. The country could not pay the debts it accrued over the war while each colony was busy issuing independent and conflicting laws and rules. In 1787, delegates of the 13 colonies held the Constitutional Convention in Philadelphia and immediately voted to drop the Articles of Confederation. They spent many months debating the form that their new government should take, until they finally found a compromise and drafted and adopted the U.S. Constitution.

This seminal document unified and guided the laws and principles of the new country's government as it does to this day. Philadelphia was the U.S. capital from 1790 to 1800, and George Washington served as the nation's first president. The northern colonies petitioned Congress to keep the capital in Philadelphia or New York, but—after a debate that Thomas Jefferson called the "most bitter and angry contest ever known in Congress, before or since the Union of the States"—the northerners were forgiven heavy debts in return for agreeing to move the capital city to a site along the banks of the Potomac River, in what is now Washington, D.C., in 1800.

POST-REVOLUTIONARY ERA

The city's economy and population experienced rapid growth as the country stabilized and had more time to focus on things other than war. However, two massive yellow fever outbreaks in the 1790s caused thousands to flee, virtually shutting down trade and commerce. The yellow fever epidemic of 1793 killed nearly one in ten residents, while most of the upper class fled to the suburbs to be safer from the disease plaguing cities. Benjamin Rush, the most famous American physician of his time, gained renown during the epidemics when he refused to flee the city and insisted on treating as many patients as possible. The work of Rush, along with that of Philip Syng Physick (the "father of American surgery") and the success of Pennsylvania Hospital, contributed to making Philadelphia the leading center for the study and practice of medicine in the United States. By 1800, Philadelphia had largely recovered from the epidemic and became one of the United States' busiest ports and the country's largest city with almost 68,000 people in the city and nearby suburbs.

However, as the largest city in the country, Philadelphia was among the most heavily affected by international events. As the British and French warred against each other, the United States tried to stay neutral, but could not. Maritime trade was interrupted by the Embargo Act of 1807, when the United States tried to stop trading with both Britain and France, and by the War of 1812, when the United States went to war against the British in an effort to reassert its independence. Philadelphia's shipping industry never recovered, and New York soon became the United States' busiest port and largest city.

While the embargo was initially bad for the city, it ultimately helped shape Philadelphia into the United States' first major industrial and cultural city. Many goods were not available due to trade embargos, so factories were established to make those goods at home. Manufacturing plants were built and the city became an important center for paper, leather, shoes, and boots. Coal and iron mines and the construction of new roads, canals, and railroads helped the city grow into an industrial power. Major projects included the Water Works, a gasworks, and the U.S. Naval Yard. Philadelphia became the financial and cultural center of the country, and chartered and private banks (including the First and Second Banks of the United States) and the first U.S. Mint opened. The Pennsylvania Academy of the Fine Arts, the Academy of Natural Sciences, the Athenaeum, and the Franklin Institute were created, and public education became available after the Pennsylvania General Assembly passed the Free School Law of 1834. Philadelphia was booming.

CRIME AND CONSOLIDATION

The population grew rapidly as immigrants, mostly from Germany and Ireland, continued to arrive. The wealthy moved west of 7th Street, and the poor moved into their former homes near the Delaware River, many of which were now converted into tenements and boarding houses. With crowded row houses filling tiny streets and alleys, the area grew filthy and smelly—like areas of London that Penn hoped his city would never resemble.

During the 1840s and 1850s, hundreds of people died each year from malaria, smallpox, tuberculosis, and cholera. The poor were affected the worst because when disease broke out in the city, the rich found respite in areas outside the city. Violence, lawlessness, and gangs became serious problems during these years. Many of the volunteer fire companies were infiltrated by gangs, and brutal fights broke out between rival gangs at fire sites, all wanting to be paid for putting out the fire.

As the city grew into an industrial metropolis, ethnic tensions also grew. In addition to Swedish, German, and British immigrants who had first established homes in the city, Philadelphia was home to strong Irish Catholic and African American communities in the early part of the 19th century. These communities established mutual aid societies, churches, and other institutions, while facing a great deal of opposition from the "Nativists." Rampant racism and violence against immigrants, especially Irish Catholics, was common in the 1840s and 1850s. The Nativist Riots between Protestant Nativists and Irish Catholic immigrants began in 1844 over a question of religious practice in public schools and resulted in injury, death, and much property damage. Violence against African Americans was common and African American homes and churches were sometimes burned.

The city didn't have the structure or government in place to handle all its problems, and additional tax revenue was required to put programs and institutions—including a police force—in place. As a result, the Act of Consolidation was passed on February 2, 1854, which united all of Philadelphia County's districts, townships, and municipalities into one big city. Through this act, 5 of the 30 largest cities in the country at the time were formed into a single municipality. This dramatically increased the size and tax base of the city, and the population grew from about 125,000 to

more than 500,000 while the total area of the city grew from 2 to 129 square miles. In addition to the crowded area along the Delaware, there were now more than 1,500 farms, woods, and wetlands in Philadelphia's new boundaries, and the city now included the townships and villages (which we now know as neighborhoods) of Germantown, Manayunk, Roxborough, Frankford, Northern Liberties, and Kingsessing. The Act meant that enough money could be generated to pay the new and much-needed police force, as well as many other public services, including water, streets, and transportation.

CIVIL WAR

When the Civil War began in 1861, Philadelphia was initially divided over allegiances. The number of blacks living in the city was just 4 percent, or 22,000—small by modern standards but far greater than in any other northern city at the time. Philadelphia served as an important stop on the Underground Railroad, housing the largest free black population in the north. Large networks of African Americans and whites, especially among the fiercely abolitionist Quakers, assisted many slaves on the way to freedom. However, many Philadelphians were against the anti-slavery movement, and abolitionists were sometimes the target of violence. Some Quaker meetinghouses were burned to the ground.

Ultimately, Philadelphia joined the Union and the city went on to play an important role in the war by supplying soldiers, ammunition, war ships, and army uniforms. More than 157,000 soldiers and sailors were treated within the city—many at Satterlee Hospital, the largest army hospital in the world at the time, which stood in West Philadelphia near the site of today's Clark Park. The Mower General Hospital in Chestnut Hill also treated hundreds of thousands of injured soldiers. Philadelphia began to prepare for invasion in 1863, but the southern army was held off at Gettysburg and ultimately the war was won. Philadelphia was less impacted by the Civil War than many other places involved in the war because it avoided the major physical destruction that many cities in the south suffered, as well as the major political and social upheavals that took place in other northern cities.

A GROWING CITY

After the Civil War, immigrants continued to arrive in the city, and by 1870, 27 percent of the population was foreign born. By the 1880s, immigration from Russia, Eastern Europe, and Italy rivaled immigration from Western Europe. By 1881, there were around 5,000 Jewish people in the city, and by 1905, the number grew to more than 100,000. The Italian population increased from around 300 in 1870 to 18,000 in 1900, and the majority settled in South Philadelphia, which remains an Italian stronghold today. In 1876, there were 25,000 blacks in the city, and by 1890, there were nearly 40,000. During the 1880s, the people moving into the city were mostly poor, working-class immigrants, and the wealthy were beginning to leave. The suburbs along the Main Line of the Pennsylvania Railroad just west of the city became a popular destination, and the area remains one of the wealthiest and most elite suburbs in the region today.

Over the course of the late 19th century, industry grew in the modern metropolis despite a great deal of political corruption and setbacks. Philadelphia became a city of homeowners, distinct from cities like New York and Chicago, where large groups of people rented tenements. The city developed to include row after row of single-family homes, which provided affordable housing for the middle class. The police department improved and volunteer fire companies were finally replaced by a paid fire department. Education reforms were implemented that served to protect the education system from corruption in politics. Opportunity for higher education improved when the University of Pennsylvania moved to West Philadelphia and Temple University, Drexel University, and the Free Library were founded.

One of the biggest events in the history of the country took place in Philadelphia in 1876. The Centennial Exposition was a World's Fair held in Fairmount Park to celebrate the United States' Centennial. Nine million people came to the city over a six-month period to take part in the carnival atmosphere and to see the landmark science exhibits, including Alexander Graham Bell's telephone and the Corliss Steam Engine. Millions of dollars went into planning the incredible event, but unfortunately many of the buildings constructed for it were left abandoned with no real purpose once the fair ended. (One of these buildings was Memorial Hall in Fairmount Park, which opened as the new site of the children's attraction the Please Touch Museum in 2008.)

Other major developments of the growing city included the construction of City Hall at the center of the city at Broad and Market Streets. The architectural marvel took 23 years to complete, and for 100 years it was the tallest building in Philadelphia. An unofficial agreement kept it the tallest building until the 945-foot One Liberty Place snatched that crown in 1987, soon to be followed by many other skyscrapers, all of which make City Hall look tiny in comparison.

City Hall was the tallest building in Philadelphia until 1987.

© KARRIE GAVIN

Another key element to the city's growth was the Pennsylvania Railroad, which expanded westward to connect Philadelphia with the entire East Coast and the Midwest. This was also the era when major department stores, including Wanamaker's and Strawbridge & Clothier, came to the city. As automobile use increased, new roads and bridges were built, including the Northeast (now Roosevelt) Boulevard in 1914, the Benjamin Franklin Parkway in 1918, and the Delaware River (now Benjamin Franklin) Bridge—which connects the city with Camden, New Jersey—in 1926. New skyscrapers were built and wired for electricity, and the first subway was constructed in 1907. The Philadelphia Museum of Art opened in 1928. The city was growing in every way imaginable.

THE GREAT DEPRESSION AND WORLD WAR II

While several economic depressions and recessions of the 19th and early 20th centuries certainly hurt the city, their effect was somewhat hampered in Philadelphia compared with other cities because of its variety of industry. But in 1929, when the Great Depression hit, Philadelphia—like the rest of the country—could not withstand the blow. The effects were devastating to the functioning of commerce and the well being of residents. In the three years that followed the stock market crash, 50 banks closed and thousands of residents couldn't pay their mortgages, making foreclosures commonplace. More than half of the savings and loan associations went out of business. In 1933, the unemployment rate was at its highest; blacks were affected worse than whites, and immigrants worst of all.

The mayor at the time, J. Hampton Moore, was considered unsympathetic to the plight of the people, blaming them for laziness. He fired 3,500 city workers, instituted pay cuts, forced unpaid vacation, and reduced the number of contracts. Many groups of workers united, and not long after Philadelphia became a strong union city, which it remains to this day.

There was a great deal of corruption and fraud in the city government throughout this period, and many had no faith in what they saw as the GOP machine. Mob activity was high, especially during Prohibition, and the city slowly started to shift towards the Democratic Party in hopes of change. The government was exposed on multiple counts of corruption and stealing, and in the 1951 election, Joseph S. Clark became the first Democratic mayor in 80 years. Philadelphia has remained staunchly Democratic ever since, with not a single Republican mayor or congressman elected in Philadelphia in more than 60 years.

The beginning of World War II helped bring Philadelphia out of the Depression as new jobs, many in the defense industry, offered new opportunity. More than 30,000 workers found jobs at the Naval Ship Yard. When the United States became involved in the war in 1941, many Philadelphia men went to serve, while women, African Americans, and workers from outside the city, who had been excluded by unions, filled in for the missing local labor force. At the end of the war in 1945, there were around 184,000 Philadelphians in the U.S. armed forces.

A SHRINKING CITY

The city's population peaked at over two million residents in 1950, and ever since, the numbers have declined while those of suburban counties have grown. After World War II, Philadelphia experienced a serious housing shortage, with many of its homes more than 100 years old and in poor condition. The phenomenon known as "white flight" began, and has continued ever since, in Philadelphia as in many other U.S. cities. Many economically disadvantaged African Americans, Puerto Ricans, and other groups moved into the city while middle- and upper-middle-class families, mostly white, moved out. Between 1950 and 2000, the city lost 26.7 percent of its population, in keeping with national trends. (Chicago lost 20 percent and Baltimore lost 31.4 percent during this time, according to U.S. census data.) Philadelphia was shrinking at a startling rate, and many manufacturing and other businesses were leaving the city or shutting down entirely, so there were no jobs for the people coming in.

The 1960s were a turbulent decade in Philadelphia, as they were across the nation. Crime had become a serious problem with drug-related gang warfare plaguing the city. A 1970 City Planning Commission survey noted crime as the city's number one problem. Police Commissioner Frank Rizzo was a controversial and polarizing figure; he was both loved and hated, depending on whom you asked. He had a reputation as an aggressive police officer, quick to use force—especially against African Americans, some said—but also as a strong proponent of law and order. He was elected mayor in 1971, after serving four years as police commissioner, and was given credit for keeping violence in check, if only by comparison to other cities at the time. He was reelected in 1975, and police and fire departments and some cultural institutions were well taken care of. Meanwhile, other areas, including the Free Library, the Department of Welfare and Recreation, the City Planning Commission, and the Streets Department experienced major cuts. Mayor Rizzo divided the city perhaps more than any other mayor in its history.

Crime continued through the 1980s, with mafia warfare taking place, mostly in South Philadelphia. Drugs, gangs, and crack houses existed in many of the city's poorest neighborhoods, and the murder rate skyrocketed. In 1984, Wilson Goode became Philadelphia's first African American mayor. Throughout the decade, development continued in some areas of the city, including Old City, South Street, and Center City, which saw several massive skyscrapers built. But due to a combination of massively reduced federal spending on cities, a shrinking tax base, and generous labor contracts, among other things, the city finances worsened throughout the 1970s and 1980s. When Goode left office at the end of the 1980s, the city was nearly bankrupt.

The very least shining moment of the entire Goode administration and perhaps all of Philadelphia municipal politics was the highly publicized MOVE incident. The police had several prior run-ins with the radical group MOVE, and a major clash in 1978 resulted in the tragic death of a police officer and nine MOVE members going to prison. The second major incident occurred in 1985 during a stand-off at the group's headquarters in Southwest Philadelphia. The police had no idea how to handle the situation, and eventually dropped a satchel bomb from a helicopter onto the house, setting off a fire that killed 11 MOVE members, including five children, and destroyed 62 neighboring houses. The handling of this unbelievable event was a shameful disgrace to the police, the administration, and the entire city.

A CITY REBORN

When Ed Rendell, who went on to serve two terms as governor of Pennsylvania, was elected mayor in 1992, he had a hard road ahead to fix the financial and social mess the city was in at the time. The vast problems included numerous unpaid bills, the lowest bond rating of the top 50 largest U.S. cities, and a budget deficit of $250 million. With charm and determination, Rendell somehow attracted investment in the city, stabilized finances, and even produced small budget surpluses.

Revitalization took place in many parts of the city through the 1990s, and in 1993, the new Convention Center was built and 17 new hotels followed between 1998 and 2000. The city began to work harder to promote its historic sites, festivals, and entertainment, and it worked; increasing numbers of visitors came to the city.

Former city council president John F. Street was elected mayor in 1999, and many aspects of the city's revitalization continued into the 21st century, although some locals don't give Street much credit for the momentum created by the Rendell administration. There were accusations of typical Philadelphia-style scandals in Street's administration, including awards, insider deals, and poor money management. There was also once again a rise of violent crime after a decline for a short time in the 1990s; it should be noted, however, that both the decline and increase have matched changes in cities throughout the country.

Many neighborhoods continued to revitalize

during Street's two terms in office and the city saw considerable progress in many areas, while it suffered in other areas. There was a condominium boom, created in part by tax breaks for new construction.

PHILADELPHIA TODAY

To look around Center City Philadelphia today is to have no doubt that the city is still growing and improving and that the revitalization that began during the Rendell era continues today. The skyline continues to expand, with the Comcast Center, built in 2005, standing 975 feet high as the tallest building between Chicago and New York. The city has seen a rebirth in arts and culture as well in recent decades, with newer additions to the Avenue of the Arts like the modern Kimmel Center and the Suzanne Roberts Theatre. As a result of updating, expanding, and marketing our many historic attractions, tourism has become a major industry and Philadelphia has garnered much national attention.

Construction projects are still taking place around the city, despite the national recession, and fewer people are leaving the city, while new people, many of them young, are moving in. Many neighborhoods, including Fairmount, University City, Northern Liberties, Graduate Hospital, Manayunk, and Fishtown, continue to experience a rebirth, as empty lots become homes and condominiums, and new businesses open in economically underdeveloped areas. As is typical with gentrification, there is concern over long-term residents being priced out of their homes, as well as other concerns that fall in line with the division of the city along class lines. Yet most Philadelphians have felt a change was long overdue, and there is generally great enthusiasm around the development.

Michael Nutter, endorsed by local media and elected in a landslide, became mayor in 2008. The West Philadelphia native was a true reformer as a city councilman and a key leader in instituting the citywide smoking ban and fighting proposed cuts to hours of city libraries and other important community resources. He accomplished much as a councilman in the face of much opposition, including frequent clashes with former mayor Street, who many felt was comfortable with the status quo whereas Nutter wanted to make a real change. Nutter

Philadelphia is a vital, growing city.

Reversing a decades-long trend, Philadelphia's population has stopped shrinking.

was elected with much enthusiasm, but his first few years in office have been somewhat disappointing. It must be noted, however, that these years coincided with the national recession and falling city tax revenues, so perhaps he had little choice in some of the unpopular moves he has made. Only time will tell what legacy he will leave as mayor.

According to the 2010 census, the population of Philadelphia has finally stopped shrinking, and in the years 2000–2009, it actually grew by 2 percent; this was the first time the population grew since 1950. The reasons some cite include: an increase in new transplants from foreign destinations and from pricier nearby Northeast cities, the 10-year tax abatement on some types of new housing, a historically undervalued housing market, improvements to the waterfront, and continuing redevelopment throughout the city. Despite the national recession and mortgage crises, Philadelphia was not hit very hard and housing prices have remained relatively stable. Here's hoping that the momentum and growth of the past two decades continues.

Government and Economy

GOVERNMENT

Philadelphia is by far the most Democratic county in Pennsylvania, with Democrats making up about 75 percent and Republicans just 15 percent of registered voters. Since 1932, Philadelphia has voted Democrat in every presidential election, and has often been the only county in the entire state to do so, as Pennsylvania is by and large Republican. Philadelphia once had six congressional districts, but as a result of the city's declining population it now has only four—all of which are Democratic. A Republican has not represented a significant portion of Philadelphia in any office since 1983.

From the Civil War until 1951, Philadelphia was staunchly Republican, and for many years,

Philadelphia was dominated by what many considered a corrupt political machine. The Republican Party rode the successes of Lincoln and the Civil War to hold onto the mayor's office through the 1950s despite wave after wave of reform movements by city activists. The machine controlled the city through voter fraud and intimidation and through extensive patronage. Reform efforts slowly changed city government, with the most significant change in 1950 when a new city charter strengthened the position of mayor and weakened the Philadelphia City Council. Other northern industrial cities elected Democratic mayors in the 1930s and 1940s, but Philadelphia didn't join the trend until 1951. While the city switched allegiances to the Democratic Party in the 1950s, the reputation of Philadelphia as a city that is "corrupt but contented" survives to this day in some minds.

ECONOMY

Philadelphia was a leading agricultural center early in its history, surrounded by rich Pennsylvania farmlands. Due to its location at the meeting of the Delaware and Schuylkill Rivers, shipyards were very successful. Farm goods were traded for sugar and rum in the West Indies, and these products were in turn exchanged for goods from England and elsewhere. Abundant natural resources, including coal and iron, helped Philadelphia become an early industrial leader, and by the 1770s Philadelphia was one of the most important business centers in the British Empire, with printing, publishing, papermaking, and textiles leading the way. Despite the national government leaving Philadelphia in 1800, the city remained the cultural and financial center of the country for some time. It also became one of the first and strongest industrial powerhouses.

The face of industry has changed drastically since its early days, in Philadelphia as in other parts of the world. The private-services-providing sectors, which are now the leading industries (including trade, transportation and utilities, information, financial activities, professional and business services, education, health, leisure, and hospitality), continue to grow while the goods-producing sectors (including natural resources and mining, construction, and manufacturing) fall, as we continue to move away from the traditional manufacturing economy. Today, Philadelphia has some of the very best education and health systems in the world, with a wealth of top-rated universities and hospitals. The tourism industry also continues to grow, and new businesses form each year to meet the needs of the increasing numbers of visitors, from hotels to restaurants to museums.

People and Culture

DEMOGRAPHICS

Philadelphia is the sixth most populous city in the country, with approximately 1.55 million people as of the 2010 census, and Center City has the third-largest residential downtown population in the entire country after New York and Chicago. The Greater Philadelphia region is the fifth-largest metropolitan region in the United States, and is home to more than 6 million as of 2010, with a total of 46.1 million people living within just 200 miles of Philadelphia—a close second only to New York City for this statistic. This means that approximately one-fourth of the total U.S. population lives within a six-hour drive of Philadelphia.

As of the latest census, the population of the city of Philadelphia is 48.6 percent white, 43.7 percent African American, 11.7 percent Hispanic or Latino, and 5.7 percent Asian. It is interesting to note that while Philadelphia has almost equal numbers of Caucasians and African Americans, the statistic is drastically different for the state of Pennsylvania, where African Americans represent only 10.9 percent and whites 85.2 percent.

It is also worth noting that two of the most subjugated ethnic groups in the city during the mid-19th century, African Americans and Irish Americans, today make up the largest groups in the city. While Philadelphia has long been considered a largely "black and white" city compared with other major cities, the number of Hispanics and Asian Americans has begun to increase over the past two decades. Philadelphia also has the second-largest Irish, Italian, and Jamaican American populations in the entire United States. The number of foreign-born residents represents about 10 percent of the city's population.

RELIGION

Since its founding, the only colony that practiced religious tolerance has attracted a wide diversity of religious sects. Many Quakers followed William Penn to his new city, where they could practice their religion without persecution, and the Quaker influence can be seen today in the many Quaker Friends' schools and meeting houses that still exist.

However, today Christianity is the dominant religion in the city, with Protestants and Roman Catholics making up the two largest sects in similar numbers. There is a significant Eastern Orthodox population, and since the early 1800s, there has been a large Jewish population that has continued to grow as Eastern European Jews immigrated to Philadelphia. However, many of the Jewish communities left the city for the suburbs during the period

PHILLY-SPEAK

Philly-speak is one of a kind. You'll surely notice the unique dialect – unless, of course, you were born here; many locals aren't aware that we say things a little differently until we leave town and someone tells us. There are many variations between neighborhoods, classes, and ethnic groups, but many of our terms cut across boundaries and are just distinctively "Philly." Here are some of the most common:

- **down the shore:** the New Jersey beach towns, including Ocean City and Wildwood, where many Philadelphians go in summer. Usage: "I'm going down the shore this weekend" (not to be confused with going "up the Poconos" to ski in winter).

- **Iggles:** the Philadelphia Eagles professional football team

- **hoagie:** a sandwich (or "samwich") on a long roll filled with meat, cheese, and toppings; referred to as a "sub" in many other places

- **jawn:** any person, place, or thing. Usage: "Pass me that jawn" (anything from a beer to the remote control); "You goin' to that jawn?" (often a party or club, but works for any event); or "That jawn is fly" (the jawn being an attractive person).

- **jimmies:** small chocolate or rainbow-colored candy that you sprinkle onto ice cream, known in most places as "sprinkles"

- **lager:** Yuengling lager. When you order a "lager" in Philly, it implies the locally brewed Yuengling brand.

- **wit/witout:** When ordering a cheesesteak, "wit" (with) means with onions and "witout" (without) means no onions, so "Whiz wit" is a cheesesteak with Cheez Whiz and onions.

- **wooder:** local pronunciation of water, as in "I'll have a cherry wooder ice," when ordering the sweet, flavored, slushy ice treat popular in Philly

- **youse** or **yiz:** plural for you, when addressing more than one person, as in "What're youse/yiz doin' tonight?"

- **The Blue Route:** I-476, the highway that cuts through Philadelphia's suburbs, including Delaware and Montgomery Counties

- **The Drive:** Kelly Drive or East River Drive

- **The Expressway:** the Schuylkill Expressway (pronounced "SKOO-kil"), the section of I-76 that runs through Philadelphia

PHILLY 'TUDE

A nasty rumor has somehow spread that Philadelphians are unfriendly, boorish, and sometimes even downright mean, and I'd like to set the record straight. Many locals are a little rough around the edges, but that is part of the local charm; this is a traditional blue-collar town after all. But unless you insult our sports teams, loudly root for another team in front of us, or play for one of our sports teams and blow the season, you shouldn't be the target of any more rude behavior than you would in any other East Coast city.

Granted, we can be loud, and maybe a little impatient − especially if you're holding up traffic while staring at a map − but beneath the tough exterior, Philadelphians are, by and large, warm, helpful, and down-to-earth people. We like to think we're just more honest here than others. At least you'll always know where you stand. If people are being nice to you, they probably really like you, and if not, they're just not in the mood, so move on to ask someone else for directions.

And just to be safe, anything negative you have to say about Philly should be said in private. While locals insult the city (and the sports teams) quite freely, visitors rarely earn the right. Oh, and one last thing − you might want to learn how to order a cheesesteak at the fast-lane cheesesteak joints so you don't hold up the line.

1950–2000, and some synagogues were converted to mosques and Baptist churches.

Smaller religious communities include Islam and Hinduism, which have seen an increase as immigration from the Middle East, Pakistan, Bangladesh, and India has increased. The small Muslim community is about 85 percent African American.

Art and Architecture

Philadelphia is one of the artistic and cultural capitals of the country, and has been since its earliest days. In the 19th century, while New Yorkers flocked to dime museums and tawdry circus acts, Philadelphians attended art galleries and public libraries. Once referred to as "The Athens of America," Philly was North America's first nexus of culture. The bustling cosmopolitan center in a rapidly growing young country was home to dozens of arts and cultural innovations, including America's first library, art school, museum, university, hospital, and much more. The evolving artistic and cultural scene continues to thrive in the 21st century, from the sparkling Avenue of the Arts to the vibrant independent arts scene.

ARCHITECTURE

Philadelphia is a living gallery for more than 300 years of architectural history—and not all of it is made from the ubiquitous red brick. More than 100 buildings are designated National Historic Landmarks, with outstanding examples of practically every notable style represented. Renowned architects who have left their marks on the city include William Strickland, Frank Furness, Daniel Burnham, George Howe, Louis I. Kahn, Robert Venturi, I. M. Pei, Frank Lloyd Wright, and Cesar Pelli.

Those who are interested in learning more about the city's architecture should take one of the Open House tours offered by the Friends of Independence, or the Architectural Landmarks tours offered by the Philadelphia Society for the Preservation of Landmarks. And anyone who appreciates architecture should visit the Athenaeum, the world's premier landmark devoted to American architecture 1800–1945. For still more information and background, Philadelphia Architects and Buildings maintains an excellent online database (www.philadelphiabuildings.org/pab/) with a wealth of information about the city's architectural gems and the innovative architects responsible for them.

17th Century

Many of the city's first settlers lived in caves built into the riverbanks, followed by log cabins, which were introduced by early Swedes. People soon began building with wood and brick with the first brick house completed in 1684. Old Swedes' (Gloria Dei) Church, completed in 1700, is the oldest surviving building in Philadelphia today. The church reflects the Quaker aesthetic for simplicity and symmetry, as do many of the city's surviving first buildings; the largest of these Quaker-style buildings is the Arch Street Friends Meeting House in Old City.

18th Century

The 18th century brought an array of more elaborate styles in architecture, including Georgian and Federal, and many of the structures in Old City and Society Hill today represent some variation of these styles. Named after several generations of kings of England named George, the Georgian style was characterized by proportion and balance. Classic examples are red brick with white trim, including Independence Hall and Christ Church. The Carpenters Company was formed in 1724 to instruct builders on these new styles of architecture.

After the Revolution, there was a deliberate move away from the English ways in many regards, including architecture. An influx of new styles came to Philadelphia, including Classical Revival, seen in the First Bank of the United States, and Romanesque Revival, as can be seen in Mother Bethel A.M.E. Church.

The Federal style was named for the Federal period in American history, when it gained popularity. During the late 18th century, the founders of the United States, after rejecting the authority of the English crown, were inspired by the ancient democracies of Greece and Rome. Marked by an intricate interior and a simple, conservative exterior, one of the city's best examples of Federal architecture is the Central Pavilion of Pennsylvania Hospital, completed in 1805. The American eagle was a popular emblem, and many buildings you'll see with this mark were built during this period; the style became a symbol for the nation's wealthy and elite class.

19th Century

The beginning of the 19th century brought the Greek Revival style to Philadelphia, along with leading architects William Strickland and Robert Mills. Strickland was responsible for the Second Bank of the Unites States, modeled on the Parthenon, and the impressive Merchants' Exchange, which offered a modern twist on classic Greek styles.

The early 1800s also saw the start of a new housing innovation: the inexpensive and efficient row house. The first row houses in the United States were part of Carstairs Row (now Jewelers' Row), named for their builder and architect Thomas Carstairs. They provided a new type of housing that was not yet available in cities like New York and Boston. The style became known as "Philadelphia rows." As the city industrialized in the 1830s and 1840s, the Delaware riverfront was lined with tenements, warehouses, and factories, some of which survive today as converted "luxury lofts."

John Haviland also worked during this period; his 1829 Eastern State Penitentiary was the first structure that so deliberately melded structure and function, and he is also credited for the design of the Philadelphia History Museum (formerly the Atwater Kent Museum), Walnut Street Theatre, St. George's Episcopal Church, and the University of the Arts' Hamilton Hall.

As the 19th century progressed, commercial buildings increased in size and splendor, and architects like William L. Johnson and G. P. Cummings made their marks. Heavily ornamented Victorian and Gothic revival architecture came into vogue, bringing ornate

the entrance to the Masonic Temple

homes, especially to West Philadelphia and Center City. A large-scale example of the style includes the Pennsylvania Academy of the Fine Arts' main building, designed by architect Frank Furness.

City Hall deserves a paragraph of its own in Philadelphia's—and the world's—architectural history. Designed by John MacArthur Jr., the mammoth structure is one of the finest examples of French Second Empire architecture in the world. It is the country's largest governmental building and the world's tallest masonry building. Sculptor Alexander Milne Calder created more than 250 statues to adorn the edifice, including the 37-foot-tall statue of William Penn atop the building. Construction of City Hall took 30 years (1871–1901), due in part to municipal corruption and cost overruns. Originally intended to be the world's tallest building at 548 feet, it had already been superseded by the Eiffel Tower and Washington Monument by the time it was completed. Just north of it stands the Norman-Romanesque–style Masonic Temple

and the Gothic Revival–style Arch Street United Methodist Church, also built during this period.

20th Century

The 20th century brought much new and notable architecture to Philadelphia. The Benjamin Franklin Bridge, designed by Paul Phillipe Cret and built in 1926, was the largest suspension bridge in the world at the time. The building that now houses the Philadelphia Museum of Art was built 1919–1928, and was designed by Horace Trumbauer and by Julian Abele. Abele was a Philadelphia native and the first African American to graduate from the University of Pennsylvania's School of Architecture; he drew inspiration for the design while traveling in Greece, as can be seen in many of the details. Abele also played a role in the Beaux Arts–style Free Library, constructed on the Benjamin Franklin Parkway in 1927. The 30th Street Station and the Franklin Institute were also built in the 1930s.

The Philadelphia Savings Fund Society

building, which now houses the Loews Hotel, was built in 1932 and designed by William Lescaze and his partner George Howe; it is considered America's first International-style skyscraper. West of City Hall, the office mega-complex Penn Center rises on the site of former train tracks (and Furness's Broad Street Station) while I. M. Pei's 1963 Society Hill Towers stand as modernist beacons in colonial Society Hill. No building could be built taller than the head of the William Penn statue atop City Hall until 1987, when City Council granted permission for the skyscraper One Liberty Place, and by the end of the 20th century, there were already seven skyscrapers larger than City Hall.

21st Century

Philadelphia remains at the cutting-edge of architecture. The magnificent, modern Kimmel Center on the Avenue of the Arts opened in 2001, designed by architect Rafael Viñoly, and west of the Schuylkill, the 28-story glass Cira Center, by Cesar Pelli, was completed in 2005. The Comcast Center is the tallest building between New York and Chicago at 975 feet. As of its 2008 completion, it is also the tallest LEED platinum-certified building in the United States, in keeping with the trend towards more environmentally friendly building practices.

FINE ARTS

Philadelphia's fine arts tradition can be traced back to its earliest days. Before the American Revolution, the wealthy merchant class began to patronize the arts, especially the portrait painters; no proper high-society home was complete without a portrait of its owners hanging on the walls. Due to high demand, fine artists gravitated to the burgeoning city, including William Williams, his son William Joseph Williams, Benjamin West, Gilbert Stuart, and Charles Wilson Peale. Peale painted portraits of many notable historic figures, including George Washington, John Hancock, Thomas Jefferson, and Alexander Hamilton, and many of them are on display in a gallery housed in the Second Bank of the United States.

the Philadelphia Museum of Art

© JOHN TOMASELLI/123RF.COM

In 1805, the Pennsylvania Academy of the Fine Arts was founded by Charles Wilson Peale, sculptor William Rush, and others in the city's arts and business communities. One of the nation's leading art schools, it is known for its vast holdings of 19th- and 20th-century paintings and for playing a central role in the education of generations of American artists.

The Philadelphia Museum of Art, one of the world's greatest art museums, was founded as the "Pennsylvania Museum and School of Industrial Art." It opened its doors in Memorial Hall in Fairmount Park in 1876 as part of the World's Fair. The landmark building that now houses it dates from 1919, and today its collection includes almost a quarter of a million pieces. The Art Museum (as it's locally known) is also the starting point for two local institutions of higher education. Philadelphia University, formerly the Philadelphia Textile School, began in its early days by offering textile manufacturers a polished education, while the University of the Arts traces the origins of its fine arts program to the Art Museum's original school.

Public art is a major part of the Philadelphia landscape. The Fairmount Park Art Association ensures that the main municipal park is a showcase for sculpture and architecture, and the much-copied One Percent for Art program requires any construction project with city funding to include public art. Meanwhile, the landmark Mural Arts Program has created more than 3,000 murals across the city—more than in any other city in the world.

LITERATURE

Philadelphia has had an important presence in the literary world dating all the way back to Benjamin Franklin. The statesman, printer, inventor, scientist, political theorist, and author published his *Poor Richard's Almanack* annually 1732–1758. It contained the standard information normally found in an almanac, as well as Franklin's own doses of wit and wisdom, much of which has resulted in sayings that still exist in American vernacular (e.g., "A penny saved is a penny earned.").

The 19th century transformed Philadelphia into a center of publishing, with major publishers like J. B. Lippincott playing a major role in local industry for decades. Philadelphia writers at the time included Charles Brockden Brown, a pioneer in the development of the American novel. Meanwhile, interlopers such as Edgar Allan Poe and Louisa May Alcott made brief stops here during their illustrious careers. Noted African American scholar, activist, and historian W. E. B. Du Bois wrote his social history *The Philadelphia Negro* in 1899, and Walt Whitman, the father of American poetry, spent much time in the city, just a quick trip from his native Camden, New Jersey, across the Delaware River.

The Curtis Publishing Company was one of the largest publishers in the country during the early 20th century. It ran its magazine empire from its historic Curtis Center building in Society Hill, publishing the *Ladies' Home Journal* and *The Saturday Evening Post,* the country's oldest magazine. Though the major publishing houses today are largely centered in nearby New York City, some domestic and international publishers still have outposts in Philly.

PERFORMING ARTS

Philadelphia's most famous performing arts space is the Walnut Street Theatre, America's oldest surviving and the world's most-subscribed-to theater. The building at the corner of 9th and Walnut Streets opened as a circus in 1809 and went through several incarnations before becoming the nonprofit regional theater it is today. Other historical theaters include Forrest, Plays & Players, and Merriam, which all date from the beginning of the 20th century when powerful national theater syndicates like the Shubert controlled the country's live entertainment.

In the music world, the Philadelphia Orchestra, founded in 1900, has established its reputation as one of the United States' "Big Five" orchestras. Several opera companies competed for attention, and in 1975, the last two merged into the current Opera Company of Philadelphia.

After Broadway tryouts left Philadelphia in the 1960s, innovative young theater companies, including the Wilma Theater and the Philadelphia Theatre Company, began filling in the gaps. In the 1990s, Mayor Ed Rendell spearheaded the Avenue of the Arts initiative, which focused on turning the stretch of Broad Street spanning out from City Hall into a true center for performing arts. At the time, the Academy of Music was essentially a loner, but since then theater groups have flocked to the new and renovated theater spaces, including the Arts Bank in 1994, Clef Club in 1995, Wilma in 1996, and the Prince Music Theater in 1999. And, of course, the Kimmel Center opened in 2001, giving a grand home to the Philadelphia Orchestra and several other resident companies, followed by the modern Suzanne Roberts' Philadelphia Theatre Company in 2007.

ESSENTIALS

Getting There

BY AIR

The **Philadelphia International Airport** (800/745-4283, www.phl.org) is approximately seven miles from Center City and offers frequent service for more than 25 major airlines and several discount airlines. It is a major hub for US Airways (www.usairways.com), and Southwest Airlines (www.southwest.com) offers daily nonstop flights from Philadelphia to numerous cities, including Chicago, Las Vegas, Orlando, Phoenix, Providence, and Tampa. Millions of dollars in renovation projects in the past decade have resulted in a generally pleasant airport experience. The Marketplace now consists of more than 150 national and local shops offering food, beverages, and merchandise, so there is plenty to do while you wait for your flight—which you often will, as delays occur frequently.

Getting to and from the airport on public transportation is easy enough on Airport regional rail line, which directly links the airport to Center City for around $7 one way. It runs every 30 minutes daily 5 A.M.–midnight and connects with other rail lines that can get you practically anywhere within the city and nearby suburbs. Taxis charge a flat rate of $28.50 for travel to and from Center City from

PHILADELPHIA TO NEW YORK ON THE CHEAP

Locals and visitors alike regularly make the short trip to our nearby neighbor, the Big Apple. The most luxurious way to get there in a hurry is to take the Amtrak train. With trips just 1-1.5 hours, tickets start at $48 each way and are much higher at peak times, so the only people who regularly use Amtrak are those with business accounts and the wealthy. The good news is you can get to New York for as little as $20 round-trip by bus in about two hours.

The cheapest way to go, and the method preferred by many locals, is to take **"the Chinatown bus,"** starting at just $10 one-way and $20 round-trip and taking about two hours depending on traffic. Originally used primarily by Chinese food purveyors buying products in New York to sell in Philly, today it is used by commuters, students, and just about everyone on a budget. Service is from Chinatown in Philly (most buses depart 55 N. 11th St., between Arch and Race Sts.) to Chinatown in New York. Service to Washington D.C. ($15 one-way/$28 round-trip, 2.5 hours) and Baltimore, MD ($16 one-way, $28 round-trip, 2 hours) is also offered. The buses are run by a variety of different companies, and you can find schedules and buy tickets at the following websites: (www.chinatown-bus.org, www.2000coach.com, and www.gotobus.com).

Another option is the **BOLT Bus** (877/BOLT-BUS, www.boltbus.com), which departs from outside Amtrak's 30th Street Station (30th and Market Sts.) and drops off near New York's Penn Station. Tickets start at $10 each way, and the buses are generally a bit nicer than the Chinatown buses, but often sell out, so be sure to book a few days in advance. In an effort to compete, **Greyhound** (10th and Filbert Sts., 215/931-4075 or 800/231-2222, www.greyhound.com) offers $10 web fares (standard fare is $19) and drops off at Port Authority and Penn Station.

If you'd rather travel by rail but can't afford Amtrak, another option is to take a local **SEPTA** train to Trenton and connect with the **NJ Transit** light rail. SEPTA departs from the major downtown stops, including 30th Street, Suburban Station, and Market East; once in Trenton, you'll wait about 20 minutes and transfer onto NJ Transit's light rail to Penn Station in New York, for a total travel time of about 2.5 hours. The trip costs around $20 one-way depending on the time of day − a bit more than the bus, but the advantage, aside from being on rails (which means no traffic and no bumps), is more flexibility in departure stations and times and arriving in Penn Station.

the airport and are always waiting just outside the baggage claim area.

Alternative airports include Newark International (Newark, New Jersey, 85 miles), Baltimore-Washington International (Baltimore, Maryland, 109 miles), JFK International (Jamaica, New York, 105 miles), La Guardia (Flushing, New York, 105 miles), and Atlantic City International Airport (Atlantic City, New Jersey, 55 miles). You'll often find the best fares by coming directly to Philadelphia, especially once you factor in time and money spent traveling from the other airports, but it is worth investigating airfares from these nearby cities, especially if you're planning a multi-city visit in the area.

BY TRAIN

Since the early days of rail transport in the United States, Philadelphia has been a hub for the Pennsylvania Railroad and the Reading Railroad. Today, Philadelphia is a hub of the nationalized **Amtrak** (30th and Market Sts., 800/872-7245, www.amtrak.com). The station is a primary stop on the Washington–Boston Northeast Corridor route and the Keystone Corridor, which connects to Harrisburg and Pittsburgh. It also offers direct or connecting service to Atlantic City, Chicago, and many other cities in the United States and Canada. All trains traveling outside the city depart and arrive at Amtrak's 30th Street Station (30th St. and JFK Blvd.). The train is the most pleasant, and most expensive, method of public transportation to nearby cities like New York and D.C., although the website often offers fare specials and there are discounts for seniors and people with disabilities.

The Southeastern Pennsylvania Transportation Authority, or **SEPTA** (215/580-7800, www.septa.org), has regional lines serving the suburbs of Philadelphia. It also connects to New Jersey Transit in Trenton, which continues to Newark, New Jersey, and New York City. Regional rail also extends south of the city to Wilmington, Delaware.

BY BUS

The **Greyhound Bus Terminal** (10th and Filbert Sts., 215/931-4075 or 800/231-2222, www.greyhound.com) offers direct and connecting service all over the country. **NJ Transit** buses (800/772-2222, www.njtransit.com) travel between Philadelphia and South Jersey, including the Jersey shore as far as Cape May at the southernmost tip. **SEPTA** (215/580-7800, www.septa.org), in addition to providing extensive local service, also offers service to some parts of southeastern Pennsylvania.

BY CAR

Philadelphia is easily accessible by car and connected to several major highways, including the Pennsylvania Turnpike (I-276), I-76, I-476, I-95, U.S. 1, and the New Jersey Turnpike. I-676 is the section of I-76 that runs through Center City and continues across the Ben Franklin Bridge into New Jersey. The Walt Whitman Bridge and the Tacony-Palmyra Bridge also connect Philadelphia to New Jersey. The usual car rental agencies can be found at the airport or in Center City, including Avis, Hertz, and Enterprise.

Getting Around

You have plenty of options for getting around in Philadelphia, between public transportation; hop-on, hop-off tour buses and trolleys; taxis; and easy-to-navigate, grid-like streets that are great for walking and biking. There is rarely a reason to drive your car in Center City when you factor in the difficulty of parking in the busiest parts of town. It's usually best to ditch the keys unless you're traveling outside of Center City, where limited public transit and ample parking make driving convenient.

PUBLIC TRANSPORTATION

The extensive public transportation network includes buses, subways, trolleys, and regional rail lines, all operated by **SEPTA** (215/580-7800, www.septa.org). While locals are quick to complain about increasing fares and delays, and the public transit system certainly has its flaws, it will generally get you to most places you need to go in the city without any major trauma. However, it can be confusing, as some trips in Philly may require a combination of bus, subway, and/or regional rail lines. The farther away from Center City you travel, the fewer direct routes you'll find, but within the central areas it is generally quick and easy. All you need is a little patience and willingness to figure out the system, or to ask for help. The SEPTA website lets you enter departure and arrival information with the "Plan My Trip" feature and will give you the best way to get from A to B—a good idea if you have Internet access and time to plan. Some SEPTA "Night Owl" routes run all night, but with a limited schedule after 8 P.M. Many lines, including the regional rail, stop running at midnight.

Buses, trolleys, subways, and subway surface cars cover the city, especially in Center City. Regional rail lines run within the city to the northeast and northwest sections, including Germantown, Manayunk, and Chestnut Hill, and to many suburbs. The eight rail lines can all be accessed through Center City stations at Market East, Suburban, and 30th Street, and all connect with the airport. These routes connect

RIDE THE 23 BUS

Not a tour bus by any stretch of the imagination, a ride on the 23 is an outing for someone who really wants to see an interesting cross-section of the city, not just the tourist spots. This former trolley route is SEPTA's most traveled surface route; it runs all the way from the sprawling, upscale neighborhood of Chestnut Hill in the far northwest section of the city into the far reaches of South Philadelphia – the historically Italian, working-class part of town. Along the way, it passes through diverse parts of the city, such as Germantown, Mt. Airy, and North Philadelphia, including some of the city's most impoverished pockets. It cuts through Center City East and past the Reading Terminal Market before continuing into deep South Philly. As you move through the different areas, you'll notice the makeup of the commuters changing along with the landscape. A straight-through ride of the entire route takes about an hour each way and is a good way to get a quick introduction to the city. If you have a day to play, hop on and off and explore whenever you see something interesting. Keep in mind, however, that this a regular commuter line, so if you want to snag a seat and avoid crowds, you should avoid traveling during the morning and evening rush hours. And since the bus is not intended for hopping on and off, you'll have to pay the fare ($2) each time, or purchase a One-Day Convenience Pass ($7), which will get you eight rides on any bus, trolley, or subway route in one day.

per day, all-day family pass $10) a convenient option. Offering continuous service every 12 minutes 10 A.M.–6 P.M. May–October, it stops at 27 attractions throughout the city. Another option is the **One-Day Independence Pass** ($11, $28 for family up to five people, available at SEPTA ticket offices or online at http://shop.septa.org). This comprehensive ticket allows you to travel on all SEPTA buses, trolleys, subways and trains, so you can get all over the city and suburbs.

Fares

Buses, trolleys, and subways cost $2 per ride and an additional $1 for a transfer, good for an additional ride on a different line continuing in the same direction. Up to two transfers can be purchased for any one trip, and are not required when transferring from one subway line to another, but are required between buses or when switching between bus and subway. If you'll be using a lot of public transportation, consider the One-Day Convenience Pass, which will get you eight trips on any buses or subways in one day for $7. Buying tokens also saves money ($1.55 each); they can be purchased in any major subway station, including Suburban, 30th Street, and Market East, and at over 400 retail locations in the city, including some newspaper stands. A weekly TransPass gets you unlimited rides on all modes of public transit in a calendar week for $22; a pass for unlimited rides in a calendar month is $83. Trips on some regional rail lines require a surcharge if used with a pass. Discounts are available for seniors, riders with disabilities, children, K–12 students, some college students, families, and groups.

Accessibility

Every SEPTA bus line is equipped with some vehicles with a wheelchair lift or ramp that can be lowered by the driver. The majority of vehicles include automated route and stop announcements that can be heard inside and outside of the bus. Route information is displayed electronically on the front and side of buses.

Regional rail cars are accessible to those with mobility devices, and many stations are ADA accessible. Many of the major regional rail

with many of the subway and bus lines, but fares for different modes of transport must be paid separately and cost is dependent on distance or number of "zones" traveled. Fares increase during peak hours: weekdays 6–9:30 A.M. on trains heading towards Center City and 4–6:30 P.M. on all trains leaving from Center City.

Those doing the tourist circuit in summertime will find the **Philly PHLASH** bus (800/537-7676, www.phillyphlash.com, $2 per trip or $5 stations, including Temple University, Market East, Suburban, 30th Street, and University City, are ADA accessible. Primary subway and trolley stations, including Frankford Transportation Center, 69th Street Station, Fern Rock, and Olney, are accessible and provide easy connections to many bus routes. More than 70 stations have elevators, and a toll-free 24-hour elevator-status number (877/797-8248) is updated when changes in elevator service occur; an Alternate Accessible Service list on the SEPTA website provides alternative options.

SEPTA also runs **Customized Community Transportation** (CCT Connect, 215/580-7145), which provides ADA paratransit services to individuals with disabilities who are unable to use regular services, along with a shared-ride paratransit program for senior citizens.

GETTING TO NEARBY NEW JERSEY

For travel to nearby New Jersey, including Collingswood and Haddonfield, **PATCO** (856/772-6900, www.ridepatco.org) offers regular service from several Center City stations. **Camden RiverLink** (215/925-5465, www.riverlinkferry.com) offers a scenic option for getting across the river to Camden in summer, departing every hour on the hour from Philadelphia and on the half hour from Camden, with additional departures during events at the Susquehanna Bank Center. It runs May–September and costs $6 for adults and $5 for children and seniors.

BICYCLING AND WALKING

Center City is compact and the grid-like streets are easy to navigate on foot or by bike. Bicycling is a quick way to get around without having to worry about parking or traffic. As in any major city with car traffic, bicyclists should exercise caution when riding on busy city streets, and a helmet should always be worn. While somewhat limited, there is an increasing network of wide bike-friendly streets with designated bike lanes. A map of routes can be found at the Independence Visitor Center or

> ## IMPORTANT NUMBERS
>
> - **Amtrak** (train): 30th and Market Sts., 800/872-7245, www.amtrak.com
>
> - **Greyhound** (bus): 10th and Filbert Sts., 215/931-4075 or 800/231-2222, www.greyhound.com
>
> - **Philadelphia Airport:** 215/937-6937, flight/gate 800/745-4283, www.phl.org
>
> - **SEPTA** (bus, subway, and regional rail): 215/580-7800, CCT connect (paratransit service) 215/580-7145, www.septa.org
>
> - **Taxis:** Liberty Cab, 215/389-8000; Olde City Taxi, 215/247-7678; Quaker City Cab, 215/726-6000; Philadelphia Taxi Co., 215/232-2000

through the website of the **Bicycle Coalition of Greater Philadelphia** (www.bicyclecoalition.org/resources/maps).

DRIVING AND PARKING

While driving and parking in Center City can be difficult, you'll usually find a parking meter even in the busiest parts of town if you're willing to search for up to 15 minutes and walk a few blocks. The Philadelphia Parking Authority's website (www.philapark.org) provides a directory of parking lots and garages. There are garages all over Center City, especially near the Convention Center and the Avenue of the Arts, but they can be expensive. Metered parking in Center City is $2 per hour. Garages vary depending on the day and time, with prices generally lower after 5 P.M. A day rate (24-hour period) is generally in the $25–35 range.

Most central areas have metered street parking. The time limit varies depending on the area but is usually 1–4 hours. Meters accept Smart Cards (prepaid parking cards the size of a credit card) and coins, and many major areas

CAR SHARE

If you're relocating to the area and you don't own a car, never fear; Philadelphia has another option. Since most city-dwellers only drive occasionally – to the supermarket, suburban malls, or for day and weekend trips outside the city – there is no need for many to own a car. You can save tons of money on insurance and maintenance, avoid the nightmare of parking in some of the more crowded neighborhoods, and still have a car at your fingertips. Environmentally friendly car-sharing programs are sweeping the world, and Philly's program is at the forefront.

Philly Car Share (215/730-0988, www .phillycarshare.org), a local nonprofit, is recognized as one of the best car-share programs in the world for its ease, affordability, and low rates, starting at just $3.45 per hour or $39 per day. To be eligible, you must be at least 19, have had a valid driver's license for at least two consecutive years, and have a clean driving record. Also, if you don't have a Pennsylvania driver's license, you must get one within 60 days of joining. Apply for an account for a nonrefundable $25 fee, and once you're set up, you can call or go online to find out where the nearest available vehicle is parked. With advanced technology, a device inside the car is synced with your key card, so you can get in without having to go pick up a key. The numbers of users, vehicles, and designated Car Share parking spaces are constantly increasing, so no matter where you live, you're never far from a car or parking spot.

now have machines so you can pay for parking with a credit card. Smart Cards are available in $20 and $50 denominations and can be purchased at any Shop Rite or 7-Eleven, or online from the Parking Authority (www.philapark .org). Be aware that some areas that have no meters still have time limits. Pay close attention to signs, especially in Center City, or you may get a ticket.

TAXIS

It's usually easy to hail a taxi anywhere in Center City, but the best place to find one is in front of a hotel or on any busy corner. Rides are metered, with the exception of the flat fee of $28.50 for trips between Center City and the airport. If you're in an area without a lot of activity, it's best to call a cab and go outside when it arrives. It generally shouldn't take more than 15 minutes, except during rain showers or at 2 A.M. when the bars close and everyone is clamoring for one. Fares are regulated, and taxis should always have a meter running so you can see how much you're paying. Fares are based on distance traveled with small increases for wait time during traffic. Your driver should be able to give you an estimate of how much it will cost to get to a specific destination.

Conduct and Customs

ALCOHOL

The drinking age is 21 in Pennsylvania, and it is strictly enforced in most bars in the city. If you look young, you will get carded, with the exception of a few complete dives (which will remain unnamed for their sake). Purchasing alcohol in Pennsylvania is not always simple. Beer distributors and state-run Wine & Spirits shops are located throughout the city and keep limited hours. Most bars will let you buy take-out beer but at a steep price.

SMOKING

In 2007, a smoking ban went into effect in all restaurants and bars in Philadelphia. There is the occasional dive bar, remote neighborhood bar, or private club where smoking is still allowed, but they are the exception. It is still acceptable for smokers to light up at most alfresco bars, restaurants, and coffee shops, as well as in subway stations and in parks. Smoking is not as taboo here as in many West Coast cities, but the recent ban has certainly changed the bar culture—for the better, according to most.

BUSINESS HOURS

Most offices, including banks, are open 9 A.M.–5 or 5:30 P.M. on weekdays. Shop hours vary greatly, but with the exception of smaller boutiques or antiques stores, which often have limited hours, most stores are open from at least 10 or 11 A.M. to 6 or 7 P.M. Monday–Saturday, and are closed or have very limited hours on Sunday. Many Center City shops stay open as late as 8 or 9 P.M. on Wednesday evening. Most restaurants serve food until 9 or 10 P.M. on weeknights and until 10 or 11 P.M. on weekends, with some restaurants in the most active parts of town (like Rittenhouse Square, Old City, South Street, Northern Liberties, and Manayunk) offering late-night menus. Many bars serve food until midnight or 1 A.M., and some Chinatown restaurants stay open until 3 A.M. Other than that, late-night dining is generally limited to diners and cheesesteak and pizza joints—some of which are open 24 hours. With the exception of a few private clubs and after-hours clubs, bars in Philadelphia close at 2 A.M. sharp.

TAXES AND TIPPING

There is a hotel tax of 14 percent, with 6 percent going to state tax and 8 percent to city tax. There is a 7 percent tax on dining out and most general sales and a 10 percent tax on liquor, but there is no tax on items considered essential, including clothing.

Philadelphians were rated the nation's best tippers in the 2009 *Zagat Restaurant Guide,* with restaurant tips averaging 19.6 percent. A 15 percent tip is usually the minimum, even when people are not particularly impressed with service. When all is good, most locals drop 20 percent. The 15–20 percent tipping rule usually applies to taxi cabs, although with more flexibility; a $1–2 tip will cover most rides within the city. For a ride to the airport, especially when luggage handling is involved, the standard is closer to $5. Bell hops and valet parkers generally get $1–2 per bag or per vehicle, and slightly more at the city's ritziest establishments.

Tips for Travelers

BUSINESS TRAVELERS

For the increasing numbers of travelers who come to the city for business—especially since the new convention center was built—most hotels have on-site facilities like fax machines and in-room Internet access. There are various 24-hour **FedEx Kinko's,** including those at 1201 Market Street (215/923-2520) and 2001 Market Street (215/561-5170). For shipping, call the local **UPS service** (215/567-6006, www.ups.com).

INTERNATIONAL TRAVELERS

Philadelphia has become an increasingly popular destination for international travelers. It is in the eastern time zone, the same as New York, and three hours ahead of the West Coast. English is the language spoken and U.S. dollars are the currency. There is an American Express office at 16th Street and John F. Kennedy Boulevard (215/587-2300), where you can cash travelers checks or change money. The **International House** (2701 Chestnut St., 215/287-5125, www.ihousephilly.org) on the University of Pennsylvania campus also serves as a great resource for international visitors. It offers information, social and cultural programming, language lessons, and affordable short- and long-term accommodations for students or anyone affiliated with a university.

GAY PHILLY

Though it's not as large or visible as in New York or San Francisco, there has long been a thriving gay community in Philadelphia. As far back as the 1930s and '40s, underground gay house parties and social networks existed not only in Center City but in West Philadelphia, Germantown, and other areas. There was also a group of mob-owned gay bars centered around 13th and Locust Streets – the area that remains the nexus of gay culture in Philly today. This east-of-Broad, south-of-Market neighborhood, also called Washington Square West, is most commonly called the "Gayborhood."

A pivotal change occurred in Philadelphia in 1965 when a group of protesters began an annual July 4 march in front of Independence Hall. Four years before the Stonewall Riots in New York ignited the worldwide modern gay rights movement, this period began the era of openness in the city. Gays and lesbians began to come out in increasing numbers and to claim their rightful place in the community.

Today, Philly's gay community is a highly visible and important part of the city, with several dozen clubs, bars, lounges, bookstores, boutiques, restaurants, and shops catering to it. Local politicians court the LGBT crowd for support and dollars, and the media gives wide coverage to various pride festivals and events, including Equality Forum in late April and early May, the Pride Parade in June, and OutFest in October.

Outside of Center City, the gay community is a little more circumspect, and unfortunately flashiness and PDA can draw unfriendly attention in some places. The Tourism Board website has a section geared towards gay visitors to the city (www.visitphilly.com/gay-friendly-philadelphia/), including gay-friendly hotel accommodations and special event packages. There are several hotels and bed-and-breakfasts in the Gayborhood, with plenty of others nearby. The **William Way LGBT Community Center** (1315 Spruce St., 215/732- 2220, www.waygay.org) is the city's largest gay and lesbian center, filled with resources and information, and the online calendar (www.phillygaycalendar.com) has the most comprehensive guide to gay-friendly events, venues, organizations, and clubs. The *Philadelphia Gay News* is a publication that offers a calendar of events and articles and is available in print or online (www.epgn.com).

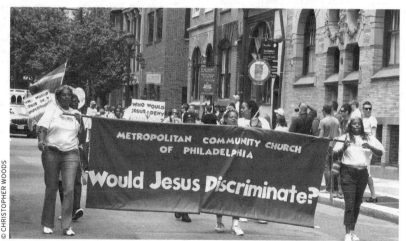

© CHRISTOPHER WOODS

Philadelphia's Gay Pride Parade

SENIOR TRAVELERS

Philadelphia is a hospitable destination for older travelers, although some may choose to avoid the hottest summer months and the coldest winter months. Senior citizens with proof of age (65 and older) ride buses and subways for free all the time and regional rail for free during off-peak hours (before 6 A.M., 9 A.M.–3 P.M., and after 6 P.M.). Discounts are available at many attractions and AARP discounts are available at many hotels. The **Independence Visitor Center** (6th and Market Sts., 215/965-7676, www.independencevisitorcenter.com) offers additional resources and information for seniors.

STUDENTS

The Greater Philadelphia region has the second-largest number of colleges in the nation and the second-largest concentration of college students living on the East Coast. There are around 120,000 students attending college in the city and nearly 300,000 in the entire metropolitan area. Including colleges, universities, and trade and specialty schools, there are more than 80 schools in the region. The biggest colleges and universities include: University of Pennsylvania, Temple University, Drexel University, The Art Institute of Philadelphia, Villanova University, Arcadia University, Bryn Mawr College, Haverford College, La Salle University, and St. Joseph's University.

Students should check for student discounts at many sights and movie theaters throughout the city. If you're considering studying in the area, be sure to check out **Campus Philly** (www.campusphilly.org) for a wealth of information and resources for students.

TRAVELERS WITH DISABILITIES

Those using a wheelchair or who have difficulty walking should exercise caution on Philadelphia's sometimes older, cracked, or bumpy sidewalks and walkways. Most of the major streets in Center City have curb cuts and handicapped parking, although parking spaces can be limited near major attractions, so allow extra time to find one. Most attractions, theaters, and all the

stadiums and newer, larger hotels in Philadelphia have elevators or ramps, but due to their old age, some of the historic buildings are ill-equipped. When in doubt, call ahead before arriving to be sure a location is accessible.

The **Mayor's Commission on People with Disabilities** (215/686-2798, www.phila.gov/mcpd) offers resources and a wealth of information, including help finding accessible parking, ATMs, health centers, and cultural events. **ARTREACH, Inc.** (215/568-2115, www.art-reach.org) connects people with disabilities to services and arts in the area and offers an online and print access guide with information on more than 75 of the region's theaters, performing arts centers, and museums. Listings include wheelchair accessibility of entrances and restrooms, phone numbers, and information on large-print or Braille materials or assistive listening devices. The guide is also available on audiocassette for the blind.

SEPTA provides detailed information on their website (www.septa.org). The **Independence Visitor Center** (6th and Market Sts., 215/925-6101, www.independencevisitorcenter.com) is helpful in providing additional information and resources.

TRAVELING WITH CHILDREN

Philadelphia is an extremely popular destination for families with children. The many kid-friendly, interactive attractions make it a favorite for school trips or for parents to teach their kids about history. With the exception of the very high-end restaurants, kids can be found dining out with parents in most of the city's restaurants. When traveling with children in the hot summer months, consider booking a hotel with a pool or visit one of the city's public pools.

TRAVELING WITH PETS

Philadelphia is a pet-friendly town, especially in Center City and in the northwest section of the city. With plenty of green spaces, and several specifically designated dog parks, there are plenty of places to walk your dog. Some hotels also allow pets, but you should always check in advance, as there may be a surcharge or limited rooms available. Some restaurants and bars with outdoor seating allow well-behaved pets to sit with you while you eat and drink. Friendly servers will often offer your dog water. Visit www.dogfriendly.com for listings of dog parks and dog-friendly accommodations and businesses.

WOMEN TRAVELING ALONE

As in most places, women traveling alone should exercise extra caution, especially at night. Most, but not all, parts of Center City are generally well lit and filled with people except very late at night. When venturing out after dark, it's always best to travel in groups or take a cab. Muggings and purse snatchings do occur, so be alert and hold your purse tightly, or better yet, don't carry one at all at night if you can avoid it. As a general rule, whenever you don't feel safe for any reason, step inside the nearest open business and wait there while you call a cab.

Health and Safety

HOSPITALS AND PHARMACIES

Philadelphia is home to several of the world's best hospitals and medical research facilities. For medical emergencies or short- or long-term care, you will find as good treatment in Philadelphia as anywhere. There are too many to name them all here, but just a few of the most renowned hospitals include Pennsylvania Hospital, University of Pennsylvania Hospital, Thomas Jefferson University Hospital, Hahnemann University Hospital, Wills Eye Hospital, and Temple University Hospital. Most hospitals are located in Center City and University City. Independent and chain pharmacies can be found everywhere in the city and you're never very far from a Rite Aid, CVS, or Walgreens. Among others, there is a 24-hour **CVS** in Center City West (1826 Chestnut St., 215/972-0909).

CRIME

If there is one statistic that Philadelphia is least proud of and most in need of changing, it is crime. Criminologists blame the high crime rate on many social and economic problems, including unemployment, gang activity, increased illegal gun trafficking, reductions in youth programs, poverty, and single-parent households. While it is impossible to pinpoint the cause or predict the future, it is a dire situation in some parts of the city, and we can only hope that this trend will change soon.

It would be remiss to say that tourists are completely safe from the violence that plagues some parts of Philadelphia, but it also must be noted that the vast majority of these crimes, especially murders, are taking place in areas most visitors and many locals never visit. While infrequent murders have taken place in practically every area of the city, most are in economically downtrodden pockets of North, Southwest, and West Philadelphia. Many of the crimes involve drugs, and innocent people that live in drug-infested areas have fallen victim.

The most likely crimes that people outside of these areas encounter are muggings, purse snatchings, and car thefts, which happen mostly at night in desolate areas. You should always exercise caution and be alert to your surroundings, especially when leaving bars, clubs, and parking garages. When in doubt, always take a cab to your destination. If you don't feel safe, get to a well-lit, populated area or step inside the nearest business and wait for a cab. Trust your instincts and travel in groups whenever possible at night.

Information and Services

COMMUNICATIONS AND MEDIA
Phones

When the number of phone numbers in the city got too large for the 215 area code to accommodate, the 267 area code became a second Philadelphia area code. The number of public pay phones has decreased dramatically as it has in most places with the advent of cell phones. The few that still do exist cost $0.50 for local calls, and most accept coins and calling cards. Dial 1 before calling toll-free numbers (those starting with 800, 888, 877, etc.). Prepaid phone cards are available at many convenience stores and cell phone stores.

Internet Services

There has been much talk of Philadelphia becoming the first city to have free wireless service everywhere, but as of yet, it hasn't happened. It isn't difficult to find free wireless access at many coffee shops and libraries throughout the city. If you don't have your own computer, public libraries are a good option for residents but aren't much help to nonresidents since you need a library card to access the system and only residents can obtain one. Many hotels and youth hostels have a computer available for free or cost for short-term use. The **ING Direct Café** (17th and Walnut Sts., 215/731-1410) has computers available for free Internet surfing.

Mail Services

Post offices are located all over the city, and the main branch (2970 Market St., 215/895-8989) across from 30th Street Station stays open nightly until 9 P.M. except for Sunday, when it closes at 7 P.M.

Newspapers and Periodicals

Philadelphia has two main daily newspapers, the *Philadelphia Inquirer* (www.philly.com) and the *Daily News* (www.philly.com/dailynews).

The *Inquirer* is considered the more serious paper, offering balanced coverage of local, national, and international news. While its popularity and ratings wax and wane, it is often considered in the top tier of daily papers in the country. Check out the Friday "Weekend" supplement for listings of entertainment and events. The *Daily News,* not generally regarded as serious journalism, is concentrated mostly on local news, with extensive sports coverage; some locals are avid fans of the easy, fun read. The *Metro* (www.metro.com), a free daily available at many SEPTA stations, is filled with short snippets of news and entertainment that range from important to entertaining to completely inane.

Many locals, especially the younger set, get their information and news from the free alternative weeklies *PW* (www.philadelphiaweekly.com) and *City Paper* (www.citypaper.net). Most stories are locally based, and both offer good listings of events, concerts, restaurants, bars, and more. You'll find them in newspaper boxes all over Center City. *Philadelphia* magazine (www.phillymag.com) is the award-winning glossy monthly lifestyle magazine for the city and suburbs, sold at bookstores and newsstands. It is an entertaining read, offering a mix of interesting features, sensational local-interest stories, and useful service journalism. Many read it for its local style, dining, and arts and entertainment coverage. The *Philadelphia Gay Times* is geared towards issues, news, and events affecting the gay community, and the *Philadelphia Tribune* is an African American weekly newspaper, the oldest of its kind in the country.

The *Philadelphia Independent Media Center* (www.phillyimc.org) is a grassroots news organization serving Philadelphia and the surrounding areas. It also serves as the local organizing unit of the global Indymedia network and was among the first of over 200 Indymedia centers in cities across the United States and worldwide. The organization's goal is to create alternatives to corporate media, with a website, online radio station, community center, and performance space.

Radio

The independent and world music station WXPN (88.5 FM) is a very popular local station operated out of World Café Live in University City. Here are some of the other local stations:

- news: KYW 1060 AM
- rock: WMMR 93.3 FM
- classic rock: WYSP 94.1 FM and WMGK 102.9 FM
- oldies: WOGL 98.1 FM
- top 40: WIOQ 102.1 FM
- country: WXTU 92.5 FM

- hip-hop and R&B: WUSL 98.9 FM
- R&B and classic soul: WDAS 105.3 FM
- classic and jazz: WRTI 90.1 FM
- smooth jazz: WJJZ 106.1 FM
- National Public Radio: WHYY 91.0 FM

MAPS AND INFORMATION

The best place to find maps and a wealth of information about what to do and where to go in Philadelphia is at the **Independence Visitor Center** (6th and Market Sts., 215/965-7676 or 800/537-7676, www.independencevisitor center.com), conveniently located in Old City near the major historic attractions. The large facility has knowledgeable staff and volunteers, as well as exhibitions, a small film theater, café, gift shop, and bookstore.

RESOURCES

Suggested Reading

Barra Foundation. *Philadelphia: A 300-Year History*. New York: W. W. Norton & Company, 1982. This is the most comprehensive account of the history of Philadelphia ever written, produced over 15 years from conception to publication. The mammoth 800-plus-page volume is a collaboration of more than 20 scholars and historians. Each chapter is written by a different expert and offers a compelling and colorful narrative of a slice of Philadelphia's history, beginning with "The Founding, 1681–1701," and culminating with "The Bicentennial City, 1968–1982." It is considered required reading for anyone really interested in local history.

Bissinger, Buzz. *A Prayer for the City*. New York: Vintage, 1998. Written by Pulitzer Prize–winning author and former *Philadelphia Inquirer* journalist Buzz Bissinger, this book intimately follows Ed Rendell, arguably Philadelphia's most esteemed and fascinating mayor both personally and politically (who went on to become governor of Pennsylvania), through his first four-year term in the mayoral office. The author was granted behind-the-scenes access to city government, and he provides a candid account of the mayor, city politics, and the lives of other diverse Philadelphians in the 1990s. A compelling read for anyone interested in the complex problems facing American cities in general and certainly for anyone interested in Philadelphia, the book is disturbing, hopeful, and very real. It is, however, more than decade out of date, so it serves as a slice of Philadelphia history rather than a current report; fortunately, many improvements have taken place since it was published.

Booker, Janice L. *Philly Firsts: The Famous, Infamous and Quirky of the City of Brotherly Love*. Philadelphia: Camino Books, Inc. 2007. This fun, entertaining little book reveals much about Philadelphia's history through its many "firsts." The city was the first in so many landmark accomplishments, from major achievements like the first hospital and first university, to the more inane, like its claim as the birthplace of bubble gum and licorice.

Du Bois, W. E. B. *The Philadelphia Negro*. Philadelphia: University of Pennsylvania Press, 1995. Originally published in 1899, this sociological study was the first of its kind to look closely at black urban Americans by examining the lives and communities of blacks in Philadelphia at the end of the 19th century. A novel concept at the time, the study did not presume that blacks lived in poor conditions due to an innate shortcoming of the race. The writer was a civil rights activist and scholar and the first black man to receive a Ph.D from Harvard University. A cofounder of the NAACP, Du Bois also wrote *Black Folk, Then and Now* (1899) and *The Negro* (1915).

Isaacson, Walter. *Benjamin Franklin: An American Life*. New York: Simon & Schuster, 2003. In nearly 600 pages, you will learn more than you may have ever wanted to know about Benjamin Franklin. The detailed, entertaining account of Philadelphia's favorite son portrays the complex figure's shortcomings, as well as his numerous accomplishments over his fascinating lifetime. Franklin spent much of his life in Philadelphia and played a key role in many monumental events in the city's history, so you will learn much about the history of the city through the life of its most prominent historical figure.

Internet Resources

INFORMATION AND EVENTS
Campus Philly
www.campusphilly.org
With more than a quarter million students attending more than 80 local colleges and universities, there are lots of resources to support the student population and enhance the college experience; Campus Philly is one of the best. The nonprofit's mission is to "fuel economic growth by encouraging college students to study, explore, live, and work in the Greater Philadelphia tri-state region." Initiatives include sponsoring career fairs and networking opportunities, a student discount program, and helping prospective students and families visit local schools. The website, geared toward current and prospective students, includes information, articles, and job and internship listings.

City of Philadelphia
www.phila.gov
The official website of the City of Philadelphia is a useful resource for new residents. This is the place to go to find out where to sign up for gas and electricity or how to find hospitals and other emergency services. A news section offers announcements, and the site offers links to many other useful sites, including public transportation, education, and employment resources.

Greater Philadelphia
Tourism Marketing Corporation
www.visitphilly.com
Philadelphia's tourism and marketing board is the ultimate online resource for visitors to the city and surrounding region, including Bucks, Chester, Delaware and Montgomery Counties. The website offers information about historic sites, tours, restaurants, nightlife, shopping, and more. It also offers suggested themed itineraries for visitors with varied interests, including couples, families with children, gay travelers, and African American visitors. The site also offers a calendar and, at times, discounts for booking hotels, events, and travel packages.

Philly Fun Guide
www.phillyfunguide.com
For nearly comprehensive entertainment and other event listings in the area, this is the place. Offering a wide range of leisure activities, including music, dance, sports, fairs, festivals, outdoor activities, tours, parades, dining, and more, it is coordinated by the Greater Philadelphia Cultural Alliance, whose mission is to increase participation and support for arts and cultural organizations in the area. Sign up online to receive FunSavers and half-price discounted ticket offers to many of the best visual and performing arts shows, exhibits, and museums, delivered to your email inbox every Thursday.

NEWS

City Paper and PW
www.citypaper.net
www.philadelphiaweekly.com

These free alternative weekly newspapers have news, event listings, restaurant and movie reviews, and more, and are written with opinion and personality. They can be found in news boxes and coffee shops across Center City or read online.

Flying Kite
www.flyingkitemedia.com

This weekly online magazine launched in 2010 and quickly became a leading source for development-related news affecting the city and suburbs.

Metro
www.metro.us/philadelphia

This free paper has a mix of local, national, and international news and a good dose of fluff; it can be found in SEPTA stations and newspaper boxes across the city and online.

Philadelphia Gay Times
www.epgn.com

Available online or in print paper, it has personals, classifieds, and event listings for the gay community. Plenty of additional events can be found at www.phillygaycalendar.com.

Philadelphia Independent Media Center
www.phillyimc.org

Philadelphia Independent Media Center is a grassroots news organization serving Philadelphia and the surrounding areas.

Philadelphia Inquirer and Daily News
www.philly.com

Philadelphia's two main daily newspapers can both be read online or purchased from newspaper boxes and stands.

Philadelphia Magazine
www.phillymag.com

The main glossy city magazine covers arts, events, restaurants, politics, and more. Popular annual issues include those of top schools, top doctors, and a general "Best of Philly" issue. With an upscale readership, the magazine caters to the suburban community and the Center City elite and can be purchased at newsstands or read online.

Philadelphia Tribune
www.phillytrib.com

Published five days a week, this award-winning newspaper geared toward the African American community can be found online or in print.

HISTORY AND ARCHITECTURE

Philadelphia Architects and Buildings Project (PAB)
www.philadelphiabuildings.org

It's the ultimate resource for architectural scholars, but the easy-to-use, accessible website is also an excellent resource for anyone interested in architecture. It brings together the collections, data, and images of The Athenaeum of Philadelphia, the University of Pennsylvania Architectural Archives, the Philadelphia Historical Commission, the Pennsylvania Historical and Museum Commission, and other architectural organizations. As of 2011, the website contains more than 131,000 images and 25,000 architects, engineers, and contractors, with an ever-growing database. If there is a local building you want to know more about, look here.

Philadelphia Society for the Preservation of Landmarks
www.philalandmarks.org

The group began in 1931, when the historic Powel House was set to be demolished and Frances Anne Wister and other supporters set out to save it. They later acquired Grumblethorpe, the Physick House, and Waynesborough, and today the organization manages the four historical museum homes and is involved in other programs that support historic preservation.

Philly History
www.phillyhistory.org

This award-winning site contains an extensive archive of photographs spanning Philadelphia's history. One of the country's largest municipal archives, it has an estimated two million photographs dating from the late 1800s. A number of different search options make it possible to find photographs from a specific time period, locale, or topic.

U.S. History
www.ushistory.org

Run by the Independence Hall Association (IHA), an organization founded in 1942 in conjunction with the creation of Independence National Historical Park, the nonprofit's mission is to educate the public about the Revolutionary and colonial era in Philadelphia. This website does just that with detailed and interesting information about the sites and history of Independence Park.

PARKS AND RECREATION
Fairmount Park
www.fairmountpark.org

The official site of Fairmount Park, this is the place to go for information on history, arts, culture, the environment, and recreational activities available, as well as maps and information about permits.

Friends of the Wissahickon
www.fow.org

This nonprofit is dedicated to Wissahickon Park, the part of Fairmount Park in the northwest section of the city. The site offers maps, activities, and trail and event information.

BEST PHILLY BLOGS
Foobooz
www.foobooz.com

With a name derived from "food" and "booze," you can guess what this blog is all about. Foobooz keeps us up-to-date on the latest restaurant and bar openings as well as events, with original content and links to articles from other local food critics. It also features great deals around the city. It was taken over by **Philadelphia** magazine in 2011, so time will tell if it maintains its independent personality.

Philebrity
www.philebrity.com

Covering "Philly Media, Gossip, Nightlife, & Politics," Philebrity is often irreverent and entertaining, and sometimes even useful. They rely on reader tips for gossip, so it can't be taken too seriously, but it is often a fun read, and the youth-oriented arts and event listings are solid.

Uwishunu
www.uwishunu.com

"Uwishunu" is not a foreign word, but a subtly hip rendering of the words "you wish you knew," all smooshed together. The younger, hipper offshoot of the Greater Philadelphia Tourism and Marketing Corporation (www.visitphilly.com), Uwishunu offers an insider's look at Philadelphia. Written in blog form by GPTMC staff and other local contributors, it highlights the latest and greatest places to eat, drink, shop, and more. Their mission is to "enable visitors to hang like locals and locals to hang like insiders."

Young Philly Politics
www.youngphillypolitics.com

With the tagline "Progressive, Young, Philly Politics, from Small to Big," this progressive political blog offers a forum to discuss and learn about current issues, with a focus on local politics but often branching out into the national level. Many of the active bloggers are passionate and knowledgeable and often have interesting things to say, and discussions are especially heated and informative around election time. Anyone can contribute by signing up for a username.

Index

Restaurants Index

Nightlife Index

Shops Index

Hotels Index

www.moon.com

DESTINATIONS | ACTIVITIES | BLOGS | MAPS | BOOKS

MOON.COM is ready to help plan your next trip! Filled with fresh trip ideas and strategies, author interviews, informative travel blogs, a detailed map library, and descriptions of all the Moon guidebooks, Moon.com is all you need to get out and explore the world—or even places in your own backyard. While at Moon.com, sign up for our monthly e-newsletter for updates on new releases, travel tips, and expert advice from our on-the-go Moon authors. As always, when you travel with Moon, expect an experience that is uncommon and truly unique.

MOON IS ON FACEBOOK—BECOME A FAN!
JOIN THE MOON PHOTO GROUP ON FLICKR

MAP SYMBOLS

▭▭▭	Expressway	▣	Highlight	✗	Airfield	♙	Golf Course
▭▭▭	Primary Road	○	City/Town	✗	Airport	▱	Parking Area
▭▭▭	Secondary Road	◉	State Capital	▲	Mountain	▰	Archaeological Site
- - - -	Unpaved Road	⊛	National Capital	✚	Unique Natural Feature	▮	Church
- - - -	Trail	★	Point of Interest			▤	Gas Station
·········	Ferry	•	Accommodation	⟍	Waterfall	◯◯	Glacier
▭▭▭	Railroad	▼	Restaurant/Bar	▲	Park	▱	Mangrove
▓▓▓	Pedestrian Walkway	▪	Other Location	▯	Trailhead	▨	Reef
▥▥▥	Stairs	Λ	Campground	✗	Skiing Area	▱	Swamp

CONVERSION TABLES

$°C = (°F - 32) / 1.8$
$°F = (°C \times 1.8) + 32$
1 inch = 2.54 centimeters (cm)
1 foot = 0.304 meters (m)
1 yard = 0.914 meters
1 mile = 1.6093 kilometers (km)
1 km = 0.6214 miles
1 fathom = 1.8288 m
1 chain = 20.1168 m
1 furlong = 201.168 m
1 acre = 0.4047 hectares
1 sq km = 100 hectares
1 sq mile = 2.59 square km
1 ounce = 28.35 grams
1 pound = 0.4536 kilograms
1 short ton = 0.90718 metric ton
1 short ton = 2,000 pounds
1 long ton = 1.016 metric tons
1 long ton = 2,240 pounds
1 metric ton = 1,000 kilograms
1 quart = 0.94635 liters
1 US gallon = 3.7854 liters
1 Imperial gallon = 4.5459 liters
1 nautical mile = 1.852 km

MOON PHILADELPHIA

Avalon Travel
a member of the Perseus Books Group
1700 Fourth Street
Berkeley, CA 94710, USA
www.moon.com

Editor: Elizabeth Hansen
Series Manager: Erin Raber
Copy Editor: Deana Shields
Graphics Coordinator: Elizabeth Jang
Production Coordinator: Elizabeth Jang
Cover Designer: Elizabeth Jang
Map Editor: Albert Angulo
Cartographers: Albert Angulo, Chris Markiewicz,
    Kaitlin Jaffe, Chris Hendrick

ISBN-13: 978-1-59880-886-5
ISSN: 1942-406X

Printing History
1st Edition – 2008
2nd Edition – October 2011
5 4 3 2 1

Text © 2011 by Karrie Gavin.
Maps © 2011 by Avalon Travel.
All rights reserved.

Some photos and illustrations are used by permission and are the property of the original copyright owners.

Front cover photo: close-up of clock atop Philadelphia City Hall © Mitchell Funk/Getty

Title page photo: A. Thomas Schomberg's *Rocky* sculpture at the Philadelphia Museum of Art © Julia Gavin

Interior color photos: p. 2 (left) horse in Elfreth's Alley © Julia Gavin, (middle) stained glass window detail in St. Monica's Catholic church © Christopher Woods, (right) Robert Indiana's *LOVE* sculpture © Julia Gavin; p. 24 (inset) Liberty Bell © peterm/123rf.com, (bottom) Swann Fountain at night © Steven Vona/123rf.com; p. 25 (top left) rower on the Schuylkill River © R. Kennedy for GPTMC, (top right) Citizens Bank Park scoreboard © Frank Romeo/123rf.com, (bottom left) Joan of Arc sculpture © Julia Gavin, (bottom right) the grand stairwell inside Pennsylvania Academy of Fine Arts © Rick Echelmeyer for PAFA; p. 26 (top) Harris Shiffman/23rf.com, (bottom) © James J. Kelly/www.flickr.com/photos/62619569@N00; p. 27 © James J. Kelly/www.flickr.com/photos/62619569@N00; p. 28 (top) © Julia Gavin, (bottom left) © Karrie Gavin, (bottom middle) © James J. Kelly/www.flickr.com/photos/62619569@N00, (bottom right) © James J. Kelly/www.flickr.com/photos/62619569@N00; p. 29 *Common Threads* by Meg Saligman, completed 1997, Broad & Spring Garden Streets, photo credit: Jack Ramsdale for Mural Arts Program © City of Philadelphia Mural Arts Program; p. 30 © msheldrake/123rf.com; p. 31 © Florence McGinn/123rf.com; p. 32 © James J. Kelly/www.flickr.com/photos/62619569@N00

Printed in Canada by Friesens

KEEPING CURRENT

If you have a favorite gem you'd like to see included in the next edition, or see anything that needs updating, clarification, or correction, please drop us a line. Send your comments via email to feedback@moon.com, or use the address above.